The Gryphon Highlord

Connie Ward

www.dragonmoonpress.com

ISBN 1-896944-18-3 Print Edition
ISBN 1-896944-63-9 Electronic Edition

CIP Data on file with the National Library of Canada

Dragon Moon Press
www.dragonmoonpress.com

Printed version printed and bound in Canada

The Gryphon Highlord

Connie Ward

www.dragonmoonpress.com

Dedication

For my parents, who gave me my first fantasy novel,
"The Hobbit."

For Martin, my computer wizard, who rescued many an errant file from the far reaches of cyberspace.

And for my husband, Tyler, who always believed, even when I didn't.

CHAPTER ONE

The summons arrived while I sparred in a courtyard with my second-in-command. Consumed in our swordplay neither of us saw the royal page right away, for pages tend to be small creatures, easily overlooked.

"Keep your blade up, Kathedra," Valleri snapped, when his unerring sword arm almost severed mine at the elbow.

Valleri took his swordplay very seriously. But I was tired, giddy, and flushed in a fever that had little to do with the heat of battle. Blocking another of his powerful strokes, I staggered away to plead through my laughter, "Mercy, Val. Mercy, I beg you!"

"Mercy?" he growled, snatching away my blade and sheathing his own. "No mercy, Kathedra. You don't deserve it. Your swordplay is lax and your concentration is…well, elsewhere." Though he tried to be stern, tried to be firm, he seemed just as distracted as I. His breath came in quick, shallow pants and his eyes glittered from behind a fall of dirty-gold hair.

Pulling me into the shelter of the castle wall, he pinned me against the stone and cupped my face in his hands. "Ahh, but then again it is so good to hear you laugh."

My arms went around him of their own volition and I stole a kiss; one of those deep, hungry kisses that inevitably leads to a dark, out-of-the way alcove.

"Let us find a place," Valleri whispered into my ear.

"Ahem."

Starting at the intrusion, we shoved ourselves apart to see that a boy stood in the courtyard with us. Possessed of that same sense of self-preservation as the rest of his kind, the page feigned selective blindness.

I swiped at a lock of hair that had escaped its plait and smoothed my crushed tunic. Indignant at this interruption, I cast a scathing eye over the boy's rumpled livery and grubby face, still pudgy with baby fat. I raised a critical brow. "You're a new one, aren't you?"

His thatch of yellow hair bobbed up and down. "Aye, Highness." Then puffing himself up with pride, he announced, "The Regent sends me to fetch the Gryphon Highlord. His Excellency wishes your presence in his audience chamber immediately."

"Ahh, what is it now?" I sighed, rubbing my temple. "Does he wish me to scour the corners of his dais for spies? Or peek under his throne for hidden assassins? Why, I just did all that yesterday. And only last night didn't I sample his spiced pudding to prove it did not contain poison and not near enough, in my opinion, cinnamon?"

The Regent's paranoia knew no bounds. Every servant was an Umagi sympathizer ready to clang him over the head with a gilt serving platter, every Halberdier standing guard at the door was a traitor waiting to poke his posterior with a spear tip.

My sarcasm, however, sailed straight over the page's head. "I wouldn't know, Highness. Please, the Regent insists that you come at once."

Of course, 'at once'. The Regent never issued an edict that ended with 'at your leisure', or 'when you have a minute'. As if I don't have enough to do.

A glance at Valleri earned me a shrug. In the pretence of returning my sword, he leaned forward and said below a murmur, "Go. See what the Regent wants. We'll meet later in your chamber, where I'll teach you the real meaning of mercy."

That last comment sent my other brow skyward.

Smiling, I watched him swagger off across the courtyard until the child's shrill voice yanked me out of my daydream. "Please, Highness. His Excellency said right away."

"Yes, yes, hold onto your—" I broke off at the sound of movement above us.

Craning my neck up at the wall, I discovered we had an audience. A pair of lesser officers watched from the boulevard. Serasteffan and Averi.

My gaze collided with the former's. A big blond giant, Serasteffan is fond of cruelties that defy comprehension. In private circles we call him the Butcher. His smarmy grin sent a rash of shivers down my spine. Averi stood beside him, his expression radiating malice, his icy stare locked on Valleri's retreating form.

Though each belongs to a separate Royal, they are more often than not found together. After all, their interests are similar-rape, plunder, torture. They share dark ambitions and even darker passions. Skilled in combat and uncommonly vicious, they are men best avoided.

How much had they seen? Nothing, I hoped. Valleri and I must learn to be more discreet, for some people frown on such things. Important, influential people.

As the officers resumed their stroll along the rampart, I exhaled the breath I held, thinking Beware, Valleri. There are men about who hate you.

I guess I turned too quickly, for the page danced aside and ducked an imaginary swat. "Easy there, boy. You're a skittish thing."

"They say you have a temper, Highness. Like a dragon's."

"Don't be silly. Unless you're an enemy spy or a horse beater you have nothing to fear from me." I can't abide horse beating. "In fact, I happen to have a high tolerance for ten-year old boys with dirt on their cheeks. What's your name?"

"Mylo, Highness."

"Well, Mylo," I said cheerfully, throwing an arm across his shoulders. "Let's not keep the Regent waiting, shall we?"

I left the page in the kitchen with a sugar dainty and a pitying glance, for who knew how long he would last? Several of the little beggars had already been turfed out on their tender keesters for the offence of being 'too watchful, too eager,' according to the Regent. Poor things. No wonder Mylo was as jumpy as a coney in a nest of adders.

Pondering His Excellency's summons, I headed for the audience chamber. I could think of nothing that might be amiss. Our enemies are in rout, our allies in thrall, and I had committed no act of gross incompetence unlike some of my contemporaries. Perhaps I am to be congratulated.

Intent on my thoughts, I rounded a corner and bumped straight into a man apparently preoccupied with ruminations of his own. Though he looked no older than twenty, with his dark hair and beardless chin, he wore a lieutenant's badge. He seemed vaguely familiar.

"Beg pardon, Highness," he sputtered, extending a hand to me where I sprawled upon the marble floor. "How clumsy of me." His features contorted in a grimace of horror at what he'd just done. Understandably so. Not only am I the highest ranking officer around, I am also the heir to the throne.

As I dusted myself off I tried to place him, for I am ill-acquainted with those outside my own Royal since there are rare occasions nowadays for officers to congregate socially. His black and white surcoat placed him among the ranks of Roche, a mercenary who drinks and wenches far more than what the castle considers prudent.

"What's your name, soldier?"

His mouth worked but no words formed. No doubt he envisioned a hundred punishments for the offence of bruising the royal derriere. Finding his tongue at last, he blurted, "Saxton."

The name didn't register, but I had no time for a full interrogation. "Carry on, then. No harm done." I patted his shoulder and walked away, well aware of his gaping stare as it followed me down the corridor. I paid it no heed, for there were other, more weighty matters on my mind.

Once outside the audience chamber I stepped over a Shouda, one of the many enormous guard dogs trained to sniff out active magic-users, where it snored before the doors, then strode into the Regent's formidable presence.

Decommission? Did I hear that right? If so, it did not sound the least bit congratulatory. Standing in the dim puddle of light before the Regent's dais, I strove to understand this bizarre pronouncement. "Beg pardon?"

The words came again, more slowly, as if the speaker addressed a dull-witted child and not the overlord of his Royals. "You are retired."

I drew in a deep breath, refilling lungs emptied by this shock that had struck me like a blow to my stomach, and opened my arms in supplication. "But…why?"

With a shrug, the Regent settled back into the purple velvet cushions of his throne and squinted at me through the veiled gloom of the room. "You have outgrown your worthiness."

Impossible I thought. After all I'd done for him? Never had I heard anything so absurd.

Swallowing a hasty retort, I searched the Regent's face for a clue to his apparent lunacy. He looked too at ease, sounded too matter-of-fact. Either he hid something or feared a confrontation. Perhaps both.

I spared a glance at the guards who stood rigid and alert near the dais, and realized my situation called for diplomacy.

"Outgrown my worthiness?" I echoed, feigning a childlike bafflement. "How can you say that? It was I who repelled the rioters at the east gate when your very own Halberdiers turned tail and fled. It was I who rallied the troops in Glanshayda when Captains Chiverly crumbled and Urharde froze. And it was I, if I may be bold enough to remind you, who warned you in advance that the alleged 'Peasants for Peace' rally in Church Grove was an ambush!"

And it was also I who, on hands and knees, inspected his royal quarters for sabotaged chamber pots, though I forbore to mention it, but just barely.

"Is this how you express your gratitude? Decommission?"

"Don't take that tone with me!" the Regent roared back, his face a magnificent shade of red. "My decision is final. You are retired."

Forgetting me for a moment he jerked his head around, barking out at his attendants who quivered nearby, "Why is it always so damned dark in here?"

Fists clenched, I battled down my dragon's temper as Mylo called it. "You can't do this. I'm your niece."

A flicker of exasperation streaked across Uncle's heavy jowls. I think he wanted to shout and rave as badly as I, but he chose restraint. Then abruptly his tone turned cajoling. "Don't take it personally, Kathedra. As I said, you've simply outlasted your usefulness. You can go no further in your present capacity. After all your accomplishments, all your victories, what else is there left for you to do?"

I knew the answer to that as well as Uncle, for he sat upon it. But I dared not say so aloud. I cast about the room for his gaggle of advisors, usually skulking in the shadows, for I was convinced he couldn't have contrived this piece of nonsense on his own, but there was no sign of the snakes.

"It doesn't make sense," I insisted. "Why now, when I am at my peak as a commander? I am your most loyal servant, commanding the most loyal of troops. They will follow with courage and pride wherever I lead them. If you pull me now, at this most critical point, you risk dissent and disorder in the ranks."

Surprisingly, Uncle maintained his composure. "Believe me," he continued, in that condescending tone which so annoyed me, "I recognize your past value, and I am grateful for your faithfulness and that which you instilled in my Royals. But the moment has come when it is no longer feasible for a woman to hold command. It is time that you married and produced an heir to carry on our family line."

That little noise I heard must have been the sound of my lower jaw as it hit the floor.

Uncle shifted uncomfortably, cleared his throat. "It's not only that, Kathedra. There are rumours, linking you romantically with..." He paused, having visible difficulty spitting out the words. "Your second."

"Lies! All lies," I lied.

Uncle didn't buy it, not for a minute. "Nevertheless, a rumour is a rumour and I won't tolerate such talk. Besides, it's bad for morale."

His statement was so ludicrous it brought a smile to my lips. Avoiding any admission of guilt, I asked, "Uncle, how can love during strife be bad for morale?" Truthfully, it did wonders for mine.

"Because soldiers take exception when one of their number is-how shall I say?-entitled to preferential treatment from their commander. It breeds discontent, resentment and hostility." Here Uncle became snappish. "Good heavens! What would happen if something unexpected happened?"

"Do you mean if I became pregnant?" I retorted flippantly.

There are three topics people are forbidden to discuss in Uncle's venerable presence. The first is pregnancy, the second fornication, and the third any mention of human anatomy such as 'breast', even if one does refer to a piece of cooked fowl.

Uncle bristled, his eyebrows arching in oh-so-delicious offence.

"Pregnant," I repeated with precise enunciation. "Isn't that what you want? Then I can retire and stay by the hearth raising heirs."

"Oh, that would be perfect, wouldn't it?" he blustered. "My unwed niece, the Princess Kathedra, Gryphon Highlord and Heir to the Throne of Thylana, bred like a heifer by her second-in-command on the eve of what may be a full scale revolt."

Rolling my eyes, I sighed, "Oh, Unc."

That is not a term of disrespect. Though his name is Bertrand and his title Regent, I just call him Uncle. He wasn't always the man he is today-a twitchy, aging despot desperately clinging to his last fraying threads of power. I can remember as a child, sitting on his knee by the hearth in the great hall, as we helped Mother string berries for our day of Holy Fest. He was happy then, almost playful, and I'd always believed he held a soft spot for me. Those days are over now, gone so long it's almost as if they had never been, though they left behind fond memories from a time when I'd called him 'Unc', an endearment of genuine affection.

I looked at Uncle now, and wondered if he recalled stringing red and white berries by the fireside. "Nothing like that will happen."

"Bloody right it won't," he snarled. "I'm relieving you of all military duties. Consider yourself banished from the stables, the armoury, and the field. You are confined to the castle proper where you shall spend the next week in preparation for your nuptials. And if I catch you within ten feet of

Valleri," he added ominously, "I will confine you to your rooms."

"Uncle, you're being unreasonable. Valleri is my second and if I have cause to—"

"He is your lover!" Uncle blustered, pounding a fist onto the arm of his throne. "My god! Do you know the sort of damage that pack of upstarts could do with such gossip if they catch wind of it?"

To clarify, that pack of upstarts is how Uncle refers to the outlaws who call themselves CRUSADERs, an acronym for Citizens Risen Up to Stand Against a Dread and Errant Regency. While I thought it showed a grand ambition and unusual creativity on the part of lowly peasants and common bandits Uncle was not impressed. He absolutely refused to give credence to a term that might imply the upstarts had a legitimate claim against him. There was also a rumour adrift in the castle that the name Citizens in Revolt Against Bertrand was also being bandied about, but I guess someone somewhere with an ounce of dignity vetoed that one.

I maintained my defiance, armoured in disbelief. "So then, tell me, Uncle. Who's the lucky man you have chosen for my consort?"

He smiled indolently, perhaps presuming I had come to my senses and would accept his lofty decree. "Lesuperis. A distant cousin and our only living relative. A man of superb breeding and excellent schooling who shall suitably secure our bloodline. He will arrive in ample time for the ceremony, which must be performed without further—"

"Lesuperis!" I sputtered, teetering on the verge of hysterical laughter. "That eel? Surely you jest! The man is the most nauseating bore I've ever met. The last time he was here he groped the cook, leered at the chambermaids, goosed the laundress, and stuck his tongue in my ear at the banquet table. If you think I'll share my bed with that letch you are quite mistaken. Distant he is and distant he stays."

"My dear niece," Uncle sneered. "Do you really think I'll permit you to marry your lieutenant, and he a commoner at that?"

I ignored the barb despite its cruel sting. "I do not wish to marry Lesuperis or anyone else. I am no man's brood mare."

"It's already settled. Accept it. You are wild and headstrong and, dare I say it, wanton. Someone needs to rein in your unseemly behaviour. You are a princess, dammit! Try to remember that. If you don't comply with my wishes you risk disinheritance."

My heart skipped a beat. Uncle had wounded me in a fashion no weapon of steel ever could. "You can force me to wed Lesuperis," I acknowledged, "but you cannot force me to conceive his child."

Ahh, the prohibited subject of fornication. Uncle winced. "True, you may pine days away longing for your old lover, but eventually you will submit to Lesuperis."

I crossed my arms. "Stubbornness is a virtue, Uncle. You taught me that.

I promise you, this union will not be fruitful."

Brave words, but a once prosperous and peaceful nation was about to fall asunder thanks to Uncle's rashness. Lesuperis was the least of my worries. "Who's to be my replacement?" I demanded. "Not that drunkard Roche, I hope? Surely not Chiverly? That bumbler can't lead a horse to water let alone an army."

"I have not yet decided."

"Not yet decided?" Truly the man was mad. "You retire the Gryphon Highlord-your most faithful officer-while your realm totters on the brink of civil war…and you have not yet decided who will replace her?"

"It is no longer your concern, Kathedra."

"It is my concern. You expect me to prepare for a wedding that might not even take place. You expect me to conceive an heir for a throne that might not even exist at the time of his birth. Uncle, be sensible! You cannot replace the Gryphon Highlord. You cannot replace me."

"No one is irreplaceable."

With effort I calmed myself, tried to think logically instead of emotionally. "You need me, Uncle," I pressed, lowering my voice. "The Cru-upstarts have harnessed the hate and resentment of the exiled Umagi. I am your best defence against the powers they may unleash against you. You invite their wrath, yet dismiss the one person who can help you."

"I don't recall asking your opinion," Uncle burbled, his need for calm forgotten. "What vanity. What pretension. Know this, Kathedra. I gave you a position of respect because you are family. But on the day your mother died, you died with her. The Gryphon Highlord is a figurehead, an instrument of fear. You are no great warrior, no battle genius. You merely follow my orders. You were useful for a time, but I have decided that such a time should come to an end. Your reign as the Gryphon Highlord is over."

His words cut deep. With that one terse statement I learned I am a fraud. I learned I am expendable. But most of all, I learned I am not loved. Everything that I had believed had turned out to be an illusion, if not an outright lie.

Rage erupted then, pushing thought against the barriers of restraint. I tried to arrest it, and almost succeeded. Emotion must never be allowed to displace thought, I reminded myself. But willpower and self-control were never my strong points. An unruly mindspell wrestled itself free. Thus an unlit torch, set in a wall sconce not two feet above Uncle's bald pate, burst into flame. Its ignition startled Uncle and made the guards jump. It also jarred me into the realization that I stood in extreme danger.

Shaken, I hastened to apologize. "Forgive me, Uncle, but you did express a desire for more illumination."

Sweat beaded on Uncle's brow. His cheek twitched, betraying his nervousness. Calmly, lest the smallest provocation on his part bring another, perhaps more deadly outburst from me, he asked, "Have you taken your tonic, Kathedra?"

"Yes, Uncle."

"Is it time for another dose, then?"

"Yes," I lied. "I believe it is."

He looked relieved. Presuming the discussion ended, he dismissed me with the curt, "Do dress appropriately for supper, as I shall be announcing your engagement."

I made no motion to leave. I did not consider the matter closed, nor had I forgotten Uncle's cruel words. "Uncle, listen to me. If you would just trust me, trust in my abilities, you could let my—"

"Kathedra, enough! The subject is not open to debate."

His arrogance grated, like the rough stone of the wall I was banging my head against. "How can you humiliate me this way? Regardless of what you say, I remain your sister's daughter. Blood is blood. Decommission me, imprison me, I am still the Princess Kathedra, and I will sit on that throne one day."

"The only way you'll ever sit on my throne," Uncle growled, his hands bunched into fists of fury, "is if you marry Lesuperis and give Thylana an heir."

The last of my self-control broke. I should point out that it is never in one's best interest to call the Regent of Thylana a greedy, pompous, moronic slug, even if one is that same slug's niece. A pair of sentries seized my arms, and after a futile struggle on my part, forced me to my knees before Uncle's dais.

"Confine her to quarters," Uncle snarled. "And see to it she receives the correct dosage of tonic."

On that ominous note, I was dragged to my feet and hauled away through the castle by Uncle's personal bodyguard, known as the Halberdiers. Only then, judging by the taunting grins of the sentries, did I begin to suspect something sinister was afoot. There was more to the forced retirement of the Gryphon Highlord than met the eye.

Over the shoulders of my guards I strained to catch one parting glimpse of Uncle. He still sat on his throne, hunched in despair and bitterness, one hand covering his eyes as if the light were too bright, or the thoughts behind them too heavy, too bleak.

Alone in my rooms, behind a closed and barred door, I pondered the wisdom of my temper. Without protest, I had accepted my tonic under the Halberdier captain's watchful glare. Only I knew it was, in fact, in addition to the two doses I'd taken that morning. Consumed in such quantity the potion gave me a headache, which I reasoned I'd have acquired anyway, given the circumstances.

Thus, I sat on my velvet settee and concentrated my thoughts on the green goblets atop my wine cart, hoping to blast them to crystal shards. But my powers were sufficiently diluted. I resorted to breaking dishes the old fashioned way. Hardly productive, but it made me feel a whole bunch better.

All is not as simple as I've made it sound, therefore an explanation or at least a brief summary is in order. I'll start with a little family history, beginning with Uncle Bertrand. As the former queen's second born, he was content to live a comfortable life in a castle and demesne of his own, complete with doting wife and loving child until the day a resident Umagi, his own hearthmage in fact, cast a simple everyday spell that went horribly wrong, discharging a lethal dose of magic. The wayward spell left the keep in near ruin and many within dead or dying, including my aforementioned aunt and cousin.

The magical onslaught caused torches and hearths to burn out of control, setting alight anything within reach, whether that be tapestry or table, and spread with deadly speed through the rushes that covered the floor. This same uncontrolled release of power also compelled portions of the keep's stone walls to crumble and collapse, trapping and maiming many unfortunates in the rubble.

Horrified witnesses also claimed that every sharp edge in the castle suddenly gained a life of its own to spread mayhem and gore throughout. As if wielded by invisible hands, swords slid from their scabbards, battle-axes leapt from their racks, and kitchen knives flew from their cupboards. Some spun at furious speed, carving circles out of the air, while others careered wildly about, slashing and hacking at anything that moved. And though Uncle never discussed the incident in detail, it was said that his young son had died with a paring knife imbedded in his throat, thrust with such strength, it severed his spine and pinned him to one of the support posts in the keep's kitchen.

When the spell had at last fizzled itself out and the poor woman had collapsed to the floor, overwrought by the chaos she had unintentionally inflicted, Uncle ordered her clapped in irons and taken to the dungeons. As the tale goes, the hearthmage's cries of remorse and anguish reached as high as the tallest tower in the keep and as far as the village that squatted in its shadow, through steel and stone and timber, for three days running. No one who heard those screams could refute the agony expressed in them, and they took pity on the woman, who had lost loved ones of her own in the tragedy.

All except Uncle who, mourning the loss of his family, ordered her execution.

Sadly enough, such incidents were not uncommon. Lack of proper training and poor concentration on the part of the spellcaster often led to a wild and violent discharge of magic, even by the most benevolent Umagi. But it was this unfortunate occurrence that birthed Uncle's hatred for all Umagi and in time led to his persecution of them.

In his stupor of grief, Uncle brought all who was left of his household from the keep he'd called, ironically enough, Idyll, here to the castle and put himself at Mother's mercy. A compassionate woman, she welcomed her only sibling and accepted him into Gryphon, where he's lain ever since, like a wounded dog, licking and snapping and snarling at an injury he won't let heal. So steeped in hatred and mistrust, he was naturally appalled when he learned the husband whom his beloved sister had taken was also Umagi. Uncle felt betrayed, this man whose reason was twisted beyond all repair by grief and rage.

Thus it came as no surprise to anyone when following my Mother's death Uncle, newly installed as Regent and named my guardian, ordered all Umagi sent from Thylana in exile. Not even the Halberdier captain at the time was above Uncle's suspicion, for he had connections to the Umagi world. He vanished soon after the edict came down, and the truth of his disappearance was never revealed. A cheerful and fair-minded man, he had a neatly forked beard as dark as the hair that curled to his nape. Val and I could always expect from him a kind word or two, and perhaps a small wooden toy. Sometimes a soldier, sometimes an animal or bird, the toy had been carved by his very hands. I'd always felt sorry for him, that he didn't have children of his own to make these wonderful toys for. And I remember shedding some few tears on the day that I learned he was gone, telling myself I cried for the loss of playthings yet to be, and not the ache in my chest that his abrupt departure caused.

As it stands, Uncle never recovered from the horrors he had seen that awful day, from the grief that ate away at his soul. I really think he had no inclination to try. After all, it is much easier to wallow in one's misery than embark upon the arduous task of getting on with one's life. There are days yet when he can be seized by fearsome rage, laying waste to anything in his path and issuing orders that no sane man can follow. Madness stalks my poor uncle, as relentless a hunter as death itself. In my opinion, his fits of lunacy are no different from the effects of an improperly cast spell.

Yet despite my Umagi heritage, Uncle was kindly disposed towards me, perhaps because I was all the family left to him, and he raised me as if I were his own. I had a roof over my head, the finest food to eat, the best tutors, and the promise of a crown. He saw to it that I lacked for nothing. Though he tried to teach me to hate my Umagi blood and the Umagi father I'd barely known, he did not succeed.

So while I revile Uncle for his actions on one hand, I pity him on the other, and love him with the loyalty of an heir who will one day take his place. No one, least of all Uncle, doubts my allegiance. I am his most trusted, his most valiant. He has made a very grave mistake indeed, to cut me from his side, as if I were a rotting appendage in need of removal.

CHAPTER TWO

That night Valleri came to my apartment through the secret passageway by which romantic interludes are possible. His appearance surprised me. I had hoped he wouldn't come, for I wanted no witnesses to my humiliation. But he possessed the loyalty of a hound.

He sat beside me at the table and took my hand in his. "I'm sorry, Kathedra."

"So you've heard?"

Valleri nodded, his expression grave. "Bertrand addressed the troops. He said you resigned in order to marry Lesuperis, that you stepped down as Gryphon Highlord because you have too long neglected your duty to give Thylana an heir."

"And you believed him?"

"I didn't believe you resigned willingly. My first thought was that you were with child." He cast me a sidelong glance. "Are you?"

"I can't believe you have to ask that," I hissed, feeling my cheeks flame as I shot to my feet.

"Sit." His hand gently pulled me back down into my chair. "I had to ask, Kathedra. The announcement was so sudden…what would you have me think?"

Shrugging the question aside, I muttered, "Well, we're in a fix now. Uncle knows about us."

"He suspects. He has no proof. Unless, of course, you admitted it."

"Don't be ridiculous. I saw no point in dragging you down with me. Uncle only retired me. He can do worse to you. Much worse." I shuddered at many a gruesome possibility. "He lied, Valleri. Does everyone believe him?"

"Not everyone. Your troops don't believe you'd ever resign, much less marry Lesuperis."

"Did he name my replacement?"

"That's to be disclosed later."

"That's because he doesn't know."

Valleri fell silent. His silence irritated me.

"It doesn't make sense!" I cried out suddenly. "The commoners mass against us. The Umagi join them. Our allies quibble among themselves. All Thylana is about to crash down around his ears yet Uncle retires the Gryphon Highlord, the one person who may be able to hold it all together, and, and, he has no idea who should replace her?"

In my frustration I slammed my palms onto the table and pushed myself to my feet. Ordering my thoughts, I paced awhile, mindful of Valleri's stare. As I passed the wine cart, I caught sight of the crystal goblets so impervious to my will, thinking, What a hideous bloody shade of green!

Finally I stopped before my window and looked out it, where I could see for miles, down upon Thylana.

"If only Mother hadn't entrusted her throne to him," I spat. "Then I would rule and none of this would have happened. Not the witch hunts. Not the revolt. None of it."

"I suppose she thought she had no choice. You were only nine when your mother took ill. She had to make arrangements…and Bertrand seemed the logical choice."

My gaze remained on the view beyond the window, though I really wasn't seeing it. "He'll never let me have the throne, Val. He says I'm too young, too immature. Yet Mother was just eighteen when she received her own crown. If Uncle has his way I'll be an old hag."

"Or never," Valleri mused. "I've warned you about this before, Kathedra. Bertrand has always questioned Thylana's law of succession, especially the point bestowing the title of Heir upon the first born, regardless of gender. He believes the first born male child should inherit the throne. He's always coveted your mother's crown. He certainly won't surrender absolute power to her daughter, not without a fight."

"Oh, Valleri," I sighed, resting my elbows on the casement. "Why must everything with Uncle be such a struggle?"

"I think you know why."

"Because he's suffered and so wants the entire world to suffer along with him?" I let out a delicate snort. "That is an old excuse, and one that I indulged because Uncle has suffered as no man should. But enough is enough, Val. The people say they have endured too long without their hearthmages, their healers, their fortune-tellers. The farmers want back their weather-weavers and forecasters. The village elders want back their rune-readers. The fishwives want back their good luck charms and love philtres."

Lowering my arms, I buried my face in my hands to murmur, "As for the Umagi…they just want to come home. And Val, I think its time that they did."

That was treason worth a trip to Gryphon's dungeons, even for one such as I. But I would not break faith with Uncle by usurping him. Treachery is not an option for me.

"Shh, Kathedra. Such talk is dangerous."

"Why? Haven't enough years passed to ease his vengeance, if vengeance is what he seeks?"

"He doesn't seek vengeance," Val said in a quiet voice, the voice he chooses whenever this subject is broached. "He wants peace of mind."

"Peace of mind? Of course. And the best way to find peace of mind is to search for it amidst the chaos and conflict of war." What the hell sense did that make?

"You know what I mean. He wants to make sure that what happened to him, will never happen again. Or what happened at Idyll won't happen here at Gryphon. To you."

Valleri defending Uncle? That was something new. As was the mention of Idyll. Normally Val avoids the topic, for he was one of the lucky few who survived the events of that tragic day, having lost his parents and a sister, and followed Uncle to Gryphon all those years ago.

As children Val and I were playmates, almost inseparable, drawn together as orphans often are. As adolescents we studied our letters and trained with sword and shield side by side, sometimes rivals but always friends. And all at the sufferance of Uncle, who was just pleased to see that at least one other child, no matter his parentage or gender, was not afraid to be with me, a fledgling Umagi.

But Val's relationship with Uncle has always been strained, uneasy. While Uncle nurtured Valleri as a boy, giving him every advantage as he did me, he also constantly criticized and berated him. Val's swordplay was mediocre, his bowmanship passable and his academic skills merely adequate. This assessment astounds me because in truth, Val was always quicker with a sword, handier with a bow, and keener with chalk and slate than I, though I manage to hold my own on a field of battle or a hall full of smarmy courtiers.

While Val never refutes Uncle's criticism or questions his decisions, I am not fooled. This ready subservience does not disguise Val's contempt for his benefactor. He lets his hatred for Uncle shape his every thought, every action, every word, which are always at war with his desire to achieve an acceptance and approval he knows he'll never win. For Uncle never lets Valleri forget that he is common, that he is something less than sufferable.

"I never wanted this, you know," I murmured. "I never wanted strife and bloodshed. I never wanted to be the Gryphon Highlord. I did not want to raise arms against my own people. But Uncle left me no choice. He gave me a sword, a helm, and told me to fight. So I did. But not for the same reasons. I fought to protect the land I love from being wrenched out of the hands of my family. I fought to protect Castle Gryphon, the only home I've ever known. I fought to protect my future throne."

"Don't be so hard on yourself, Kathedra," Valleri said by way of comfort. "You've done all you can. I know it's difficult for you to see Thylana in such turmoil, for you to watch the innocent suffer. You risk your life with mercy missions, spiriting in sacks of meal and medicines to those in direst need...and it works to your advantage. Now is the time to engender a sense of respect and admiration in the people, so you won't be reviled later when you become queen."

He made it sound so mercenary. Compassion and pity move me foremost. To my people I can be generous. To my enemy, remorseless.

My anger returned tenfold. My voice shook and my whole body trembled with it. "He's ruined everything, Val. By retiring the Gryphon Highlord he's eliminated the only person who cares. My influence maintains reason and restraint when Uncle's Royals would slay the weak and try the innocent. My presence forestalls the retaliation of wizards who can just as easily inflict chaos. Mine, Valleri. Mine."

I heard Valleri leave his chair and walk toward me. "Be calm, Kathedra," he said in that clipped tone which always made me feel like a small child. "You're still reeling from the shock of it. It will pass."

I spun, his words sounding like so much nonsense. "Be calm? My world has come crashing down around me and you tell me it will pass?"

Too long repressed, too long leashed, my powers erupted, overwhelming rational thought. I couldn't stop it. Maybe I didn't want to stop it. Vulnerable to my will, the horrible green goblets exploded to scatter a spray of crystal splinters at Valleri's feet. In that moment a look crossed his features, almost as if he were recalling that day at Idyll. Then just as quickly it was gone. His jaw tensed beneath the masked expression, and the sky-blue eyes went a shade deeper. He backed away a step.

I caught my breath, stunned by what I had done, appalled by what I'd seen in his face. I held out a shaky hand. "I'm sorry, Valleri. I didn't direct it at you."

Lifting his chin he regarded me warily, as if not quite knowing whether to believe me. I'd never lost control before in his presence. He'd never seen me so wild, so helpless, and I'm sure he didn't know what to do.

"Please, Valleri," I begged. "Don't be afraid of me. Now, more than ever, I need you not to be afraid."

Until today, grief and fear and uncertainty were things I'd always hidden from Valleri, controlled by either sheer will or my tonic. My display of emotion touched him deeply. More importantly, he realized that I needed him like he'd never thought possible.

To my relief, he stepped forward and pulled me into his arms. I clung to him, grateful for his compassion.

After a while he withdrew to hold me at arms length. "Beautiful, tempestuous Kathedra. You have been caged for so long it is truly a wondrous thing to see you fly."

His words moved me, for it was the first he'd ever revealed his heart to me. In some ways we are very much alike. But the words he spoke next caught me unprepared.

"I love you, Kathedra."

It was then that I realized I loved him as well. "Truly, Valleri?"

"Truly. I didn't want to love you. Our dalliance was meant to be a diversion, a way to forget duty and war, a way to escape. Though it wasn't supposed to get so complicated, I think it was inevitable. Even natural. We depend on each other for everything, even survival. We share the same terrors, the same triumphs. How can I not love you?"

I clutched at him fiercely, ashamed that he should see me this way. "I'm so humiliated, Valleri. Are all the terrible things Uncle said really true? Am I so expendable there's no need to replace the Gryphon Highlord? What a fool I am, in my pride and arrogance. Uncle's right. I'm not indispensable. I merely take my orders and pass them to you. You, Valleri, are the warrior, the strategist, the true commander. The glories, the victories, all belong to you. I'm just a figurehead, a symbol without substance or reality."

"That's not true," Valleri admonished, tilting my head back so my eyes met his. "The Gryphon Highlord is a symbol, but a very important one. You give us courage when we lose faith. You give us strength when we feel beaten. But most of all, you give us pride. We are the finest of Gryphon's Royals because of you. We follow you into battle. We rally around your standard. There are times when you become more than a symbol. I've seen you fight to the death defending that standard. Don't let Bertrand's shackles fail your spirit. Don't let them fetter your heart."

His speech cheered me enough to risk a smile. "I'll miss you, Valleri."

"Miss me? Whatever do you mean? Once Lesuperis is dead we can continue to be together."

I drew back, chilled by his tone. "Once Lesuperis is dead?"

"Of course," Valleri crooned, nuzzling my neck. "You didn't think I'd let that lout marry you, did you? I'll take care of him."

I pushed him away with more force than I intended. "No, Valleri. I want no family blood spilt."

There is one ancestral law I refuse to break, one commandment I revere above all others; family blood is sacred. To shed it would bring me a dishonour I could never bear.

Once upon a time, when the first rumblings of revolt broke loose, I had an advisor. When I had railed in vain against Uncle and this needless conflict, my advisor suggested the only way to avoid bloodshed and save the throne was to assassinate Uncle. I had the man quietly executed. I have not appointed another advisor since.

Valleri had argued with me then, chiding me for my hasty action. He argued with me now.

"Do you really consider Lesuperis family? The man has barely a thimbleful of royal blood in his veins. Neither he nor Bertrand has any honour worth considering."

"Then I shall have enough for us all. I will not sanction his murder. You must swear that no harm will come to him. Swear it."

"I swear," Valleri sighed with more than a hint of belligerence, "no harm will come to Lesuperis not of his own doing."

Not exactly the oath I had in mind, but I did not press it.

Valleri snorted and strode to the window. Facing me, he leaned against the casement and folded his arms over his chest. "Whatever shall I get you for a wedding gift?"

I sensed beneath the bitterness his pain at the thought I should be given to another man. His anguish both touched and amused me. Smiling, I went to his side. "Oh, Valleri. There isn't going to be a wedding. I'm sure Uncle will rethink his brashness and come to his senses. I need only be patient."

"You deceive yourself if you think Bertrand will relent."

"At least I am giving him the chance, which is more than he gave me."

"And if he does not reconsider? What will you do then, Kathedra?"

I hadn't given that any thought, confident of Uncle's capitulation. "I don't know. But I won't wed Lesuperis, even if the price of defiance is disinheritance. There are people in Thylana who still believe I am the rightful heir, those who would see me on the throne. Perhaps I'll join the Crusaders. Who knows? They might even win me my crown."

I jested, of course. But Valleri took me seriously. "That may not be wise. While there are those who would resurrect you to the throne, there are just as many, particularly in the Umagi camp, who would rather see the Gryphon Highlord's head on a stake. I can see the benefits in switching sides, but too many Crusaders I fear, have long memories and won't forget you once fought against them. They won't trust you. You'd probably be executed."

"Valleri, it's a jest. You talk as if it's an option."

"Forgive me, Kathedra. I'm just not thinking straight, is all." He shook his head and pushed himself away from the window. "I'm tired of talking. I'm tired of arguing. It's all too mind-boggling to comprehend right now. Perhaps we should sleep on it. We'll be able to think more clearly in the morning."

"I'll be a long time falling asleep." I glanced up hopefully. "Can you stay tonight? I really don't want to be alone."

"Sorry, no. I can't risk being here." Grinning, he slipped my hand into his. "But I'll linger awhile, until you fall asleep."

The door was bolted, so we need fear no intrusion. Valleri has a way of making me forget my troubles. He did not disappoint me this night. It was easy to lose myself in his embrace, to fall under the spell of urgent hands and eager lips. Yet, afterward, I could not shake the feeling this tryst had been our last.

I guess I slept. For in the morning, Valleri was gone.

I spent the next three days pondering my tumble from grace. Meanwhile, I continued to receive my required dose of tonic. This I succumbed to meekly, for it is administered by the one person I fear even more than I do Uncle. Grezalia-my former governess, now my jailor.

A stern old spinster she covers herself head to toe in drab robes that serve only to emphasize her ample girth. Tall and stout, she towers over my slight stature and probably weighs twice as much. She wears her dark hair, now peppered with grey, in a tight, modest bun, the pain of which I assume accounts for her surly disposition. In addition is an ever present smirk-a smirk that has stretched considerably since my disgrace and subsequent confinement.

My fear is rooted in childhood, when her formidable shadow loomed over me, threatening the imperial posterior with a switch. I view her still with the eyes of a twelve year old girl, who'd never committed any offence worse than filching honeycakes from the kitchen, but who now, over a decade later, faces down a horde of Crusader fanatics on any given day.

"This is all your father's fault," she huffed, watching as I drank the concoction. "From the moment that witch man set foot inside this castle I knew he'd cause nothing but problems."

"I see," I replied with sugary venom, feeling particularly brave today. "Not only are you a governess and a jailor, you're also a prophet."

"It doesn't take a prophet to tell it is that very same insolence which has brought you to where you are today. Hmph. An Umagi trait, I suppose. Your father was no different, so arrogant, so…" and she was off, foaming at the mouth.

With an ease born of practice, I shut her out and let my thoughts turn inward. It is her inclination to blame everything on my father, for it was from him that I inherited my Umagi powers.

Father was Teki, a member of that branch of the Umagi family tree whose magical source derives from telekinesis, the most mysterious and unpredictable of all Umagi talents. Thus, it is paramount that Teki children are able to learn young how to control and wield their extraordinary powers. As a five-year old I can remember the early lessons he taught me: Will must control thought. Power is the strength of will. The walls separating emotion from thought must never be breached, or chaos ensues. Alas, my father, a respected Umagi healer, broke that cardinal rule himself while tending a farmer severely injured in a fire. So badly did he want that man to live, desire over-rode will, and he let slip too much power. His patient survived, but he didn't.

Devastated by his loss, which followed closely behind the disaster at Idyll, Mother was prone to manipulation. In the turmoil following these events, she was pressed by some, not just Uncle, to restrict the Umagi and their powers. But she didn't believe that protecting one segment of her subjects by sacrificing another was the answer. In my case, however, she bent beneath the pressure when it was pointed out that Thylana might not accept a witch-queen. Thus, to appease her brother and his supporters, she gave the apothecary permission to concoct a tonic to repress the manifestation of my powers.

"No, it's Uncle's fault," I blurted, interrupting Grezalia's tirade.

She glared down at me with the visage of an avenging harpy. "Impudent witch child! How dare you? Have you no respect for your uncle, for your sovereign?"

Ahh, poor deluded Grezalia. She's had hopes of snaring Uncle for herself ever since he arrived, bemused and distraught, on Gryphon's doorstep with orphans, widows, and wounded in tow. Maybe she thought she could ease his heartbreak, and in time make him swell with new life, but her efforts went wasted. Uncle might as well have lost his sight along with his heart at Idyll, for he never saw another woman since the loss of his fair Pepet.

In vain attempts to woo his attention, she has taken boot kissing to an art form. But if she believes her mental torture of me will set her in Uncle's good graces, she is mistaken. She is just a bitter old woman who has thrown away her life, pining for a man who repays her devotion with ignorance, who neither knows, nor cares, that she exists.

Nevertheless, I could tolerate Grezalia's impertinence no longer. "Get out," I snapped. "Take your medicine vials and vulgar comments and get out."

Collecting her tray, she stalked to the door where she paused to throw me the taunt, "You know, if you had any honour at all, you'd cut your wrists."

"Rot you," I muttered, plucking a toy horse from its shelf and hurling it at the closed door. I was rewarded with a solid, satisfying thud, for the piece was constructed of a sturdy wood and had weathered well similar treatment.

Regretting my temper, I retrieved the horse and stroked the fresh nick in its glossy, timbered hide as I pondered Valleri's words. Had he spoken them out of sincerity or kindness? Either way, did it matter? Regardless, they filled me with renewed doubt and suspicion.

Perhaps it is self-pride, but I believe my role as the Gryphon Highlord more than just a symbol. While it is true I rarely participate in hand-to-hand combat, I recall frequent times when we underestimated the Crusaders' ingenuity and I was forced to enter the fray. I fought on horseback when challenged and I dismounted to engage in swordplay when my braver enemies thought themselves superior enough to take my standard-an insult I will not endure, a victory I will give no one.

So if Valleri spoke the truth, how can Uncle retire me? Surely my duty to produce heirs can wait until the Crusaders are vanquished and Thylana is secure once more. Certainly Uncle can overlook gossip about my romance with Valleri if it means deliverance for Thylana. Still, Uncle's abrupt dismissal puzzles me. Beyond a doubt I am the most valuable of his officers, the majority of whom are useless cowards.

So why do I sit behind locked doors, like any common prisoner, awaiting marriage to a man I despise?

A riddle I have only four days to figure out.

CHAPTER THREE

My third day of captivity and still no apology from Uncle. The door remains barred except when Grezalia brings my tonic, or dear sweet Cook arrives with my meals. My wedding gown has been delivered, along with silk slippers and matching veil. I hated it on sight. It is very beautiful, all lace and satin, trimmed with pearls and fancy bows. But it is virgin white. I distinctly recall telling the head seamstress scarlet, for I wished to make a statement. Uncle wouldn't allow it. No veil, then. I shredded it to ribbons.

Fretting that Uncle would not relent, I sent messages pleading for an audience, but he refused them. His rejection hurt, so much that if not for my tonic I'd have wept buckets. This is what has become of the glorious Gryphon Highlord.

At last, on the fourth night, Valleri came to visit me in his secret fashion, for I am denied personal visitors. I could barely contain myself, so starved was I for news of the world beyond my prison walls. Still, I felt it only polite to inquire first into our military situation.

In terms of warfare the revolt began over a year ago, despite the fact that unrest had been brewing since Mother's death. It began with small demonstrations or marches against the Regent's purported oppression, then progressed to civil disobedience with the perpetration of such acts as vandalism, looting, and arson against those who supported Uncle's edicts.

Mind you, all the great armies are gone now, having devoured one another on the fields of blood three centuries ago. Only one kingdom rose from the bones of the dead: Thylana. Nevertheless, Uncle retaliated the only way he knew how. After several decades of domestic peace, he reinstated the office of the Gryphon Highlord and divided his castle troops into Royals, then sent them out to quell the violence and muzzle the outspoken. He put me in charge because I was the only person he trusted, not because I was necessarily most qualified for the job.

But to Uncle's everlasting dismay, the Umagi refused to be herded back into exile and the commoners only grew more aggressive. Soon the Citizens Risen Up to Stand Against a Dread and Errant Regency was established, which had money to hire, of all things, mercenaries to back up its lofty ideals. Head firmly planted in the sand, Uncle dismissed the organization as rabble and denounced them as outlaws. Too late he realized the Crusaders were serious.

The castle troops had previously spent their time patrolling the borders, quashing poachers, and ridding the countryside of bandits. Their duties included policing fairs and market squares, on the alert for thieves, cutpurses, and drunken troublemakers. To be truthful, the Royals knew little about real warfare, but we were learning, as were the Crusaders. Learning too well I feared.

I don't believe Uncle had ever wanted to kill anyone, but there was blood on both party's hands now, and he would do anything to restore order, to save his throne. Even if it meant making war on his own people.

As it stands now our military might is spread pretty thin. While raiders from across the far northern sea continue to wreak havoc on the borderlands, the Royals are hard pressed to contain what Uncle insists is an outbreak of unrest instigated by a misguided few. But we try. When the Crusaders seize towns, we drive them out. When they block roads, we open them by force. When they waylay merchant caravans, we cut off access to the highways. But always more towns are seized, more roads blockaded, and more caravans robbed. Thus, this tug of war has escalated and will continue until one side or the other loses patience and launches an all out assault.

"Any major developments?" I asked, affecting a tone of interest.

Valleri seemed distracted. "Tock broke the impasse at the southern crossroads. He dealt the Crusader commander there a telling blow. It's believed he is permanently out of action if not dead. Still no word from our spies, however. I fear our agents are being discovered and dispatched before they can contact us."

"But that's good news," I chirped. "It leaves us one less outlaw champion to worry about. Without its leaders the organization will fall apart. Tock has scored a major coup."

"Good news for Bertrand, yes."

He fell curiously silent, forcing me in my impatience to demand, "Well? Have you heard anything? What is the rumour in the castle?"

"It's not good, Kathedra," he replied, his tone ominous as he slumped into a chair.

My shoulders sagged, and though I sensed the worst, I asked anyway. "Uncle hasn't changed his mind?"

"And I'm here to tell you that he won't."

I nodded, accepting that answer with my body but not my heart. "Has he named my successor?"

"No, not yet."

"What about our allies? What is their position? Have you spoken to Uncle's advisors? Perhaps they can be petitioned to sway him."

"How, Kathedra?" Valleri snapped. "How can I know what our allies think? How can I move Bertrand's advisors? I'm a lowly lieutenant. I'm not privy to such circles."

"What about Arial? Surely he won't sit by and allow this outrage to occur."

He slid me a sideways glance. "The Regent ordered Arial's Royal north to Shipsford to investigate an increase in bandit activity. He won't be back any time soon."

Well, that was convenient. I repressed a shudder at the mention of Shipsford. Arial was welcome to it. I recalled riding through there last summer, after repelling a particularly savage raider assault. One minute the villagers were hailing me a hero for saving their homes and farms from the dreaded northern invaders, the next they were calling me oppressor and setting my horse's tail on fire. There is just no pleasing some people.

I bit my lip to keep from bursting out in frustration. It would serve no purpose to alienate my sole ally. "Have you found out anything at all?"

"Oh, yes, Kathedra," Valleri murmured in a tone that said he was not happy with me. "Oh, yes, indeed." His eyes glinted with something akin to anger. "I overheard a pair of guards talking. It seems you 'tried to incinerate the Regent's head'. Is that true?"

"Please," I snorted, waving a hand. "If I'd really wanted to send Uncle's bald pate up in flames I could have done so."

"That's not the point."

"It was an accident."

"An accident?" His gaze hardened to granite. "Like the other night when you destroyed that set of goblets?"

"No. I mean, yes. Oh, what's the difference? I didn't mean to do it. It just slipped. It won't happen again."

"But it's happened before."

I turned my back to him, indignant at the thought I need explain myself. "Just forget it, Valleri. I don't want to discuss it."

"We must discuss it, Kathedra."

"I fail to see what this has to do with my plight. You're supposed to be helping me. I want to know why Uncle has done this."

"You already know. You just don't want to believe it. The drug is losing its effect. It can no longer properly restrain your powers."

"True, my tonic is not as potent in its present measure, but the dosage needs only be increased."

Valleri got to his feet and placed gentle but firm hands on my shoulders. "Kathedra, you know that will not work-has not worked. You've been upping the dosage on your own and it hasn't helped."

I tried to deny it but Valleri's hands only tightened. "No, Kathedra. Don't lie to me. I paid a visit to the medicinal stores where your tonic is housed and discovered a...discrepancy. You've been stealing it and administering it to yourself without telling anyone. How long has this been going on?"

Though his discovery of my perfidy came as some relief, I began to tremble with uncertainty. "I've done so for almost six months now, ever since I noticed my need had grown."

"How bad is it, Kathedra? How far has it gone? On the day you broke the goblets, how much did you take?"

"My regular dosage plus two."

I felt Valleri tense, heard his gasp of surprise. "Three full doses and they did not last the day?"

Twisting in his arms, I saw the shock roll across his face and hurried to reassure him. "Yes, that's true. But I've been experimenting, Val. I can control my Umagi talent. Well, a little anyway. I've let it slip forth in small increments. Remember our victory at Alags Field three months ago? Remember the earth tremors, the hailstorm that whipped up seemingly out of nowhere? I did that, Val. I did. Didn't you see how the enemy fled in droves?"

"Yes, and don't think I didn't see that half of our men fled the field right alongside them."

"It needs some tweaking, I admit. But, Val—" I clutched his arms with barely reined excitement, "I'm learning to channel my powers, to direct them where I will."

Gently, he disengaged himself from my grip. "It doesn't matter, Kathedra. I don't think you should take up the study of telekinesis upon a battlefield. And I'm sure most everyone else will agree with me, Bertrand included."

"Maybe not, but I need to learn." My fingers caught his sleeve. "Listen, Val. I don't have a choice now. The drug has become practically useless. In order for it to continue working, the dose has to be so high it leaves me a veritable zombie, incapable of consciousness, let alone the ability to function. While Uncle may suspect my dose needs to be increased, he doesn't have to know the whole truth of it. All I have to do is—"

"Too late, my dear. He knows. Your clandestine forays into the dispensary haven't gone unnoticed on the apothecary or Bertrand. This is the ultimate betrayal, worse in his eyes than even what your mother did."

The shock of that rendered me momentarily speechless.

Valleri wrapped his arms around me, resting his head on my shoulder. "Oh, Kathedra," he whispered. "Don't you realize that was the worst thing you could have done? Bertrand was afraid there might come a time when the drug would lose its potency, but he expected you to tell him. He doesn't trust you anymore. Why did you hide it from him? From me?"

"Because I was scared-scared something like this might happen." My voice caught, tripping over my fear. "And it has!" I tried to shrug out of his grasp but he held me all the tighter. "Val, I can settle this uprising for him, for Gryphon. I know I can. All he has to do is trust me."

"And you expect him to do that now, after what you've done? Kathedra, my love, you are in such danger you can't imagine. Your drug dependency was intended to last a lifetime. You were never, ever, supposed to wean yourself from it, let alone learn to wield your Umagi powers."

"Why not? If Uncle wouldn't be so stubborn, I could throw away the tonic, and concentrate on my magic. How can he deny me that? Hell, Valleri, you said yourself that he doesn't want what happened to Mauranna to happen to me."

A glazed look came over his features, like he'd gone somewhere else for just a moment. With a shudder, he came back to me. "This has nothing to do with what happened at Idyll. It has to do with this revolt, and more pointedly, yours. Bertrand will never forgive the people for turning on him, for taking the side of the Umagi over his. He will tolerate neither magic nor insurrection in Thylana, including yours. Tales have been taken back to the throne room, Kathedra. He knows your views concerning the Umagi. He knows your allegiance is shifting. Do I really need to spell it out for you? You're the next best thing to a traitor."

"No, Val, I'm not. You know that."

"But there's more, Kathedra. Think about it. If the tonic no longer controls your powers, that means Bertrand no longer controls you. As you are now-untaught and inexperienced in the ways of magic-you are unpredictable, unmanageable, even dangerous. But once you master your Umagi talent, and learn to work it to your will, you will truly be formidable. You will become a threat, his worst nightmare come true."

"A threat? How?"

"Whether you realize it or not, your telekinesis, once tapped and properly channelled, could become an awesome weapon. You caught a brief glimpse of that power at Alags Field. You can turn on him, challenge him, and if he resists, you can use your own Royal, together with your magic, to put him down. That's why you were retired. You've become too powerful with all your influence, winning the undying loyalty of troops whose first loyalty should be to the Regent. In time, you could rally all of Castle Gryphon's Royals to your banner, then crush him and his Halberdiers. The people of Thylana would call you a hero."

I was appalled. "That's preposterous! I would never betray Uncle. I would never violate the high laws of my ancestors. Never."

His patience lost, Valleri snarled, "The day will come when he pushes you too far and you will be forced to retaliate. However, that day may come too late. Even now, he hastens to bend you to his will while you are still within his thrall, forcing you from your post of command into an arranged marriage so you will be in less of a position to rebel against him. If he waits until you gain total mastery of your powers you won't stand for it."

I railed against him, not wanting to believe a word of it. "If it's true that I pose such a threat to him, why didn't he send me from Thylana in exile, too? Why, when insurrection broke out, did he bestow upon me the most coveted title in Thylana and grant me all the authority that goes with it?"

"Because maybe in the beginning Bertrand hoped your magic could be of use to him, an instrument to be forged into a great weapon. He knows well the destructive capabilities of Umagi talent, witnessed it first hand. But he can't control it any more than he can control you."

A spreading numbness crept through me, cold and debilitating. As Valleri suspected, I had known in the back of my mind the cause of my downfall. There was no reason now, since the truth had been spoken aloud, for me to continue denying it. I was a weapon with the potential to grow so proficient that I must be destroyed.

Light-headed, I swayed and reached out for Valleri's arm to steady myself. He took my hand, lending me his strength. Gently, he murmured, "You must leave, Kathedra. If you want to save yourself, your only hope of escape from Bertrand is to flee Thylana."

"Leave?" I repeated, dazed. "I can't leave. I can't leave my home. I can't abandon Thylana to Uncle's mercy. If I flee, I will be disinherited. Then I will never sit on the throne. I will never get the opportunity to right all Uncle's wrongs. But if I remain, if I bend my knee to his will and marry Lesuperis, he may forgive my defiance. He may even—"

I heard myself babbling. Valleri's stern voice cut in above mine. "If you remain, you will never sit on the throne." His eyes narrowed into angry slits and his grip tightened about my shoulders. "Do you honestly believe that once you give birth to Thylana's heir you will live out the day?"

"Uncle wouldn't dare! He must abide by the laws of our ancestors. To shed family blood is a sin too vile even for him." I tried to disengage myself but his grip was too strong. I wanted to throw something, anything, hurl it at the wall or pound away at the stone bricks until they crumbled into dust. I felt the confusion welling up inside me and fought to curtail any random thoughts, thoughts that without purpose or direction might find release in dangerous and violent ways.

"Listen to me," he hissed, his face a scant inch from mine. "Blood and honour and law-none of it matters to Bertrand. He seeks only to preserve himself and everyone else be damned. If you want to save your throne and your life, you must leave."

"No!" I cried, over and over, a litany of shock. "No!"

Above us the iron wheel and its host of candles swayed upon its chain. The dishes on the table jiggled and bounced, tinkling musically against one another. My coat rack toppled to the floor. Books tumbled from the shelves in my bedroom. Even the tapestries on the walls shifted askew.

"Kathedra, stop it." Spinning me around, Valleri shook me until my teeth rattled in my head. "Control it," he commanded. "Turn it. Force it down. You must. You can do it, Kathedra. Just concentrate."

I tried. Focussing all my will, all my strength, I struggled against the tide of power surging up inside me. My fingers balled into fists around Valleri's hands, my nails drawing blood. With supreme effort I thrust my rage and frustration aside. Slowly, rational thought returned. The tableware ceased their impromptu dance and the iron chain swung to a standstill.

Perspiration soaked my clothes and matted my hair. I felt cold all over. Exhausted, I lifted my gaze to Valleri. His eyes were wild, his hair and skin as damp as mine. "Help me," I begged. "Valleri, please. Help me."

His eyes lost their feral look and his features relaxed. He even managed a weak smile. "I'll help you, Kathedra. Have no fear."

He guided me onto my settee, then poured us each a measure of wine. We drank it down quickly and he poured again. As I sipped from my second cup, I asked, "Where will I go?"

"Zigores, I think. It's a known haven for Umagi renegades. When you get there ask for asylum from Bertrand, but under no circumstances reveal your true identity. You'll have coin enough to pay your way, as well as to apprentice yourself to the best Teki adept you can find. You can stay there, studying and learning, until I deem the situation in Gryphon safe for your return."

"And how will I know when it's safe?"

His hand stole across the space between us to cover mine. "I will come for you myself. I will find you. Come fire or brimstone, flood or famine, I will find you, and bring you home. The only problem I see will be getting you to Zigores in the first place."

Zigores. I allowed a wry smile. None of Uncle's agents had been able to infiltrate the place. Maybe I would succeed where a hundred others had failed.

"Getting there, yes." I sipped my wine, reflective. Zigores lay many miles east. But in the east, so lurked the Crusaders. I had every confidence I could get there, once I got out of Thylana. Trouble is, can I get out?

"You will be hunted," Valleri observed, as if reading my thoughts. "Bertrand will not permit you to escape his yoke. He won't let you run around loose. Here, under the influence of your tonic, you are like a leashed hound. But now that leash is severed. Dangerous you will be in your own right if you decide to turn on him, but you will be a formidable weapon against him in the hands of his enemies. For your own sake, you can't allow yourself to cross paths with the Crusaders."

One question still puzzled me. "How will I get out of the castle? I'm under house arrest, remember? I'll never get past the sentries."

"You will if we plan your escape for the night of your wedding."

"That's leaving it to the last minute, don't you think?"

"Yes, but it's the best time. As tradition dictates, the ceremony will take place in the evening, which shall provide us the cover of darkness. Since it's an atmosphere of celebration security will be lax. There will be plenty of noise and confusion, what with entertainers and guests all making merry. The bailey will be deserted. By the time the wedding party arrives to collect the bride, you will be in the secret passage on your way to the stables."

My spirits lifted at the thought I'd be going to Zigores, a place far from the turmoil and strife of Thylana, there to be among fellow Umagi. A place where I'd be able to study magic without interference from Uncle or drugs.

Only one thing worried me. Would I ever be able to return to Thylana and sit on my mother's throne? Uncle was not the only obstacle in my path. There were the Crusaders, as well.

My consternation must have shown on my face, for Valleri set aside his goblet and slipped onto the settee beside me. "Don't worry, Kathedra. The Crusaders are no match for the mighty Royals of Thylana. They will be quickly and thoroughly vanquished. Castle Gryphon will never fall. She will await your ascension to the throne, when you return to Thylana as sole mistress of your powers and challenge Bertrand for what is rightfully yours. Then no one, not even Bertrand, can oppose you. And I, with all your loyal troops, shall stand beside you."

Smiling, I reached out to fondle a strand of his hair. "But what of you, Val, in the meantime? If Uncle discovers you helped me escape he will not be lenient. I will live in constant fear for you."

"You mustn't. I'm insignificant and agile enough to sidestep Bertrand."

I counted myself lucky to have Valleri for my trusted friend. But such loyalty is not always a good thing. He would lie, cheat, steal, and risk himself for me. He would do anything for a cause he believed in. Even kill. I must resign myself to the ugly fact that Uncle and I have become enemies. I know that one day I will have to oppose him if I ever want to reclaim my homeland. I also know that I will use my magic against him if forced, as much as I hope it doesn't come to that.

It would take many years to heal the land, to regain the trust of the people, and to restore my family's good name after all the injustices Uncle had wrought. But even after learning he had conspired against me for years, I would not make him pay the price for his treachery with his life.

"Valleri, I ask you to protect my interests here in Thylana. Keep my name alive in Castle Gryphon. Do whatever you can. Everything, I mean, short of murder. I don't desire Uncle's death. Promise me you will do nothing rash."

Defiance flickered in his eyes but quickly passed. "I swear I shall not harm a hair on his head."

That oath would not suffice, for Uncle's head was balder than a baby's bottom. "Val, your word."

As expected, he balked. Apparently he had plans of his own for Uncle. Nonetheless he relented. "I promise, Kathedra. You have my word. But I will do everything within my power, short of killing him, if he in any way threatens your return or sabotages your throne."

"So be it." I began to worry Uncle may have an 'accident'. Twice, I had extorted promises from Valleri. I would not risk a third.

"You'll have to rely on your own ability to control your powers. You must conceal them from everyone you meet during your journey to Zigores. You can do it, Kathedra. I know you can. You have great strength and willpower. You need only remain calm and patient."

Therein lay the problem. I've learned to control my Teki blood under normal circumstances, but as my outbursts in Uncle's throne room and here in my own prove, I am hard pressed to do so when agitated. Valleri had more faith in me than I did.

Forcing a confidence into my voice I did not feel, I said, "I just hope that one day I'll be able to reward you for all your loyalty."

"The only reward I need is to see you crowned queen." He surprised me by dropping to a knee at my feet and taking my hand. "Don't despair, Kathedra. You will sit on Thylana's throne. I promise you."

"Promise me one more thing, Val," I urged, squeezing his fingers. "Promise you will be there at my side…my consort."

He bowed his head, the image of abject humility. "I am not worthy. My blood is not yours. I am fortunate to serve as your second. I am too lowborn to share your dais, to share your bed."

"Ahh, now I see," I purred, sliding into his lap and pushing him down to the leopard-skin rug. "But you are not too lowborn, not too humble, to share the Gryphon Highlord's bed? I shall be the one to judge your worthiness, Noble Knight." Bending to nibble his ear, I murmured, "You are more than worthy."

"Truly, Highness, you are too kind." He grinned and drew me down to him, his fingers finding the laces of my tunic.

But at that moment an idea occurred, and I wondered why I did not think of it sooner. "Valleri," I breathed, drawing up his coarse, homespun shirt to expose his chest, "come with me."

"Hmm?" he queried, taking no time to unfasten his mouth from my throat.

"Come with me."

His back stiffened beneath my hands, and disengaging his lips, he leaned his head against the floor to stare up at me with furrowed brow. "What?"

"To Zigores. Oh, please, Val. I can't bear to be separated from you."

I smiled a dreamy smile and bent to kiss the tattoo stamped just below his heart, acquired in his early days as a Halberdier, the existence of which I had only cause to discover recently. Of peculiar design, it depicted an eagle's widespread wings clutching in their talons a bloodied heart, wreathed in chains. For the life of me I don't understand why men choose to mar their bodies so, but Valleri tells me I should be flattered. According to him, the imagery symbolizes his bond of service to the house of Gryphon, and by extension me.

"We shall live in exile together."

Amazement flashed across his face. He pulled himself up so abruptly that I was forced to sit. "Kathedra, this is no romantic adventure you're undertaking. You're fleeing for your life."

His sharpness startled me. "I know. I just want you with me. I need you, Val."

"You need me here. Who else will look after your interests? Who else will protect your throne? Who else will be here to open the gate when you return?

Who will if not I?"

"Then you choose not to go with me?" My disappointment would not be disguised.

"It's not that I don't want to go," he clarified, gently smoothing the hair back from my cheek. "I wish with all my heart I could. But it's just not possible. Please understand. I can do you the most service here."

I nodded, feeling somewhat sheepish. "I'm sorry, Val. What you say makes sense. I'm being selfish. I want you with me because I don't want to be alone. Because dragging you along would be easier than saying good-bye."

Pulling me to him, he rested his chin upon my head. "I know, Kathedra. It is not easy for me either. But we must say farewell and I must leave. If we spend this night together, it will only be harder on us both. You might be tempted to stay and I might be tempted to go. Neither of which will do us any good."

He was right, of course. We'd already had our last night together, its memory sweeter because we had spent it in blissful ignorance.

Rising, Valleri tugged me to my feet and kissed my brow. "When I come for you, be ready." Then taking his torch, he slipped into the tunnel, where its dark length soon swallowed him up.

I closed the panel, replaced my teak and silk screen, then returned to the settee, certain that I'd never felt so alone.

CHAPTER FOUR

The day of my wedding dawned sunny and warm. Standing at the window I gazed east into the rising sun and plotted my course. A thousand acres of parkland surrounded Castle Gryphon. The main road from the keep led south, well out of my way. The greatest concentration of Crusaders, however, sat beyond the castle's boundaries, between the highway and the edge of the forest. They controlled the entire southeast from a secret location, which no Royalist had been able to unearth, to Uncle's chagrin.

My most obvious route was to cross the park and head east, straight into the forest, the other side of which would deposit me in rich farmland, leagues away from Uncle and Crusaders both. With a little luck the light of a full moon would guide me. I could then continue on to my final destination, taking care to skirt roads and towns. The hardest part would be escaping the castle itself, which was beyond my control. I'd just have to trust that to Valleri.

I was still in my robe when Grezalia arrived with my breakfast and tonic. She greeted me with her customary scowl, which I ignored. Miffed that her ugly mug had not cowed me, she sneered, "How is our blushing bride-to-be this morning?"

I made no reply, wary of her scathing tongue. Instead I surveyed my bland meal and the tiny medicine bottle beside it. The vial, I noted, contained three doses. Ah. My conspirators had caught on. But what they did not know was that a mere three doses would lose their effect before the day was out. My powers would be fully restored by the time Valleri came to collect me.

I poured the potion into my juice and gulped it down under Grezalia's arched brows. Then, poking at my eggs, I dismissed her with a wiggle of my pinkie.

But upon her departure she paused at the door, turned and said with more cheer than any sane person could possibly muster at so early an hour, "Another vial will be brought with your supper."

I damned near choked on my eggs and the shrew did not move an inch to save me. "But…that will be six doses," I sputtered. Four doses in one day gave me an excruciating headache. What would six do?

"Your skill at arithmetic is astounding." Her smirk stretched into an ear-to-ear grin.

"I shall have to be held up at the altar!" I shouted.

"That is the point, of course. His Excellency can't risk any disruption of the service. I do pity your poor bridegroom, however, for he may have to wait a day or two to consummate the marriage."

"He'll wait a hell of a lot longer than that!" But I raved at a closed door.

I spent the afternoon trying to rally my Teki powers, in vain. Desperate to find a solution, I wondered what advice my father might have for me. As an attentive, eager five-year old, I can still hear him saying, "Random thoughts lead to random words, Little Red. Therefore, if you can't think anything nice…"

As promised, Grezalia delivered a second vial of tonic with my supper. She also brought a friend, the Halberdier captain, all rigged up in his dress uniform.

"I don't recall inviting you to my wedding, sir." A sarcastic jest. In truth, I hadn't invited anyone.

He stiffened but otherwise gave no indication he heard. Although the captain and I are healthy rivals, there is no malice between us. I doubt it came easy for him to serve as my keeper. We have no squabble with each other. The captain minds his own business and doesn't involve himself in castle politics. His duty is to protect the Regent and that's what he does. But in doing his duty he uses it as an excuse to overlook unpleasant details, such as the brutish tendencies of his men and the inanity of Uncle's orders. I can fault him only for his lack of backbone. My cause would receive no sympathy from him.

Grezalia tapped a large wooden spoon on the flat of her palm. I wondered what mayhem she intended with such a powerful weapon, and whether the captain perhaps carried a bloodthirsty whisk.

"Drink up," she ordered, indicating my cup of …water?

Ignoring the command, I lifted the lid of my bowl. "Broth and water?" Uncle not only wants me submissive, he wants me emaciated. "What kind of 'last meal for the condemned' is this?"

"Cook has prepared a sumptuous feast to follow the ceremony. You may eat then, if you are able, with your guests." Grezalia aimed her terrible weapon at the vial. "Drink it. I won't ask you a third time. The captain will."

Having no choice but to comply, I poured the tonic into my cup and watched it turn the water a sickish green hue. But as I brought the goblet to my lips, I hesitated. Normally, my juice disguised the unpleasant odour and diluted the obnoxious taste, but water is…well, merely water.

I drank half the cup, and unable to finish it, lowered my hand. Quicker than a striking viper, Grezalia slammed her spoon onto the table, barely missing my fingers. "All of it!" she barked.

I obeyed, but only after giving the woman my best withering glare. Gagging, I forced the rest of the foul liquid down my throat.

"Now eat your broth. The seamstress will be here soon to dress you."

I surveyed her dull, shapeless robes. "Shall I assume you won't be in attendance at this farce tonight?"

She beamed a grin of triumph. "On the contrary, a horde of sabre-toothed hobgoblins couldn't keep me away."

Well, I guess not. They'd probably welcome her as family. "In that case, do dress appropriately for the occasion," I harrumphed, dipping a spoon into my soup, "or I shall have you tossed out."

Chuckling merrily to herself, she trotted out the door, the Halberdier captain trailing at her heels like a sullen puppy.

By the time the head seamstress and her assistants arrived I felt like I'd drunk a keg of ale. Fortunately, I bypassed the headache and went straight to the nausea. As the women fussed and hovered over me, I warned them twice to fetch me a bucket. Twice they ignored me. Therefore I vomited all over my pretty petticoats, scattering my attendants like a flock of squawking geese.

It did not take long for them, however, to regroup and resume my torture. Naturally they could not overlook this opportunity for gossip. While the head seamstress chided me at great length for ruining my veil, the girls speculated in low tones about my unexpected illness. I let them say and do what they would. It was pointless to protest even if I could, for a strong lethargy had come over me, sapping my will.

Their evil work complete, my tormentors settled me on my settee and arranged my train about my slippers. Though they tried to make me sit like a lady, I could manage only a half-hearted sprawl. My head lolled over the backrest, prompting me to marvel aloud at the intricate network of cobwebs that adorned the ceiling.

"Oh, my," cooed one of the girls to her accomplices. "She looks so pale, so sick. Do you think she'll be all right?"

Another chimed in, "She's fine. All she needs is a rest and some air."

Then, "Poor, little dear. Do you suppose she's with child? Perhaps that's why she's being married so hastily to that snivelling whelp."

"Maybe we should stay with her until the bridal party arrives."

"No," I croaked out, raising my head so quickly I saw stars. "Leave me. All of you."

I must have sounded more menacing than I felt, for they fled the room without a backward glance.

Left alone I discovered I was famished. I dragged myself upright and tottered to a cabinet, stomping like a great white pachyderm all over my lovely gown. There I retrieved the box of honeyed almonds Cook had given me as a wedding gift-the only one I'd received-smuggled up to me between a stack of fresh linens by the chambermaid. Prize in hand, I slunk back to the settee and stretched out. Then, hoisting my gown, I dangled my legs over an armrest and kicked off my slippers.

Again the lethargy, the feeling that nothing mattered, settled over me. Forgetting what a mess of sticky honey can do to white satin, and forgetting Uncle, I devoured half the box before I dozed off.

I awoke the instant the door cracked open. Grezalia poked her head around it and took a half step into the room. She wore a frilly pink gown with matching cape and slippers. She'd topped off her already ridiculous outfit with a floppy mauve hat. She looked for all the world like an exploding bouquet of petunias.

Splayed upon my settee, I regarded her from behind drowsy lids. Beyond the door a contingent of guards stood at attention. Uncle wasn't taking the chance that I might bolt.

"You've crumpled your gown," she sniffed. "His Excellency won't be pleased." Her nasty smirk appeared. I got the feeling Uncle's displeasure with me would give her great joy.

"The bridal party will arrive soon. Do try to put on your slippers."

"Hag," I muttered, as the door slid shut behind her.

When I was certain she'd gone, I slunk from my perch and slid the bar into place, then set about ripping the yards of satin and lace from my body, scattering a fortune in pearls all over the floor.

Once extricated from the cumbersome garment, I fled to my bedroom where I'd readied my clothes the previous night. I had donned my breeches and just shrugged into a shirt when I heard my teak screen scrape across the floor and knew Valleri had arrived.

"Kathedra," came his hushed voice. "Where are you?"

Struggling into my boots, I hopped around the corner to find Valleri staring at the torn remnants of my gown. "Here. Help me."

He gaped in disbelief. "Why aren't you ready? The bridal party has already begun its procession."

While I fought with laces and he strapped on my sword belt, I told him what had happened.

"Fiends," he growled. "I knew they might increase your regular dosage but I had no idea they'd try to incapacitate you. Are you all right?"

"Yes, yes," I muttered, fumbling with the clasp of my cloak. "But I can't summon my powers."

A sudden rap on the door made us jump. Uncle's voice bore through the thick wood. "Kathedra, unbar the blasted door! Your groom awaits."

When he received no reply Uncle began to pound on the door, sacrificing regal dignity. "Kathedra, I order you to present yourself at once!"

"Hah!" I grabbed my pack stuffed with a change of clothes and food squirreled away from a week's worth of untouched suppers. "If you want me, you'll have to come in here and get me!"

Indeed, the door started to quake with Uncle's fierce pummelling. Then the banging abruptly ceased and Uncle bellowed for a battering ram.

Seizing my arm, Valleri whispered, "Come. It will hold until they bring the ram. They'll be awhile knocking it down but we must hurry."

We slipped into the secret passageway. Valleri secured the panel behind us so it might provide us a head start, then snatched up the torch set in a wall bracket and led me down the tunnel.

Not until we had turned a corner and the torchlight caught the flash of metal badges did I notice he wore formal attire. “You would actually attend my wedding?” I asked incredulously, my voice bouncing off the stone in eerie tune with our hurried footsteps.

“I am your second,” he reminded me. “Bertrand ordered me to attend. I think he seeks to punish me for our indiscretion. After all, what could be more suitable punishment than forcing me to watch him give you to another man?”

Touched, I started to spout some silly, sentimental drivel but Valleri silenced me with a gesture. We had reached the tunnel’s end. Cautiously, he pushed open the small portal, concealed behind a row of barrels, in an alley near the granaries. We emerged into the darkened bailey, deserted save for the few lonely sentinels pacing the battlements. Except for the troops alert at their posts and the servants at work in the kitchens, everyone in Castle Gryphon awaited my arrival in the chapel, not yet aware of the mayhem I could well imagine was this minute erupting outside my tower apartment.

Keeping to cover and taking care to avoid the guardroom, where Uncle’s personal henchmen, ever vigilant, amused themselves with dice, we stole across the bailey toward the stables. Since all was controlled chaos here, with the arrival of so many extra horses and their attendants, we were able to sneak unnoticed into the rear of the building and to the stall housing my charger. While I quieted him with soothing words and slipped on his bridle, Valleri saddled him.

Something warned me that stealing away in the dead of night on a white horse was not too darn intelligent. But when I questioned Valleri about it he shrugged off my apprehension in that blithe way he takes with everything. “Nonsense. He is the fleetest mount in Gryphon’s stables.”

True, my charger was sure-footed and swift, but I’d never needed to escape pursuit before. I’d just have to take Valleri’s word for it that speed was more important than stealth. Besides, we didn’t have time to ready another horse.

The moment of farewell had arrived.

Embracing, we whispered our partings. “Come with me,” I begged one last time, loath to leave Valleri behind. “You can still change your mind.”

My plea held no sway. He stood stiff and erect, his face grim in the gloom of the stables. “Kathedra, you know I can’t.”

“But if Uncle discovers you aided my escape—”

Valleri hushed me with a kiss. “Don’t worry about me. I can take care of myself.”

Heavy of heart I mounted, and taking the reins in one hand, leaned down in the saddle to touch his cheek. In doing so, I caught sight of something disturbing. “Val, is that blood in your hair? What happened? Are you hurt?”

Stepping beyond reach, he snapped, “It’s nothing. I cracked my head on a protrusion of rock in the tunnel when I came to fetch you. I’m fine. Now go. There’s not much time.”

There were a thousand things I wanted to say but the words would not come. So I said only, "Thank you."

Smiling, Valleri rested his hand on my leg and squeezed my knee. "Remember, Kathedra. No matter what happens, I will always love you."

I believed him. Despite the aura of doom surrounding that statement, I believed him.

He led the charger to the stable door, gave me a cocky salute and grin, then ducked out of sight.

Prodding the horse into the bailey's shadows, I surveyed the gate. The portcullis remained up, politely accessing tardy guests, but a cluster of soldiers milled beneath the archway. I had only seconds to reach the gate.

Strangely enough I felt calm, confident nothing could thwart my escape. I donned my helm and nudged the animal's flanks. We catapulted into the light.

A cry from behind startled me nearly out of my seat. I hauled on the reins and the horse reared, alerting the guards who stood in the archway.

"Drop the gate! Drop the gate!"

Wheeling to face the speaker, I saw the Halberdier captain run from the castle proper as he shouted to his men.

I heeled the stallion and he leapt forward, tearing at breakneck speed across the bailey. Initially I had hoped to take the guards by surprise and send them scattering, but now they were forewarned.

"Drop the damned gate!"

Spurred to action, the guards atop the battlements ran for the tower to engage the windlass. Meanwhile, the soldiers in the archway looked twice at my speeding charger and collected their wits. Some flew into the tower to help with the portcullis while others drew their swords and formed a line before the gate.

"Stop her!"

There came the whine and screech of ancient ironworks as the men struggled to close the gate, but it was too late to stop. The horse bolted straight for the soldiers. A few, seeing I hadn't slowed my charge, dove for cover, but the rest held their positions. The latter, I'm afraid, got trampled.

Keeping my head low on my mount's neck, I thundered beneath the arch as the portcullis was midway down. It crashed to the ground behind me, too quick for anyone to cross before it. The captain's cry changed to "Raise the gate! Raise the blasted gate!"

Slowing to a canter, I threw back my head and laughed in triumph, my cloak whipping out behind me.

But my euphoria did not last long. Halfway across the park I heard the alarm raised. I glanced over a shoulder to see a knot of horsemen charge from the castle and head in my direction.

I urged the stallion into a fresh gallop.

We streaked through the park, my white steed and I, as brilliant as a diamond in the velvet of the night-time sky. I'm sure my pursuers had no trouble keeping us in sight. Upon reaching the forest fringe, I paused to check the horsemen's progress. I heard rather than saw them, the clang of armour and jangle of harness a deafening cacophony to my ears.

I darted into the sanctuary of the forest, where I hoped I could lose them. Instead, I lost myself. It soon became the longest night of my life.

CHAPTER FIVE

I had not realized the enormity of the forest until now. Its dark maw engulfed me, though I had ventured only a few dozen yards inside. Dense foliage made footing treacherous. When the charger blundered onto an overgrown deer path I gave him free rein in the hope it might steer us clear of the bush into country I recognized.

I rode with my sword across my lap.

Time seemed ethereal in this netherworld of gloom, where the glow of the full moon barely penetrated. I couldn't tell whether hours or minutes passed, everything was so still and silent. The forest canopy obliterated the stars, my sole source of navigation. Soon I lost my bearings entirely, following the wretched deer trail, yet having no idea where it led. Though I detected no sign of pursuit, I did not lessen my caution, for I couldn't be sure that I did not just wander in circles. Every tree looked the same, every thorn bush and dead stump.

But I was far from alone. Fear and dread were constant companions. I flinched at the horse's every stumble or whenever a twig cracked under hoof. I tried to invoke a mindspell of protection, weaving it strong with threads of terror and desperation. Of course I had no way of knowing whether or not it worked, unless the absence of pursuit thus far was any indication. Nevertheless, I couldn't maintain my concentration, as every owl hoot and creak from a branch instantly scattered my thoughts.

Then I heard a sound that made my blood run cold; a low rustle rippled out toward me. I paused, every sense alert as I strained to identify other noises emanating from the tangle of growth. Uneasy, the charger grunted and flattened his ears. Despite my soothing words, he only grew more agitated. Too slowly I recognized the sound as the hushed voices of men. Although I should have bolted at the first sign of danger I'd dithered instead. Now, it was all I could do to gather the reins in my trembling hands and try to sneak away.

There was a shout, then a great hue and cry, as men on horseback crashed through the underbrush. In no need of prodding, the stallion leapt forward. Ignoring the narrow path he chose the most direct route and charged into the foliage with Uncle's soldiers bellowing in pursuit.

Brambles raked the horse's flanks and low boughs battered my helm, obscuring my vision. I caught only glimpses of huge hardwoods, their gnarled limbs seeming to open in embrace as I flew past. Panic distorted my perception. Each sapling that sprung up was a soldier reaching for me, each thicket a crouching man. Hanging creepers threatened to knock me from the saddle. My imagination ran wild, turning shadows into concealed soldiers ready to pounce.

Clinging to my mount as he careered through the undergrowth, I willed strength into the spell. Indeed my terror was so great I should be invisible. But my pursuers kept coming, baying at my heels.

Oh, they were relentless! Twice, I lost them in the forest cover and slowed my panicked horse for much needed stealth-listening, watching, hoping. But each time, I heard them nearby, blundering through the bushes on all sides. And each time, they caught sight of me, my white stallion shining like a beacon in the gloom, to resume the hunt with renewed fierceness.

I can't say how long the chase lasted. An eternity it seemed. Nor had I any idea where I was, though the vegetation looked a little less dense and the trees more widely dispersed. Finally, just as a ray of predawn light seeped between the trunks off to my right, indicating the forest edge, my pursuers overtook me.

Flanking me, horsemen attempted to dislodge me from my seat. They knew I wouldn't come easily, but I don't think they were prepared for the savageness with which I resisted them. My blade swept out, cutting down the rider to my left. Veering sharply, I drove the stallion into the horse on my right, smashing its rider against a sturdy elm. All to no avail. I was surrounded.

There were a dozen altogether, members of the Fourth Royal, judging by their colours. Greatly outnumbered, I opted for diplomacy.

"I warn you," I announced in a strong voice, "I won't go back to Uncle willingly. Spare yourselves the trouble and let me pass unhindered."

To my amazement they all looked at one another and laughed. A couple even dismounted. Their mirth subsided, however, when the leader barked from his mount, "Drag the bitch off her horse."

I was astonished that any soldier of Castle Gryphon would address me with such insolence. I became even more astonished as the two unmounted guards proceeded to do their commander's bidding. When the nearest tried to lay hands on, I kicked him into a thornberry bush, then brandished my sword at his companion. Wisely, the man backed away.

"How dare you speak to me so?" I demanded of the officer. "Uncle would have your head if he knew."

The officer ignored me. I could see nothing of his face, hidden behind his helm, nor did I recognize the voice despite its familiar ring. Sparing a glance at the pair of dead soldiers, he drawled, "Come now, boys. The sooner you unseat her, the sooner the fun can begin."

The remark proved to be of some incentive to the others, for the trio of horsemen behind me urged their chargers closer. The thick undergrowth and proximity of the trees allowed me no room to manoeuvre on horseback, making any attempt to break their circle impossible. Thus, it appeared my best position of defence was on foot.

Jumping to the ground, I situated myself so only the corpses were behind me. A threatening lunge forced the chargers to retreat and a menacing gesture held the unhorsed soldier at bay. "Call off your dogs before someone else dies," I spat at the officer.

He glared at me through the narrow slits in his helm. "Drop your sword, Kathedra. You cannot stand against us."

That was all too obvious to me, but I was determined to do whatever I must to avoid going back to Uncle. Not once did I entertain the notion they would do me serious harm, for they would suffer grievously at Uncle's hands if I returned to him injured.

"Fools! I will fight you to your deaths."

The officer motioned to the horsemen at his side. "Take her weapon."

They dismounted and advanced, swords drawn. I braced myself, blade held at the ready, and waited for someone to make a fatal move. They approached with caution, respecting my skill with the sword. None of them wished to die for the sake of my capture.

The boldest of the lot rushed me. He braved a formidable thrust, but his aim was too high and slightly wild. I got two hands on my hilt and blocked the blow. Sparks ignited. I broke off and leapt back as he darted in low. Again I parried effortlessly. He feinted right, but I had anticipated the move and did not try to intercept. Instead I slid aside and drove my blade deep into his torso. Staggering, he let out a yelp, which I cut short with a thrust through the heart.

The other two circled me warily, then advanced together. I met the taller man first, who possessed the longer reach, turning his blow and sidestepping his companion's lunge. I felt my hair stir as his steel whizzed past my temple. The former recovered and got in a couple of good whacks before I slipped under his guard and punched my sword through his thigh. He toppled like a giant oak.

The next was altogether a better swordsman, his blows coming fast and hard. I parried furiously, retreating farther into the brush with every swing of my arm. Once, I dodged him too slowly and his blade sliced into my sleeve, nicking my elbow. Pain lanced through me; I welcomed its presence, hoping it would provoke a telekinetic response. An earth-shattering tremor perhaps, or at the very least a violent whirlwind. But…Nothing. My powers were so diluted I could not summon an ounce worth to save my life.

Meanwhile, my opponent continued to rain blows down upon me. We exchanged an exhausting volley. When his recovery grew sluggish, I took the opportunity for a low feint. He faltered, hesitated just a moment too long, and my blade swooped up to meet his jugular.

I stepped away just as another horseman approached, but I held his skittish gelding at arms length with my gore-drenched sword. Before I could catch my breath, someone grabbed me from behind and wrenched my sword arm back, an elbow locking across my throat. Damn, I'd forgotten that soldier in the prickly bush.

"Drop the blade."

Choking, gasping, I tossed my sword to the ground.

My captor relaxed, his arm slackening around my neck. I still had one free hand. Before anyone could shout a warning, I snatched the dagger tucked under my shirt and stabbed his leg. He screamed, his grip loosening enough for me to twist and drive the knife up between his ribs. As he slumped to the mossy floor, I turned and ran, plunging through the brush like a madwoman.

"Seize her, you useless curs!" the officer raged. "Seize her!"

Blood-smeared knife in hand, I broke free of the forest. Frantic, I paused to collect my bearings. A red ball of fire teetered on the horizon, and I realized it was the rising sun. My desperate flight had deposited me on the eastern edge of the forest. Below the gentle rise wound a desolate tract. If I could just make it to the road, it may take me to a village or…

"There she is!"

A backward glance saw soldiers emerging from the trees. I sprinted for the bleak ribbon of road…but to what avail? The highway provided no traffic where I might lose myself, no pedestrians who may come to my aid. Perhaps it even hid lurking Crusaders, who then would have us all in their stewing pot.

The thunder of hooves drummed through me. Though I knew I couldn't outrun the horses, I lengthened my stride, for the moment still free. Nevertheless, the charger quickly bore down on me. I heard its snorting breath, the mad laughter of its rider. I swerved repeatedly, but the country was too open and the horse overtook me with ease.

As the gelding drew alongside, its rider leaned down in the saddle to scoop me up. I flailed out with my dagger and got in a telling blow, the steel biting deep into my assailant's arm. He screeched in surprise, promptly losing control of the reins. We toppled to the ground and rolled clear of each other. Knocked breathless, I looked up to spy the gelding prancing ten feet away. Hope rising, I crawled towards it.

Then something closed around my ankle, squeezing, hurting. Crazy laughter drifted out behind me. "Got you! I got you!"

Rolling onto my back, I lifted my free leg and bashed the man two or three times in his snout. But the bastard hung on, grinning like an idiot.

Miraculously I still retained my blade. I stabbed at the oaf, only to have him release my leg and snatch my arm instead. Throwing all his weight atop me, he slammed my wrist against the rocky ground until the knife flipped out of my hand.

I was dragged to my feet and shoved up the slope ahead of him, all the while treated to his lewd commentary.

We met the officer riding towards us. He vaulted from the saddle before his horse had even stopped. "Give her to me."

My captor pulled up short, his fingers gouging the flesh of my arm. "But, sir," he whined. "I caught her. I should—"

"Shut-up. She's my catch. My prize. I want her to know who brought down the mighty Gryphon Highlord before you hounds scramble her wits. Now hand her over."

The soldier grunted something and shoved me into his superior's arms. Though I struggled, the man held me to him in a bone-crushing grip. He tore free my helm and threw it to his sullen underling as the rest of his henchmen loped into view.

A gloved hand stroked my cheek, then brushed a tangle of hair from my face. "Ahh, the fair, the proud Kathedra," he whispered. "Still beautiful in all her defeat."

That voice. I knew it, I was certain. A voice I should recognize, but one I was unable to identify. Even now.

Unflinching, I met the dark eyes peering out from behind the visor. "Unmask yourself, you coward."

When he pulled off his helm, I gasped in disbelief. "Averi?"

How ironic that out of all the men who could have been charged with my capture, Averi had won the draw. My nemesis. There was some very negative energy flow between us, although for my part it wasn't personal.

Averi and Valleri were once rivals for the position of my second. While both were skilled swordsmen and able strategists, Averi was too arrogant and brutal for my liking, so I gave the position to Valleri. Chiverly, however, had wasted no time snapping up Averi for his own Royal. I had no cause to believe Averi would be especially pleasant towards me.

"You were wrong to choose Valleri over me," he breathed into my ear, clutching me tighter. "You shouldn't have done that. Val, too, was wrong to keep you all to himself. He will pay. You both will."

His words alarmed me, implying he was in a position to threaten me without risk of reproach from Uncle. But I refused to reveal any sign of that fear to Averi. I matched his murderous stare, repulsed by the hatred in his eyes. His face, the mere sight of which was enough to make the castle wenches swoon, was hard like flint. There was no mercy, no forgiveness, in that iron expression.

He bent closer, his long black hair grazing my face, his breath hot against my cheek. The stench of perspiration and stale mead smothered me. I clung to the idea that he was merely toying with me, trying to scare me, with no intent of actual harm.

Averi pulled me to him in a vulgar pose and his hands fumbled beneath my cloak. Recoiling at his touch, I gathered my nerve and reached down into the well, groping for one last tendril of power.

"Unhand me, sir," I said, managing some venom, "or I'll—"

"You'll what? Hurl a fireball at me? Command the earth to open up and swallow me?" Averi laughed, a harsh sound containing no mirth. "Your demon powers are dead, Kathedra. Without them you are nothing. You hear me? Nothing. How does it feel to be worthless? Helpless? Now you know how it was for me, rejected and scorned by you, forced to watch you play the whore with Valleri, yet unable to do anything about it. Now, Kathedra, it's my turn. Powerless, beaten, you cannot stop me."

That was true. The well was apparently dry. Not a drop of power remained.

Hoping to instil the terror of my uncle I attempted to reason with the lout. "Averi, I urge you not to do anything rash. Harm a hair on my head and Uncle will make you regret it. If you release me now, however, I shall neglect to mention my mistreatment and allow you to take me back to Castle Gryphon with no further resistance."

"Take you back?" Averi sneered. "Who said anything about taking you back? Our orders, straight from Bertrand's mouth, are to stop you, Kathedra. Stop you any way we can." His sneer stretched into a malevolent grin. "If that means putting an arrow in your back, then so be it."

"Uncle would never issue such orders. You lie."

"Our orders are explicit. Under no circumstance should you be allowed to fall into enemy hands. Why, a Crusader could pop up any minute! Bertrand can't let you turn traitor. And he certainly won't permit you to roam around unleashed. Believe me, Kathedra. I can take you back to Gryphon, where you'll rot a slow death in her dungeons…but I am not without mercy."

Snatching a fistful of hair, he pulled my head back to whisper close to my cheek, "Behave yourself, Highness. Don't fight me too hard. Afterward, I'll let you live." Then his lips clamped over mine.

Though stunned by his words, I hadn't lost my wits entirely. I tried to squirm free, succeeding only in cleaving myself closer. Distasteful as it was, I had no choice but to bite him.

Averi pulled away, blood dribbling down his chin, and dealt me a vicious backhand. I hit the ground hard, the air once again sucked from my lungs. Leering down at me, he wiped his mouth with a fist and said, "I've always wanted to do that, Kathedra." He removed his gauntlets, then his sword belt. "And something else, too."

His men gathered in a semicircle to chant and shout crude suggestions. I got an inkling of what heinous crime Averi was about to commit, and was horrified. The beast was going to dare Uncle's wrath for the chance to make me sorry I'd ever spurned him. I'd sooner go back to Uncle, begging his forgiveness on my hands and knees, than endure Averi's idea of mercy.

Averi fell upon me, pinning my arms above my head. His body covered mine as his hands groped and tore at my clothes. I remained motionless just long enough for him to think I wasn't going to resist. Then I brought up my knee.

He rolled away, groaning and clutching at himself. I scrambled to my feet, swung in the direction of the road but again his brutes were there to block me. They caught me easily enough, and proceeded to bounce me around some, amusing themselves until their leader recovered from his paralysis. Laughing, jeering, they flung me back into his arms. Dazed from the abuse suffered at his minions' hands, I barely noticed the blows Averi delivered. Satisfied I was beaten into submission, he shoved me once more to the ground.

Shutting out the taunts of the soldiers I heard only the creak of Averi's leather, my eyes squeezed shut. Then, miraculously, just as I expected the worst, something struck Averi with such force, it lifted him into the air and flung him against the trunk of the nearest tree, knocking him cold.

The hilltop erupted in chaos. Averi's men scattered, some going for their blades, others going for their horses, but not a single one going to the aid of their stricken commander. I remained where I lay, frozen with fresh terror. It had been no beast, nor any sort of mortal weapon that had flattened Averi. A smell like scorched earth floated on the breeze, one I instantly recognized. The scent of spent magic.

A man leapt over me, brandishing a sword and bellowing challenge to my fleeing attackers. "Gutless bastards! Do you know no other sport than attacking defenceless travellers? Stand and fight!"

A couple did just that, taking after my saviour with a vengeance. He made short work of them, however, slicing off the hand of one and skewering the kidney of the second. They fell back, howling and shrieking their agony to the world.

I had no idea how many potential rescuers had arrived, but there were at least two, for a second voice called from somewhere off to my left, "Behind you, sir!"

The swordsman spun, deflecting a blow from a soldier that would have half-severed his neck. A fierce show of swordplay ensued, though I missed much of it. I slipped in and out consciousness, the din of clashing blades just an echo from another reality. I cannot be sure that what followed next was real or hallucination. At one point the second rider dismounted to join in the fray. But he was not as handy with a blade as his companion; he staggered under the strike from a sword hilt that dropped him to the ground, rendering him even more nonsensical than myself. Meanwhile, my saviour fought on, pressed front and back by a pair of soon-to-be-dead men.

At a noise from behind, I managed to tip back my head in time to see Averi rise from the base of the oak, and spying his embattled soldiers, begin to slink from the scene. Helpless, I watched as he bent to collect his sword belt, then climb aboard his horse and heel it back up the slope.

Feebly, I croaked out, "He's getting away."

With a motion too swift to follow, the swordsman dispatched first one foe, then another, his blade flinging blood and gore, before turning in the direction of my wobbly finger as Averi galloped for the trees. Seeing this, the survivors of Averi's patrol abandoned the fight and ran for their mounts. The swordsman hurled a slue of curses after them, but did not give chase. Instead he knelt by his injured companion, a youth not yet out of his teens, who roused at his touch.

The man helped the boy gain his feet, then together they made their way towards me. It was about that time that I felt safe enough to give in to the beckoning darkness.

CHAPTER SIX

When next I opened my eyes, Uncle's barbarians were gone. But I was not alone. My rescuers stood looking down at me, perhaps wondering if I had expired. My whole body ached so badly I wished I had died. Every breath was torment, every eye blink agony. I noticed my face was wet, and thought it must be raining, although I distinctly recalled the morning sun rising into a clear blue sky. Thus I was shocked to learn I was crying. I hadn't cried in years.

But the sky I saw was no longer clear. Dark grey clouds had rumbled in, banishing the sun. Soon it did begin to rain. I thought it fitting.

The swordsman, a tall, brawny fellow dropped to a knee beside me. As he reached out to roll me over, his breath caught on a stifled oath. I suppose I was no pretty sight. What did it matter? I had no dignity, no pride left.

"She's alive," he pronounced.

The boy, cradling a hand to what must be the grandmother of all goose eggs, grumbled, "I think she'd be better off dead."

I was inclined to agree with him.

"And to top it off, it's raining," he added in an undertone, as if somehow I'd ruined their day. "We can't go tracking in the rain."

His companion admonished him with an exasperated shush. "Nevertheless, I think she can be saved."

"But, sir…we can't take her with us."

"Jory, if you're not going to help me," my saviour snapped, withdrawing an object from his pocket and passing it to the boy, "ride on ahead and fetch a healer."

"Yes, sir," Jory demurred in a voice that said he was more than happy to leave. He mounted a pretty piebald grazing nearby and turned her muzzle down the slope.

Drawing me into an upright position, my rescuer held a flask of water to my lips. I sputtered and choked, but managed a swallow or two. Up until then I had been unable to see much of his face, hidden beneath a rain-sodden hood. But as he leaned over me, I saw it was strong and kindly, framed by strands of curly black hair. An easy smile peeked out from between a neatly trimmed beard and moustache. His eyes were a deep brown, warm and friendly. I guessed his age to be somewhere on the nether side of forty.

Gently, he smoothed a snarl of hair from my eyes, "What's your name, girl?"

It is only natural when someone asks your name to reply unthinking, and I had lost the wits to be careful. I told him, instantly regretting it. His expression grew suspicious. A glance at my battered field jacket, which I'd had the arrogance to wear, and comprehension lit his features. "The

Gryphon Highlord?"

Though I pretended not to understand, the man was not convinced.

He stared at me in disbelief, his dark brows knitting themselves into a knot. "Who were those men?"

"Gryphon's troops," I choked out, resigned to the fact I could not dissuade him of my identity.

His arm swept the length of my body, his face paling with shock. "Your own men did this?"

I don't think he believed me. Not at first. "Not mine but those of the Regent's, yes."

"Why?"

Why? The answer eluded even me. I blurted out what had hurt most. "Because I have become expendable."

He appeared thoroughly repulsed.

"You're a Crusader," I said, for I could see enough of his attire to recognize it as a uniform of sorts.

"Umagi," he clarified.

"And a Teki."

He hesitated a moment, as if he might refute it. "Of modest talent, I assure you."

Then to my astonishment, he began to rip the insignias from my jacket. Uncle's badge, my rank identification, along with every last button and stitch of piping came away, thrown into the muddy waters of the ditch. As a result my costume, now drab and nondescript, resembled any other traveller's. Strangely enough, stripped of Uncle's trappings, I felt freed.

Even as I understood that he tried to conceal my identity I never believed it would work. I clutched at his sleeve, straining to pull myself up. "Kill me," I whispered. "Please. I beg you."

The man plucked my fingers free of his arm to take my hand in his. "I cannot," he replied solemnly.

"You can. Use your sword. End my shame, my pain. Else your Crusader friends will surely do it for you."

He shook his head, eyes steeped in sadness. "I won't kill you. Nor will I allow anyone else to kill you."

"Please, friend. You do not know how very desperately I want to die."

"On the contrary," he smiled, stroking my bruised cheekbone, "I know how very desperately you want to live."

"What have I to live for? The things I value most are gone. My home. My throne. My pride." A tear slid down the side of my nose. "My powers."

"Your Teki powers?"

"Yes. They are…I mean, they have…"

"Grown beyond Bertrand's ability to control and so he sought to render them inert?"

I gasped. "You can't possibly know that."

He flashed me an all-knowing sort of grin. "We guessed, when certain inexplicable losses began to effect us. It's no secret that you carry Umagi blood. Nor is it a secret that Bertrand employs a potion to suppress your powers. News of that magnitude is nearly impossible to guard. Fortunately for you, Bertrand has failed."

I perked up a little at that. "He has?"

"Abysmally, I'd say. Let me guess. Back in the trees you attempted a shielding or cloaking spell of some sort?"

"Well, yes. But I think its pretty clear that it didn't work."

"Not necessarily." He lifted an arm to the dull grey sky. "Do you see? The rain, the clouds, they obeyed your command, your desire for camouflage. They came a little late, but they came. Not the most subtle of spells, I'll admit, but that's to be expected from a novice such as yourself."

Could that be true? Had my powers been restored? Self-pity and hopelessness had blinded me to the obvious. Hope soared anew. I laughed weakly, rejoicing in the discovery all was not lost. I lived still, and so, too, did my Teki ability.

I looked up in awe at my gallant rescuer and squeezed his hand. "Who are you?"

A sombre cast came over his face then, and his voice adopted an air of pain. "You do not know me?"

"Should I?"

He lowered his hood. The rain shone in his raven hair and sparkled like tiny diamonds in his beard. "It's me," he whispered. "Sestus. Have you forgotten?"

"Sestus?" The name did seem familiar. I let my eyes stray to the faded red emblem stitched over his heart. A memory from early childhood surfaced, images of happier times, when laughter and song filled Gryphon's great keep. Grass had grown in the courtyard, when it was a place for hide-and-seek and tag instead of a barren and dusty parade ground, which was its current incarnation. A maypole stood in its centre, entwined with ribbons of every colour, where young girls flocked and twittered like geese. Mother sat on a blanket, flowers in her hair, which were offerings from the children. Father stood nearby, smiling at their antics. Another man, his features young and carefree, laughed as he bounced a small child on his knee. A mane of dark curls spilled around the collar of his uniform. He gave the child a wooden toy horse and called her…

"Little Red," I murmured. The family's pet name for me.

"Yes!" Sestus cried, his eyes brightening. "You do remember." Hugging me to his breast, he kissed my filthy brow. "You always were my Little Red."

I returned his crushing embrace as best I could, though pain ripped through every part of me. But I didn't care, intoxicated by the smothering horse smell of his coat and the warmth of his arms, smiling like a fool.

After a time we looked up to see each other weeping tears of joy. Sestus laughed, just as he had that day in the courtyard under the maypole. "Ahh, Kathedra. I never thought I'd live to see you again." He wiped the tears from my face and sniffed away his own. "My word, what have they done to you? Come. Let's get you somewhere safe."

Reality intruded, in that rude way it has about it. "Sestus, you forget. I'm not one of you."

"Not to worry," he assured me, even as he removed his cloak to wrap it around my shivering body. "I'm sure between the two of us we can contrive a plausible story. For starters, you'll have to decide on a new name. Any ideas?"

Only one came readily to mind. "How about Ruvie?" It was a common enough name among the peasantry, but not obviously so.

He nodded. "We'll say you were attacked by ruffians attempting to flee the castle."

Well, that was not so far from the truth.

"You can fill me in on what happened later, when we've got time." He patted my leg. "Meanwhile, say nothing. They will understand if you're too delirious to talk straight."

Although I began to worry who they might be, I trusted that Sestus knew what it was he did, trusted he would do everything in his power to protect me. I had no other choice but to trust him.

As he lifted me onto shaky legs however, I thrust him aside. "My horse, my sword," I muttered, reeling in the direction of the trees and scaling the slope at a determined totter. "My helm."

"No, Kathedra. They're gone. There's nothing up there. No sword. No horse. Nothing."

Halfway up the hillside I collapsed, too weak, too heartsick to go on. Sestus was right. My possessions should lay scattered across the slope, but it was empty. That bastard Averi had taken everything of mine. Trophies, I presumed. But the most precious of his plunder was my dignity. Drifting back into oblivion, I vowed to reclaim it, along with everything else that was mine.

"Ho, Sestus!" hailed a cheery voice. "What the hell happened to you? Jory lit out of here like his tail was on fire. Left you something, too."

A horse's broad back swayed beneath me, where I rode safe and snug in Sestus's arms. I roused at the sound of this new voice, belonging to an old man in farmer's attire, complete with straw hat and newly patched boots. Leaning against a broom, he stood in the doorway of a rundown barn, perched on a knoll dotted with spring flowers, a smaller outbuilding nestled a stone's throw away. As Sestus dismounted, the man passed him a small opaque object possibly fashioned out of glass.

"That's breaking the rules, you know, Sestus."

"Yes, Erol. I know," Sestus said in response to the gentle admonishment. "But thank you so much. It won't happen again."

Sestus clucked to his horse and led it by the reins into the barn. Despite my throbbing head and the pain of a bruised jaw, I gave the man what I hoped was a friendly smile. He didn't smile back, eyeing me with a look of speculation and chewing on a blade of grass. Though he hadn't objected to my presence in so many words, I got the feeling I wasn't exactly welcome.

From between swollen, half-shut lids, I studied the barn with its walls of timber and roof of thatch. Though in good condition, it appeared abandoned; the only sign that livestock once inhabited it were the bits of hay and petrified horse droppings scattered throughout. Sestus led us all the way to the far end to another door, closed and fitted with a lock mechanism. Here, he inserted the object Erol had given him, which I now recognized as a key. There was a metallic ching, then Sestus returned the key to a ring on his belt. Who locks a barn?

"Are you ready, Ruvie?"

I answered his wink with a puzzled frown. "Ready?"

He pushed open the door, admitting a lusty breeze redolent with the scent of wood smoke from the cookfires and forges of the sundered castle in the vale below. Though we emerged on the opposite side of the barn, the scenery was different. Where there should be a stand of evergreens was a sprawling meadow dotted with sheep and-.

Sundered castle?

Despite having never set foot in the place, nor even having seen an artist's rendering of it, I knew exactly where I was.

Idyll!

A prudent man, Sestus kept his back to me as he guided my mount down the slope, more to conceal his amusement at my slack jaw and glazed eyes than to spare my dignity. My shock was absolute, my brain wholly incapable of absorbing the revelation that the Crusaders not only had the audacity to occupy Uncle's former demesne, the source of all current strife in Thylana at the moment, but that Idyll was almost two hundred miles from Castle Gryphon.

I twisted in the saddle to find the barn was the same, only the location had changed. This was sorcery of the highest calibre, and yet there was no evidence of such. I fixed my gaze on the crumbling stone edifice growing closer with the horse's every stride and struggled to get my mouth closed. Our approach afforded me an excellent overview. The main keep was in near total ruin, but the outbuildings, stables, and workhouses appeared to be in good repair, which is where the Citizens Risen Up to Stand Against a Dread and Errant Regency had set up shop.

A hundred questions popped into my mind, the first and foremost being a tossup between why and how. The latter won out. "Sestus…how is this possible?"

He slid me a smile over his shoulder as we continued down the slope. "An Umagi dabbler in teleportation created it. It's called a teleportal."

"You mean Erol?"

"No. Erol's the caretaker. The lookout. If any outsiders should come nosing around, he'll alert us. But unless one has a passkey, the barn's just an ordinary barn, and the teleportal can't be accessed." His smile turned sheepish. "I guess I really shouldn't be telling you all this."

No, Sestus. You really shouldn't. That didn't stop me, however, from listening. I better understood the reason behind the caretaker's reproach. While an impudent and clever device, the teleportal, if discovered, would land Uncle's Royals on the Crusaders' doorstep with little or no warning.

But the conversation was at an end, for we had reached the keep and our arrival had caused a stir. People rushed up to greet Sestus, making his horse shy, and soon a babbling, curious mob ringed us. It would seem that Jory had wasted no time spreading the tale of their encounter on the 'other' side.

A dozen eager hands reached up to take me. Sestus passed me down to them without compunction, shouting orders above the turmoil. Despite my protestations that I could walk, a burly man carried me through the throng and into a ramshackle building of wood and roughly hewn stone. He took me past the main room and into one smaller, more sparsely furnished, where he set me down on a rickety cot. Then, doffing his cap to wring it between his hands, he asked, "Can I get you anything, miss?"

"A physician might be nice."

"Oh…yes, miss, right away," he stammered, and proceeded to back out the door straight into Sestus.

"Has Ginger returned?"

The man jumped aside. "No, sir. Not yet."

Sestus looked relieved, muttered something like, "Small miracles."

"Sir?"

"Never mind. Let me know the minute he does." Sestus clapped him on the shoulder and the man departed, only to collide with someone in the outer room.

Another voice, brazen and insistent, from beyond the doorway, commanded, "Out of my way. Let me pass. I said move, you big lug!"

A stout woman, in a flowing frock and tattered shawl, armed with an assortment of bags, shouldered her way past Sestus, the same gangly youth from the hillside trotting in her wake. "Bloody Crusaders," she frothed, waddling toward me where I cowered on my cot. "Think they don't have to move their arses for simple folk like me. Bah!"

"Ahh, Biddy," Sestus sighed. "How nice to see you."

"Up yours, Sestus, you old goat," Biddy snapped. "Just you keep out of my way."

Sestus grabbed Jory by his collar to hiss into his ear, "You had to bring her?"

Jory flushed and babbled some excuse, the whole time trying to squirm out of Sestus's grasp.

Ignoring them, Biddy dropped her gear and placed stubby hands on ample hips to glower down at me. Wispy threads of greying brown hair dangled at her temples, having strayed from the bun beneath her crooked hat. "You look like hell," she declared, her face bloated and red with temper.

"So do you." It seemed the only appropriate response.

She arched a brow, and a wry smile appeared. "I like her, Sestus. She's sweet."

Still unconvinced the woman was not a raving lunatic, I asked, "Are you a doctor?"

"I am not," Biddy retorted with indignation. "I'm a herbhealer. And the best damned one this hellhole's got."

I watched as she rummaged through one pack then another, searching for who knew what. I thought about begging Sestus to take me somewhere, anywhere, else. I even considered crawling for the door myself, but it was an effort simply to breathe. Sestus and Jory, however, seemed unconcerned, peering inquisitively over her shoulder.

Realizing she had an audience the old shrew rounded on the men in a fit of outrage. "Stop gawking at the poor girl! She's been through enough already without having to put up with your rude stares. Well, just don't stand there like a couple of lackwits. One of you fetch me a tub of hot water and some towels. While you're at it, bring a few blankets. Not those old, ratty ones neither, but the good ones you save for the horses. And make it snappy."

Jory scurried out the door, eager to obey Biddy's orders. Smiling reassurance, Sestus came to my side and stroked my brow. "It's going to be all right."

Biddy thrust a jar of weak blue solution at me. "Drink it. It will make you sleep."

I drank, submitting to Biddy as I would to Grezalia. Soon a feeling of lassitude settled over me, banishing all my aches and pains. I fell asleep, cradling Sestus's hand in mine.

CHAPTER SEVEN

I awoke slowly, wary with the sensation of being watched. Without warning I snapped open my eyes. Well, actually, only one eye. The other was covered with a dead fish. Three faces swam into focus, all hovering close. Unpleasant memories of Gryphon soldiers resurfaced. I shrank away, trying to duck under the blanket.

"Get your ugly mug out of her face, boy," a woman's voice spat. "You're scaring her."

Firm but gentle hands took mine and tucked the blanket under my chin, that same grating voice murmuring, "There, there. You're safe here." As full awareness returned I recognized the voice as Biddy's.

I opened my eye again, relieved to see Sestus smile. "How are you feeling, Ruvie?"

Ruvie? Ahh, yes. I said something that sounded more like, "Thbltt." My mouth felt as if it were full of marbles.

"Don't try to talk," Biddy admonished as she readjusted the fish. "Your lip is still pretty swollen. I'd say you're damned lucky to have all your teeth."

I struggled onto my elbows but a stab of pain lanced through my chest, making me wince.

Biddy nodded. "That'll be your poor ribs. Can't do anything about them, I'm afraid, except bind you up. But that will only make you more uncomfortable. Just be thankful they aren't broken."

Looking down, I saw myself clad in a flimsy nightgown. I'd been bathed and my hair washed. A hint of lavender hung in the air. I felt clean and refreshed, despite the ache of my body and a warm, sleepy feeling. "Thank you, Biddy," I managed, overcome with gratitude. "I don't know how to repay you."

"Bah," she snorted. "Don't you worry about that. Payment is up to Sestus."

She removed the fish from my eye to a chorus of oohs and ahhs. "What are you two groaning about?" Biddy demanded, her healer's fingers probing a sizable bruise. "The colour is coming out nicely."

Sestus wrinkled his nose. "What's with the fish? It stinks."

"That's for me to know and you to find out." She flung the corpse into a bucket, passed it to Jory. "Feed it to the dogs. No sense wasting good food. Go on. Out with you."

Once the boy had fled, Sestus asked, "Are you hungry?"

Hungry? Try famished. I envisioned roast chicken with wine sauce, fresh leeks, and thick slices of bread plastered with butter. What I got was a bowl of broth and a cup of water, much like my last meal in Castle Gryphon.

Biddy poked a slender reed between my fingers. "Drink up. Use the straw so you don't dribble down yourself. It's good beef broth. You should start light. Maybe later you can have a nice pork pie."

Recollecting my manners, I smiled my thanks. I had forgotten this was a poor Crusader outpost, not Gryphon's dining hall, where I was accustomed to sumptuous food and drink. I slurped my broth, conscious of Sestus's ill-concealed grin.

Biddy packed away her herbhealer's paraphernalia and set a basket filled with odds and ends on the table, then rattled off a list of instructions. "You're to rest in bed for a couple of days. I've stitched the gash in your arm. Sestus can change the dressing tomorrow. There's an ointment of comfrey for your cuts and bruises, and a solution of chamomile to put in your tea if you have trouble sleeping. You have no serious internal injuries, but go easy on your ribs."

With that, she closed up her last bag and held out her palm to Sestus. "My payment, if you please."

Sestus dug around in his purse, coming up with two coins, which he dumped into her outstretched hand. At her quizzical squint, he said, "It's all I have."

As the woman continued to eye him dubiously, Sestus snapped, "Plus the three hens I promised. Is it enough?"

Biddy slipped the coins into an apron pocket. "It will do."

Damn, these people were poor. All thanks to Uncle, and his stubborn refusal to forgive and forget. I'd never felt so ashamed.

As Biddy flounced out the door, I could see she was tickled pink with her meagre payment and somehow that made me feel worse. I stared down at my half-finished broth, my appetite gone. "I can't let you do this, Sestus. I can't accept your kindness and hospitality. Not at your expense."

Concerned, he sat down on the stool beside me. "What do you mean?"

"I mean, you gave that woman your last two coins."

A dazzling smile appeared. "I'd have given her my horse had she asked. Don't worry yourself over a few pieces of silver."

"No," I growled, shaking my head. "You don't understand. Biddy deserved more for her trouble."

Sestus laughed. "Don't you worry about Biddy. All her remedies and herbs add up to a small fortune. She's probably the richest peasant in the place."

"Exactly. You all have so little. And I have…had…so much. It doesn't seem fair I should take your charity. Me, an enemy, of all things."

"An enemy no longer, I'd say. After all, we both have a common foe in Bertrand."

I turned away, unable to bear thoughts of Uncle right now. Though it was correct to assume he and I were now enemies, I had not yet come to terms with his treachery.

"Your friends might not see it that way, Sestus. If I am discovered, my presence also endangers you. From what I know of the Crusaders, they won't approve of your bringing a wolf into their fold. I can't allow you to put yourself at risk for my sake."

Sestus seemed amused. "Do you really believe you have a say in the matter, Little Red? Do you think you can do anything to stop me? I dare say you couldn't walk to the door." He set my bowl and reed on the table, then taking my shoulders, eased me back down under the blanket. "Rest, Kathedra. We'll talk later."

I slipped an arm under my head, but as he stood to leave, I said, "I don't understand, Sestus. You should hate me for all I have done, all Uncle has done. You should want me dead. Why are you helping me?"

He sank back down onto the cot beside me, smoothed a hand over my newly washed hair. "Why wouldn't I help you? You are my best friend's daughter. To not help you would do a great injustice to his memory. The Gryphon Highlord may be dead, but I will do everything in my power to keep Kathedra alive."

With that he rose and strode to the door. "Rest now, Little Red. We have much to discuss in the morning."

"Wait," I implored, mustering a firm voice. "I will repay you, Sestus. For all your compassion and generosity, I will find a way to repay you."

"Get well first, Little Red. Then we can talk about payment."

The door closed behind him, leaving the word 'payment' reverberating in my head. For all his noble words, Sestus planned to use me somehow. In that fashion I would be expected to render payment. Of course, anyone in his situation would be a fool not to take advantage of it. The sudden and rather timely advent of the Gryphon Highlord was an opportunity too lucrative to pass up. I represented both Uncle's greatest fear and the Crusaders' best chance at victory. After all, I possessed invaluable tactical secrets. I had knowledge of Castle Gryphon's defences, weaknesses, strengths, strategies…there was no limit. More so, I commanded perhaps the most important weapon of all in this revolt against Uncle-my Teki powers.

Hence, two problems for Sestus and me to puzzle out. Will I cooperate? And, if so, how to conceal my identity from the Citizens Risen Up Against a Dread and Errant Regency?

But Sestus is wrong about one thing. The Gryphon Highlord is not dead. She is very much alive, in temporary exile only. If Uncle should learn of my survival, Averi will wish Sestus had finished him. For my own sake, I prayed he doesn't-not until I am ready to pull the gold-braided cushion out from under him.

I have never indulged in cruelty, but that does not mean I do not understand it. My years in Uncle's company and on the battlefield taught me it. Excruciating tortures await Uncle and Averi-torments of the mind. I want them alive to witness my triumphant return, to watch me retake Castle Gryphon. Most of all, I want them to see me seated on my throne, Mother's crown upon my brow.

I did not see Sestus again for the rest of the day, nor anyone else, save Jory when he delivered my pork pie. I had plenty of time alone with my thoughts-all confused, all unpleasant. Ever present on my mind was Valleri.

I missed him terribly, yearning for a comfort only he could provide. This ache for Valleri, deeper and stronger than physical pain, troubled me beyond sleep. Finally, I weakened and added Biddy's chamomile sedative to my tea. It soothed my nerves and numbed my mind, enveloping me in a warm fog, which soon deepened into slumber.

Indeed, the potion worked so well I slept through the night and far into the morning, never stirring until a commotion in the adjacent room woke me with a start. Alarmed, I pushed myself up on my cot, straining to hear the voices of men, all talking at once. My heart was in my throat when purposeful footfalls approached the door. It opened without a knock of warning and a man stepped through it.

A gasp escaped me before I'd realized who entered.

"I'm sorry if I startled you," Sestus said, closing the door. "How are you feeling?"

"Much better, thank you. What's going on?"

He swept a hand through his dark curls and sighed. "I've just received word...Ginger is on his way. He'll be here tomorrow. I'm glad to see you're awake. We have a lot to cover before his arrival."

His agitation surprised me. He seemed more haggard since last I saw him. I gathered his anxiety had something to do with how this Ginger person would react to my presence. "Who's Ginger?"

"A Crusader captain. This is his post, which he shares with Repachea. They're both coming."

I slumped under the blanket. Perfect. Just what I needed. Not one outlaw leader but two. How many were there? Sestus talked as if there were more posts, therefore more commanders. How can this be? Either Castle Gryphon's intelligence operates on the same level as a simpleton's or I had not been privy to all the facts.

"Anyway, Ginger is upset," Sestus continued. "And if there is one person I do not want to be around when he's upset, it's Ginger. He and Repachea left a week ago to lend their assistance in a standoff with one of Bertrand's Royals near Bolta. I can only assume something went wrong."

I slid further beneath my blanket, wishing I could disappear, sick with the feeling I'd just been kicked in the stomach. Sestus did not need my silence to alert him to the possibility I knew something he didn't. He need only recall who I am. He caught an inkling, and jerked up his head like a hound on the scent of my guilty conscience.

"I don't suppose you'd happen to know something about this?" he queried, folding his arms across his chest.

"Um…not much, I'm afraid," I stalled, trying to recall Valleri's report. "Only that Captain Tock defeated an enemy commander at the southern crossroads. He is reported grievously injured if not dead. I considered it a major victory for Uncle since I believed there to be only two outlaw leaders of significance. But now I know different, and I wonder if perhaps I was given misinformation."

Sestus muttered an oath. "Belvemar is one of our best, a fearless Crusader. And a good friend, too. No wonder Ginger is fit to be tied."

"Bad tempered is he?"

"Did I give you that impression?" he snorted. "Let's just say he's about as forgiving as Bertrand."

"I can't wait to meet him. Remind me to watch my step."

"It won't be that easy." Sestus's cow eyes took on a sombre cast. "Ginger's Umagi, too. Wizard calibre."

A wizard? That sickening sensation in the pit of my stomach moved all the way up into my throat. I began to wonder which of the Fates I had offended to earn His or Her personal grudge. Sestus was right; it would not be easy. How to conceal my erratic Teki powers from a full-blown wizard who was, in all likelihood, several times more powerful than myself?

"Yes," Sestus agreed, reading my alarm. "You see why it is so urgent we talk? First, I have some questions for you. And," he added in an undertone that suggested he had long experience in matters of interrogation, "I expect straight answers."

"Yes, by all means. You deserve them. But I have a question to ask of you, Sestus." Indeed, it was a question that had popped into my head and stayed there since our reunion in that roadside ditch. "Why did you desert me? Why, when Mother died and Uncle launched his mad quest for justice, did you abandon me?"

"Kathedra, I did not abandon you. I—"

"Yes, Sestus," I interrupted, trying to control the anger that rose inside me, anger I hadn't even known existed. "You did abandon me. You were a surrogate father to me and…well, you just left. You can call it nothing else."

"You're right," he admitted. "And I'm sorry. I did leave you."

"And Val," I muttered. "You left him, too. We grew up together, never trusting anyone but each other."

Sestus sighed. "Yes, and Valleri, too. I did not mean to hurt anyone. But try to understand, Little Red. It was not safe for me to remain. Bertrand had lost all reason, all sense of right and wrong. Although I possessed very little in the way of magic, it made no difference to him. I had to flee. I had no choice."

"Yes, you did have a choice," I hissed, struggling for composure. "You could have taken us with you."

That must have struck him with all the impact of a broadaxe, for he slumped back in his chair, a shocked expression on his face. Wonderingly, he said, "Kathedra…you know that was impossible."

"Do I? You knew what I was, an Umagi, a Teki just like you. You know better than I do what can happen to an untrained, unskilled mage when ill luck and inexperience collide. You can see for yourself what Uncle has done to me, what his hounds tried to do to me. Could life as an exile with you have been any worse?"

His tone of disbelief matched mine. "Kathedra, think. Had I taken you and Val from Gryphon, Bertrand would have hunted us to the ends of the earth and beyond. You are the rightful heir to your mother's throne!"

I dismissed his words with a shrug. "And yet still an exile."

After a quiet moment, he said, "Don't be angry with me, Little Red. I swore to myself that I would return to set things right, to avenge myself, and Mauranna, and all Umagi. It is a vow I intend to fulfill even now, all these years later."

"Is this your revenge, Sestus? To incite unrest? To birth a civil war?"

"I didn't start it. You know that, Kathedra. It started a long time ago, back when Bertrand ordered Mauranna's execution. It's only been recently that a handful of brave souls, tired of his tyranny and madness, decided to end it. I merely offered them my assistance. As a former Halberdier captain I could provide invaluable aid. So I dug out my uniform, dusted off my warrior's skills, and recalled long-buried memories."

"But don't you see? None of this has solved anything. It has only done more damage. Instead it's divided a realm, inflicted untold carnage, and sullied my family's name. Look at me, Sestus. I have lost everything."

"You still don't understand, do you, Kathedra? No, I can't expect you to; you consider yourself my enemy. My role here has nothing to do with you. I stand with the Crusaders for the same reasons as Ginger or Repachea or anyone else-to free Thylana from Bertrand's hands, to defeat the oppressor and to liberate the oppressed, to ensure a decent life for our children, to take back our homes."

Though his face remained expressionless and his voice calm, I saw clearly the grief and torment the years had etched into his eyes. "No, Little Red. I need no revolt to exact my revenge. My only instrument of vengeance will be the knife I use to plunge through Bertrand's black heart."

One does not change loyalties overnight. Sestus's tirade still sounded like so much treason to my ears. Nor could I justify bloodshed with more bloodshed. That might seem silly coming from a soldier, but it was how I felt. How I'd always felt.

"You don't approve?"

"Revenge is a very personal thing. Heaven knows I have reason enough to carve my name in Uncle, but because he broke the law of our ancestors does not give me the right to break the same law."

Sestus smiled. "I've known others who thought much the same as you. That is why they are all dead. That is why you very nearly died as well. But, go on. Tell me. What are your plans for revenge?"

"I, too, want only to take what is rightfully mine. The difference is I want Uncle alive to watch me do it. Otherwise, it would not be half as sweet."

Sestus pulled up a chair, sat down and crossed his legs, prepared to stay awhile. "Perhaps I would better understand if I knew the whole story."

I did not necessarily agree. Though I owed Sestus an explanation, I was reluctant to recite to him the intimate details of my downfall. I felt his eyes upon me, so irritatingly patient, and wished for a convenient interruption to forestall the inevitable for a little while, at least.

Somehow, somewhere, someone heard my unspoken prayer, for at that moment the outer door slammed open and a voice shrieked, "Where are you, you no good, lowlife, rebel pirate? Sestus? Sesstuss!"

I nearly laughed out-loud in giddy relief. Sestus rolled his eyes. "Oh, what does she want now?"

Biddy burst into the room, overburdened with her herbhealer's supplies and…a chicken? Yes. A white, black-speckled chicken. She dumped the bird into Sestus's lap, where it clucked peevishly and struck a dignified pose, looking for all the world like it thought it belonged there.

Sestus leapt to his feet, unseating the startled bird amid a flurry of flapping wings and flying feathers. The chicken fluttered an erratic path to my cot, then lighted near my legs and began to preen its ruffled plumage. Cursing, Sestus dusted himself off and gave Biddy the evil eye. "What the hell is the matter with you?"

Biddy glared icicles. "Oh, stop it, Sestus. You know you make me tingle all over with your sweet talk. Save it for your bedroom. I mean business."

She dropped the rest of her stuff and pointed to the chicken, where it pecked at my toes beneath the blanket. "You promised me three hens. That is a rooster. Can't you tell the difference? Or did your mama not tell you the facts of life? Think you can swindle old Biddy, eh? I want my hen!"

"Now?"

"Yes, now. How, pray, am I supposed to get eggs from a rooster?"

"Well, it's not my fault. I'm to blame because that lackwit of a boy grabbed a rooster by mistake?" Sestus stamped around and glowered at the cock. "Can't you just cook it and eat it?"

"There's no meat on a blasted rooster, you birdbrain!"

"Oh, all right. I'll get someone to fetch you a hen. Meanwhile, keep the rooster. On me."

"I don't want the rooster. I want only the hen. See to it." Her gaze narrowed as she glanced at me. "Did you change her bandage like I told you?"

"No, he didn't," I piped up, stroking the bird's feathery breast.

"See? I can't trust you to do nuthin!" Biddy pushed Sestus out of her way with the back of her hand. "Now go fetch my hen while I tend to the poor girl's arm. Men. Useless, witless things, the lot!"

Sestus grabbed the rooster and tucked it under his arm, ignoring its squawk of outrage. "I'll be back," he told me. Then, with a final scowl at his nemesis, he stomped out the door.

As Biddy washed her hands I let a giggle or two escape. She glared at me from across the room. "What are you laughing at, girl?"

"Just you and Sestus. You act like an old married couple."

She snorted and reached for a towel, but I thought I saw a blush of pink colour her cheeks. "Don't go putting a hex on me, now."

"You like him, don't you?" I coaxed.

"I can't stand the man."

That was an out and out lie. "He likes you, too. I can tell."

"You don't know what you're talking about, child."

"Oh, don't I?" I smiled complacently. "It's all so obvious. Sestus gave you the rooster, knowing full well you'd return it, which you did. Likewise, you told Sestus to change my dressing, knowing he wouldn't and you'd have to come do it yourself. You both got exactly what you wanted, which was to see each other again, and yet never actually had to say it."

Scowling down at me, Biddy took my arm and began to unwind the bandage. "And how does a chit like you presume to know so much?"

"It's a game. I've played similar."

She tossed me a look that I'm sure curled my toenails. "It's not a game at all, dearie. It's war."

"Well, I'm sure it's not that bad. Are you saying a ceasefire is out of the question?"

"It is out of the question and off the page." She said this almost proudly, as if it were a point of honour. "Sestus doesn't like to talk about his shortcomings, or his mistakes, let alone own up to them."

Well, that was harsh. "What on earth did he do?"

"It's not what he did. It's what he didn't do." She paused in her work, watching me with a mingled expression of hurt and anger. Whatever the cause of their conflict, she cared a great deal for Sestus. Animosity is a way of covering up pain. And where there was pain, there was yet an ability to heal. I knew this from Uncle's example. Not even he was beyond hope of recovery.

Ducking my glance, she resumed her handiwork. "And when the war has gone on this long, it turns into a contest of wills. No one wants to be the first to give in, the first to apologize, so it continues."

I shook my head in mock disappointment. "You had your chance. You could have ended it right now."

"Oh, really? Think you're smart, eh? Do tell, wise one, what should old Biddy have done?"

"You should have cooked that rooster and invited Sestus to supper."

CHAPTER EIGHT

Sestus returned late that night, so late I'd thought he wouldn't come at all. Thus, he caught me out of bed, parading around in Biddy's oversized nighty. "Should you be walking around like that?" he asked.

I looked down at myself and fingered the hem of my gown. "If you mean walking around in this silly shift, no. I'd prefer a decent change of clothes."

"You know that's not what I meant. Get back into bed."

"I just need a bit of exercise," I protested, crawling back beneath my blanket. "You don't expect me to spend the rest of the revolt in bed, do you?"

"Of course not. I just don't want you to push yourself." He withdrew a bundle from behind his back and presented it to me with a sly grin. "I managed to scrounge you up some clothes. I hope they fit. There aren't too many women around here, so you'll have to take what you can get."

"Thank you, Sestus." I took the clothes from him and started poking through them, inexplicably thrilled with the motley assortment.

"We didn't get much of a chance to talk earlier, did we?"

There was no doubt I owed Sestus the truth after all he'd done for me. He had jeopardized the Crusaders' security by bringing me here, as well as his good standing with his cronies. "No, we didn't."

Briefly, I told him of my forced retirement, my imprisonment, my short engagement to Lesuperis, and lastly, my flight from Averi and his henchmen. When I'd finished, Sestus donned a puzzled frown. "How did you flee Gryphon? It's a veritable fortress. Surely Bertrand would have taken extra precautions to ensure you could not escape."

"Apparently Uncle did not think it necessary. He believed the tonic would be enough to render me submissive." Sestus still eyed me dubiously, suspecting I withheld something. "And I had help, of course," I snapped.

"Ah-ha. Now we're getting somewhere. Who helped you? Was it Valleri or your second-in-command?"

I thought I detected a leer in his voice. "Valleri is my second-in-command."

That shocked him into a full minute of speechlessness. Twice he looked ready to venture a prying question but refrained. Finally he just shook his head, as if trying to push away an obnoxious thought, and said, "So Valleri did help you."

"Surprised?"

"Surprised he helped you? No. It's the least I'd expect of him. After all, you were childhood friends. It's just…" Sestus let the remark slip away.

"Just what?"

"Nothing. I heard a rumour once. It's of no importance. I had no idea

Valleri was your second. Why did you choose him?"

"He was the only man I trusted. Do you think it a poor choice?"

"Not at all. I'm sure Valleri proved himself a worthy lieutenant and a faithful friend. But if he's as devoted as you claim, and he suspects foul play on Bertrand's part once he learns you never reached your destination, he may set in motion his own plans for revenge."

I shared a similar thought but kept it to myself. "Valleri is loyal, ruthless, but not rash. He won't make a move until I give the word or he sees a body. As for avenging my death…" I let the thought trail away, now not so certain all those oaths I'd extorted from Valleri mattered. No doubt, if he believed harm came to me at Uncle's hand, he would consider them void.

Sestus's expression turned grave. His eyes spoke volumes of sorrow and regret. "What's wrong?" I asked. "Isn't that what you want? Uncle dead? Does it matter whether Valleri or you holds the blade?"

"You've missed the point, Kathedra. The death of Bertrand will not mean the end of this."

"What are you saying?"

He leaned forward in his chair and rested his elbows on his thighs, his clasped hands a writhing knot of fingers. "Understand," he implored, "if Bertrand dies now, before this is brought to a resolution, there is only one person under your ancestral law who can take your place as heir."

"Yes. The Gryphon Highlord traditionally takes the title if there is no heir present. But in my case there is neither."

"Exactly. Think about it for a minute. Logically, who would replace you as commander of Gryphon's elite troops?"

"Logically, tht would be my second. Therefore, Valleri. But Uncle doesn't think logi—"

"And from there?"

He let the question dangle in mid-air. I recalled Uncle's steadfast refusal to name my replacement. From the moment I'd been imprisoned in my rooms, my captaincy went vacant. For obvious reasons, not just any officer could assume leadership of the Twelfth Royal. Well, there weren't really twelve Royals, but twelve sounded more impressive than, say, five. Anyway, that position was a step away from that of the Gryphon Highlord's and from there…

"The throne?"

Sestus made no reply, only continued to stare at me with those sad, sombre eyes. "But that's impossible," I snorted. "Valleri can't take the throne. I'm still alive."

"Yes, Kathedra. But if you're presumed dead…according to law, Valleri, as the Gryphon Highlord, stands next in line."

"How? His blood is not mine. If anyone can lay claim to Thylana it's Lesuperis. He still possesses noble blood, remote as he is."

Sestus donned a sardonic grin. "I really don't think Lesuperis would be an issue. From what you've told me, Valleri will have no compunction about removing that weasel from the race."

Agog, I whispered, "Are you insinuating Valleri would seize my command, then use it as a means to murder Uncle and claim the crown for himself?"

"I believe it's a possibility."

I took some time to absorb that. For lack of a replacement, Valleri may take immediate command of my Royal but I can't see Uncle allowing him to retain that position permanently, considering his contempt for Val's common bloodline. "If-and I do mean if-that comes to pass, it would be to your benefit. Val is a reasonable man. I'm sure he would be willing to negotiate terms acceptable to both sides."

"It would resolve nothing if Valleri usurped Bertrand. The Crusaders will not trade one tyrant for another, nor will Val surrender his newly won power to an enemy he has fought so hard to repel. He will continue to fight us with renewed determination."

"Sestus, I would hardly call Val a tyrant. Once he learns I am alive he will yield. He will stand down in favour of me. He will agree to any terms with which I agree. I know he will."

Sestus, I saw, was skeptical. But how could I convince him further without betraying my lovers' secret?

"Sestus, trust me. I know Valleri better than anyone else does. He swore to do everything in his power to see me on Thylana's throne. I believe him. He will defer to me, and to the Crusaders as well, if I say that's how it must be. The revolt will be over."

"On the contrary, the throne will be in contest. Thylana will split into three factions-Bertrand's Royalists, Valleri's sympathizers, and yours. Before all this happened there were many Crusaders who supported your claim to the throne, but feared you were too loyal to Bertrand. Now…that may have changed."

I was secretly pleased not all Thylana had abandoned faith in me, but the revelation also brought disappointment. "I never wanted the throne this way, Sestus."

"Well, I fear it's beyond your control now." He leaned back in his chair and regarded me curiously. "Tell me, Little Red. Where had you planned to go when you fled the castle?"

"Zigores. Valleri thought if I could infiltrate the city as an Umagi, I could hide myself away from Uncle. There I would be able to study and learn how to manage my powers without his influence."

"You realize, of course, that's out of the question."

"Am I a prisoner here?"

"Not exactly. You see, Zigores is a myth. It doesn't exist. We invented it to explain away certain things that we didn't want the castle to learn. In Thylana there is no safe place for the Umagi, Kathedra. You more than anyone know that. Most especially not in some fictional city."

I sat a moment in stunned silence, wondering at all that might mean. At last I said, "I can find Zigores on a map, Sestus. Don't tell me it doesn't exist."

"The city known as Zigores, a sprawling cesspool perched on the edge of nowhere, exists, yes. But as a secret haven for Umagi? No."

My heart sank. Not only was my hope of finding sanctuary lost, but also my faith in Gryphon's capacity to determine fact from falsehood. With a sigh I set aside the clothes, my exuberance gone. "I'd intended to return someday to Thylana in full command of my powers, to challenge Uncle for all that is mine by birthright, to take back Mother's throne, to re-establish her rule and to heal Thylana. But…that's all rubbish now."

Sestus, however, was having none of my self-pity. "Return when, Little Red? To what? You would leave Thylana, abandon her as I once abandoned you? Perhaps never to return? And if you did someday return, it would not be to the Thylana you once knew. Anything could happen in your absence. Bertrand could crush the revolt and rise to such power you may never sit on the throne. Or we could usurp him and you would see strangers ruling your land, in it a stranger yourself. You could even be forced to challenge Valleri for Thylana. You have to stop running. Castle Gryphon is your home. She needs you. You have to stand up to Bertrand with the rest of us. Like it or not, you are one of us now."

I digested his words in silence, realizing their truth very much against my will. I wanted to stay with Sestus, to seize the opportunity to strike back at Uncle and restore Thylana, but I could not shake the cold, hard fact I was among my enemies. "It's not much of a choice, is it? You cannot guarantee me that if I decide to join you I will ever be permitted to take my place on Thylana's throne. Your Crusader friends may have something else in mind."

"True, there are no guarantees. But my Crusader friends, as you call them, are not out for personal gain or glory. They want to restore Thylana to a just and productive rule. In the days preceding the revolt there were those in Thylana who yearned to see you, the rightful heir, supplant the Regent in the hope your reign would prove as harmonious as your mother's. If we gain momentum, the fact that the Gryphon Highlord herself changed sides and chose to serve the Crusader cause must be taken into consideration, and that sentiment may be reborn. It is to your advantage to help us, because if there is one thing I can guarantee, it is if Bertrand is not soon vanquished, you will never be queen."

I frowned. "I don't know how much help I can be to you. As I've said, I can't be sure whether I was given all the facts, nor how much of that limited information is false. Uncle has deceived me from the start. I may do your side more harm than good."

"Perhaps, but it will be up to us to decide for ourselves what is true and what is false. You possess knowledge other than campaign secrets. For instance, you can read and write. There aren't many here who can. Those skills alone will be of much value. You are also trained in warfare. And, you fled Castle Gryphon after having lived there your entire life. It's been a score of years since I last walked those halls. A lot has changed. Together, you and I can accomplish much."

"If you say so, Sestus," I sighed, certain I had no other recourse.

Sestus relaxed, an ear-to-ear grin spreading across his face. "I do. But we can't reveal who you are now. There are still some Crusaders around who'd rather execute you. We must convince them of your loyalty to our cause first. We'll have to give you a new identity, but one that will allow you to supply us with vital information without arousing suspicion."

Hmmph. Easier said than done.

Sestus mulled it over. "I'll say you are the daughter of a friend I knew at the castle. Someone I respected and trusted beyond reproach."

I cautiously agreed. "We can say I grew up in the castle, educated and privileged due to my father's position of…what?"

"Scribe?" Sestus suggested. "Yes, we'll make him a royal scribe. Close family?"

"All dead." No lie. If not for Uncle's royal blood he'd be a stranger. "We can keep it simple that way."

"The question could be raised whether or not you knew the Gryphon Highlord."

"Not personally. She had no friends." No lie again.

"We need to find you an occupation, an explanation for how you spent your days in the castle." He tapped his chin with a finger. "A chef?"

"Sestus, I am hard pressed to boil water."

"A food taster?"

"Be serious."

Sestus tipped his head in thought. "Your mother-she read a lot, didn't she? Poetry and history were her favourite subjects as I recall. She had a whole room filled with shelves of books where she could sit and read undisturbed."

"She read less and less once she became sick," I said, saddened by the memory. "But the room you speak of adjoins Uncle's briefing room."

"Does someone look after those books?"

"Oh my, yes. There's a whole staff dedicated to Mother's library. They dust the books, sort them, repair them and whatnot. I frequented it myself when I was in need of geographical or historical texts. It's a quiet, restful place."

"Then you're a librarian."

"Honestly! Do I look like a librarian?"

"It doesn't matter. People around here don't even know what a librarian is."

"That still doesn't explain my access to privileged castle strategies. How would a humble librarian know that Captain Fleurry's next assignment is to take his Tenth and establish an observation post in Pixley? Or that the mercenary captain Roche broke his hip falling dead drunk off his horse and was not wounded in action as claimed in the official report?"

"Is that true?" Sestus demanded.

"Why, yes. I saw it happen. Roche had been up all night drinking cheap wine with his cadre of hardcore hangers-on when—"

"No, no, no. Not that. About Fleurry."

I shrugged. "Hard to say, now. But that's what was said at the last briefing I attended."

"What was your next assignment?"

"I hadn't received new orders at that time. My troops were in barracks for a rest. But I still need a reason explaining why I left the castle."

"A leak was discovered. People began to point fingers at you. They suspected you may have overheard military secrets while dusting books in the next room and had sold them to the Crusaders. In fear for your life you fled, hoping to reach Glanshayda and distant relatives. But you only got as far as the highway, where you were attacked by a gang of bandits…and you know the rest."

"Might not someone suspect I'm a spy?"

Sestus shook his head. "Not once I explain how I came across you."

It actually sounded as if it might work. "So, I have my disguise. But one other thing troubles me: Ginger. I might be able to fool everyone else but he's a mage. If he suspects I'm lying, he may have a method of extracting the truth from me."

"Ginger is not an easy man to fool, but I have seen no evidence that suggests he possesses that sort of power. Besides, he has bigger things than a fugitive librarian with which to concern himself."

"One other thing, Sestus. Is it possible Ginger may somehow sense my Teki powers, even dormant?"

"It's highly unlikely. You didn't detect my presence back on that hill, did you? And to me you appeared as any other hapless traveller fallen prey to brigands. Unless, of course, you release some tendril of magic. Deliberate or otherwise," he added pointedly. "If you lose control, if you let it slip out, as you have before, upon the battlefield for instance, he'll catch wind of it and trace it back to you like a bloody Shouda."

"But that's just it, Sestus. I don't know if I can. I have no training, no instruction. I've been stumbling along on my own for so—" An idea occurred. "But you can help me. You can show me."

"What? Oh, no. No, way, little girl." He started waving his hands back and forth, retreating from me. "I possess just enough magic to keep my sword sharp without the need for a whetstone. I am so not qualified to be your teacher. You need someone more learned in the art of telekinesis than I. I could inadvertently do more damage than good."

"Not a teacher, per se. But a mentor. Someone to guide me."

"No." Sestus seemed unpleasantly adamant on that point. "I will, however, show you how to repress your powers, to not use them, and without the aid of drugs."

Well, that was better than nothing. Later, with the proper employment of guile and begging, I might get more out of him.

"And no one can recognize you as the Gryphon Highlord?"

"None save you. Unless you have a spy in your midst or other…turncoats," I added, stumbling over the word.

My last public appearance had been at nine years of age, shortly before Mother's death. Claiming it was for my own protection, Uncle had confined me to the castle and its grounds until his reinstatement of the Gryphon Highlord. From that time on, I viewed the world from behind a helm, from horseback. No Crusader has seen me without full armour.

Sestus considered it. "I am aware of no Royalist deserters or sympathizers in this vicinity. As for spies, it's believed we eradicated them. There is, however, another matter we should address. Once news surfaces of the Gryphon Highlord's disappearance, your arrival here may seem a bit too coincidental for some people's liking."

I shrugged it off. "I don't think we need worry about that. It's my belief Uncle will cover up the entire business. If word got out that I was missing, it would only encourage the Crusaders to search for me. And that is a scenario Uncle will try to prevent at all costs. It would be to Uncle's advantage to let the outlaws and everyone else continue to believe the Gryphon Highlord is retired, but ready to be called into service at any time."

"True enough, Little Red. But often news of such magnitude is nearly impossible to keep under a lid."

We talked well into the night, refining my disguise. Ginger and his fellow Crusaders would have many questions and I could not permit a single slip-up, no matter how minute, for the slightest mistake would arouse suspicion.

I intended to give the Citizens Risen Up to Stand Against a Dread and Errant Regency everything they required to topple Uncle. But that did not mean my betrayal was complete. Come what may, I would not turn on Valleri. Where he was concerned, my lips were sealed. If Valleri honoured his oaths to me, the Crusaders need never know of his existence.

But before Sestus left, as his hand was poised on the door latch, I asked, broaching the subject with him for the first time, "About you and Biddy. I admit I don't know what's happened between you two, but I wonder…is there no hope for a reconciliation?"

He did not turn around to answer me, saying under his breath, "No, Kathedra. No hope at all."

Hardly a Crusader mantra. But maybe I could fix that.

CHAPTER NINE

I rose swiftly the next morning, anxious to meet the two Crusader captains, and struggled into the clothes Sestus had brought. Tailored to fit the male body, the trousers were too tight in the hips and too baggy in the waist, the latter I fixed with a belt. The shirt I chose was no better, a huge, billowy garment overlong in the sleeves, ranging all the way down to my knees. I pulled on my boots, then stepped into the other room. Sestus awaited me at the table, a meagre breakfast before him.

He gestured me to sit. "You should eat something."

Complying, I helped myself to a pot of sticky oatmeal. "Any sign?"

"Scouts sighted Ginger's party an hour ago. He'll be here soon."

I wolfed down my tasteless breakfast, then reached for the kettle to pour myself a cup of tea, aware of his ardent stare. "What's the matter?"

He smiled. "You're far too pretty, Little Red. Even with a black eye and a bruised jaw. I fear Ginger and Repachea will have trouble believing your story. I would myself, if I had not been the one to come across you."

I do believe I blushed.

"Perhaps you should tie up your hair."

I shook my head so the mass of my hair fell along my purpled jawbone and shadowed my swollen eye. "I admit I'm a vain woman. I'd rather not emphasize my injuries. But maybe you'd like to slap me around some. You know, so I look a little ragged around the edges." I was being facetious, of course. The next man who thought to brutalize me would soon be a dead one.

Sestus betrayed a crooked smile. "That won't be necessary. I have more than enough witnesses. But I warn you, Repachea has an eye for the ladies."

"And Ginger?"

"Put it this way. Ginger won't waste his time on a pretty face. He won't waste his time, period."

"He sounds like a barrel of fun."

"More like a barrel of determination with a bucket of petulance sitting on top."

"Ahh, I sense an interesting tale."

"Suffice it to say he has a personal grudge to settle with Bertrand. It's his sole purpose in life. He will allow nothing to divert him from that course."

I dropped the subject, unwilling to press Sestus at this time for details. In truth, I had suspected there was more to learn about Ginger, suspected Sestus withheld information. The man was Umagi. That was all I needed to know about him.

The drum of approaching hooves outside interrupted our conversation. A dozen horses, at least. Sestus shot to his feet. "Hurry, Kathedra…I mean, Ruvie. Damn, I've got to work on that. Wait in the other room. You're something I must tell them myself."

I gulped down my tea with such haste I scalded my tongue, allowing Sestus to push me into my room. I heard the muted sounds of men dismounting beyond the outer door just as mine slammed shut. Intending to eavesdrop, I hovered near.

The Crusaders made a noisy entrance, with much boot stomping and backslapping as everyone greeted one another. Then their voices lowered as they discussed their comrade's fall in Bolta. I strained to catch their words, my ear pressed up to the door, struggling to make sense of the dialogue.

It seemed hours passed before Sestus finally got around to explaining my arrival. A prolonged hush ensued, then the conversation heated up once more as the outlaw leaders uttered their protests. Unable to bear the suspense any longer, I cracked open the door just enough for me to poke my eyeball through. The Crusader nearest me was of medium height, with a slim build and a sweep of raven-dark hair. The other stood with his back to me, taller and a tad broader across the shoulders. Their clothing bore signs of recent battle and a hard, dusty ride.

The dark-haired man had much to say, things like what were they to do with a woman and having an extra mouth to feed, all the while insisting he commiserated with my plight. Sestus countered by pointing out my usefulness, trying to persuade him I was a risk worth taking. As he continued to debate the issue with the first Crusader, the second grew ever more restless yet contributed little to the discussion. Patience deserted me. I yanked open the door.

"Enough."

All three men jumped at my unexpected entrance, then froze, save for the taller man, whose hand flew to his sword hilt as he spun round. My gaze travelled up the length of his arm to his face, where it met the baleful stare of piercing, steel-grey eyes-mage eyes. But that wasn't the worst of it. Long, mink-coloured hair framed angular features, the flesh of which at some previous time had suffered the passage of flame. Patches of red, tautened skin spattered the right side of his face, from cheekbone to chin. Though this disfigurement detracted little from a certain masculine beauty, it came as a shock just the same.

His gaze sharpened at my startled gasp, turned challenging, daring me to look away. But I held my bold stare, unflinching, until his companion spoke.

"Ruvie, I presume?"

I tore my gaze from Ginger to fix it on the speaker. "You presume right."

Repachea leaned against the table, crossed his legs at the ankles, and lifted a hand, stained with dried blood, to rub his tired eyes. "Oh, Sestus. I swear I'm in no mood for this. It's one damned thing after another."

"Bad timing is all," Sestus sighed.

I glanced at Ginger, still glaring, still clutching his sword hilt, then said to Repachea, "Never mind, captain. I'll make it easy for you. I know when I'm not welcome. Loan me a horse and I'll be on my way. Forget who I am and what I can give you. Perhaps that will improve your mood."

I brushed past him, ignoring his look of astonishment. A transparent bluff, however one I intended to push. For a moment I thought Repachea would call me on it. But just as I reached the door a sword scraped from its scabbard, and Ginger's blade barred my path.

Taking my elbow, Sestus pulled me beyond reach of the mage's sword arm. "Then you're in agreement, Ginger?" he asked.

The mage sheathed his blade with a curt nod.

Sestus turned back to Repachea. "You know we can't cut her loose. If she falls back into Bertrand's hands she can lead him right to us."

Repachea allowed a wan smile. "And why is that, Sestus? Because you can't resist bringing home stray puppies. You know this is a monumental breach of the rules."

"You would have done the same. I know you too well. She can give us information. Give us the edge we need. We'd be fools to dismiss such an opportunity."

"All right. You twisted my arm." Repachea pushed himself away from the table. "If Ginger agrees, how can I object? But first, we have another matter in need of our attention. Belvemar wants to see you."

Sestus was startled. "Belvemar? You brought him here?"

"We had no choice. The doctor in Bolta could do nothing for him. Our only hope is Biddy. Her herb-lore is his last chance." He gestured to me and headed for the door. "Bring her."

By the time we reached the tiny infirmary, located in an older section of Idyll's former barracks, Biddy was already there, crouched by a pallet where the injured commander lay. Our entrance did not disturb her, so intent was she in her work. We huddled in the doorway while Sestus and Repachea conversed in hushed tones.

"How bad is he?"

"He should be dead," Repachea said. "I thought the ride here would kill him. In fact, it would have been a blessing if it had."

"How long does he have?"

"Hard to say. It's an ugly leg wound. He may linger for a week or two if his heart doesn't give out. He lost a lot of blood and infection has set in." Repachea shrugged. "Like I said, he should be dead. Ginger can do nothing more for him except numb the pain. It's up to Biddy to heal him now. If she can."

"Repachea?" came a shaky voice from the pallet. "Is that an angel you've brought for me?"

"Uh…not exactly, Belvemar."

"Come. Let me see her for myself."

Glancing my way, Repachea said, "I hope you have a strong stomach."

I thought that was a stupid thing for him to say to me. "I know what horrible things men can do to each other, sir," I sniffed. "I also know what horrible things they can do to women."

Repachea had the decency to look abashed.

The three of us approached the sickbed with all the enthusiasm of going to the gallows. Ginger hung back, less eager than the rest of us. A man lay on a blood-soaked cot, his face ravaged by lines of pain. He was a big, strong-looking fellow, his hair and beard streaked grey. A little older than Sestus, he was probably fifty-something. Biddy had finished dressing the wound and now applied compresses to his fevered brow. But at our approach he thrust her hand away with surprising strength and offered us a jovial smile, his eyes alive with a not yet failing light.

Lifting an arm, he beckoned me to his side. A conspiratorial smile touched his mouth as his gaze flickered from Sestus to Repachea. "Now, which of you virile, young bucks has been keeping so delicious a secret from old Belvemar, and with good reason?"

Both men chose to overlook the remark. Sestus said, "Her name is Ruvie. She's a refugee from Castle Gryphon."

Belvemar looked at me sidelong, noting my black eye and purple jaw. His expression darkened. "Ruvie's agreed to help us," Repachea spoke up, forestalling an inquiry. "She has intimate knowledge of the castle and the Royalist offensive strategy."

"She will serve you well, I think. She has…trustworthy eyes." He managed a feeble grin. "Of course, that is the opinion of a dying man, delirious with pain and fatigue."

"Don't talk like that," Sestus chided. "You're not going to die."

Belvemar reached out a hand and Sestus took it in a firm clasp. "Oh, Sestus. I am glad I lived to see you again. It is good to die in the company of my most treasured friends."

Though Sestus struggled for composure in the face of his friend's imminent demise, he could not prevent himself from blurting, "You stupid, old ox. I told you not to go. I begged you. We should leave this to the youngsters, to Repachea and Ginger."

"No." Letting his hand fall, Belvemar turned his face away with a grimace that could have been one of disdain or pain. "If it is truly my time to die I intend to go out fighting. So I'm a little older, a little slower, but I never wanted to take my last breath in a rocking chair. I deserve a warrior's death."

Biddy returned the compress to his forehead and flashed Repachea a weighty glare, having until now maintained an unusual silence. "I think you should leave now. My patient needs rest."

No one argued, not even Belvemar. Once Sestus and Repachea had made their farewells we retreated, leaving Ginger and Biddy to their tasks.

A sombre trio, we retired to Repachea's quarters, just across a breezeway from the hole in the wall I shared with Sestus, where the outlaw leader rummaged through a chest, discarding pieces of clothing until a pile lay at his feet. Sestus and I exchanged a dubious glance. Finally, Repachea found that which he sought and spun around to face us, holding aloft a vintage of wine not seen since my mother's reign.

"I was saving it for a special celebration," he murmured, caressing the jar. "To share with Belvemar upon our victory. But it seems that is not to be."

He set three goblets on the table and began to pour. He offered the first to me, but at my polite refusal gave it to Sestus. I had yet to be interrogated and I did not need the influence of wine to fuddle my brain.

We sat at the table in silence, waiting, I gathered, for Ginger to rejoin us. I became conscious of Repachea's marvellous blue eyes on me, not so much studious as appreciative. Already his lusty male mind swarmed with ideas. I thought if I appeared cold and indifferent he'd be discouraged.

My aloofness, however, served only to arouse his curiosity. "So, Ruvie? Are you married?"

"Not yet," I replied, the irony lost on him.

"Ahh, wise girl," he tsked. "A fate worse than death, I can tell you. I've been married three times myself."

"I hardly think you take marriage seriously then."

He fashioned a grin obviously meant to dazzle me. "Seriously enough to consider a fourth time."

The arrival of the mage spared me further drivel. Sestus asked, "How is he?"

Ginger's only response was a shrug and a tired-sounding grunt.

By way of comfort, Sestus said, "It is enough you can ease his pain."

Repachea threw off his dusty coat and raked a hand through his hair. "Right, then. Let's get this over with."

I had expected a formal and rigorous interrogation, but it was more of a debriefing, as if I were a scout returned from a routine mission. The atmosphere was intimate, relaxed, and might even have been comfortable if not for Ginger's oppressive silence. Repachea did all the talking. His questions, mostly of a personal nature, were endless, referring to my family background and social station in Castle Gryphon, all of which I answered just as Sestus and I had rehearsed.

At Sestus's prompt I spilled Uncle's campaign secrets. Repachea bombarded me with questions. Through it all Ginger stood in a corner, staring at me with those shrewd mage eyes, and never uttered a word.

By nightfall the Citizens Risen Up to Stand Against a Dread and Errant Regency knew everything of strategic importance the Gryphon Highlord knew, which, when I thought about it, was not a hell of a lot.

"It's my understanding," I said, "that in the beginning Bertrand and his advisors never considered your revolt anything but minor unrest. It would pass. A shove here, a nudge there, would put the unruly in their place. Even when you evolved into a nuisance they didn't consider you a real peril. After all, what threat could a rabble of exiles pose to the might and will of Castle Gryphon? No one seemed to worry until mercenaries began to appear."

"It was a mistake for the Regent to ignore us," Repachea growled. "We will make him rue it."

"Nevertheless, the Regent has lost patience. The Citizens Risen Up to Stand Against a Dread and Errant Regency have proven themselves dangerous. It is no longer a matter of subduing you, but one of eradicating you completely. He is done playing games. He means to kill the Crusader movement for good."

"The Gryphon Highlord won't let him," Repachea replied, managing to startle me.

"How so?"

"Through everything, she has remained tolerant. There were times when she could have run us into the ground, but she refrained. She is torn between her people and the Regent…and that will undo her. The Gryphon Highlord is weak. She lacks conviction. Though she does not realize it she has crippled the Royalists with her own indecision, her inability to do that which is sometimes necessary. Her guilty conscience is our greatest asset. While she dithers, pleading for leniency, pleading for compromise, we grow bigger, stronger, smarter, until Bertrand is no longer in any position to stop us."

I went rigid with indignation. Is that truly how the people of Thylana perceive me? As weak? Spineless? Wishy-washy? Is it strictly a Crusader point of view or simply Repachea's?

It was then I resolved to show them all-Crusaders, Sestus and Uncle-a thing or two. By the time this was over, no one in Thylana would ever underestimate the Gryphon Highlord again.

Repachea sat there in his chair, looking so smug, so superior, I actually considered letting him and his assortment of Crusader know-it-alls go down with their sinking ship. But if they continued to rely upon the Gryphon Highlord's indecisiveness it would mean the end for us all. Therefore, I swallowed my pride and decided to set them straight.

"You will need to readjust your strategy." I chose a tone as smug, as superior, as Repachea's expression. "The Gryphon Highlord is no longer a factor. In the days preceding my flight from the castle, rumours circulated she was to be retired."

That wiped the smirk from Repachea's face. His expression darkened, turned suspicious. "Why would Bertrand clip the wings of the Gryphon Highlord?"

I shrugged. "I know only that the Regent announced her betrothal to a distant relative named Lesuperis."

"Marriage? Unbelievable! When?"

"Probably as we speak she is already a married woman." It unnerved me to think that such a statement would be true had I remained at Gryphon.

Repachea turned thoughtful. "Retirement, eh? You can bet she did not go willingly. But why would Bertrand deliberately put her out of action at this most crucial stage? It doesn't make sense. Her Teki powers are an invaluable asset to the Regent. Surely he knows this. We respect her presence on any field of battle, wizard and woodsman alike. True, she is young and inexperienced as a commander, but her finesse amply compensates. She grows bolder, stronger…"

He paused, twisted in his chair to face Ginger. "Could that be it? Is it possible her powers have grown in strength, become harder for Bertrand to restrain?"

"Or maybe," Ginger murmured, "Bertrand fears his darling niece has grown powerful enough to challenge his claim to the throne and bring about a peaceful end to the revolt. A marriage would serve as a clever means by which to get her out of the way."

Well, they were half right. It was in my best interest to let them draw their own conclusion, if it led them away from the truth.

Warily, Repachea asked me, "Why didn't you mention this earlier?"

"You didn't let me finish," I reminded him. "As I was saying, the Royalists think there are only two outlaw commanders of any significance. They believe one is dead or permanently out of action-Belvemar. The other they believe is in Pixley, where Fleurry will post his Tenth."

"We must warn Gregaris," Sestus mumbled.

Repachea flashed him a glare. A silent rebuke, I surmised, for name-dropping in my presence. "That is precisely what we want them to think."

"I don't follow."

He regarded me a moment, then seemed to decide that if I were indeed a Royalist spy, I was no danger while in their custody. "There are two other teleportals in Thylana, concealed in a manner similar to this one. They were, until now," he said, pausing to direct another sharp glance at Sestus, "inaccessible to outsiders."

I began to see the broader scope. And frankly, I was startled by the Citizens Risen Up Against a Dread and Errant Regency's ambition, not to mention a little scared. "An audacious strategy. Let the Royalists believe the majority of the Crusaders' strength is concentrated in Pixley and so divert their attention. Meanwhile, you gather your supporters and launch an assault on Castle Gryphon via these teleportals."

"Smart girl." Repachea unleashed his winsome grin. "But the retirement of the Gryphon Highlord changes things. You see, she had unwittingly bought us time. We are not yet fully prepared to mount a siege. If what you say is true, we have some serious re-planning to do."

A palpable silence followed while Repachea's insinuation hung in the air, as decisions were being weighed and balanced. Finally he turned to Sestus. "Do you trust her?"

"Implicitly."

I had yet to determine Sestus's position in the Crusader hierarchy, but his opinion obviously carried a lot of weight. Repachea nodded. "That's good enough for me. We'll grant her second level clearance. We can put her in charge of the map room. The place is a dump. She can clean it up, file stuff away. After all, isn't that what a librarian does? Organize and sort? While she's at it, she can act as your assistant. You know, keep track of reports and duty rosters, things like that. But remember, Sestus. She's your responsibility."

"I understand."

A knock came at the door then. Ginger opened it at Repachea's cue. A frazzled, tired-looking Biddy shuffled into the room. Blood splattered her apron, and a few strands of grey-shot hair dangled down her brow. Fearing the worst, the men greeted her with a barrage of questions.

She silenced them with an impatient gesture. "Be quiet. All of you," she snapped. "I'm in no mood for twenty thousand questions. I know as much as you do, which, when I stop to remember that you're all a bunch of lunkheads, is nothing to brag about. All I'm going to say is he's asleep and resting comfortably, thanks to Ginger."

Nevertheless, Repachea demanded, "Did you talk to him? Did you explain the severity of his injury? Did you tell him he should be at home with his wife and daughter and grandchildren instead of rotting a slow death in this hellhole?"

"Yes, yes, yes. I told him. He won't listen. He's just as stubborn as the rest of you. You who call yourselves freedom fighters, liberators, crusaders, and all that rubbish. You're all the same. Only know how to kill and maim and destroy. If he wants to die here, if you all want to die here for the sake of your own stubbornness, then I say rot the lot of you."

"Calm down, Biddy," Sestus cooed. "You're just upset."

"Stuff it."

"Don't blame yourself. You can't help someone if he doesn't want to be helped."

Sighing, she slumped into the chair Repachea had vacated. "I know. But I feel so bloody useless. I've been here, how long? watching friends die. I can't take it anymore. I just can't." She pulled a crumpled hanky from her pocket to dab at her puddling eyes. "I hate to admit it, Sestus, you old fool, but when you die your blasted hero's death I'll cry for you, too. After I dance my jig, of course."

Sestus smiled, touched I think. His smile brought some light to Biddy's weary face. She composed herself, sniffed a last sniffle, and glanced at Repachea, her belligerence restored. "Well? Have you decided what you're doing about the girl?"

"We're keeping her." Repachea grinned. "Sestus's stray puppy has put us on a whole new scent to victory."

Biddy rolled her eyes, conveying her limited faith. "Anyway, I'm glad. I have a job for her, if that's all right with you." Not waiting for permission, she turned to me. "I want you to help me take care of Belvemar."

Taken by surprise I babbled, "Oh, Biddy, I don't think that's such a wise idea. I don't know much about that sort of thing."

"Well, I can't do it all myself, can I? I have other patients to look after too, you know. I have to sleep. I have to eat. I just need some help, is all. Someone to feed him and bathe him, or just keep him company. Someone to ease him through these last few days"

"Why me? Isn't there anyone else who can help you?"

"Take a look around you, girl. There's not much to choose from. Soldiers aren't any good for anything but soldiering. Besides, Belvemar requested you."

"I think it's a great idea," Sestus spoke up, to my dismay. "C'mon, Ruvie. What do you say?"

I looked from him to Biddy, swayed by the plea of her woeful eyes. Reluctantly, I agreed.

Biddy's smile said she'd never doubted my compliance. "Thanks, girlie. Come see me tomorrow, when you get a minute. I'll be in the infirmary if anyone wants me." She rose, gave Sestus her customary parting scowl, and rejuvenated, marched out the door.

Repachea wore a strange look. He did not seem happy with Biddy's decision to enlist my aid. Nevertheless, he had not objected and did not bother to do so now. He returned to the trunk and began to stuff a pack with the clothes he'd previously dumped on the floor. "Ruvie can take my quarters if she likes," he told Sestus, without glancing up. "I imagine it's pretty cramped in yours."

"Not really. I have some extra…wait a minute. You're leaving?"

"I won't be gone long. The better part of tomorrow. But I'll be in and out of Idyll a lot in the weeks to come, so my quarters will just go to waste. I'll bunk with Ginger. Anyway, we passed a sad, destitute little village on our way back. Looks like they had a tough winter and could use a few sacks of meal and other foodstuffs. I know we don't have much, but it's still more than they've got. Since Ginger's field of expertise requires him to be here, it seemed only right that I should be the one to go. Or do you think otherwise?"

"It's fine with me."

It wasn't really, but Sestus chose not to disagree. An objection might arouse suspicions. I didn't like it either. I'd rather see Ginger gone on a mercy mission than Repachea. He would be easier to bluff than the mage.

"Thank you, captain," I said. "That's kind of you."

"Yeah, well, don't get too attached. I'll want it back eventually. 'Course, that doesn't mean you'll have to move out." Again with the lecherous wink.

As Sestus and I rose to go, Repachea told my benefactor, "I'll head out at noon, but I think the three of us should meet first." He tossed a meaningful glance at the mage. "Ginger and I might have a few more questions."

Well, they weren't the only ones. I had plenty of my own. But while they had the luxury of directness, I did not. My position called for diplomacy and discretion. Therefore, I would choose a gentler, subtler approach. Sestus would not, could not, tell me everything. But I was confident that with a little tactfulness and a lot of patience, I would eventually possess the information I required to manipulate the circumstances to my benefit. I need only listen and observe...and control my restless Teki blood.

CHAPTER TEN

I awoke late the next morning, stiff and sore, thanks to my ribs, but otherwise refreshed. I dressed quickly and emerged from my room to find Sestus already gone. I stepped over the pallet he'd prepared for himself by the hearth and helped myself to the pot of gruel on a hook above the fire. I ate, thinking on Valleri. My mood soon soured. I would accomplish nothing sitting around feeling sorry for myself.

Ignoring my pangs of guilt I poked around Sestus's quarters-Sestus, who had been so kind and generous to me-looking for what, I didn't know, yet convinced I'd recognize it once found. I uncovered nothing of enlightenment, just some books of leisure and a drawer full of letters from Biddy, chiding him for some reason or another. No documents. No personal journal. No confidential reports.

But my search was not entirely fruitless. At the very back of a cupboard, I discovered my benefactor's secret stash of contraband. His horde contained spell books, grimoires, charms-all sorts of magical texts and devices that Uncle had ordered banned and confiscated. I sifted through it with reverence and painstaking care. I had never seen such oddities, such wonders, though mundane they must seem to any other Umagi. The thought occurred, or conceit really, that if Sestus refused to instruct me in the ways of magic, I might teach myself.

My education would have to wait, for the moment. Sestus was due back from his meeting and I had a previous obligation to Biddy. Replacing my treasures, all save one, I headed for the infirmary to seek out the irascible herbhealer. Looking pale and weary, she sat alone with the wounded outlaw leader. Belvemar's condition appeared unchanged, while Biddy seemed on the verge of collapse.

Rising awkwardly, she snagged my arm and drew me a prudent distance from the bedside. "Glad you could make it," she grumbled. "I've bathed him and changed his dressing. He's asleep now but if he wakes, you can give him some broth. What's that in your hand?"

I shrugged. "Oh, it's just a book I found in Sestus's room. I thought I might read to Belvemar, if he's agreeable."

Biddy pulled on her ratty shawl with a snort. "Suit yourself. But remember, he needs his rest. I'm going home to get some shut-eye, then I have a delivery to make. Here's the key to the dispensary if anyone needs anything. I shouldn't be long." With that, she stomped out the door.

"Is she gone?" asked a voice behind me.

I smiled at my patient's eager tone and slipped the key into my pocket.

"Yes, sir. Biddy's gone. I thought you were asleep."

Belvemar winked a mischievous blue eye. "Nah. I only pretend to sleep so she'll leave me alone. Don't get me wrong. Biddy's a fine, hard-working woman, and dedicated to her craft. But it's nice to see a fresh, pretty face and hear a sweet voice for a change. Come. Sit with me."

I pulled up a stool and lifted the lid on a steaming bowl of broth. "Hungry?"

"Only if it's not that rat soup of Biddy's."

"Oh, it's not so bad." I fed him a spoonful and wiped his lips with a cloth. "I had some myself when I was…" I hesitated, regretting my loose tongue.

"Incapacitated?" Belvemar finished for me. "Yes, I know your story. Biddy got it from Sestus. She told me all about you. Don't worry. I won't pester you with bothersome questions. I'm sure you got your fill from Repachea."

He paused long enough to let me spoon him another mouthful of broth. "You're a sweet girl to do this for me. After all, I know you have no reason to be feeling kindly towards a man, even if he is a bedridden, harmless old fool. But if I must lie here dependent on someone else for my every need, it comforts me to know it is someone who understands my pain, and yes, my humiliation. Someone who survived and can give me courage. I hope you don't mind."

"Not at all, sir."

"Don't call me that. I've always hated it."

He chatted easily between swallows, keeping the conversation light, and once he'd eaten, I fluffed his pillow and urged him to sleep.

"Plenty of time to sleep when I'm dead."

"Now, Belvemar," I cooed. "Don't be stubborn. You know you need rest. Look." I held up the book I'd brought. "It's a collection of heroic ballads. I thought you might like to hear one or two."

He smiled. "Yes, I do believe I would."

Flipping through the pages, I selected a verse at random and began to read. An hour passed before Belvemar started to doze, and even once he dropped off to sleep I continued to read aloud for the company of my own voice. Thus occupied, I did not hear the infirmary door open.

"Well, now. Aren't you a clever girl?"

I stopped in mid-sentence and looked up to see that a young man leaned against the jamb, eyeing me with a huge grin. "Who taught you to read? And so eloquently, I might add."

"My father," I said, embarrassed. "He was a scribe, and a collector of books."

He nodded, then pushed himself away from the door and walked towards me, his head tipped in a pose of consideration. His grin widened. "I'm Ragsey. I don't think I've had the pleasure..?"

I ducked my chin, feigning shyness in an attempt to guard my appearance.

I wanted to avoid meeting too many new people. The lower my profile, the better. "I'm Ruvie."

"Oh, the librarian," he said, shaking my hand. "I should have guessed. Ginger has the annoying habit of omitting details he considers trivial. He neglected to tell me how pretty you are."

Silly, gullible me, I sat there blushing.

Ragsey misinterpreted my reaction. "Don't get me wrong. Ginger isn't a gossipy old hen. But I am his personal courier. I carry messages to and from the other camps. Naturally, I'm kept informed."

"I understand. It sounds like a very important position."

"Aye, dangerous too. It can get damn scary sometimes, having to sidestep several different Royals at once. But I have no complaints. I've been with Ginger since the beginning of the revolt. He's a good man. There's not another like him I'd risk my neck for."

I filed that away in the back of my noggin for future reference. A man who inspired such loyalty and confidence had all the makings of a great leader. Ginger would prove a formidable foe. Therefore, it would be in my best interest to make him a friend. That, however, would be no easy task. Such men had only allies and enemies.

"How's Belvemar doing?" he asked

"Holding his own."

"I never doubted he'd pull through. He's tough." Ragsey crooked a thumb at the anteroom. "I just came in to get a herbal balm. Did Biddy leave you the key?"

Nodding, I set aside the book and accompanied Ragsey to the annex where Biddy housed her medicinal remedies. "Sorry to bother you," he said, as I unlocked the cupboard, "but Biddy's salve is the only thing that soothes my back after a long day in the saddle."

"No bother."

Once Ragsey had selected a jar of ointment labelled in Biddy's chicken scratches and I'd locked up the cabinet again, I led him to the door. There he turned to apologize once more, his boyish grin in place. "I'm really very sorry for being such a pest. I hope you'll forgive me."

"There's nothing to forgive."

"Good. Maybe we'll see each other again soon."

"Maybe," I said, smiling to myself as I closed the door.

Biddy returned soon after, looking cheerful and spry as she carried in an armful of supplies. She went straight to Belvemar's side and held a hand to his brow. "No improvement, huh?"

"Oh, I don't know. He ate a whole bowl of broth and he seemed to enjoy the book I read to him. His spirits were good and he talked—"

"No, I mean the infection. I think it's spreading."

"I wouldn't know," I mumbled.

"'Course not. Never mind. That's for me to worry about." She trotted into the anteroom with her bags. A moment later she exclaimed, "All right, who filched a jar of Biddy's peppermint balm?"

My word, but she was observant. I hastened to explain. Irritably, she muttered, "Well, I hope he paid you."

"Um, actually, he didn't. I never thought to ask him for anything."

"Damned soldiers," she huffed, slamming her bags onto the cupboard. "Always trying to cheat old Biddy out of her fair share. Always trying to get something for nothing…" Then she was off, frothing like a rampager at the bit, unpacking her bottles and jars with furious energy.

"Well…I'd best be going."

I sidled nearer the door, hoping to slip out unnoticed, with limited success. Repachea was there, quick with a winsome grin. "Ahh, just the little lady I was looking for."

"Uh…"

Taking my elbow, he leaned around me to shout at Biddy, "I'm borrowing Ruvie for the rest of the day if that all's right with you?"

"…and another thing. I'm getting just a wee bit sick and tired of having to tramp through this cesspit making all these deliveries. What's wrong you people? Your legs are younger than mine!"

Repachea responded to Biddy's tirade with a shrug and a wink, then tugged on my arm. "C'mon. I've arranged a little diversion."

Since no one had bothered to ask my consent, I allowed the captain to drag me from the infirmary and out to the stable yard, curious to see exactly what his definition of diversion was.

"I don't suppose you've ever ridden solo before?"

The question startled me, for it was ridiculous in the extreme, until I remembered that I was a fugitive librarian of little means, accepting sanctuary from people not much better off than myself. "Uhm, well, I…"

Not too articulate for a keeper of books. I should work on my vocabulary skills some.

"That's what I thought," he replied, stopping us before a spirited black gelding, saddled and bridled and snorting its impatience. Repachea leapt lithely to its back and extended me a hand. "Up, my girl. We don't have all day."

I hesitated, not at all certain this was a good idea, and stole a glance around the yard whereupon I noticed several other pack animals, loaded with sacks and bundles of all sizes, and recalled Repachea's mercy mission. Apparently, he was taking me along for company.

Reaching for his hand, I let him pull me up behind him onto his blowing mount and made myself comfortable. He wheeled the beast and signalled our escort to head out, just as Sestus came huffing and puffing from his quarters. "Don't worry, Sestus, old man," Repachea called out cheerfully, forestalling any objection my benefactor may voice. "I'll have her back before dark."

I had time to give Sestus a brave smile before Repachea prodded his mount into an easy trot, pack mules and escort in tow.

We reached the village in good time, though we did not have benefit of a teleportal. Repachea had not exaggerated about its degree of destitution. A knot of villagers, among them frail, old men and dirty, rail-thin children, emerged from their huts, sheds, and nearby fields to greet us. The outlaw leader dismounted, breezy smile in place.

I slid from the gelding's back to stand behind Repachea, just on his periphery, uncertain of my business here, watching as people clustered anxiously around him. The escort began unloading the mules so I went to assist them. Turning with an armload of goods, I found myself ringed by eager villagers. I passed out loaves of bread, crates of eggs, and baskets of fruit, all generously put together by volunteers from Idyll.

When we were done, a man too weakened by malnutrition to open a jar handed it back to me. How the men of my Royal would chuckle to see, if they could, the illustrious Gryphon Highlord with a jar of beets between her knees as she tugged on a stubborn lid. How that fop Chiverly would sneer in disgust to see the Princess Kathedra wrestling with an ornery mule over a sack of carrots, only to end up pitched face down into the dust of the road.

For a moment I had to step back from the frenzy, the emotion. While it was true that I had delivered mercy missions of my own to starving villagers, I had done so from the back of my horse, a prudent distance removed, watching my men distribute the food and feeling noble, feeling smug, with my good deed. But today was different, a stark contrast. A mother to a brood of six touched my sleeve and thanked me with her eyes. A greybeard squeezed my hand in silent acknowledgement, too moved to speak. Their gratitude was a palpable thing, and it humbled me to think that by doing something so simple, I had made these people so happy.

I looked at Repachea, efficiently directing the distribution of supplies, and recognized for the first time the nobility in him, observed the glow of compassion on his face, even hidden by a week's growth of black stubble. His jokes, his conceit, and his easy going manner had blinded me to the lines of care and hardship etched onto his features, and he a man still under thirty.

I might have broken down on the spot had Repachea not approached to kneel beside me.

He watched, an indulgent smiling playing about his lips, as a trio of scruffy young boys took great fun in breaking up the wooden crates for kindling. Then he turned back to me and said in his most sprightly voice, which seemed all the more ominous considering the subject, "These people are what I'm all about, Ruvie. Sadly, they and thousands like them are caught in the crossfire between us and the Regent. Sometimes they become forgotten by Royalist and Crusader both. I come from a village such as this, prosperous at one time but made impoverished by the effects of the revolt. Ginger fights for an erroneous chance at revenge. Sestus too, though he hides behind his banner of the liberator. The others prattle on about glory and justice and freedom. But this is what I do. It's one objective the Princess Kathedra and I had in common. And now she's not even in the equation. That leaves just me to care about what happens to these people. I fight for them, and them alone. I will allow no further harm to come to them by either side, for any reason."

The smile had faded, and the cheerful tone had gone flat. Piercing me in his earnest gaze, he said, "So, if you betray me, if you give me reason to doubt your allegiance, rest assured it will be the last thing you do."

His warning chilled me to the bone; I took it to heart. I rode back to Idyll with a far different man than with whom I'd ridden out. Or at least my perception of him was different.

If I had been harbouring any thoughts that Repachea, as a rake and a jester, amounted to little more than a brash young insurgent, eager to find eternal glory on the end of a Royalist blade, then they were promptly banished. He would make me a foe every bit as terrifying as Ginger. But also a staunch ally. Loaded with convictions and principles, Repachea possessed a selflessness and gallantry that a woman in my position would find impossible to dismiss.

CHAPTER ELEVEN

By the end of my first month in Idyll, I had begun to sift through the mess of documents, maps, communiqués, and scribbled notes that encompassed the Citizens Risen Up to Stand Against a Dread and Errant Regency's strategic hardware in an effort to put the map room into some semblance of order. My initial task was to verify the information already assembled. No easy feat. It seems the Crusader intelligence is as dull as Gryphon's. I spent most of my time correcting misinformation and deleting discrepancies. The Crusader spies had collected an alarming amount of knowledge, but for a hindrance here, a dead end there, had been unable to implement into their grand strategy.

Slowly, methodically, I began to fill in the blanks.

I toiled by torch glare in a corner of Idyll's former dungeon, which was one of the few areas of the castle still intact. While serving as a workstation it was also capable of housing the present population in the event of a Royalist siege. Here the physical evidence of Crusader plots and activities are safe from prying eyes and inquisitive ears. This is what Repachea so reverently referred to as second level clearance.

That oblique designation, however, did not grant me access to everything I wished to know. It frustrated me to be fed these tantalizing morsels, which whet my appetite but did not sate my hunger. For instance, I learned there are six outlaw leaders. Ginger, Repachea, and Belvemar I already knew, and I had heard of the captain Gregaris, whom Sestus had implied headed a force in Pixley, which was Fleurry's next destination.

As Repachea had mentioned, there are two more teleportals, but their locations remain a mystery. That information, I assume, is accessible only to those with first level clearance, men like Sestus and Ragsey. Information I may be able to obtain from Repachea if only I can swallow my distaste. Each teleportal has its own guard and is activated by a passkey identical to the one Sestus used in the barn. In addition to Sestus, each outlaw leader also possesses such a key, the usage of which is governed by strict rules, rules that if broken carry stiff penalties. Sestus had broken the cardinal rule by loaning his to an unauthorized person. But Erol, apparently, was no snitch.

Of course, the Umagi wizard who originally erected the teleportals did not require a passkey, nor did the mages who shared the responsibility of maintaining the energy necessary to sustain the operation of each teleportal. According to Sestus, the keys were created simply for the sake of convenience.

In essence, I became little more than a glorified housekeeper. It was honest work, however, and kept me out of trouble, as Sestus would say.

Repachea was being kind when he'd called it a dump. Dishevelled and cluttered, the place was in sore need of a meticulous hand. I don't know how they found the map table half the time, let alone Royalist outposts. In librarian-like fashion, I straightened out the confusion, developed a system of organization, and had genuine fits of hysteria when someone, usually Ragsey or Repachea, messed it up. I tacked maps to the walls and rearranged mismatched markers, to the chagrin of scouts and messengers alike. I dusted and sorted and filed and tossed anything extraneous into the fire. My efforts drew praise from everyone. Everyone except Ginger, who was cross because I'd unintentionally consigned to the flames his unfinished treatise on the importance of dragonfly wings in the preparation of illumination spells. I mean, really. I thought it was a joke!

Thus, my time became divided between working in the map room and visiting Belvemar. The wounded captain showed sign of neither improvement nor decline. He seemed to hover in stasis, much like myself. Unlike Biddy and Sestus, however, I maintained hope for his survival. Weeks had passed and still Belvemar clung to life, which was miraculous in itself.

True to his word, Sestus introduced me to a variety of ways by which I could learn to master my Teki powers, including meditative studies, mental exercises, and something he called 'crystal intervention'. He gave me a small, rough-around-the-edges gemstone, purple in colour, worn smooth on one side, bearing a definite thumbprint impression.

"It's an amethyst," he told me, a tad sheepish. "Such stones are renowned for their ability to create inner peace and harmony, as well as influence psychic abilities. As you can see, I've sought its intervention on many occasions. The adepts scoff and sneer at what they deem tripe, saying that a Teki who professes true mastery of his or her powers does not require such mundane tools. Anyway, I find that it has helped me in moments of anxiety, or dare I say, panic. I've kept it in my pocket all this time, ever since my father gave it to me at the age of ten. But you know what? I can't recall the last time I needed to use it. Consider it yours now. Put it under your pillow at night, if you like. Use it in any fashion that helps."

His kindness touched me, and even helped to alleviate my disappointment, for I'd been looking forward to pouring over spell books and experimenting with actual magical devices, which had been beyond my reach since Uncle had declared them contraband. Crystals and meditation seemed, well, boring. But I accepted Sestus's advice with grace and the promise I'd try his methods. I even fashioned a little wire cage for my amethyst and fixed it to a slender chain, so I could keep it in the pouch at my belt, within easy retrieval should I feel the need.

Though I had Sestus's benign influence to guide me, those early days in Idyll were still tough. It was a rocky adjustment for me to make after spending all my life conditioned to the strict social structure of Castle

Gryphon. One thing remained unchanged; I was an outcast here as well, an outsider who had to carve her own little niche before she could fit into Idyll's community and be accepted as one of its own.

That is not to say I was lonely. Far from it. Indeed, I had next to no privacy at all. Between Ragsey's friendly chatter, Repachea's sly innuendos, and Sestus's and Biddy's constant bickering, I feared for my sanity. My only source of tranquillity was the time I spent with Belvemar, and he slept through most of my visits.

To make matters worse, Repachea suggested that as a meek and mild librarian living the life of a fugitive in a Crusader outpost, I should learn how to defend myself. To my horror, Sestus agreed with him, pointing out that it did seem a logical argument. Repachea, I'm sure, had an alternate agenda. Nevertheless, I bowed to their wishes, thinking it an ideal way to keep my fighting skills sharp.

My lessons started immediately, with Repachea as my tutor, of course. I must say the outlaw leader has a curious method of instruction, which involves (in my opinion) unnecessary oratory and constant close physical contact. The man also has a rather high opinion of his skill in swordplay, but it is well deserved, as he demonstrated to me one dismal day on the soggy practice field following an evening's rain.

To his surprise Repachea took a few nicks and whacks, which his male ego dismissed as beginner's luck. After one particularly close call, he looked at me askance with that crooked grin of his and declared, "I think, my dear, you indeed have some talent for swordplay," then proceeded to lecture me on the finer points of swordsmanship.

"As you may or may not be aware there are four S's to the art of swordplay. Speed. Strength. Stamina. And…and…bloody hell, what's the fourth?"

"Strategy?" I offered helpfully.

"No."

"Stealth?"

"Unh-unh."

"Self-discipline?"

"Nope, but that's a good one. Ah! I've got it." He made a grand flourish with his rusty practice sword. "Style."

Of course. This was Repachea, after all.

"One needs to fight with precision and dexterity, yes. But a little grace, a little finesse can't hurt. If you can't look formidable, you can at least look elegant." He waved at Ragsey where the man stood a short distance away pitching throwing stars into a wooden post with frightening accuracy. Stowing his missiles, he trotted over. "Allow me to demonstrate," Repachea told me.

I handed over my practice blade to Ragsey, who suddenly went white-faced, and adjourned to a nearby stump to watch the proceedings, which if not especially enlightening, were at least entertaining. As for style, I had to agree that Repachea delivered Ragsey's ass kicking with distinctive flare. Then again, I could have dealt Ragsey a good punishment myself. Once Repachea had disarmed his flustered opponent, the demonstration degenerated into a wrestling match. Truth be told, the courier should stick to his throwing stars.

Repachea emerged from the muddied field, flushed and breathless, but triumphant, leaving his vanquished foe sprawled in the muck, sputtering curses. I flung him his discarded jerkin, which he used to wipe his face. "You see?" he panted cheerfully. "Style is everything. Oh…hey, Ginger. What's up? You want to have a go at me next, old man?"

I glanced over a shoulder at the mage who, in keeping with his style, had come upon us unannounced. Without a word to me, he tossed a scowl of disapproval at Repachea and jerked a thumb towards the stable before stalking from the field.

Repachea gave me an apologetic shrug. "Well, I guess that's it for today, Ruvie. I'd better go see what he wants." As he moved to pass by me, he said, "You know, you might want to tie back your hair or cover it next time. Having it long and loose like that might be dangerous in a real fight. But on second thought…" He paused to tuck a stray wisp behind my ear. "It's too beautiful to hide away."

The man never misses an opportunity.

While Repachea trotted after Ginger, I went to fish Ragsey out of the mud. I must say he took his thrashing with his customary good humour. "You see how I dazzled him with my lightning reflexes, flummoxed him with my fancy footwork?"

"Yes, well done," I laughed. "Perhaps you could teach me." I was about to quiz him, discreetly of course, on the mage's boorish behaviour, when a sudden commotion distracted me. Biddy and Sestus had emerged from the infirmary, squabbling as usual. "What now?" I wondered aloud.

Ragsey got to his feet, shedding slime and clods of soil. "What? Oh, them. Ignore it."

Judging by their angry gesticulations and the pitch of their voices, for I could not make out their words at this distance, it sounded vicious. "Doesn't their carrying on bother you?"

"Not as much as Repachea's superior combat skills do."

"What's their story?"

His eyes, big and startling white in their rings of dirt, narrowed with suspicion. "Why?"

"I want to help if I can."

"Leave it be, Ruvie." He shook his head, flinging clumps of sod from his hair. "It's old and bitter. Hatred and rage is all they know. It brings relief from the pain. I gotta go…clean up. But, hey. Maybe you and I could spar some time." He stepped back with a wry grin and opened his arms to indicate his sodden apparel. "I could use the practice."

"Sure. I'd like that."

As I scooped up the practice blades to clean and return to the armoury, to the accompaniment of Biddy's and Sestus's fussing in the background, I knew I'd heard their sad refrain before in Uncle's tale of lament.

Throughout all these antics Ginger is ever present, his watchful spectre lurking in the shadows, although he never speaks to me. In the beginning I thought Ginger a quiet, circumspect fellow, the sort who only talks when he has something important to say. Then as time progressed, I came to suspect he did not trust me enough to speak in my presence. But when we'd meet alone, face-to-face, and he'd not even utter a polite hello I took it personally.

So when I mustered the courage to demand an explanation from Sestus, I was embarrassed to learn the truth. We sat at the huge worktable at the time, sorting through the latest scout reports from Ragsey. At my inquiry, Sestus stopped reading and glanced up. "Well, in case you haven't noticed, women intimidate Ginger. Pretty ones, especially. They usually don't look at him long enough to strike up a conversation. But you?" He allowed a low chuckle. "You sort of knocked him off-balance."

"Yes, well, you might have warned me about that."

Sestus shrugged. "To be honest, I never thought to. I mean, we've grown so used to the way Ginger looks, we just tend not to notice it any more. It's no different than the blacksmith's limp or the wart on the tip of the laundress's nose…no, wait. Bad example. We do notice that. Really, it's hard to—"

"So what you're saying is that Ginger is just shy?"

"Yes. Shy. Or bitter. What have you."

"Sestus, those aren't the same. Which is it?"

"Bitter then, I guess."

"Why? Because of what happened to his face? What did happen to his face? Was it some kind of accident? Was there a woman involved?"

"Uhm, yes and no. You know, of course, that in the year following your mother's death, Bertrand outlawed all magic and banished those Umagi who refused to comply. Due to what happened here at Idyll, his fear and mistrust included all magic-users."

"He banished all save one," I reminded him.

"Yes. You were spared." Sestus shook his head. "Why? I don't know. Perhaps even then he retained a shred of family honour, or perhaps he realized you could be of future use to him. But I suspect you were saved persecution because you reminded him in so many ways of his dearly departed sister. You cannot know how much you resemble her, Kathedra. Your eyes, your voice, even your gestures. God only knows where you got your red hair."

Smiling, he reached out to ruffle the short tuft that had usurped my red-gold mane, for I'd taken Repachea's words to heart and chopped it all off.

"But I digress. Naturally, there were those who defied the Regent's proclamation and refused to be forced into exile. They remained, living always one step ahead of Gryphon's huntsmen and their hounds, stirring up rebellion and unrest."

"And Ginger was one of these?"

"Not in the beginning. First off, you should know that Ginger was present here on that fateful day. The son of the stable-master, he was about the same age as the young prince, Ivor, your cousin, and they became close friends. In fact, he was standing with Ivor in the kitchen, prepared to execute a daring raid on the pantry along with some other boys, at the time that Mauranna's spell went horribly awry. In the same instant that the knife had hurtled through the air to impale Ivor, the hearth fire flared violently, belching up a gust of hot ash and liquid flame that struck Ginger's face. Spell-born, the fire was no ordinary fire, burning long and deep. Miraculously Ginger survived, thanks to a gifted Umagi healer, but Ivor perished."

I digested all that in a shocked sadness, marvelling at the coincidence that Ginger had known my cousin, a relative I had never even met.

"Upon hearing of Mauranna's execution and fearing further retribution against the mageborn on your Uncle's part," Sestus went on, "Ginger's parents spirited him from Idyll, for during his efforts to save the boy's life, the Umagi healer had uncovered their son's budding magical talent."

Sestus tipped his head, his expression thoughtful. "Now one might think that such a tragedy would cause Ginger to forsake his newfound craft. Instead, it only fuelled his desire to learn. He nurtured his powers under the guidance of an old enchanter, studying long and hard despite constant, nagging pain that haunted him through the rest of his youth. Then Dundurn happened."

I waited expectantly, for what had occurred at the town of Dundurn had been a pivotal moment in the history of Thylana.

Sestus cleared his throat, continued, "While studying under the enchanter, Ginger met a fellow Umagi, a fellow student actually, just about the time the outlawed wizards began to trickle back from exile. Her name was Nelia, and she didn't care about Ginger's disfigurement or his turbulent past. They fell instantly and completely in love. Anyway, their youth and exuberance led to stupidity when a radical Umagi faction formed a protest in the streets of Dundurn and they joined in. As you know, an uprising ensued; nothing serious, but Bertrand panicked and sent in his troops."

That much was true. There are those who argue that if not for this single unfortunate episode, a more peaceful resolution might have been made between Uncle and the Umagi, one satisfying to both parties.

"Ginger joined the more vociferous protesters, and although the Royalists stick to their claim the Umagi used magic against them, Ginger denies it. As he tells it, the Umagi only retaliated with thaumaturgical means after Gryphon's troops attacked them. As it happened, sporadic scuffles escalated into a full-blown riot thanks to the Royalists' aggressive tactics. Without any weapon of his own, Ginger soon found himself face to face with a Royalist blade. Somehow, Nelia got between them and in the confusion that followed was impaled on a pike. She died from her injury on the pavement of Dundurn, becoming the first official casualty of the revolt. Dundurn turned into a bloodbath from there. Ginger never forgave himself. He's always felt he should have died instead of Nelia."

The rest of the puzzle that was Ginger slid into place. "So motivated by guilt and rage and hatred he plans to visit revenge on Uncle?"

He paused, sliding me a stern look. "I'll be frank. Ginger not only intends to usurp Bertrand, but to ensure his lineage never again sits on Thylana's throne. Now do you see why it is imperative he does not discover your true identity?"

"That's ridiculous," I snorted. "I can understand why Ginger is eager to punish Uncle, but why me? I was still taking lessons from my arms master when all that happened. He can't blame me for the atrocities of my uncle."

"Ginger is not a rational man. He does not think as we do. He has a single purpose in life, one reason for living, which is to see the reign of your family swept into oblivion."

I stared at my fingers, knotted on the table before me, and wrestled down my anger. "Don't you think this is something you should have told me from the start? Or did you fear I might refuse to aid a fanatic's cause?"

"I did what I thought best," Sestus replied, making no attempt at apology. "I believed the truth would frighten you. Fear often leads one to make mistakes, mistakes you can't afford around Ginger. One tiny slip-up can cost you your life. If he discovers who you are too early, he may think to kill you."

"And there is nothing you could do to stop him?" I gasped, astonished. "Are you saying you and Repachea and Belvemar are powerless to oppose Ginger's will? It is inconceivable I should be held responsible for the transgressions of the Regent, even if I am his niece. Where are your noble higher principles now? I can't believe you would permit a lunatic to lead your celebrated Crusaders."

Sestus remained calm, unflinching before my righteous fury. "You're wrong, Little Red. Ginger is not supreme commander. He shares that position with five other Crusader captains and myself. Together, we form a democracy. No one man has absolute authority. In the event of a dilemma, a vote is held and the majority rules."

"That is how you hope to keep a madman like Ginger in line? Are you ready to gamble that theory with my life?"

"In the end Ginger will decide for himself," Sestus conceded. "He is a man who will die to fulfill his obligation. He is the single most dangerous obstacle in your path to the throne. Therefore, you will need to win his confidence, to earn his trust and to prove your loyalty to our cause. Perhaps then, once we gain the victory, he will see that you truly deserve to wear the crown by deed and not by right. Time is your ally. Use it to your best advantage."

It galled me that I, the Gryphon Highlord, the rightful heir to the throne, should have to prove to anyone I deserved the role I was given by birth. But did I have a choice? Here? Surrounded by my enemies?

I got to my feet, prepared to take my leave. "He's mad, you know. How can he not be?"

Sestus shook his head. "Not completely. He need only be brought back from the brink. Either he jumps, or we pull him back."

CHAPTER TWELVE

"Bloody hell!"

Repachea stared up at me from the trodden sod of the practice field, arms splayed behind him, a mixture of surprise and bewilderment on his face. I hooked the hilt of his fallen sword with the toe of my boot and tossed it to him. He caught it awkwardly, still reeling from the shock that his pupil had bested him.

Dusting off my palms, I said politely, "Touch me like that again and I'll break your fingers."

He climbed to his feet, still dazed with disbelief. "Where did you learn that little trick?"

"Not from you, surely. Do you think you're the first to try that lame move on an unsuspecting female? You ought to be ashamed of yourself." He really should be. It was a measure of his desperation for a rake of Repachea's calibre to have to resort to adolescent ploys. I expected better of him.

The rogue somehow managed to appear sheepish despite his dazzling lupine smile. "You're jealous."

Only strapped to a rack would I confess to the sliver of annoyance at learning that I was not the wolf's sole prey. An incorrigible flirt, Repachea spent a good deal of his spare time wooing the pretty dairy maid who came with her father twice a week to sell us milk and cheese. Not that I had the slightest intention of accepting his advances.

"I'm wearing you down, Ruvie. Go on. Admit it."

I gave him my back and busied myself with polishing rag, grateful there were no racks in the vicinity.

I considered our practice session ended. And not a moment too soon, apparently. Horses appeared in the stable yard, saddled and loaded with overnight gear, most notably Repachea's black gelding. Whirling on him, I exclaimed, "You're leaving?"

He grinned his foxiest grin. "Just a little plunder party. Won't be gone long. Hardly time enough for you to miss me."

A single snowflake drifted down between us, the last of the season. Winter in this part of Thylana was mild enough, consisting of six or eight weeks of moderate cold and sporadic flurries of snow, followed by a cool, soggy spring. The weather never slowed our practice sessions, nor did much to deter Repachea's zeal for mischief and mayhem.

"You weren't going to tell me, were you?" So keen was my petulance I almost stomped a foot in outrage. For months now I'd been hounding Repachea to allow me to accompany him on a raid. Plundering a supply caravan destined for Fleurry's command post or looting a storehouse filled with luxurious 'necessities' for Chiverly had been a secret fantasy of mine, even when I was a Royalist. But always Repachea gave me the same tiresome answer.

"Ruvie, I'm sorry," he began, shaking his head, "but no. You're just not experienced enough. I don't want to have to be worrying about your safety when I'm supposed to be sacking and pillaging."

That of course was the biggest crock of horse manure yet out of his mouth. The fact that he had the gall to say such a thing after I'd just knocked him ass over tea cosy was indicative of the man's enormous ego. But Repachea was good at what he did, which was ambushing caravans and plundering supply depots. He lived for raids, for skirmishes with the enemy. I blush to think that maybe even I had lost a wagon or two to the knave.

I ached to be able to tell him that I had pillaged and plundered with the best of them, but all I could say was, "I can take care of myself."

"Ruvie, I said no." His tone actually sharpened, though he softened it with a smile and reached out to tug at a tuft of my shorn hair. "You did that, cut your hair I mean, just to spite me." Then he withdrew, gathering up his practice blade and shredded dignity, leaving me with a fey wink. "Defiance. Jealousy. I like it. Keep it up."

I stood there, pouting, and watched him leave. So. Repachea was gone, along with Ragsey, who was off on a reconnaissance mission. A feeling of desertion set in. I trudged off the field, dragging my sword behind me. I thought of seeking comfort with Belvemar. A visit with him never failed to cheer me up. Sestus, however, was usually in the infirmary at this time of day, and I was holding a grudge.

My anger with the former Halberdier captain had been reduced to a low simmer, bubbling just below the surface. While we continued to work together in the gloom of the dungeon, our easy banter was noticeably absent. Indeed, immersed in piles of maps and stacks of minutia that seemed to go on without end, I began to view it as a true prison, its dismal walls haunted by Ginger's ominous presence.

Ginger, the enigma who had only a few short days ago been a source of infinite wonder and terrible fear to me, had turned into a dreadful bore. Not only did he not speak to me, he did not smile. Nor did I see any evidence of his diabolical powers, save for the teleportal, whose energy I assumed he maintained, though no one had said so in as many words. He merely hovered, ghost-like, glaring and disapproving.

I soon tired of his arrogance, his me-against-the-world attitude, and came to pretend he didn't exist at all. I ignored his sullen gaze, his critical frown, even his oppressive silence, which seemed to bother him immensely. I do believe he actually expected me to cringe under the touch of his menacing mage eyes, and scurry from his path like the rest of Idyll. He got the message, and I think he was even disappointed that his attempts to cow me had failed.

Truly, death by boredom was my only fear. Even my Teki powers flowed tranquil and serene, tamed by the monotony. How I longed for Valleri. Charismatic, vivacious, always exciting Valleri. To hear his voice or see his smile would be a breath of heaven here in this dull life of exile.

Things were destined to liven up, however. Although not quite in the manner I would have chosen.

It was hard to stay angry with Sestus, especially when he flashed me those sad hound eyes. I missed his company during meals, but more so his cooking. The time had come to make up. It only seemed sensible to do so over supper.

Hence, one night after I'd seen to Belvemar's needs, I borrowed a jar of wine from Repachea's private store and strolled over to Sestus's quarters. He answered my knock quickly enough, yet did not seem so eager to welcome me inside.

"Oh. Ruvie. This is a surprise." He spoke to me through a crack in the door.

"I know," I admitted. "But I want to apologize for my behaviour. I realize you were only trying to protect me. I want us to be friends again. You're the only one I've got."

He gave me a lopsided grin. "Only friendship, Little Red? It seems to me you'll starve if you have to eat much more of your own cooking. Well, I'm sorry, but you'll just have to suffer."

"Oh, Sestus. Don't be like that. Look." I held up my booty. "I've even brought a peace offering."

"It was a nice thought, but I'm on my way out."

Too slowly I got the feeling Sestus hid something. I sniffed the air. "Is that woodruff I smell? Why are you all dressed up? Why won't you open the door?"

He began to protest but an outraged squawk interrupted him. I pushed open the door to find the white, black-speckled rooster tugging on his bootstrap. "What's going on?"

Sighing, Sestus scooped up the troublesome bird. "Biddy invited me to supper tonight. I can't imagine why, unless it's to poison me."

"And the rooster?"

He looked at the bird where it pecked at the metal doodads ornamenting his uniform. "I don't know. She just said for me to bring it. I expect she's changed her mind, after all."

It seemed Biddy had taken my advice to heart. "Here," I said, giving him the wine. "Take it to share with Biddy." I started down the wooden steps.

"Wait, Ruvie."

I turned around to see Sestus trying to juggle the bottle, the rooster, and the door. "Why don't you come along? You know, so I'll have a witness when she tries to put snakefoot in my tea."

"No, thanks. I don't think Biddy will welcome my intrusion. She'll want you all to herself."

"Yeah, that's what worries me."

I shuffled off to my own quarters, resigned to another bowl of gruel, and several pots of wilted plants, dying on the windowsill, for company.

A voice next to my ear startled me out of a sound sleep. "Don't be frightened," it intoned.

It was a voice I'd rarely heard before. When I opened my eyes I realized why. Ginger had materialized beside my pillow. I sat up on my elbows and blinked at him in the gloom. It did not occur to me to be scared, although I was fully aware I lay half-clothed, weaponless, and alone in the presence of perhaps the most dangerous man in Thylana.

To my surprise he gave me a tentative smile, one that only a chosen few ever saw. "Forgive the intrusion," he said in a softer, less officious tone, "but there's not much time. Where's Sestus?"

Still groggy I mumbled, "Isn't he in his quarters?"

"Obviously not, else why would I have come to you?" I opened my mouth to answer but he cut me short. "Never mind. I guess I'll just have to settle for you. Get dressed. I'll wait outside."

"Where are we going? It's the middle of the night."

"Out."

I dressed hurriedly, fumbling about in the dark for my clothes, then rejoined Ginger on the doorstep where he gazed at the waning moon. "Will you please tell me what—"?

"Follow me."

Grumbling to myself, I trudged after him to the stables. There he saddled two horses and bade me mount with the surly order, "Just be quiet and follow my lead."

We rode from the slumbering keep, my docile mare following the stallion into the dark, sprawling countryside. There was no conversation, no sound save for the horses as they trotted steadily afield. Ginger paused once to test the breeze, then veered north. I had begun to doze off when he called a halt.

We tethered the horses in a stand of poplar, then Ginger pointed our way farther north. "Stay close."

I shivered in the chill night air and marched after him, still having no idea where we went or why but not daring to ask. As I tramped alongside the mage, a frightful thought occurred. Had Ginger somehow discovered my true identity? Heavens above! Did he plan to-?

A touch on my arm nearly made me scream. I gasped and jumped away, trembling. Ginger gave me a stern warning glare and brought a finger to his lips. He stared at me a moment longer, eyeing me with clear contempt. "What's the matter with you? Don't tell me you're scared of the dark."

"Of course not," I hissed, regaining my composure. "I just find it a little strange."

"Get down," he snapped, shoving me to the ground. I landed on my belly with a mouthful of twitchgrass, the wizard down beside me. "Don't make a sound."

With painstaking care we inched ourselves over the rise until we looked down onto the valley below. Ginger gestured with his left hand and it seemed the veil of night lifted to reveal a shade of twilight. A troop of horsemen snaked along a distant road, moonglow glinting off armour and weaponry. At a glance I recognized Castle Gryphon's elite troops.

Ginger crept closer. Our elbows touched. "Do you know whose Royal that is?"

Mine, I wanted to shout, though I managed to restrain myself. "The Twelfth. The Gryphon Highlord's."

"You're certain?"

"Quite."

He nodded, satisfied. "That was my guess too, but I wanted to make sure." His finger lifted ever so slightly to indicate the rider in the lead position, just ahead of my standard-bearer. "Is that her?"

"No."

"How can you tell?"

Oops. I did some fast thinking. "That's not her armour. Nor is that her horse. Hers is white."

So, I had been replaced. But by whom?

"Do you recognize the commander?" Ginger persisted.

I wished he'd shut up so I could think straight. "No, the distance is too great." Not only that, but his light-spell had begun to fail. "Besides, he wears helm and armour."

"Well, he's astride a black charger. Sound like anybody you know?"

I gave him a withering look, which went wasted on the gloom. "That's not much to go on."

"Fleurry, maybe?"

I shook my head. "He should be in Pixley by now." My fists clenched in fury. By damn, if Uncle had given my command to that lout I'd die of shame. Calmly, I uncurled my fingers and battled down my temper, fighting restless, dangerous thoughts.

"Where do you think they're going?" he wondered.

"You'd know better than I."

"Well I don't." He nudged my arm. "C'mon. We have to find Sestus."

We slithered back down the hillside and hurried to our mounts. During the return trip I pondered this latest discovery. My Royal had received new orders and now marched under a new commander. But whom had Uncle chosen to replace me?

Belatedly, I realized I had not seen Valleri. He did not ride beside the commander in what is traditionally my second's position. I began to fret something terrible had happened to him. Uncle may have learned of his role in my escape and had him imprisoned, or executed, or worse.

When Sestus didn't answer Ginger's knock at the door we let ourselves inside. His quarters were empty, his bed undisturbed. We stood there in the dark and squinted at each other, perplexed by his disappearance.

"He'll turn up in the morning," I yawned.

"I don't have until morning." The mage sounded agitated. "When did you see him last?"

"This afternoon. He was on his way to Biddy's for supper, but he should be back by now."

"Should be. It's nearly dawn. Where could he..?"

An absurd thought occurred, nudging aside Ginger's words. Did Sestus have reason to suspect Biddy may be plotting his demise, or was his comment only in jest? True, their ongoing feud could be nasty at times, but I'd been convinced they really cared for each other. Had Biddy poisoned Sestus? Was she, this very minute, burying his corpse in her garden, between the herb bed and last year's tomato stakes?

"Ah, this might sound silly, but before I left him Sestus said something about Biddy plotting to poison him, something about snakefoot in his tea. He asked me to go with him, but I thought he was joking and…" I broke off, aware of my hysterical babble.

Ginger glared. "You're right. It does sound silly."

"Well then, where is he?"

Five minutes later we pounded on Biddy's door, calling Sestus's name. Ginger is not a patient man. He did not wait for an answer. I watched, incredulous, as he forced the door, its latch giving way under his brute strength. We stumbled inside just as a lamp ignited, the sudden light scorching our eyeballs. The illumination, however, gave us a startling view of the situation.

For there on the bed sat Biddy, her hair strewn about her pale shoulders. And before us stood Sestus, wearing only an expression of horror.

I apologized profusely to Biddy and Sestus, neither of whom was amused by our brusque intrusion. But after I'd explained, the tension subsided and all was forgiven. Biddy actually got quite a hoot out of it, and laughed until tears came to her eyes. Sestus too, grudgingly admitted a grin once he got over his embarrassment. Only Ginger failed to see the humour.

The advent of the sun, heralded by the crow of a familiar white, black-speckled rooster, completed the interruption. Biddy insisted we stay for breakfast, and she cooked us all a hearty meal of eggs and sausages. Ginger ate hurriedly while he and Sestus discussed the sighting of the Royalist patrol.

At one point he mumbled something I did not catch, for Sestus suddenly blurted, "You're leaving? You can't leave, Ginger. We need you here."

"I have no choice. We must learn what the Royalists are up to."

"How long will you be gone?"

Ginger shrugged. "A week, maybe two. Surely, you'll survive without me for a fortnight."

"You can't go alone," Sestus protested. "It's not safe. We've never seen a patrol in this area until now. It could be a trap to lure you out."

"I'll take Ragsey with me. He's due back any minute. I assure you my tracking skills are more than adequate enough to elude any Royalist patrol. Or do you lack confidence in my talents of wizardry?"

"Of course not. It's just your talents could be put to better use here. Hell! We've already lost Belvemar. It's anybody's guess if we'll see Repachea again, knowing his bent for misadventure and self-destruction. Now, you? It's too dangerous."

Ginger smiled, but it was a hollow, jaded sort of smile, very different from the shy, almost friendly one I'd seen earlier. "I appreciate your concern. But danger, my friend, is the name of the game."

"I agree with Sestus. I think you should remain here."

I don't know why I said that. Certainly it would be safer for me with Ginger gone. Perhaps, deep down, I feared the mage would learn things during his reconnaissance I'd prefer he didn't.

I glanced up from my meal to see both men staring at me. Sestus glared icy rebuke. Ginger was not nearly as pleasant. His grey eyes had hardened to stone, unmistakable malice etched in them. Then in a voice thick with soft menace he said, "You have no say in the matter, precious."

My back stiffened at his arrogance. I am not used to not having a say in matters. Nor am I accustomed to being told so. In Castle Gryphon my word had been second only to Uncle's.

I returned his baleful stare but held my tongue, aware I could not openly challenge his authority, though it galled me to no end.

"Why is it so important you go?" Sestus asked.

"There's a chance the Gryphon Highlord may ride with them. If I can bring her into our custody, she may prove to be a strong bartering tool with the Regent. She is, after all, Bertrand's blood heir."

"Bertrand doesn't care about his niece," I snorted, as much as it hurt to admit. "He's already retired her."

"That's merely rumour. I've neither seen nor heard evidence to substantiate it."

"That's irrelevant. I've already told you the Gryphon Highlord did not command that patrol, or does my word mean so little?"

"It can't hurt to make sure. She may ride incognito."

Now that was truly absurd, but there was no way I could persuade him otherwise. It did, however, prompt me to think I might have overlooked Valleri. Maybe he led the patrol. Maybe he didn't believe me dead and searched for me. Maybe I could somehow let him know I lived.

"In that case, I'll go with you."

"You will do no such thing," Ginger snapped.

"I see no reason why I can't. It may even benefit you to have me along. I can ride some, as you know, so I won't slow you—"

"Be silent. You'll stay right here and help Sestus until I return." Fury smouldered in his eyes, trembled in his voice. "So long as you are here in Idyll, accepting our hospitality and our protection, you'll damned well do as I say. Is that clear?"

From the corner of my eye I caught a glimpse of Sestus teetering on the verge of a conniption. I could push my defiance no further. "Yes."

"Yes, what?"

I clenched my teeth. "Yes, sir."

Ginger stood, said to Sestus, "I'm leaving within the hour and there's nothing you can say or do to stop me. I'll be back just as soon as I can. In the meantime, perhaps you'll be able to teach her some discipline."

The mage spared me a last, poisonous glance and stomped out the door.

Biddy tried to alleviate the awkward silence left in his wake by quizzing me on my botanical charges. "How are those seedlings I gave you, Ruvie? It'll be planting weather soon. Maybe you can help me track down the hoes and rakes."

I wasn't really paying attention, glowering at the empty doorway. "Hmm? Oh, yeah, the plants. Sure, they're fine. No problem."

In truth, the seedlings had withered and the potted seeds of thyme and lavender had failed to sprout altogether. I couldn't even bear to look at the shrivelled towers of ferns, and I feared the henbane had caught a chill. The only thing germinating was my dislike for Ginger.

Back in my quarters Sestus muttered and grumbled, pacing like a caged beast. "Well, you very nearly mucked it all up, Kathedra. All our carefully laid plans almost went up in smoke."

"Ruvie," I reminded him.

"Ruvie. Yes. Thank you. As I was saying…you haven't done yourself any good with Ginger, I can tell you that. Nor have you made it any easier for me. I'm responsible for you, remember?"

Sulking, I sat in Repachea's leather chair and stared out the window. "I'm sorry."

"Sorry nothing! When will you learn you're no longer in command? Ginger gives the orders around here. Not you."

"I am the Gryphon Highlord. I take orders from no minor lunatic."

"You were the Gryphon Highlord," Sestus reminded me, none too gently. "You're not in the castle anymore, Ruvie. You're going to have to set aside your pride and adopt a lesser role."

"This is not an easy adjustment for me," I retorted. "It's bad enough I must eat food the royal hounds would not touch, and wear second-hand rags day in day out, and live in quarters the size of my closet. I've lost my command, my throne, and my inheritance. My dignity is in shreds and my powers in thrall. All this, I think I've accepted better than anyone could possibly expect. But I cannot, will not, take orders or withstand insults from an overbearing, thick-witted, in-love-with-himself madman. I swear, when this is all over I'll have him flogged!"

Sestus smiled at my tirade. "Yes, well, first things first, Little Red. If you hope to rise to your former glory as the Gryphon Highlord, you'll have to humble yourself for the time being. I know it's hard for you right now, but you will adjust. You carry the blood of a Gryphon queen and an Umagi adept. That is a combination of which you can be proud."

He concluded his pep talk with the wry remark, "Do try to curb your tongue around Ginger. He thinks you talk entirely too much for a librarian."

CHAPTER THIRTEEN

With Ginger absent I felt liberated, like a great weight had been lifted from my shoulders. Gone was the oppressiveness, the aura of gloom, which seemed to permeate everything when he was near. I no longer walked on eggshells in the fear an unruly thought might break loose and alert him to my deceit. I caught myself humming as I went about my duties, at ease with my new surroundings, adjusting, as Sestus had predicted, to my lesser roles of librarian and nursemaid. People were friendlier toward me, armed with smiles and words of greeting.

But I was not the only flower that blossomed in the sunlight since the dismal thundercloud that was Ginger had departed. Belvemar's condition improved every day. He grew stronger, his spirits high, and his pain tolerable. Biddy thought she had the infection under control and there was no sign of gangrene. The fact he still lived did not seem so miraculous.

Of course, the greatest miracle of all was that Biddy and Sestus had called what could be loosely termed a truce. Oh, they still bickered and sniped, but their hearts weren't really in it, almost as if they acted out of habit than true animosity. The discord remained, not always evident, lying just below the surface. I resolved to get to the bottom of it. Meddling, Ragsey said. Nonetheless, I was determined that they should find happiness together.

For the moment, I basked in Ginger's absence. Idyll itself seemed to heave a collective sigh of relief, freed from the tension and despair emanating from the dour mage.

My work in the map room progressed smoothly enough, and soon became routine. Of course, I had Sestus for companionship despite constant interruptions demanding his attention. I had yet to determine his placement in the Crusader command structure. Although he did not hold a captain's rank, he boasted a position of some authority, and served the outlaw leaders in the capacity of an advisor/mediator. But with both Ginger and Repachea absent, and Belvemar incapacitated, Sestus was the man in charge.

So it happened one day, while Sestus and I worked together in the dungeon blissfully free from disturbances, the subject of Valleri again arose.

Some time ago Sestus had produced a set of obsolete interior plans of Castle Gryphon. It became my task to update these maps, marking everything from the new servants' quarters to the labyrinth of tunnels burrowing beneath the foundation. He studied each of my completed copies with thoroughness and asked pertinent questions. On this particular occasion he placed before me the most recent of my reproductions and pointed to the area of his concern.

"This passageway, Kath...dammit, Ruvie," he began, scratching his head.

"Where does it lead? You've shown it exits into the bailey, but I can't identify its point of origin."

Avoiding his glance I answered, "My apartments."

"Ahhh…Ah-ha!" He hid his smile very badly. "So all those rumours about you and your second are—"

"None of your business," I finished for him, smiling a secret smile of my own.

Sestus chuckled to himself, pleased with his deductive reasoning, until he recalled the identity of my second-in-command. His amusement disintegrated. "You and Valleri?"

"Yes, Sestus," I said wearily. "Does that surprise you?"

"Frankly, yes. The idea never occurred to me. Although now, I must admit it seems only natural. Why didn't you tell me?"

"I thought you would disapprove."

"Because he's your second?"

"Yes," I sighed, hoping a confrontation was not at hand. "Understand, Sestus. Valleri was my lieutenant first. I appointed him to that position because he was strong, fearless, reliable. It was only later, for lack of someone else, I took him for my consort. I know it is a breach of some unwritten military code to allow this intimacy between captain and second to develop, but I didn't care. It never affected my judgment, never interfered with duty. For that reason, and the fact Valleri was not of royal blood, we were forced to be discreet. Our entanglement would have been a source of embarrassment to Uncle. We knew if he ever found out, he would put a swift end to it, which he did, although it was merely an excuse to disguise his true motive."

I turned my back to him, wishing for a window to look out. "So, please. Don't lecture me, Sestus. I've paid the price for my indiscretion with a broken heart."

"Love," Sestus groaned. "It is a bond that enslaves entire armies."

"What do you mean by that?"

"Only it complicates matters for you."

I smiled, rueful. Sestus had not been born yesterday. He perceived my love for Valleri as a serious kink in the Crusader strategy. "You have good cause to question my loyalties. I've studied the maps. I've read the communiqués from Pixley. I've heard Ragsey's reports. Your counterstrike is bolder than I first thought. The Crusaders plan to storm Castle Gryphon and usurp the throne by brute force. Negotiation is not an option. They plan a massacre. I probably can't prevent it. I will, however, do everything in my power to protect Valleri. I will not sacrifice him in order to grant your friends a victory, nor to regain my throne. I've betrayed Uncle. But, please, don't ask me to betray Val. I can't. I won't."

"You may find, Little Red, in the end, it will be either a matter of you betraying Valleri or Valleri betraying you."

"Never," I declared. "Valleri would never, ever, betray me. He'd sooner die."

I was with Sestus in the dungeon, perusing a magic text entitled, 'Mindspells For the Novice', when Repachea breezed inside, looking mangled and mauled but high on the euphoria of victory. In a manner I hoped was unobtrusive I tucked the grimoire under a pile of maps to retrieve later.

Repachea had not returned to Idyll empty-handed. Reaching into the sack he'd brought, he withdrew a bent tiara, glittering with an array of gemstones, and planted it on my head. "There you go, my girl. Closest we'll get to royalty, I'm afraid. Still, not too shabby, eh?"

He reeled away, pulled another sparkly diadem from the bag to perch it precariously on his own head, then slouched into a chair, well pleased with himself. Tossing a red velvet cap at Sestus, he crowed, "Sestus, you won't believe who I had the good fortune of bumping into on the road south."

Then, launching into his tale with unbridled enthusiasm, Repachea explained how he and his raiders had overtaken the unsuspecting escort to the Earl of Hundley, a staunch supporter of Uncle's yet also a braggart and boor whose company I could have done without several times. Hundley was a noteworthy man for two reasons, the first being the heft of his purse, and the second his prowess in the bedchamber. His escapades there had produced seven daughters, every one a stunning beauty and of marriageable age, which had conspired to cause the earl more than one grey hair. Thus, imagine Repachea's surprise and elation when upon opening the gilded carriage, he found within no bearded and pot-bellied earl, but instead three of Hundley's splendid daughters twittering behind their wimples, the commander's reputation apparently having preceded him.

Suffice it to say, the escort put up a vigorous fight but in the end Repachea and his gang looted the baggage wain and made merry with the Earl's happy-to-oblige daughters, now of questionable virtue.

"Charming girls. Simply charming," he mused with a chuckle. "Bertie's going to have his hands full coaxing old Hundley down from the rafters."

"Well, as long as you had fun," Ginger droned from the doorway, fresh from his own foray. I waved a greeting at Ragsey, who waved back over the mage's shoulder.

Repachea was immune to that famed Umagi glower. "Oh, hey, Ginger, old boy. Sorry. All out of fancy hats. But I've got a couple of nice bracelets and a gold pisspot if you're interested…no? Well, your loss. You really need to get out more, my friend."

"I was out. Working."

Ginger placed a special emphasis on that last word, as if implying Repachea was simply out having a lark.

"Oh, now this I've got to hear." Repachea shrugged at the mage's churlishness and flashed me a knowing grin. I returned it, tickled silly with my souvenir.

"Did you find out what the Royalist patrol is up to?" Sestus asked, massaging his temples with thumb and index finger.

"Not exactly." Sliding into a chair, Ginger pulled out a deck of divination cards and began shuffling them. "Though we did get close enough to eavesdrop. Information has surfaced proving Castle Gryphon is indeed bereft of her beloved commander."

"Ruvie already told you that."

"She said the Gryphon Highlord was to be married and put out to pasture," Ginger clarified. "But the marriage never took place. It seems neither holy wedlock nor retirement appealed to her. Instead, she opted to escape."

Uh, oh. Either Uncle is not as good at keeping secrets as I'd hoped, or Castle Gryphon is rife with spies.

"Escape?" Sestus echoed with a credible inflection of surprise. "How did she manage that?"

"Not very well. She's dead."

"Dead?"

"Stop repeating everything I say," Ginger chided. "According to our informants she fled the castle on the eve of her nuptials. A patrol was dispatched to fetch her back, but when they picked up her trail they found her murdered."

"Murdered?" Sestus gasped, ignoring Ginger's previous remark. "By whom?"

"The castle claims we found her first and killed her."

"But…but…that's ludicrous!"

"Of course it is. You and I both know that patrol executed her, acting on Bertrand's orders. She played right into his hand. When she fled the castle it gave the Regent an opportunity to kill her and blame it on us. The whole sordid affair hasn't made us any friends. A good portion of Thylana's citizenry remains loyal to the Princess Kathedra."

"Are you sure she's dead?"

Ginger nodded. "The patrol, including a few casualties, returned with her helm, her horse, her sword, and her body-what was left of it. She must have put up a hell of a fight. She was bludgeoned almost beyond recognition. But they were able to identify her as Kathedra."

A body? How in the world had Averi managed that? I risked a glance at Sestus. His expression was neutral but his jaw had clenched, and I could see he pondered some deep thought.

"I'm sorry, Sestus," Repachea said with genuine sympathy. "We all know how fond you were of the princess as a little girl."

Sestus shook off the words. "Do you know who identified the body?"

"Who else? Her second-in-command. After all, he was her lover."

What? Did everyone know? Poor Val. He must be beside himself with grief. Averi must have done some ghastly work on that woman he murdered to fool Valleri.

"That's not the half of it." Ginger paused, turning to look directly at me. "You might find this of interest, precious. I've learned who's replaced the Gryphon Highlord. He led that patrol we encountered."

"Who?" I tried not to appear too eager, praying it wasn't that prig Urharde.

Ginger shot Sestus a triumphant look. "Her second-in-command. Valleri."

Val? I couldn't believe it. My own lover had replaced me? Sweet, loyal Valleri had taken my command? Impossible!

"That's interesting…considering he's not of royal stock."

"Isn't it?" Ginger's gloating grin was ear-to-ear. "Not only that, but Bertrand named him his heir."

His heir? I shuddered. Everything was falling into place just as Sestus had predicted.

Repachea sniped, "Ouch! I bet that hurt old Bertie."

"What does that suggest to you?"

Sestus shrugged in response to Ginger's question, taking pains to avoid my gaze. "It seems a logical choice. After all, Valleri is next in command."

Ginger shook his head, impatient once more. "It suggests rather he was in league with Bertrand."

"What are you saying? I can't believe Valleri would plot against his own commander."

Nor can I. This little fable grew more fascinating by the minute.

"It's quite believable once you stop to think about it. Bertrand noticed his niece's powers had grown and decided to hobble her before she challenged him for the throne. But he needed help, so he approached Valleri. In return, he offered him the title of heir. How could the man refuse? Valleri pretended to be Kathedra's devoted lover, gaining her confidence, her trust, then betrayed her to her very own uncle. Ohh, they were a subtle pair."

"Valleri hates Bertrand," Sestus huffed. "I can't understand why he would help him to do anything, let alone murder Kathedra."

"Honestly, Sestus, it's so simple a child could grasp it," Repachea chimed in. "The throne. With Kathedra dead, Valleri has only to kill Bertrand and the throne will be his. He's a diabolical genius. He's gotten rid of his biggest rival and he's a footstep away from plunging a knife through Bertrand's black heart. I almost like the man."

"Bertrand is not stupid," Sestus pointed out. "He is not blind. Surely he must suspect Valleri of ulterior motives. So if he suspects, why would he name the man his heir?"

"Bertrand may not suspect. Has not Valleri just proven his loyalty by betraying Kathedra?"

Silence descended as Ginger's question dangled in the air. Sestus's face grew grave, his eyes filling with resignation. "I see what you mean."

I couldn't believe Sestus was actually buying this rubbish. How could

Ginger make up such terrible lies about Valleri? They had to be lies. Val is not the devious, ruthless fiend Ginger would have us believe. Or…is he? A swift, angry thought nearly got the best of me. As if in answer, a menacing rumble of thunder reverberated down from the surface.

Ragsey opined, “Sounds like a storm’s brewing.”

“A storm indeed,” Repachea mused. “When do you think Valleri will strike?”

“Hard to say,” Ginger replied. “He’s still got some work ahead of him. First he’ll try to woo the Royals to his standard while he simultaneously undermines Bertrand’s Halberdiers. He’s far cannier, far more dangerous, than anyone’s ever suspected. He’ll prove to be just as charismatic, just as seductive, as his predecessor. Gryphon’s Royals will flock to his banner. Once that’s accomplished, he’ll slay Bertrand and take the glory. All Thylana will call him a hero. With the Princess Kathedra dead, Thylana will accept Valleri as its rightful king.”

“Really, Ginger? Would it be so bad with Valleri on the throne?”

The mage fixed Repachea in a fierce glower. “Personally, I don’t care who sits on Thylana’s throne as long as it’s not Bertrand or his kin. But know this: Bertrand’s death won’t end the revolt. Valleri won’t compromise. He’s too proud, too greedy, to give up absolute power once he wrests it for himself. Considering the lengths he has gone to in order to get it, he will go even further to keep it. We must move soon if we hope to accomplish our objectives before he achieves his.”

Fanning out the deck on the worktable, the mage motioned me to pick a card. I flipped one over…and had to bit my tongue in order to stifle a yelp of surprise. I had drawn the queen of swords, which could be interpreted to represent Ginger’s enemy, therefore me, but with subtle, sinister differences. In any card deck I’ve ever seen, the queen of swords carries, well, a sword, and she glares out from the background with a clear, cold-eyed gaze. But this card showed her blindfolded, with hands bound behind her back. The figure from the mage’s deck had been altered, whether by magic or some other unknown mystical force, I don’t know.

“A good sign, Sestus. A very good sign.” Leaving the cards spread before us Ginger got to his feet, grinning his cruellest grin. “But the Gryphon Highlord’s premature death is a terrible shame. I had so looked forward to seeing her again.”

Sestus watched the mage stalk out the door. Frowning, he asked no one in particular, “What’s he talking about?”

“He’s met the Gryphon Highlord before,” Repachea muttered.

Really? What utter fantasy.

“Or do you forget, sir?” Ragsey added. “She routed him at Laurelac.”

Laurelac? A bolt of revelation struck me. Laurelac. Ragsey was right. I had indeed encountered the wizard before.

I remembered Ginger now. The Crusaders had launched a daring attack on that harbour town, hoping to disturb the river trade and annoy Uncle at the same time. My Royal chased them out. But during a pivotal moment in the struggle, I eagerly spurred my mount up a nearby hill for a better overview of the situation, outdistancing my standard-bearer. Apparently, the Crusader captain had the same idea. We crested the knoll almost simultaneously from opposite slopes and nearly collided.

Startled, we reined in and stared at each other over the ears of our chargers from not ten feet away. The skirmish waged on below while we sat frozen, each waiting for the other to make the first move. Ginger gave no evidence he was a mage, but I felt his hatred. It hit my brain like a physical force. Though partially hidden by his helm his face was grim, streaked with sweat and grit. He held a sword while mine lay snug in its scabbard. Strangely enough, I felt no fear, no rage, no inclination at all to summon my Teki powers. Only surprise and a detached curiosity. My thoughts flowed serene. He had the advantage over me and yet he hesitated. I sensed his fury dissipate, replaced by something I can only call wonder.

But below his ragtag collection of Crusaders had begun to collapse, their courage faltering as Valleri pressed them fearlessly. The outlaw leader had to make a decision, either to waste precious time battling me or try rallying his survivors and beat a hasty retreat.

In the end he flipped me a mock salute, slammed down his visor and drove his charger back down the hill.

At the time, I'd assumed he was merely another Crusader commander. I had not known a wizard, a mad and near omnipotent wizard, held an officer's rank. It seemed miraculous we should meet again and yet not know it was not the first time.

A shiver slithered down my spine. Such an occurrence reminded me just how much of my disguise relied upon luck. I had worn light battle armour-a mail shirt, a blue surcoat emblazoned with the gold gryphon of Thylana, a cloak, and a helm. Ginger could see nothing of me save my eyes, nor could he recognize my voice since I had not spoken. There was no possible way he could connect me with the woman atop that warhorse.

Nevertheless, I remained in a precarious position. It would be next to impossible to persuade Ginger I did not deserve the same fate he intended for Uncle. His ego would not permit him to forget the defeat at Laurelac. He had a personal grudge to settle not only against the Regent, but the Gryphon Highlord as well.

I waited until both Repachea and Ragsey had gone, before retrieving the queen with trembling fingers. Sestus tried to reassure me. "It's just a card trick, Little Red. Ginger does them all the time. It doesn't mean anything."

"No? I think it means the threat to him, or what he perceives as a threat, no longer exists. That means I no longer exist, as the future queen, as the

Gryphon Highlord."

"I really think you're reading too much into it."

"Yeah." I returned the card to the deck. "Maybe."

That night I spent hours walking around the shattered skeleton of the castle in an effort to soothe my rattled nerves. I needed to be alone, away from Sestus and the mage, so I might sort my thoughts and sift the truth out of Ginger's garbled information. I had little in the way of success, but if nothing else the peaceful evening air helped restore my equilibrium. When I returned to my quarters around midnight, Sestus awaited me.

"Where have you been?" he growled.

"Just out for a stroll." I threw off my cloak and collapsed into Repachea's far too comfortable chair. "I wanted some time alone to think."

"I don't suppose I have to guess who it is you were thinking about?"

"Ginger is wrong about Valleri."

"Wrong? The man conspired against you, stole your command and usurped your position as heir to the throne. How can Ginger possibly be wrong?"

I sighed. "Ginger has an over-active imagination. He has distorted and manipulated the facts to serve his own ends. Whatever Valleri has done, he has done so in my best interest. I will not entertain the notion he has ulterior motives."

"How can you defend the man after all he's done?"

Ginger was a lunatic, Sestus too, if he believed the mage's mad delusion. The explanation was really very simple once I'd given it due consideration. "First of all, Valleri did not conspire against me. He helped me escape, remember? Nor did he steal my command. Uncle gave it to him because he is the most qualified person for the position. Lastly, Val was named heir for lack of anyone else. Everything has fallen into place according to his plan."

"Plan? Which plan would that be?"

"The one that will resurrect me to my throne."

"Resurrect you?" Sestus laughed, a high, giddy sound. "Valleri didn't help you escape. He led you right into what was supposed to be your death."

"But I didn't die."

"Partly due to my intervention," he snorted, "in case you forget."

"Maybe, maybe not. Haven't you asked yourself why Averi substituted my body?"

"Because he failed to carry out Bertrand's order of execution and needed to cover his tracks."

"Not exactly. Averi had orders to return me to the castle, had the authority to kill me if I resisted, yet he implied otherwise. Therefore it's possible he received counterorders. Counterorders from Valleri. Val substituted my body, not Averi, by which to convince Uncle I was really dead, otherwise he would have ordered the hunt continued until I was found."

Sestus was quiet a long moment, unable to make sense of this particular riddle. "You think Valleri located a look-a-like for you and murdered her? Is Valleri capable of such an act?"

"Oh, yes." I remembered the slain woman's blood in Valleri's hair, which he'd overlooked when he'd washed and changed clothes that night of my escape.

When Sestus made no reply I continued, "Valleri probably thinks I'm on my way to Zigores by now, ignorant of the fact I'm trapped in a Crusader stronghold. He should have known better than to trust Averi. It's safe to assume Valleri doesn't know what liberties Averi took with those counterorders. Val's made some errors in judgment, Sestus, that I'll concede. But he did what he thought necessary in order to help me. He's in the best possible position to protect my throne."

I did not reveal it to Sestus, but I was furious with Valleri. Small things that would have alerted me to his plot I had ignored, such as his insistence I take my white charger, so Averi would not lose sight of me, and his adamant refusal to flee with me. Val had been right not to divulge the full extent of my escape plan, for I would never have agreed to it. I would not have sanctioned the murder of that poor girl whose misfortune it was to bear a resemblance to me, nor would I have allowed him to enlist Averi's aid for fear of his treachery. But I suppose to Valleri, who was desperate to see me safe from Uncle, he had no alternative.

"I think maybe we should tell Ginger about you," Sestus said.

I stared at him in disbelief.

"If Castle Gryphon believes you're dead, you've become a valuable asset to us. I think in light of that, Ginger would be willing to set aside his personal vendetta for the chance to use you against Bertrand."

"He'll use me against Valleri," I protested. "That's where Ginger sees the true threat. Once I've served his purpose he'll discard me or worse. I'll be a weapon for his cause, true. But I'll still be his prisoner, and that means he'll see to it I never gain my throne."

Sestus chewed his lip, still warring with that part of him suspicious of Valleri. "Do you believe, beyond a doubt, Valleri acts on your behalf?"

"Yes, Sestus. Absolutely."

"You harbour not the slightest suspicion he plots against Bertrand to seize the throne for himself?"

"None. If he does, why would he go to such lengths to help me escape, even contrive my death?"

"Perhaps when the order finally came from Bertrand to kill you, Valleri just couldn't go through with it. Have you thought about that? His love for you may hamper him, just as yours for Val cripples you."

I dismissed the notion. "Regardless of what you and Ginger say, the only thing Valleri is guilty of is loving me. Make no mistake about that, Sestus."

"Nevertheless, Ginger is right about one thing. Whether Valleri wants the throne for you or himself, he still schemes against Bertrand. That much you can't deny."

Sadly, I could not. The oaths I had extracted from Valleri meant nothing. It is a question of who will reach Uncle first. Will Valleri hold the executioner's blade, or some Crusader captain? Either way, will it bring me my crown?

"It's too soon for Bertrand to die. We're not ready. We still have to build our assault teams. In the meantime, Ginger intends to prevent Valleri from doing anything rash."

"As do I. Uncle deserves to pay for his crimes, past and present. He is unfit to rule Thylana. But he does not need to die in order to do penance." Even after all he'd done to me, I would not stoop to his level of vileness. I would not commit regicide, nor allow anyone else to, whether he be Valleri or Ginger.

Sestus rose to leave. "Well, if nothing else, at least one good thing has come out of this."

"What's that?"

"Ginger believes the Princess Kathedra is dead. That makes your position here a great deal safer. But that doesn't mean you can afford to be careless."

I understood. "Did Ginger happen to find out where Valleri's Twelfth is headed?" Those words cost me dear to say.

"He said the new Gryphon Highlord has orders to harass Naren in Shanasea, but first he has to pick up reinforcements in Church Grove. Bertrand hopes to cut off Naren's food supply. A message has already been dispatched to Shanasea. Naren will be prepared. Why?"

"Just curious."

Once Sestus had left, I crawled into my bunk to ponder the Gryphon Highlord's orders. Naren is the fifth of six outlaw leaders. I recalled a briefing in Castle Gryphon several months ago with Uncle and the available captains, about where to strike next. I suggested Shanasea. Everyone, including my second, vetoed me, claiming Shanasea was too trivial a concern. A small, unremarkable town, it was not important enough on which to waste time and money. If the Crusaders wanted it, they could have it. Let them tie up men and arms in a place of no interest to anyone.

Thus I received orders to rout the enemy at Laurelac, which I did, to Ginger's embarrassment. I consoled my bruised ego with that victory and never gave Shanasea another thought.

Until now. During my last few weeks in Castle Gryphon I had heard nothing to suggest Shanasea had become of sudden importance. What had changed to turn Valleri's attention toward it?

I suppose I should have told Sestus about it, but I merely assumed Uncle had withheld information from me and a shift in strategy had come at a time when I was no longer privy to Royalist secrets. It seemed too minor a detail to mention. At the moment I was more concerned with how I felt about Valleri commanding my Royal. Angry thoughts surfaced. Swift and violent angry thoughts that demolished Repachea's favourite item of plunder, a well proportioned sculpture of a writhing and naked woman.

CHAPTER FOURTEEN

Some days later I had the opportunity to quiz Biddy myself on the matter of her feud with Sestus. I was in the infirmary, attending to the grim task of trimming Belvemar's toenails, when I heard what sounded like muffled sobs coming from the dispensary. Excusing myself, I went to investigate.

I peeked around the door. "Biddy? Is that you?"

She spun, red-eyed and teary, from the cupboard she'd been leaning against, to swipe at the moisture staining her cheeks. "What are you doing, girl, sneaking up on me like that?"

"I'm sorry. I didn't mean to sneak. It's just that I heard—"

"Well, go away. I'm busy."

"Busy feeling sorry for yourself?"

She sped me such a fierce glare that had I been any nearer I'm sure she'd have swatted me. I stepped into the room and closed the door. Though prickly and over-bearing at times, Biddy had a warm heart and a sensitive nature, like most healers. It took only a sympathetic look on my part for her story to pour out.

Apparently, once upon a time, when the organization dubbed the Citizens Risen Up to Stand Against a Dread and Errant Regency was still just a daydream, she and Sestus had been sweethearts. Her brother, Cadwell, an aspiring Crusader, introduced them. As the story went, Cadwell and Sestus took a trip into the woods to hunt deer. Uncle's deer, mind you, but I forbore mentioning it. Anyway, they came upon a wild boar, unwittingly cornering it. Such a beast is dangerous and best left alone, but before the men could retreat, the boar spotted them and charged. It went after Sestus first, bearing him to the ground. Cadwell came to his rescue, putting every arrow in his quiver into the boar, but still the beast did not relinquish its hold. In desperation, Cadwell dove onto the animal's back and fumbled for his hunting knife. It's attention diverted, the animal left off Sestus to battle Cadwell. A monumental struggle then ensued between man and beast. Although Sestus had lost his arrows in the battle, he still, of course, had his magic. But according to Biddy, he didn't use it.

"Why not?" I asked, recalling the flashy telekinesis spell he had unleashed that day in the glade when he'd saved me from Averi and his men.

Biddy looked up at me, blew her nose into her apron. "Because the Regent had forbidden it."

Oh. All this had occurred at some time after Uncle's pronouncement outlawing the use of magic. Nevertheless, the revelation came as a shock to me. Perhaps as a former Halberdier captain Sestus had felt some sense of duty to obey the Regent's edict. To Biddy, however, it seemed like out and out cowardice. I certainly was no one to judge Sestus's action. Or inaction. It had taken me years to summon the confidence to defy Uncle, and then only upon Valleri's encouragement.

Thus, frozen with indecision, Sestus watched as his friend was gored by the boar. Only Cadwell's cry of pain prompted Sestus to act; he hurled a mindspell at the beast and while it lay dazed by the blow, thrust his dagger through its heart. But it was too late. Cadwell had been mortally wounded.

"Things change, I know," Biddy continued, dabbing at her eyes. "Now there's open rebellion against Bertrand and Sestus uses his powers almost daily. So why not then? What was the difference? He could have used them for something good. Now he just uses them, as does every other Umagi, to help get himself killed. I can't forgive him, Ruvie. I just can't."

I put an arm around her in sympathy. Wracked with sobs, she finished her story, telling me that Sestus had brought her brother home to her, where she had employed all her healer's skills to save him, but it wasn't enough. At last, I understood.

Wasn't it true, that from that day forward Sestus continued to bring her home casualties, wounded Crusaders one after the other, and her efforts never seemed to be enough? But Sestus alone wasn't to blame. Repachea did it, and so did Ginger. The woman's needle and thread knew no rest, her potions and poultices always in demand. This wasn't just about Cadwell. Sestus and his cronies were just too blind to see it.

Right from the beginning, Biddy was not a staunch supporter of the Citizens Risen Up to Stand Against a Dread and Errant Regency. She didn't understand their principles, nor their greater purpose. Biddy was here simply because she was needed. She tended to the starving, the bleeding, and the dying. As far as she was concerned, the world would be a much better place bereft of both Royalists and Crusaders.

"Well, 'nough of my blubbering," she said with forced cheer, patting my knee. "I've got something for you. Give this to Repachea when you see him later."

With that, she plucked a vial from the cupboard above us and pushed it into my hand. Nonplussed, I stared down at the container of shimmering fluid. "See him? I have no plans to get together with him. He cancelled our sword practice for today."

"That's probably because he's busy packing."

"Packing? Is he going somewhere?"

"Only clear across the countryside. You mean he didn't tell you?"

No one told me anything around here! It wasn't much different than being in Castle Gryphon.

"You will say good-bye to him, won't you? I dare say Repachea would be insulted if you didn't. He fancies himself something of a heartbreaker, he does. He'd be quite hurt if you didn't drop your ice shield and fall swooning at his feet."

"But...Belvemar's toes—"

"Oh, leave those daggers of his to me. Just go." And she sent me on my way with a saucy wink and not so gentle shove.

As Biddy had suggested, Repachea was packing when I arrived in the quarters he shared on occasion with Ginger. He turned to greet me with his usual grin. "Ahh, Ruvie. Come to see me off, have you?"

"Where are you going?"

"Just away. For a while. I'll be back."

"Where?" I persisted. His evasiveness irked me.

"Hmm...I can't tell you that."

"You're going to Bolta. You're taking over for Belvemar, aren't you? That's insane, you know."

I knew about Bolta, the site of Belvemar's injury, the place where he and nearly fifty other Crusaders were wounded or slain by a combination of Tock's strategic brilliance and dumb luck. Now Repachea was going back.

"I'm taking over for Belvemar, yes. His men need leadership and encouragement. I can't tell you where I'm going, but it's not Bolta. We're moving on from there."

Un-huh. I lifted his hand and slapped the vial into his palm. "Biddy asked me to give you this."

Frowning, he looked down at the tiny decanter then shoved it into his sack. "Biddy's extract of...oh, who knows what. Truly, I don't know what I'd do without it. The road turns me into a homicidal insomniac."

I shoved the coin that he flipped me into a pocket. Despite myself, I could commiserate with him. I remembered the long, sleepless nights spent in strange towns and siege camps, lying awake, staring at the ceiling or tent roof, whichever the case may be, my over-tired mind full of dread and doubt, wondering what the next day would bring. A victory. A defeat. Or even death.

"I know what you mean. The night seems to bring out all the uncertainties that never see the light of day. It's like me, trying to sleep here, in these drafty wooden barracks when I'm so used to the stone and mortar of Castle Gryphon."

"No, Ruvie. You've got it all wrong." Repachea chuckled and threw me a come hither glance. "My problem is, I just don't like to sleep alone."

That, I was certain, was an invitation. I sidestepped it. "Do you know anyone who does?"

He seemed to give the question considerable thought. "Ginger. Ginger likes to sleep alone. Not me. I don't like to be alone. But you must understand that. Surely, you've left behind a sweetheart at Gryphon."

It was the first he'd ever broached the subject to me. No doubt he'd come to conclude that I spurned his advances because I was unavailable. I must have looked guilty, for he smiled and said, "Do you miss him?"

"Sometimes." It was a lie. I missed Valleri with an intensity that bordered on grief, his absence something akin to death.

"Was it serious?"

I shrugged. "It was never a romance. More of a recreation, a pastime. A way to forget the daily grind, to shut out the ugliness of the world and ease our troubles. When a relationship is meaningless, it is somehow simpler, more carefree. But if it's allowed to continue too long, invariably it will grow complicated."

I paused, considering my relationship with Valleri. It had started simply enough, then had evolved into a full-blown love affair. We should have ended it long ago, when we first suspected our attraction was something more than physical. Now, torn from him, I had reaped more grief and pain than I had purged.

"As it happened, it never had the chance to go that far," I finished.

Repachea hefted his pack and strode to where I stood near the door. "I think I understand you. We are alike, you and I. Two kindred spirits." He tipped his head, wistful. "No demands. No commitments. No restrictions. Keep it simple. My style exactly."

Then suddenly, he asked, "Would you like to come with me, Ruvie?"

"You won't tell me where you're going, yet you'd invite me along? Sounds like you don't trust me enough to leave me behind."

"You know that's not true. Really, luv. It's your swordplay. It's terrible. I'll live in fear for your safety every day that I'm away."

I laughed at that, as he'd intended, for he knew that little Ruvie the librarian was fast becoming a proficient swordswoman. Though Repachea could not possibly know how badly I wished to cross swords with the nearest Royalist, it was not safe at all for me to be by his side. Therefore, I tried to let him down gently. "Sestus and I have much work to do here."

"You could be just as much help to me. I could use your knowledge and expertise, too."

"What about Biddy and Belvemar? They need me as well."

Laughing, he held up a hand. "No excuses, please. You're right. It's better this way. No harm in asking. Take good care of Belvemar while I'm gone."

I leaned against the open doorway and watched as Repachea mounted his black gelding before bidding his farewells to Sestus and Ginger. A crowd of well-wishers lined the main thoroughfare to wave and shout farewells. As he drew abreast, he gave me a smart salute, his blue eyes sparkling behind his helm's visor. I could not know then, when next we met, the circumstances would not be as favourable.

Since my sword practice with Repachea was at a standstill, I was able to bask in the luxury of some free time. So taking advantage of the recent spring-like weather, I decided to explore the ghost that was Idyll, to acquaint myself with a part of my history, a part of my family I never knew. Though there was little but bones left of the original keep, I was undeterred. A single stone watchtower remained, but proved uninteresting as the entire bottom floor now housed livestock. I avoided altogether the empty ruin that had been the kitchen, unwilling to disturb the site where so many had died, Uncle's beloved Pepet and Ivor among them.

As I navigated the rubble that was the main keep, I tried to get a sense of Uncle in this place, tried to conjure his image here, and failed. Of course it was a task made more difficult by the fact that nothing of his remained. Not a stick of furniture, not a single tapestry or piece of crockery. Looters had ransacked the wreckage, followed by scavengers, long before the Crusaders had staked a claim to it.

Idyll was a relic from the past, a monument to the dead, which Uncle would accuse the Crusaders of desecrating, if he knew. Subscribing to the 'out of sight, out of mind' theory, he had left it untouched, forgotten. Nevertheless, I found it amusing to tell myself that perhaps it could be restored. Upon my coronation as queen, I could bequeath it to my most loyal champion. Sestus, perhaps. Not Val. Instinct told me he would not care to have it.

Chill splats of rain forced me to take shelter, encouraging me to seek out subterranean entertainment. I poked around some in the armoury, where I really wasn't supposed to be without reason, astonished by the stash of weapons the Crusaders had accumulated. Lances, swords, axes, bows, and daggers of all description and degree of repair nestled snug in their racks and crates, protected from the dampness by oilskin rags and leather sheathes. A shame that so many Crusaders had no idea how to use them.

From there I tiptoed past the dungeon, where Sestus snored over a stack of duty rosters, and headed down a passageway that in Castle Gryphon would have taken me to the wine cellar but here led to the crypt. Not exactly a desirable destination on any tour. Dark. Dusty. Dreary. Here, with the weight of Idyll's skeleton bearing down on me, I realized it was no accident that had brought me there. Before me rested a sarcophagus, one smaller than the rest, that of a child's. Carved onto the face of the stone lid was the effigy of a boy, his eyes closed in a semblance of peace, a bouquet of flowers clasped in his hands.

Even before I saw the name etched in the stone lid, I had no doubt that the tomb belonged to my cousin, Ivor. Reaching out a tentative hand, I placed it on the cold, unyielding slab…and all at once became aware that I was not alone in that place. A living, breathing, flesh and blood entity shared that musty space with me.

I looked up, off toward the deeper shadows. Movement stirred the cobwebs there as Ginger stepped into the torchlight. Despite my conviction that I had every right to be here, more so than even him, I froze. My initial thought was that he spied upon me, but then realized it was I who had intruded upon him.

"What are you doing here?" he demanded in a low, unhurried voice.

I couldn't tell him the real reason, of course, so I replied with a half-truth. "Just exploring." Then, emboldened by his silence, I asked, "What are you doing here?"

"Paying my respects to the dead." His tone of censorship was unmistakable.

Then I understood. Ivor had been his childhood friend. Perhaps he did have a stronger claim than I. The situation was rapidly growing awkward. Searching for conversation, I observed, "The sarcophagus is new." It had to be. Uncle had not lingered in Idyll long enough to see his family properly honoured before fleeing to his sister in Gryphon.

He touched the first letter of the name carved in eight inch characters at the foot of the sarcophagus, allowing the distraction. "A stone-carver owed me a favour. Ivor was my friend. I figured it was the least I could do for him."

"It's lovely." It really was. The workmanship was exquisite, the detail and precision far beyond any I had seen elsewhere. It must have been one hell of a favour, or a ton of guilt on Ginger's part. After all, he had survived the maelstrom of magic when Ivor hadn't. In fact, I bet he spent a good deal of time wandering lost around Idyll, in a manner not all that dissimilar from mine. And why shouldn't he? It had been his home at one time.

It's at times like these that I like to say something profoundly stupid. "Why did the Crusaders choose this place? Idyll, I mean. Just to rub salt in the Regent's wound?"

His expression went as hard as the granite beneath my hand. Only the light thrown by the pair of torches softened it, made it human. At the moment I was glad for the barrier of stone between us. But his voice, when he spoke, was devoid of all emotion, even annoyance. "It just made sense. We knew Bertrand would avoid it like the plague, and so far he has. It's the last place in the world he'd suspect."

I couldn't agree more. The revelation that Idyll was the Citizens Risen Up to Stand Against a Dread and Errant Regency's centre of operations had blindsided even me, the top Royalist officer. Then again, my rank probably didn't mean a thing in regard to such matters.

He started to come around the corner of the sarcophagus, then paused to lean one hip against the stone. Head tipped to one side, he studied me with those shrewd, feline-like eyes. All-assessing. All-knowing. And what he said next made my heart stop.

"Have we met before? I have the impression whenever I look at you that we have."

I assumed he was experiencing a feeling of déjà vu from Laurelac, and that was unnerving enough until I recalled where we were, and who lay between us, tucked to sleep in his crypt. With a near debilitating horror, it began to sink in that I just might resemble my cousin in some way. My gestures. My features. My voice. Sestus had even remarked that my shorn locks lent me a somewhat boyish appearance.

I tried to steal a glance at the figure carved on the lid, but the mage's shadow blocked it. Frantic, I fumbled for words, for an excuse to get out of there. "Oh, um, no. Don't think so. Ever been to Glanshayda? I have family there." Stiff with fright that at any moment he would lunge around the slab of stone and grab me, I began to edge my way toward the door.

Long, elegant fingers scratched at the stubble on his chin. "No, but I was at Laurelac. Were you ever—"

"No. Never. Definitely not. Where? Actually, I've never heard of it."

Now one might be tempted to think that a princess, or a general, or a princess who was once a general, might demonstrate a degree more composure than this, but the man so unhinged me, I couldn't manage a straight thought, the reasons for which went beyond the fact that he was my enemy, that he was Umaji. Reasons that I pray at night will go away.

A frown further puckered the scarred face as he tried to remember, tried to recall places and people.

"I have to go," I mumbled. "I need to water some plants."

"But…it's raining." He sounded perplexed.

"Not in my room." At least I hoped not. But given the circumstances, considering my inner turmoil, it was entirely possible.

Two weeks following my encounter with the mage in the crypt, I found myself again straddling the back of the gentle mare, only this time bound for a place called Edenwood, with both Ragsey and Ginger for travelling companions.

"Uh, Sestus, are you sure this is a good idea?" I asked the crack in Sestus's rear as he bent over my mount's front hoof, inspecting its shoe.

I had avoided the mage and his haunts around Idyll this past fortnight, afraid he'd make a connection between Ivor and me, afraid I'd fall apart and confess everything if he looked at me sideways. I was much more comfortable in his presence when he hadn't bothered talking to me at all.

"Of course it is." He straightened and smoothed a hand over the horse's sleek neck, producing a happy nicker. "There's nothing wrong with her foot. If she's limping, its because you're such a poor rider."

He passed me a packet of rations and the dagger that Jory had dug up for me. "Now, stop dawdling."

I accepted the knife, slim-handled with a puny, six inch blade, and fastened the sheathe to my belt, swallowing my disappointment. I had hoped for a sword.

"Ginger trusts me with a weapon?" I wondered aloud. "And tell me again why he wants me along?" I just couldn't wrap my head around the mage's sudden change of heart.

"I told you already," Sestus sighed, sounding much put-upon. "According to the messenger, the Royalists have Gregaris pinned down pretty tight in town and he's looking for some relief. His agents confirm that Fleurry has set up his command post in Edenwood, just outside Pixley, as you previously suggested. He thinks you'll be useful. He thinks you'll be able to identify faces."

This was not the adventure I had envisioned, which was a war party, armed to the teeth, riding forth to deal Fleurry the ass-kicking he deserved. Repachea, it seemed, nabbed all the juicier assignments. "Still, I wish you were coming, too."

"You know I've got to stay behind and mind the shop." Sestus slid me a censorious look." This isn't a full out assault, Little Red. Gregaris just needs a little breathing space. Ginger says he can handle it himself. You know, throw some chaos spells around, tamper with equipment, make a nuisance of himself."

Well, I'm sure he'd have no trouble with that last part. Needless to say, this took the wind out of my sails. Subterfuge wasn't my style, although I seemed to have developed a knack for it. Guile and stealth had always been Val's forte.

"There's a rumour going around that Valleri might show up." He spoke this as an afterthought, a detail too minuscule to be considered.

"Valleri? I thought he was on his way to Shanasea."

"His reinforcements have already left Church Grove, but he's making a detour." Sestus took the mare's bridle, clucked to her and led us from the stable to the yard. "The meeting will take place on the Festival of Ofaedea," he continued. "That gives you four days."

"That's convenient," I snorted. The Festival of Ofaedea is a spring holiday dating back hundreds of years to a pagan celebration of the Grain Goddess. In those days it was celebrated with fairs and tournaments and the ritual sacrifice of maidenheads to Ofaedea's priests. It was supposed to be one big fertility rite, beseeching the goddess to bless the soil and bring the rains in preparation for a bountiful harvest. Nowadays, it had degenerated into a celebration of the Grain Goddess's most revered crop-ale. Everyone celebrated it by getting thoroughly soused.

"For everyone involved," Sestus agreed. "The festival atmosphere will provide so much chaos and confusion no one will notice a covert delegation of Crusaders slipping into Edenwood."

"Will Idyll be celebrating Ofaedea's festival?"

He flung me a withering glare over his shoulder. Their little uprising had seriously impeded the Crusaders access to ale. "There will be plenty of inns nearby where you can stay without fear of discovery. But you'll have to get there early to claim a room. Nevertheless, you must take care to conceal yourself. There will be plenty of Royalists roaming about who may recognize you. You might want to cover that red head of yours. It's a dead giveaway."

"I'll wear my hood," I promised.

"Make sure you do. Fleurry's Royal is billeted near the market district, in a long- abandoned warehouse. The shops will close by sunset in observance of the holiday, but the streets and inns will be jammed with revellers all night, providing you excellent cover."

Sestus drew the mare alongside Ragsey's sturdy roan. Here, he released the bridle and passed me the reins. "Ginger will fill you in on the details. Good luck."

On impulse I reached down to grab Sestus's hand. "Tell Belvemar I said good-bye. Don't forget." For some inexplicable reason I felt guilty for leaving in such haste, as though I abandoned him. Over these past few months, I had grown fond of the old Crusader.

Ragsey gave me a big friendly grin. "All set for our grand adventure, Ruvie?"

"Is that what you call it?" Despite my misgivings, I returned his smile. The man's cheerfulness is contagious, kind of like the plague, or to a lesser degree a mild summer pox. Just more annoying. Only Ginger is immune.

He thundered up behind me, astride his huge stallion, and skidded to a halt, dancing the fiery beast before me. His glance raked me in a cursory inspection. I shivered in the cool dawn air and drew my cloak tighter, partly to ward off the chill, and partly to thwart those grey mage eyes.

Irked by my stall tactics, he inquired with false chipper, "Are we ready, precious?" I don't know why he called me that. Probably because he knew it irritated the hell out of me.

He spurred his horse into a gallop and charged from the yard. Ragsey laughed, and with a whoop of maniacal glee, urged his mount after the mage. My mare followed at a more sedate gait, too dignified to kick up her heels like her fellows.

Ginger took point, which suited me just fine except Ragsey drove me crazy with his incessant chitchat. We stopped only once during the day, to rest the horses and refill our water flasks from a brook. All in all, it had started out to be a boring and uneventful journey.

Long past dusk, Ginger called a halt for the night. We made camp in a stand of elm and ate a late supper of cold food since the mage advised against a fire. It would be a chilly slumber without a blaze to fend off the evening air, but not unbearable. I curled myself in my bedroll, as far away as I could get from the men, lest either of them got the idea to snuggle. It wasn't that damned cold.

Admittedly, I was wary in their presence. People I had known well had committed unspeakable acts against me, and these two men were almost total strangers.

I awoke with a start not an hour later thinking I'd heard a noise. Too many nights in siege camps had made me a light sleeper. I glanced across the ring of elm. Ginger sat up, but Ragsey snored on. The mage's voice drifted across to me, "Did you hear that?"

I nodded. The sound came again: a sort of whuffle and snort, creeping through the brush beyond the trees. Ginger heard it too, and reached for his sword. As it happened, he didn't have time to draw it.

Something as big as a small pony shot past me from out of the darkness. Snarling and snapping, it headed straight for the mage. I scrambled to my feet and shouted at Ragsey. He was up before I got out his name. Ginger rolled away from the hurtling beast and scooped up a fallen branch. As the monster wheeled for a second charge, the mage swung the bough like a cudgel and sent the creature yelping into a tree.

Ginger's voice was frantic, filled with rage. "Shouda!" he yelled, sounding close to panic. "Bertrand's dogs! Get off the ground!"

The dogs. Shouda, they are called, canines specifically bred to track down the spoor of spent magic and kill the Umagi responsible. Uncle had turned hundreds of them loose upon escalation of the revolt. Castle Gryphon crawled with the dogs; fortunately, they are trained to attack only practicing Umagi. As long as I'd taken my tonic, I was safe. Since I had not summoned any magic, the culprit must be Ginger. At the moment, they had sniffed out his spell and traced it to him. I had no doubt they would kill him if someone did not intervene.

Two more emerged, circling and growling, wary of the bone-crushing weapon the mage held. Ragsey had scampered up the closest tree. He watched the scene below with horrified eyes. I remained where I was, breathlessly still, and tried to recall the commands.

The Shouda are trained to obey voice commands. Originally a gift to Uncle from a desert chieftain, the dogs had been taught commands spoken in the language native to their former masters. Wracking my brain, I searched for foreign words. For obvious reasons, I'd never handled Shouda personally.

Ginger bellowed, "Ragsey, use your stars!"

But Ragsey was frozen, so petrified he couldn't even shake. He himself was in no danger. The Shouda would not attack him unless he first attacked them or tried to interfere with their quarry.

Without warning one of the pair leapt at Ginger. He bashed its snout and it sprawled, stunned. But the first Shouda had recovered to limp in from behind to rejoin its mate. Together the two advanced. Seeing no other alternative, Ginger flung his club at them and turned to climb the handiest tree.

The closest dog lunged and grabbed Ginger's arm in vice-like jaws, dragging him down. Without a thought, I rushed forward, yelling, "No!" Then, "Stop!" And finally, "Tarush ka!" I don't know what made me say that, but it seemed to have some effect.

The nearer Shouda stopped in its tracks and swung its craggy head to look at me. "Tarush ka!" I yelled again. The dog sat down abruptly and whimpered.

It came back to me then. Tarush ka meant 'stop' or 'desist'. I shouted the command again, over the Shouda's ferocious snarls as it tore at the flesh of Ginger's arm. Man and beast writhed on the ground, locked in mortal combat. He had no time or opportunity to loose a spell, even if he possessed one appropriate for the situation. Belatedly, I realized the animal's killer instinct had too firm a grip on the Shouda for it to respond to tarush ka.

Another command popped into my head. "Sasha ro!" It meant 'bad' or 'mistake'. "Sasha ro!"

The dog stiffened and paused in its attack, but did not release its hold on the mage. I stomped over and bellowed, "Sasha ro!" with all the authority I could muster.

Its jaws slackened just enough for Ginger to yank free his arm. But the dog remained poised above its prey. It growled menacingly, blood dripping from its enormous fangs. I gestured in a manner that I hoped appeared non-threatening to the Shouda for Ginger not to move.

"Tarush ka," I intoned firmly, but with less harshness. The Shouda retreated in confusion, no doubt wondering what it had done wrong, wondering why it was suddenly 'bad' to do that for which it had been trained since puppyhood.

I pointed towards its fellow and said, "Jammi ja," which in common tongue is akin to 'at ease'.

The dog obeyed, muttering under its breath, and settled beside its panting companion. The first Shouda shook its daze, struggled to its feet. I flung a surly jammi ja its way, just to be safe. Then I knelt at Ginger's side to see what I could do.

He tried to ask a question about the dogs, but I shushed him and proceeded to examine the wound. It wasn't as bad as I'd feared. The punctures were not deep and no bones were broken, but he'd lost some blood and the flesh was rent in a jagged fashion.

"There were lots of Shouda on the castle grounds," I said by way of explanation. "I learned a smattering of commands." That seemed to satisfy him.

I turned to see Ragsey still perched in the tree, his face pale, his whole body trembling. "Get down and help me," I ordered, annoyed by his inertia. "Get the medical bag." Surely Biddy would have packed us some herbal remedies and bandages.

"Move it!"

Ragsey snapped out of his stupor to babble, "The dogs…"

"They won't hurt you."

He shook his head in refusal.

I wanted to set his tail alight, managing to curb the notion just in time. I tore off what remained of Ginger's sleeve and tied it around his arm, then placed his other hand atop it. "Squeeze it tight. It will stop the bleeding. You know what to do." I stamped off to retrieve the medical supplies myself.

I calmed the frightened horses with soothing words while I rummaged through their packs and collected my necessities. On my way back I paused by the Shouda, all seeming content to relax and watch me. I praised them profusely.

"Kuka he. Good dog. Kuka he." It was important they felt happy and secure while I was too busy to keep an eye on them. I could not remember the phrase that would make them go away.

I dug through my gear, sorting bandages, vials, and salves. "What is the matter with him?" I snarled at one point, throwing a caustic glower Ragsey's way.

"Don't be too angry with him," Ginger said with surprising benevolence. "When he was a boy he saw his baby brother mauled to death by a pack of wild dogs. He's had a mortal terror of canines ever since. Curse him all you want, but he won't come down."

Oh.

There was no herbal potion to numb the pain, but Ginger said it was tolerable and he could use his limited healing skill to fight infection. Nevertheless, he worried whether or not I knew what it was I did.

"Relax. I've seen Biddy do this sort of thing a hundred times." I'd also assisted on battlefields, but I couldn't tell him that.

I wished aloud for a fire and some hot water. Ginger told me to do without. "A fire might attract more of them," he said, watching the dogs with a mistrustful eye. His faith in my ability to control the Shouda was not implicit.

I cleansed the wound as best I could, then laboriously stitched a couple of the more serious gashes with needle and thread. Me-who had never even sewn a button on a uniform. Ginger was exquisitely brave throughout the procedure, holding a candle for me while I toiled.

Thinking to distract him with some chitchat, I asked, "What sort of spell did you cast back there?"

He gave me a blank stare.

"I'm not stupid. The Shouda attacked you because they picked up the scent of a magical discharge and tracked it to the source-you. It wasn't a heat spell because I distinctly recall the chatter of my teeth as I crawled into my bedroll. Nor was it one of illumination. Which makes me think it was a protection spell of some kind. If so, I'd say it needs a little work."

I'd tried to sound light-hearted, but it came out as a reprimand.

"Actually, it was a protection spell. But not against Shouda. Against you."

Really? The meek and mild librarian has the big bad wizard quaking in his boots? I could have said that and got mind-slapped for my effort, but I knew better. "So, you still don't trust me?"

"I don't trust easy. Sestus does. Repachea, too. Everyone's an enemy, Ruvie, until they prove otherwise."

Not very liberal minded for someone who claimed to be a liberator. Nevertheless, I saw his point, even if his words came several months too late for me.

I said no more as I smeared his tortured skin with a greasy concoction that Biddy often used to speed the healing process, then expertly bandaged his arm.

Ginger's belligerence seemed a good sign, though I remained concerned. The mage's face had gone an unnatural colour, at least that part of it not seared shiny with scar tissue. His normal complexion is swarthy, like a deep tan over dirt. But now his pallor was ashen and he felt cold to my touch.

I covered him with every available blanket and sat with him sort of sprawled in my lap, his head on my chest. We both faced the dogs. I bade him sleep with the promise I would stay awake just in case the Shouda got ideas or if any more appeared. Either he believed me or he simply couldn't fight it. He slept.

Wide awake for all of five minutes, I then had to struggle to keep my eyes open. There is not a surer cure for insomnia than trying to stay awake. Snoring again, Ragsey slept in the crotch of the tree. Needless to say, it was a long night for me. I amused myself by attempting to recall the command to get rid of the Shouda. I tried every syllable I could think of meaning retreat or disperse, including a few desperate scadaddles and get losts. All I got in response was a couple of sublime yawns.

One of the Shouda, perhaps reasoning I attempted to communicate, came over to curl up beside me. I scratched its ears and combed my fingers through its shaggy coat, listening to the thump-thump of its tail. I presumed Ginger to be in a deep sleep, for the proximity of the dog did not disturb him. As for myself, I wasn't afraid of the Shouda. I had grown up with generations of them at my feet, and for a lonely young girl who'd had no friends, they had been my sole companions. Except Valleri.

Val. How I missed him. Memories of him filled my head with warm and pleasant thoughts. They made me drowsy. Unintentionally, I drifted into slumber, forgetting who and where I was.

A nightmare visited. I dreamt of racing through a forest atop my white charger, hunted by terrible men who, when they caught me, made me scream in pain and fury. I dreamt of rescue by a man from my childhood and exile in a sundered castle. There was another man, an archmage made insane by pain and grief, beautiful and mysterious, but tainted with a hatred so violent it turned my blood to ice. Shoving away the horror, I fought to wake up.

Dully, I stirred to feel a weight in my arms that I hoped was Valleri. Alas, it was too much to wish that it had all been a dream. I opened my eyes to see it was Ginger I held. Sorrow overwhelmed me. Clutching him fast, I rocked his poor hurt body in time with my own, and wept hot, silent tears of anguish.

CHAPTER FIFTEEN

When morning came I was on the verge of collapse. Ginger roused and immediately spotted the Shouda curled all around me with snuffling canine snores. Although he did not speak I sensed his contempt for the beasts.

"How do you feel?" I asked, rubbing my eyes.

His speech was very precise, very controlled. "I'll feel better once we get out of here." He got stiffly to his feet and threw a stick at Ragsey. The man awoke with a start and nearly toppled from the tree. "Get down. We're leaving."

"Are you able to ride?"

I was treated to the mage's surliest glare. "I've ridden days with injuries far worse than this."

I worried that his injury may jeopardize our mission. Like many Umagi, Ginger relied heavily upon hand gestures to employ his magic. Now, one of those tools was impaired if not useless. "Maybe we ought to turn back."

"Don't patronize me," he snapped. "I'm not incapacitated, merely inconvenienced. We'll continue on as planned and finish the job."

Who am I to argue?

It took some coaxing and pleading, but we finally convinced Ragsey to come down from the tree. I tossed the Shouda scraps from my rations, hoping to whet their appetites and thus encourage them to go hunt for their breakfast. The dogs had been taught to forage and fend for themselves in the wilderness, so did not need to rely on people for food. They did not seem hungry but politely ate my vittles, probably having feasted on a kill the previous night. Despite all my efforts I could not get rid of them.

Naturally, when we tried to ride forth they followed. I cursed. I shouted. I stamped my feet. My tantrum had no effect. The Shouda were determined to lope along behind us.

They would not follow long. Each pack of Shouda had its own territory, its boundaries clearly defined by the men who had trained and released them. Once we reached the edge of their domain they would not cross it.

Come the thousandth time I glanced back, I saw they had stopped on a hillside. One hound howled forlornly, as if deserted. Another barked and ran off the way they'd come. His fellows followed, yipping and cavorting like pups in play. Both Ginger's mood and Ragsey's improved drastically once the Shouda had gone.

The men ate a cold breakfast on horseback. I refrained, having had nothing better to do all night except nibble. But I was so tired I just couldn't keep my eyes open. The gentle sway of my mare and the countryside's solitude, together with the sunshine, soothed me like a lullaby. I dozed off and on, struggling to stay in the saddle.

Fearing I might tumble off, Ragsey rode near. More than once he saved me from a headlong dive by a timely snatch of my coat. He voiced a complaint to Ginger.

The mage dropped back beside me. "Want to hitch a ride?"

"I can manage."

"Maybe. But if you fall off and hit your head you could sleep forever. Climb aboard." He reached over with his good arm and dragged me behind him onto his mount.

I caught Ragsey's disapproving frown. I would not be surprised if he considered the mage a rival for my attention. Ginger I don't think noticed. Safe and settled, I leaned my head against a bony shoulder. I slept like a baby in her mother's arms.

The remainder of our journey passed without incident. We arrived in Edenwood at sunset of the next day. We took a room on the west side at an inn dubbed the Dragon's Lair. The only troops we saw belonged to Fleurry, stationed near the market square as Sestus had promised.

We enjoyed a hot meal that night in the tavern's common room. A real feast for us weary travellers, consisting of leek soup and roasted mutton. I'd tucked up the remnants of my once flowing red mane under Ragsey's battered cap and tried to pass myself off as androgynous. No one paid any attention. It did not take long for the inn to fill up with travellers come to celebrate the Festival of Ofaedea.

Since the incident with the Shouda I now commanded a great deal more respect from my companions, especially where Ginger was concerned. A new entity existed between us, one he placed great value in: trust. But it was hardly more than a delicate thread. I would have to be careful if I wanted to keep it intact and eventually strengthen it by some pretence of friendship.

On our first night in Edenwood the boys gallantly offered me the room's single bed. Ragsey bunked down on the floor beside it, and Ginger sprawled in a chair. I don't know what the innkeeper thought of our arrangement, but no one questioned us.

Ginger left early the next morning to scout Fleurry's makeshift barracks. After a breakfast of cold ham and hard boiled eggs, Ragsey and I retreated to our room to play a game he'd taught me, requiring dice and wooden chips. By the time the mage returned, I had accumulated all of Ragsey's chips and a fair chunk of his ego to boot.

Ginger informed us of his findings. "It's a big, square, one level place. Catwalks and platforms span the area above, accessed by a single flight of stairs. From up there we can look down and see everything below. It suits our purpose perfectly."

"Which is?" I ventured.

He shrugged. "Just a little nocturnal recon in and around Fleurry's headquarters."

"Aren't you forgetting the little matter of his soldiers? Fleurry's not known to set a lax camp."

"He's got them all tied up and spread pretty thin at the moment. In exchange for use of the warehouse, the captain made an agreement with the magistrate to keep order in the streets tonight. It's too much for the local guard. Trust me. We'll have no problem."

The mage went downstairs to get something to eat. Ragsey tagged along. Left to my own devices I repaired the hem of my cloak. I figured if I could stitch Ginger's flesh, I could do that. As I toiled the not so distant roar of the fair just down the road kept me company. When I was done, I inspected my handiwork with a self-satisfied grin, thinking how proud Valleri would be of me. I had even learned to cook a little.

My attention next became drawn to the hubbub beyond my window. Pushing open the shutter, I looked out upon the inn's courtyard. A pleasant place, it was neatly cobbled and landscaped with flowering shrubs and trees. There was even a quaint wrought iron bench.

The jubilant voices of fair-goers and the excited shrieks of children drifted on the air, along with the delectable smells of freshly baked pies and pastries. I imagined spitted pigs roasting over fires and brightly coloured pennants waving in the breeze, in addition to all the carnival games and buffoonery associated with the fair.

I longed to be able to go down to the square and join in the excitement. Although I'd been freed of the confines of the castle, it seemed ironic that such an opportunity still lay beyond my reach. I could not parade about town in broad daylight like a tourist. Edenwood teemed with Royalists, any one of whom might recognize the former Gryphon Highlord.

"Would you like to go down there?"

Lost in my daydream I had not heard anyone enter the room. Startled, I turned from the window to see Ginger stood behind me.

He meant the courtyard. The mage had already expressed his concern to me about strolling the streets. He feared I might blunder into a soldier who could finger me as Castle Gryphon's librarian, and thus apprehend me as a possible traitor.

"Where's Ragsey?"

"He's gone to the market to fetch supplies for the return journey. We may have to depart Edenwood in a hurry."

Ah-ha. So the mage had not been blind to Ragsey's jealousy. He wanted some time to converse privately. Whatever he had to say, I could listen to it just as well outside in the sunshine.

The courtyard sat empty since everyone, except the innkeep and us, attended the fair. Leaving room for Ginger, I settled on one end of the bench, but he remained standing. Pretending to admire the scenery, I tried not to appear as uncomfortable as I felt. What did he want to say? Why did he want me alone? Did he know something he shouldn't? Had he sensed some tendril of my Teki powers stirring?

"I want to commend you on your actions of the other night. You kept your head and took control. You displayed uncompromising valour, and that's a rare trait in most people."

I tried to appear pleased by his compliment, and accepted his praise with feigned modesty, playing my role of follower instead of supreme commander. Some things one cannot hide, especially when confronted with a crisis. My battle training and field experience had conditioned me to take charge of difficult situations. I hoped it was not obvious to Ginger I had reacted more like the Gryphon Highlord than a mild-mannered librarian.

"I owe you my life."

That admission astonished me almost beyond speech. Shaking my head, I stammered, "No…no, you owe me nothing." The mage struck me as a man unaccustomed to owing debts. I did not want him to perceive me as some sort of threat to his masculine pride.

"The Shouda would have killed me if not for your intervention, and only the Fates Themselves know what may have happened if you had not so swiftly tended to my wounds."

"I would have done the same for Sestus or Ragsey or anyone else. Was it any more than you might have done for me if our roles were reversed?"

Ginger did not bother to respond to that. Just as well. I may not have liked the answer. "Don't argue with me, Ruvie. Just be gracious and accept my thanks."

He smiled then. Not the shy half-smile I'd seen before, nor the sinister grin I'd seen more often, but something in between, suggestive of respect and camaraderie. It was also the first time he'd called me by my name instead of the derogatory moniker 'precious'.

At my nod he fell silent, satisfied. But I sensed there was more he wished to say.

"The kindness you've shown Belvemar is admirable," he continued. "I want you to know it's appreciated. He's a good man and a fine soldier. He doesn't deserve the ending he has been dealt. He responds better to you than he does to Biddy or me. I truly believe if not for you, he'd be dead."

"It's the least I can do. After all, if not for Sestus's kindness, I, too, would be dead."

"Sestus is like you. Kind. Compassionate. Those sentiments deserted me long ago when Nelia—" He broke off suddenly, as if having said more than he'd wanted.

"Nelia?" I prompted.

"A friend. She didn't deserve her ending either."

Although I did not press, I must have looked guilty for Ginger said, “Sestus told you.” Not a question, but a statement of fact.

He slid wearily onto the bench beside me. “There were so many times I should have died. But always someone intervened, sometimes at great risk to themselves, even to the point of sacrificing their own life.”

He flinched then, as if pricked by a needle of pain, and I knew he was angry. “I don’t understand,” he went on. “I never expected it of them. It makes me wonder why I am so special while others like Belvemar and Nelia, who are far worthier of life than I am, are permitted to suffer or die. What grand purpose do the Fates hold in store for me that I should be spared, sometimes by a stroke of luck?”

Guilt consumed the man. Perhaps that is why he is so angry, so close on the verge of madness. “You know what your purpose is: to destroy the oppressor and free the oppressed.”

“And then what? Once Bertrand is dead my life will be over.”

“Maybe it is your destiny to rebuild Thylana and to help establish a new era of peace. Your association with the Crusaders may be only the beginning.”

“There’s not much hope of that now the Princess Kathedra is dead. Without her temperance, Castle Gryphon will be free to mass its Royals and launch a major assault, which we will be unable to repel any time soon unless we find some way to turn the cards in our favour.”

“Your optimism is overwhelming.”

“It’s hard to be optimistic when you’ve seen as much senseless death as I have. My greatest fear is I’ll never avenge Nelia. I wanted to take Kathedra away from Bertrand, the one thing whose absence might touch the bastard and make him hurt, just as he took Nelia from me. But he robbed me even of that small pleasure.”

His venom for Kathedra should have frightened me, but her alter ego, Ruvie, could not repress a twinge of sympathy. Ginger sat so close, so steeped in despair, the temptation to comfort him was great. Resting my hand on his, I said, “You can’t let your vengeance rule you. You can’t let your hatred get in the way of your objective. If you do, it will only obstruct your judgment, and ultimately, destroy you.”

I spoke from experience. I had as much reason to hate, to avenge, as Ginger. But somehow I had not been left as demoralized as the mage. I’d risen above my fury and grief, freeing myself to concentrate on my future. But Ginger’s single-minded obsession had left him no future.

“I don’t think Nelia would want to see you in such pain.”

His fingers tightened around mine. “I really loved her. But…I never told her. I couldn’t.”

“She knew, I’m sure.”

“You have no reason to want to comfort me.” His grey eyes, suddenly warm and soft, tilted towards me. “You are much like Nelia. She had your compassion and tenderness. And like you, she was made of the strongest steel."

Then to my surprise, he leaned forward and kissed me. It was a sweet, chaste kiss, gentle and innocent, like one exchanged between friends. But I sensed something deeper, spawned of long-unsated hunger, straining to break past the anger and fear that chained it.

Strange how things can change almost overnight. Only days before we couldn't bear to be in the same room together. Mutual mistrust and disdain had dissolved with a single kiss. I had known since that meeting in the crypt that Ginger is not as repugnant to me as I'd wish. And that is not necessarily a good thing.

Our fingers were still entwined, our eyes locked together, our lips separated by the space of a breath, when Ragsey entered the courtyard. His intrusion was not subtle. He did not pretend he hadn't seen anything.

Ginger withdrew and got to his feet. Although he said nothing, I felt his disappointment as keenly as I felt my own. Neither of us owed Ragsey an explanation. Nevertheless, we could not help but feel we'd been found doing something obscene. I stared hard at my hands, clasped in my lap, and tried not to blush.

"The innkeeper told me I would find you both here," Ragsey said in an accusatory tone.

"What is it?" Ginger asked, a barely audible murmur.

"I thought you should know there's a Royalist patrol out on the street."

Ginger nodded. "You're right. We should get inside, stay out of sight."

I agreed. As I rose from the bench to follow the mage back inside, Ragsey approached, a broad grin on his boyish features. "What do you say, Ruvie? Are you up for another game of Hares and Hounds?"

"Sure. We've got time, I guess. Should we ask Ginger to join us?"

"Nah. Ginger doesn't play games."

Oh, yeah? That's what you think. I fought to control a know-it-all smirk. His games just have higher stakes.

CHAPTER SIXTEEN

We left the Dragon's Lair at dark while the celebration was at its peak, and forced our way through the boisterous crowd. The streets were clogged with revellers, the public squares and inns unable to contain the flow. The town had quadrupled in size, the local peasants having flocked inside to attend the festivities.

It took some time and a lot of patience but we managed to push ourselves through the throng into the market square. Torches had been lit and the area was packed with people drinking, dancing, and singing. Ragsey got a kink in his neck trying to ogle all the pretty girls.

The warehouse stood isolated at the end of a lane leading from the square, only a few torches pushing back the gloom where sentries kept watch. Slipping from the crowd, we ducked into the deeper shadows. Ginger indicated a back entrance too conspicuous not to be locked. Ragsey muttered something.

Ginger replied, "I removed the locks earlier and replaced them with a spell that will make the door seem secure to the guards. We'll have no trouble getting inside."

We waited for the sentries to complete their circuit, then headed for the door under a charm of misdirection. Going by feel, we climbed the rickety staircase to the very top. We were so close to the rafters that we could not straighten fully, to my back's constant complaint. The view of overhead walkways and platforms made my head swim. In days gone by, when the building had stored precious merchandise, guards could oversee the entire shipment from this superb vantage.

I tugged on Ginger's sleeve. "Aren't you worried Fleurry might post guards on the catwalks?"

"He won't. The warehouse is awaiting demolition. Only a fool would stand up here." He grinned impishly, then gestured to Ragsey to remain on the landing. "You're the lookout."

The mage led me along the walkway to a wooden platform. I clung to the rail, battling a sudden bout of vertigo. Ginger peeled away my hand and forced me to lie down on the dusty planks, where I could peer over the edge. Only a few inches of worm-eaten wood and a couple of cross beams lay between me a three-story drop onto about two dozen Royalists below.

Then I saw the rats. Several sat on the rafters above, seemingly content to watch us with beady black eyes. Another hunched in shadow just three feet from my elbow. I tried to shoo it away but it wouldn't budge. With effort, I ignored it.

Ginger sat in the platform's centre, arranging concealment spells around us, and probably others he hadn't told me about. I surveyed the scene on the ground, tallying Royalists and scanning for faces I knew. Fleurry was present, of course, sitting at a desk thrown together with planking and empty crates. I wondered if he was aware of that little bald spot.

He and his second had their heads bent over an unfurled map, plotting, I presumed, their attack on Gregaris. While they conspired, several more men entered the building, stopping to identify themselves to the guards. Ginger peppered me with questions.

"Who's that, the one in the Gryphon livery?"

"Um, not sure. Scout, maybe."

"And the short guy beside him? With the lady's sword?"

Lady's sword. Ginger-slang for rapier. "Looks like a liaison from the castle."

Another soldier slipped inside, strode unimpeded past the checkpoint and straight to Fleurry, passing him a leather satchel.

"What's that? What's in that packet? More maps? Codenames?"

I squinted for a better view, the oily black torch smoke that spiralled upwards stinging my nose. "Ahh. Oh, my."

"What?" the mage hissed. "What?"

"It looks like…his supper. Yes, some thoughtful underling has fetched the captain fare from the local tavern. A wrap of hard cheese. A loaf of black bread. A jar of stew, and its still hot—"

Ginger's glower stopped me in mid-sentence. I guess whatever earth-shattering revelation he hoped to uncover here had little to do with Royalist metabolic timetables. Hey, you're the one asking the questions.

Fleurry opened the jar and the pungent aroma of mutton stew wafted up to us, mingling with the smoke that hung thick and lazy in the air. The visitors stopped by the checkpoint apparently gained entrance, for they materialized at the captain's elbow as he slurped his supper. They did most of the talking, discussing supply issues and Arial's impending arrival with reinforcements, which should appear within the month. Fleurry swallowed hard over a chunk of meat in reaction to that last, and let out a much put-upon sigh as he picked a piece of fat off his spoon.

"Can't he speed it up?"

"He's trying, sir, but the Gryphon Highlord has expressed a difference of opinion on the matter and so—"

"I don't give a shit what that toad Valleri said. Who's in charge? Him or Bertrand?"

"Uhm, maybe you can ask the general that when gets here. There's a rumour circulating that Chiverly and Urharde take orders only from him."

Fleurry sputtered and cursed, spewing broth all over the sleeve of the liaison, who ogled it with distaste. "Bloody hell! I knew it. I goddamned knew it!" He pounded his fist on the desk for unnecessary emphasis, shattering a support crate into splitters. Although the desk titled dangerously

Fleurry didn't seem to notice. "That venomous worm. The usurpation has already begun. I warned Bertrand about the sneaky bastard but he ignored me. The ingrate. Nobody listens to me."

A refrain similar to my own.

There was a minor commotion at the door as someone tried to barrel his way past the checkpoint. Harsh words were exchanged and the guards stepped aside. As Fleurry shot to his feet I thought excitedly Val's here!

But no. That fop Urharde sauntered in, two underlings in tow, his helm tucked under an elbow, all for show. I can't recall an instance when Urharde actually entered an arena of battle. Fleurry grumbled and sat back down, his deflation as acute as my own.

Urharde chuckled at the captain's obvious malcontent. "Tut, tut, Fleurry, old friend. Such dramatics! You've been out of the castle too long. There's been developments since you took to the field."

Fleurry is as tough as they come, a grizzled, hardened old warrior of fifty or more. His experience and plethora of battle-scars allow him the privilege of complaint and dispute when it comes to dealings with the Regent. No doubt he considered Valleri's newfound influence with Uncle unwarranted and unwelcome. He levelled a glare on Urharde that would have made anyone with an iota of sense cringe.

Urharde broke into a grin. "As for Arial…"

One of those people who revel in their role of bearer of bad news, he let the words hang in the air, dangling them like a bone before Fleurry as if the captain were a starving dog. Fleurry's eyes narrowed, perhaps on the assumption he wasn't going to like what he was about to hear, and with a wave of his hand, dismissed the men crowding his desk. Everyone but Urharde and the liaison went.

Ginger nudged me with an elbow, whispered low, "What do you know about Arial?"

Ahh, Arial. A pure delight. Not young, not old, in his mid-thirties. He had a skid-load of experience and know-how behind him. Sensible. Thrifty. Reserved. The sort who thinks before he acts. A no-nonsense, by-the-book commander. Neither a coward nor a blowhard. All his risks are calculated, all his losses minimal. He treats his men decently, and he's well liked by his peers. We got along just fine. Better, even. He'd won his command from Uncle on merit, not by wealth or favour like so many others.

I relayed most of this to Ginger in hushed tones, but he didn't seem impressed. I attributed his ignorance and indifference to the fact he'd never had a run-in on the field with the Royalist captain.

Finally, Fleurry snapped, "Arial what?"

"Arial's been relieved of duty. Bertrand gave him his walking papers."

"Bertrand did?" Fleurry's bafflement was genuine, bafflement I shared. Even the castle liaison didn't seem alert to the situation. "I find that hard to believe. Surely the Regent is aware of Arial's worth to him in terms of loyalty and effectiveness."

Urharde shrugged. "Well, it seems Arial wasn't seeing eye-to-eye on a few things with the new Gryphon Highlord, so he got the boot. I didn't get much in the way of details."

I mulled that over. Valleri was a risk-taker, sometimes a hothead. And yet he was decisive and ruthless at times when I couldn't be. It was not out of the realm of possibility to conclude that Val and Arial had butted heads.

"Just like Kathedra," Fleurry muttered. "Everyone's expendable, it seems."

"Yes, something you should keep in mind."

"Is that threat?"

"A friendly warning, is all. Bertrand is useless. Valleri is, for all practical purposes, the Regent of Thylana. Bertrand dares not oppose him."

"Valleri murdered the princess, didn't he?" Fleurry shot the captain a rueful smile. "The damned Crusaders had nothing to do with it."

Urharde shrugged, as if my death were of little consequence. "Valleri has ambitions of own. Kathedra moved too slowly for him. She was a restraining hand on his shoulder. He could not act with her around. Valleri is free now to take charge. When he gets finished, there won't be a Crusader left alive. And you can bet it won't take him another year to do it. Whatever his humble pedigree, at least he knows how to get things done."

Fleurry shoved aside his meal, half-finished. Poor man. All he'd wanted was five minutes to eat his supper in peace.

"Where is Arial now?" the liaison asked.

"Nothing's official, but I presume he's a guest in Gryphon's dungeons. He wouldn't have gone quietly."

"Did your source happen to mention his replacement?"

My blood ran cold as I recalled Arial's second-in-command. I reached out, consumed with a near-debilitating dread, and grabbed Ginger's arm.

"His lieutenant. Someone called Serastaben. Sarastuffit. Sara—"

"Serasteffan," Fleurry finished for him. "That low-life? The man's an idiot! What the hell is Valleri thinking?"

I echoed the sentiment. A cold-blooded killer like the Butcher had been given a command? Beside me, Ginger tried to prize away my fingers. "I take it you've met this Serasteffan?" Dark mirth edged his tone.

I nodded. "And pray that you never do." My hand clenched his tighter. "Promise me one thing. Promise me you'll keep your Crusaders out of his way."

He stared at me a moment, all amusement flown, my terror having transmitted itself to him. "I'll pass that along."

"So, you're my reinforcements?" Fleurry was saying, sounding less than enthused.

Urharde's grin only widened. "Sorry, no. You're on your own here. I'm just passing on the message." He signalled to an underling to take his helm, then pulled on his gloves. "Can you perhaps recommend a decent place to eat near here? One that serves something besides goat?"

"What?" the captain sneered. "You're not staying to hear what Valleri has to say?"

"Oh, I do beg pardon. I forgot to mention; Valleri's not coming. He has business elsewhere."

For one heart-stopping minute I thought Fleurry was going to fly across the desk at him. Then, displaying admirable restraint, the captain said, "The Boar's Head down the block serves an edible pigeon pie. Don't let me keep you."

I jabbed my elbow into the mage's ribs. "We've been duped. We have to get out of here. Now." I struggled to get up but Ginger caught my sleeve.

"No. We have something to do first."

I snatched away my arm. "What's that?"

"I'm going to bury this place in rubble."

Somehow, I had expected it. This was no reconnaissance mission. He'd planned this from the start. Except now he would be deprived of his prime target.

Livid, I stared at Ginger. He stared back, his eyes impassive, his face set in grim determination. "You'll kill us all," I hissed.

"We'll have several minutes to reach cover, I promise. Just do as I say. Get ready to move."

I glanced at the rat that was no rat at all, but some sort of sorcerous mine awaiting Ginger's detonation spell. Several more, similarly disguised, lurked in the rafters. How many more, concealed as scraps of junk, littered the warehouse below?

Urharde had gone and Fleurry was grumbling to the liaison. "...bastard's allegiance blows with the wind." It was a shame Urharde would enjoy a reprieve, but it only made good strategic sense for the Crusaders to rid themselves of an adversary as dangerous as Fleurry.

Ginger returned to the platform's centre, knelt and traced a pattern in the dust of the planks. His lips moved, muttering mystical words of sorcery though I caught only one in ten.

Naturally, something went awry. The spells backfired in Ginger's face, the saboteur himself sabotaged.

A thunderous concussion rocked the building. Sparks flew. Ginger reeled away from the explosion, engulfed in smoke, sputtering and choking. A second convulsion shook the platform, the force so great I lost my balance and fell to the boards. As I lay there, I noticed the dust was no ordinary dust but a fine scattering of powder. Beside me, the rat had been reduced to a pile of ash.

"Hang on!" Ginger yelled, urgency in his cry. Past the haze of smoke, I caught a glimpse of the mage clinging to the rail and gasping for breath. "Hurry, Ruvie," he beckoned, holding out a hand.

Cautiously I inched toward him, feeling the platform lurch and sway with the shift of my weight. I was four yards away from the mage when the thing groaned ominously and pitched to a sharp slant. There was nothing to hold on to. It happened so fast I didn't even have time to scream. I slid along the planks feet first, plummeting toward Ginger and certain death below.

A wrench in my right shoulder tore a grunt out of me as Ginger snatched my arm. I dangled in mid-air, suspended high above the stunned Royalists, the world below me spinning crazily.

"Grab the rail!"

I looked up into the mage's face, tracked with sweat and taut from exertion, and noticed that he held me with his injured hand. "Oh, drat," I groaned. "Please, don't drop me."

"I won't. Just grab the rail."

Wriggling about like a fish on a hook, I managed to wrap my fingers around the gnarled wood. Then, hoisting me enough so I could swing my legs onto the catwalk, Ginger helped me to my feet and supported me with a steady arm.

"Where's Ragsey?" I gasped.

Ginger glanced down at the Royalists as they began to pick themselves up off the floor and pulled me towards the stairs. "He should be to the door by now. C'mon, let's go."

The Royalists had recovered their wits. "Stop them!" Fleurry bellowed to his men, as he crawled out from under the remnants of his desk. "Kill that blasted mage!"

We skidded down the steep flight in darkness, bouncing over the last few steps on our bottoms. Hoping to beat the soldiers, we burst through the door and out into the night. Escape lay only a sprint away, except I sprinted left and Ginger sprinted right.

"Ruvie! This way!"

Too late. Urharde's escort rounded the far corner. A bunch of Fleurry's soldiers flew out the door and, spotting Ginger, streaked after him. In flight for his life, the mage ran for the sanctuary of the crowded market square, a dozen guards giving chase.

Panic seized me. I froze inside the feeblest of shadows below the wall. If Urharde caught me, he would surely kill me. His words echoed dully in my brain. *Kathedra moved too slowly. She was a restraining hand on his shoulder*.

As the soldiers pounded towards me, I held my breath, hoping they wouldn't see me, pouring all my Teki energy into that one thought. They bore down, weapons drawn. I shrank against the wall and gathered shadows around me.

And to my astonishment…they ran straight past. Not a soldier glanced my way. They charged after their fellows in pursuit of the mage.

Relieved, I took a deep breath and edged warily toward the corner. Fleurry stood outside, ranting in high dudgeon, but the distance muffled his words. I watched while he and his cohorts mounted and rode off in the direction of their barracks.

Only when I was certain everyone had gone did I make my way back to the square and blend into the mob. Once, I spotted a group of Fleurry's soldiers as they bickered among themselves, frustrated at having lost Ginger's trail. Finally, they split up and were swept away by the flow of the crowd.

Since I lacked Ginger's skill for covering my tracks, I took a roundabout route back to the Dragon's Lair. Swallowed up in the press of bodies, I allowed the lazy, meandering stream of traffic to carry me to safety.

Miraculously avoiding Royalist patrols, the crowd deposited me on the tavern's doorstep. I pushed my way inside and through the rowdy throng. Over the heads of the mob I strained for a glimpse of my companions and spotted Ginger almost immediately, slumped at a corner table. Ragsey sat across from him, leaning forward, I presumed, so no one might overhear them. As if anyone would hear a lion roar above the din. From the set of Ginger's face, they argued.

My knees felt suddenly weak and my legs turned to jelly as the absurd notion struck me that if I did not reach Ginger I would collapse and be trampled beneath several dozen drunken feet. I shoved and flailed at the bodies surrounding me, ordering them to move. I lost my hood in the press and tore the hem of my cloak as some clumsy oaf trod on it.

At last the sea of flesh parted and Ginger caught sight of me threading a path towards him. He blanched, his eyes widening. Clearly he had not expected to see me again. Then…he smiled.

I hurried forward. Without thinking, I elbowed a man in his face as he groped after me, then stomped a woman's toes, heedless of the curses she flung at my back. All that mattered was reaching Ginger.

I was only a few short steps from him when Ragsey stood up and blocked me. Incredulous, he said, "Ruvie, we thought we'd lost you!"

His arms came around me, whisking me off my feet in a bone-crushing bear hug. My whole body trembled with relief as I realized just how narrowly I'd escaped. At that moment it did not matter that he wasn't Ginger. Giddy, I wrapped my arms around Ragsey's neck and kissed his cheek. But over his shoulder I saw the mage had risen. His smile was gone, his face slack and sombre. What shadow was that crossing his features? Disapproval? Disappointment?

When Ragsey released me, Ginger did not welcome me into his arms. He greeted me stiffly and gestured me into a chair. Without asking, I grabbed his ale tankard and drained its contents.

"How did you escape the soldiers?" he asked.

"I took cover beneath the wall," I said, wiping ale from my chin. "The shadows were too dense for them to see."

Ginger stared at me, his gaze level and penetrating, as if seeing me for the first time. His eyes contained a glimmer of disbelief. I dropped my own, afraid he suspected some inkling of the truth. The only reason I'd eluded capture was because my Teki powers had erected a shield of invisibility.

Ginger leaned back in his chair, thoughtful. "Well, I suppose it's possible a fraction of the concealment spells held."

I nodded. "Yes, that must be it." Then fixing the mage in my sternest glare, I asked, "What happened back there?"

"I don't know exactly. All I can think is that when I detonated the spell a foreign entity present in the warehouse caused it to collapse on itself."

"Magebane," I concluded. The word is a general term applied to any number of substances that deflects or repels sorcery. Anything from a powerful amulet to simple diamond dust like that which powdered the platform. "Why didn't you detect it?"

"I wasn't looking for it." Ginger seemed embarrassed. "Fleurry's not as incompetent as I'd hoped. He took precautions. I won't underestimate him again."

I rubbed my eyes. "We have to leave Edenwood. Now."

"Why?" Ragsey protested. "No one saw us. No one can identify us. We're in no danger here."

I sped him a dark look. Could it be he didn't want to leave because he'd taken a fancy to our pretty bar wench?

"That's not the point," Ginger hissed at him. "Valleri wasn't at the meeting. Sounds like maybe he had no intention of coming here at all. He may already be in Shanasea, perhaps engaging Naren even as we speak."

Ginger was worried, and with good reason. But I didn't think he understood the full import of what Valleri's absence implied.

"We have to return to Idyll and report our failure. We must figure out what to do next."

"Not only that," I interrupted. "But at any minute a Royalist could walk in here with a Shouda and it would be all over for us."

Ginger's head jerked up, a flicker of surprise in his grey eyes. He had not considered that possibility. I arched a brow, silently chiding him for his oversight, and pushed away the empty mug.

We slipped out of Edenwood at dawn while the town slept off its collective hangover. We rode in silence, each of us angry for one reason or another. I considered the escapade a complete disaster, my relief giving way to disgust. Ginger was a madman and a fool. It galled me to think he would risk our lives to serve his own ego.

At noon Ginger sent Ragsey to scout ahead. The mage guided his mount close beside mine. "I can't say how relieved I was to see you again." His tone was gentle and shy, like a little boy's. "I was afraid the Royalists had caught you."

"Afraid why?" I snapped. "Because you feared for my life? Hah. You feared I'd give away all your precious Crusader secrets."

"That's not true. If keeping secrets were my only priority I would have let you fall to your death when that platform gave way. I was afraid they'd captured you, to torture and kill or who knows what else? I shouldn't have left you behind."

He'd had no choice, of course. The two of us would have been unable to fend off all those soldiers. We'd both be dead. Nevertheless, I could not shake the irrational feeling he had deserted me. Nor the conviction Ragsey had deserted us both.

"Is that why you were so glad to see me? So you wouldn't have to live with your guilt?"

"Why do you have to twist everything I say? Why are you so angry?"

I jerked on the reins, halting my horse. "You abandoned me," I spat. "You were relieved, yes, by my return. But I saw no tears spilling into your beer. Don't pretend to care what the Royalists may or may not have done to me."

He stared at his hands where they clenched the reins. "I did not abandon you. Not intentionally. I wanted to go back for you. Ragsey argued. He said it was too dangerous." He raised his gaze to mine. "I would not have left Edenwood without you."

As much as those words startled me and set my silly heart aflutter, they did not assuage my anger. "It doesn't matter. We never should have embarked on this mission. It was doomed from the very start. You risked our lives needlessly. For what? A chance at the Gryphon Highlord? A chance to be a hero? You can't continue to think everyone is as stupid as you. Did you ever once stop to consider the possibility that the whole thing was a trick to draw you out into the open?"

Ginger was speechless. He pinioned me with a look that said he wanted to strangle me. Unafraid, I continued, "No. I can see not. I don't know why I waste my breath talking to you."

I prodded my mare but Ginger snagged my arm. He dragged me from the saddle and leapt from his own. "How dare you admonish me? If I wanted your opinion I'd ask for it. Just who do you think you are anyway?"

I wanted to shout, 'I am the Gryphon Highlord! I am the Princess Kathedra, heir to the throne!' But I restrained myself. Barely. The arrogance of the dog! I was outraged he'd dare manhandle me in such a fashion when he should be on his knees in my presence. It took all my self-control to keep from mindspelling him into the nearest ditch.

Setting my teeth, I ground out, "I am someone who is trying to help, if you would only swallow your pride and let me. If you wish to aid your comrades and their cause you must put aside your own ambitions until a more auspicious time. You must learn patience. It was pure folly to undertake this mission thinking yourself so much cleverer than the Royalists, thinking yourself so invincible. What have you accomplished? Furthermore, what will the Gryphon Highlord accomplish thanks to your blunder?"

His gaze grew stormy, his fingers tightening around my arm. "I will concede I gambled wrongly. But had my plan succeeded, it would have meant a major victory for us. I took a chance, and I admit I made a mistake. But I don't need you to point it out for me. You must learn to mind your place."

My thoughts whirled, colliding with each other inside my head, screaming to be vented. I forced them still with the consolation the mage would one day kneel before me and beg my forgiveness.

A nice fantasy. Ginger would sooner have me torture him a hundred different ways than bow down and call me queen.

Glaring at his fist where it gripped my arm, I demanded, "Unhand me." Later, when I'd been crowned queen, I'd have it cut from his wrist.

"Apologize first."

"I will not." I yanked myself free. "It is you who owes me the apology."

"I owe you nothing."

"You owe me your life," I reminded him.

"I repaid that debt by saving yours!"

"Whose fault is it that it needed saving?"

Ragsey appeared then, interrupting our shouting match as he rode back toward us at full gallop. He hauled his mount up short before us, a wild look in his eye. "I hate to break this up, but there's a Royalist patrol heading our way. About six of them, I think. They must have followed our tracks."

"Shouda?" I asked, scanning the area for suitable cover, but the closest was a clump of trees a mile away.

"No, thank heaven." Ragsey looked scared, more so than during the Shouda attack, though his hand on the reins was steady and firm.

"We're going to have to fight," Ginger muttered.

"With what? I don't have a sword."

He hesitated, still struggling with the part of himself that didn't trust Ruvie the librarian. He exchanged a glance with Ragsey, who came to my defence. "She can fight, Ginger. I've seen her take Repachea down."

The ground began to tremble with the drum of Royalist hooves. I held the mage's tepid gaze. "Or do you think they'll spare me because I'm a girl?"

That brought him around. He gave me his spare blade then tossed me the reins to his horse. Ragsey and I watched, a little anxiously, as the mage plucked a bottle from his magicks pouch and proceeded to pour liquid the colour of onyx onto the ground before us. When he was done, an iridescent line about a dozen yards long separated us from the charging Royalists.

Next he snatched the reins from my hand to lead his horse towards the streak of glistening fluid. Five feet away the stallion balked violently, almost dragging the mage off his feet. The beast wheeled and ran back to its fellows, clipping grass at a prudent distance. Ginger gave us our instructions. "Stay back, behind the line. The potion is a bane to horses and other dray animals. Smells like blood and fire to them. They'll come up against it as if they hit a wall and refuse to cross it."

"Won't they go around?" I asked.

"They won't know its there until it's too late, and by then we've already done some damage. Ragsey, get ready with your stars."

The Royalists were almost upon us. Their uniforms blazed the colours of the Tenth. Oh, was I looking forward to this, a chance to strike back at Uncle. I tested the weight and balance of the sword, which was a tad heavy but I could compensate. I itched to take on a Royalist blade, eager to test my mettle after so long a lapse. I pulled my hat lower and donned my hood, betting the Royalists would not recognize me with my shorn hair.

We braced ourselves, stood our ground. Excitement churned my blood, alongside a nervous anticipation. I practised the mental exercises Sestus taught me, for if I allowed the tiniest mindspell, Ginger would know it. His feelings for Royalists left me no delusions. My free hand crept to the pouch at my belt, extracted the crystal on its chain to rub it between thumb and forefinger in hopes of encouraging serene and pleasant thoughts. Baby deer gambolling in a field of daisies. Puffy white clouds in the shapes of hearts and kittens. Thumping the mage's thick head against a brick wall, if we survived that is.

The horses came up against Ginger's barrier of fear at full speed. Less than a nose from the line, just as I was about to dive for cover, they stopped. Rearing, lunging, screaming, they tried to twist away and instead collided with their neighbour. Two of them dumped their riders immediately, and Ragsey took out another horseman with a clean throw to the man's throat.

Despite his wounded arm, Ginger waded in among the chaos of flailing hooves and tumbling men to cut a Royalist from his saddle as he fought for control of his terrified horse. Ragsey went after one of the soldiers on the ground and I took the second, booting him in the chin as he tried to gain his feet. Knocked onto his back, he managed to raise his blade against me. My blow struck him hard, breaking his grip and sending his sword aloft. After a quick glance to check that both Ragsey and Ginger were distracted, I ran my blade through the soldier's arm, producing the desired scream, then cracked him senseless with my hilt. I didn't have it in my heart yet to kill a Royalist who, in reality, had been one of my own.

I looked around the field of battle. Ragsey had winged another rider with a star, though had succeeded only in pissing the man off. The Royalist jumped from his horse and took after him with his sword. Ginger had his hands full with a soldier wielding an axe nearly the mage's height. Not exactly a standard-issued weapon, but I guess regulations had gone to hell in my absence.

The sixth Royalist had managed to get his horse under control. He backed it up, away from the turmoil, and fumbled to load a crossbow. I ran at him, my blade reaching for his torso, but he lifted a foot from his stirrup and planted it in my shoulder. My sword flew; I hit the ground with such force constellations exploded in my head, and looked up to see the rider's bolt trained roughly on my chest area. I was aware then that my hood had fallen back, exposing my hair and face, and the man's eyes that a moment ago had been narrowed with concentration went wide with shock and recognition.

His mouth opened, a name shaping his lips, a shout, I'm sure, gathering in his throat, when Ragsey stepped between us, knocking aside the crossbow. The bolt discharged, but skewed harmlessly into the sod three paces away. I scrambled to my feet, hunting for my lost sword, but a gurgling scream told me Ragsey had already dispatched the fellow. And just in the nick of time, too. Another second and my true identity might have been revealed.

"Thanks, I owe you," I said to Ragsey, who merely grinned and went off to help Ginger with the axeman. He fell upon the Royalist from behind, blade slicing deep into his back even as the mage's sword sliced his head from his shoulders.

Afraid that more Royalists might be on their way, we did not tarry to loot the dead. Neither Ginger nor Ragsey looked that close at the soldier I'd knocked cold. As we collected our horses, Ragsey remarked to the mage, half in jest, "A teleportal would come in handy right about now."

I couldn't agree more.

CHAPTER SEVENTEEN

Sestus greeted us upon our return to Idyll, his cheerful smile soon vanishing once he saw our grim faces. Ginger and I had exchanged less than ten words over the course of our journey home, which suited me just fine. The encounter with the Royalists had only added fodder to my disgust with the mage. I dismounted and strode straight past Sestus, not bothering to conceal my displeasure.

"Ruvie? What's wrong?" he called after me.

Never breaking stride I flung over my shoulder, "I'll talk to you later." Let Ginger speak his piece first. Then I'd have my say.

Eager to see Belvemar I went to the infirmary. He'd been in my thoughts constantly during the ride home. Did I say home? Yes, Idyll is my home now.

Biddy met me in the doorway. "How did it go?" she asked in her gruffest tone.

"It was a disaster."

"Hmmph," she snorted. "I could have told you that and saved you the trip."

"How's the captain?"

She shook her head, a cloud darkening her features. "The same, though depressed. He talks about dying when he talks at all. He's giving up."

"Not if I can help it."

Brushing past her into the infirmary, I knelt beside Belvemar's cot. The old Crusader stirred when I called his name and his eyes fluttered open. I smiled. "I'm back."

"Oh, Ruvie," he moaned. "I'm so glad to see you. Are you all right? Where's Ginger? Was your mission a success?"

I clutched his frail hand in mine. "It did not go as Ginger hoped," I replied with a certain amount of satisfaction. "We are no further ahead than when we left. Ginger will give you the details. I just want to know how you're doing."

"Better now that you're here, safe and sound," he sighed. "I missed you all these long days with nothing to do but worry. I feel so useless lying here. I'm a burden to everyone."

"Hush. You're going to get well again and help us kick some Royalist butt. Until then I want you to stop talking rubbish." I gave him a dastardly grin and a big hug. He brightened considerably.

"So tell me," I said, pulling off my riding gloves. "Has Sestus heard from Naren?"

"A dispatch from Shanasea arrived this morning. Naren says everything is quiet up there. Too quiet. But he's ready for a Royalist siege. He can hold out indefinitely."

I nodded, thoughtful. “Repachea?”

“There hasn’t been word from him in a while. He’s not much on writing reports. Why do you ask?”

“No reason.” In truth, a growing misdoubt had set up residence in the pit of my stomach.

Belvemar smiled, his eyes gently teasing. “You are concerned for the handsome young captain, yes? Well, don’t worry about Repachea. He’s as safe as a fledgling in the nest. He also commands the finest gang of mercs in Thylana.”

I was concerned, but not solely for the handsome young outlaw leader. Valleri was going to strike somewhere and I didn’t think it would be Shanasea.

Belvemar suddenly let out a groan. His smile faded, his eyes quivered shut. Biddy appeared and pressed a vial to his lips, making him drink. She pulled me away to whisper, “It’s for the pain. So he can rest.”

“How’s his wound? Is it healing?”

“Yes, but slowly. It takes all his strength. He’s very weak and tires easily.”

“I understand. I’ll visit again tomorrow.”

I returned to my quarters, where I unpacked my things, including the dagger, which I tucked away in a secret place for future access. Then I bathed and changed into fresh clothes. By the time I finished supper it was full dark. Exhausted, I sat before the hearth and sought insight in its dancing flames while I awaited the inevitable knock at the door.

Finally it came. I steeled myself for the confrontation with Sestus.

He pushed his way inside. “I know what you’re thinking, and I understand your anger, but you’re wrong. I had no idea Ginger would pull something like that. I had no part in it. I told him it was a stu—”

“Stop it,” I interrupted, my tone cool and authoritative. “You haven’t the slightest idea what I’m thinking. Otherwise, you’d be speechless with horror. Sit down.”

He tossed me a questioning glare, but sat.

“I don’t care whether or not you knew about Ginger’s sabotage plan. It doesn’t matter. The fact is we shouldn’t have gone to Edenwood. Do you really think Valleri is so inept a leader? Do you really think he would leave himself vulnerable to leaks and spies in the first place?”

Sestus stared at me, struck dumb by my tirade. My alter ego, the Gryphon Highlord, had resurfaced and she had rebuked him as she would any other Royalist officer who’d made a serious tactical blunder. Perhaps I overstepped myself, but I refused to back down. His recklessness had nearly cost me my life.

Recovering his tongue, Sestus said contritely, “Look, Little Red. I admit we made an error in judgment. We underestimated Valleri and Fleurry both. But it was an opportunity too good to waste. We had to try and seize it.”

“An opportunity too good to be true is what it was,” I snapped. “Ginger’s arrogance and your haste led us into a trap. We haven’t done

Gregaris any good either."

"Trap?"

"What else? Someone planted the rumour that the Gryphon Highlord was going to be in Pixley. The presence of magebane suggests they were expecting us."

Sestus shook his head. "Wait a minute…you think Fleurry deliberately lured Ginger to Edenwood?"

"No. I think Valleri did. Fleurry didn't seem to know that Val wasn't coming until Urharde told him. Obviously the Royalists realize the Umagi pose the greatest threat. So the question remains…was Ginger their chosen target, or would the assassination of any mage do?"

Sestus waved the question aside, his face darkening as he began to understand the broader implication. "If the leak was engineered, that means the information claiming Valleri is headed for Shanasea is also false."

"Exactly. Naren reports no sign of him."

"He could be anywhere, ready to launch a sneak attack." Sestus bolted to his feet. "I've got to get out a warning."

I placed a gentle hand on his arm. "It's too late, Sestus. He's probably already done his damage. You just haven't received word yet."

Word came two days later in the form of an exhausted and bedraggled messenger. He'd ridden hard for a week straight, collecting a fresh horse in every Crusader outpost along the way as he spread his grim news. He'd nearly killed his last mount in his urgency to reach Idyll.

Valleri had scored himself a major, if bloody, victory. He'd destroyed the teleportal assigned to Repachea's protection and decimated the outpost called Killary. The Gryphon Highlord's elite troops had swept into camp in the dead of night and birthed a massacre. The wizard-calibre Umagi stationed there was the first to die, leaving Repachea bereft of magical influence with which to defend the outpost. He himself had barely escaped slaughter, rallying his troops into a fighting retreat.

Valleri had taken no prisoners. He slew everyone within reach, then razed the place. The messenger had witnessed it all and related the horror in minute detail. So keen was my disappointment I wanted to weep. Not only for the Crusaders' loss, but also for the loss of the Valleri I had once loved. He had become a monster.

Repachea was limping back to Idyll with fewer than a hundred survivors. Most were Belvemar's mercenaries, who had fought valiantly, the messenger said, against the terrible odds.

The news spread like wildfire through Idyll. Shock and sorrow touched everyone within. Sestus was stunned almost beyond the ability to function. Ginger flew into a violent rage. He swore, he paced, he threw and broke things. Then he secluded himself in his quarters, where he refused to see anyone for two days. He didn't speak for three. He and Sestus blamed themselves for Repachea's misfortune.

Belvemar's reaction, however, was the most surprising. I'd expected him to despair at the news of the massacre, but he didn't. He just got angry. Anger fuelled his desire to live.

Since I appeared so far removed from the effects of the repercussions, the responsibility of running Idyll fell on my shoulders. I single-handedly fielded the flood of communiqués, dispatched couriers, and oversaw the daily operations of the camp. Somehow I still found time to help Biddy in the infirmary, where she did double duty herself. While everyone else wallowed in self-pity, Biddy and I exhausted ourselves. Finally, on the third day since the messenger's inauspicious arrival, I decided it was time for Idyll to snap out of its mourning.

So that evening I went to see Sestus. Dispensing with the pleasantries I said, "We must talk. This can't go on. Your revolt is in peril. You and Ginger have to figure out what to do next. You must ignore this latest setback and regroup."

"I know," Sestus sighed as he stared out the darkened window. "It's just I'm still trying to figure out what happened."

"It's partly my fault." Briefly I explained my earlier misgivings in regards to a Royalist attack on Shanasea. "I should have guessed it was a plot to mislead you. Killary was Valleri's target all along."

"That doesn't explain how Valleri knew the location of the teleportal."

"Well, logic would dictate that the leak originated from the Crusader camp, not that of the Royalists."

He snorted dismissively. "We eliminated all Royalist spies long ago."

"Perhaps not them all," I replied, irked by his complacency. "Could it be the spy is not a Royalist? Could it be he is one of your own?"

"A Crusader? That's preposterous."

"Is it?"

"Look, Ruvie. Only a select group of people knew about that camp. All of them beyond suspicion."

"Then I suggest you get together with Ginger and have a second look at that select group of people. Perhaps they are not as trustworthy as you think. Find out where they are and who they may have told, then track it from there. A spy with access to such privileged information must leave a trail a mile wide. It's possible Ginger can use his sorcery to find him."

Sestus nodded, reluctant to admit I was right. "I'll speak to Ginger. But if I were you, I wouldn't mention the word spy aloud. Heads might turn to you."

"Me?" I burbled.

"Yes. You appeared roughly about the same time our luck began to sour. Certain people might grow suspicious and start asking questions. People like Ginger."

"What do you mean?"

"Must I spell it out for you?" he hissed. "You sit safely here in a Crusader outpost, having faked your death while your second, who is also your lover, undermines the Regent. With the Regent rendered impotent, Val crushes the revolt, then recalls his lost paramour from hiding to take her rightful place on the throne."

"You know that's not true. I had no part in—"

"I know that," he interrupted. "But how can I convince everyone else? If your identity is discovered now, it will look like the two of you cooked it up together. So if you want to save your life and any chance you have at the crown, you must make a decision."

"What decision is that?" I snapped. "I've already proven my loyalty to you by betraying Uncle."

"Bertrand is irrelevant now. He cannot stand against the combined might of Castle Gryphon. Therefore, if you do not stand against Valleri, you stand against us."

I sat down, my mind awhirl, knowing what my decision must be but unwilling to accept it. Sestus was right. In order to save myself I had to take a stand.

"Ask yourself this, Little Red," Sestus urged in a gentler tone. "Is it worth it to sit idly by and watch Bertrand murdered, your friends slaughtered, only so Valleri may seize the throne for himself? Or will you fight him for it? Perhaps you should consider something else, too. If you allow Valleri to usurp it for you, no Crusader will ever accept you as queen."

"What do you want me to do?"

"You must publicly declare who you are and on whose side you stand. You must let Valleri know you won't be his puppet."

"But I should instead be yours?" I shook my head, saddened by his coercion of me. "Still you don't trust me. You think me weak and foolish. I assure you, things are different. My heart no longer blinds me. My eyes are wide open. I understand now it doesn't matter what Valleri's intentions are. Only that his ambitions will be achieved at the expense of Uncle, the Crusaders, and my own honour. Nevertheless, to ask me to denounce Valleri is too much. I've agreed to help you, agreed to support you. I am the Princess Kathedra. Why is my word not enough?"

"It's enough for me, Kathedra. But it's not enough for Thylana."

"What about Ginger and Belvemar and Repachea? Will they accept me?"

He looked at me with eyes betraying volumes of despair. "They have become desperate men. They will be ready to compromise, to bargain with the lesser evil."

The lesser evil. Me. Not exactly how I wanted to begin my reign as Thylana's queen. But I, too, had opted to serve the lesser of two evils. I had chosen the Crusaders over Uncle.

"Betray Valleri, you say. So simple. So easy." I could barely speak for the sorrow constricting my throat. "I will consider it. I just need some time, is all, to adjust."

"Don't wait too long. Time is not with you."

"Nor with you, Sestus. Think on this; if Valleri knew about one teleportal, he probably knows about the others, or soon will."

It had been a long, tiring day that had allowed me no spare moment to visit Belvemar. Nevertheless, I felt obliged to stop by and check on him. It might even take my mind off my impending treachery of Val.

As I strolled through the deserted lanes of the castle on my way to the infirmary I gazed at the distant stars, wondering where Valleri was and what he did. Did he feel remorse for the bloody attack on Killary? Did he perhaps, at this very minute, think of me even as I thought of him?

When I reached the infirmary I found that the door wouldn't budge. A temperamental thing, it always stuck in the hot muggy weather, and then opened abruptly when pushed, so one fell ungracefully inside. I leaned my weight against it and nudged it with my shoulder, but it was stubborn. Finally, I kicked it, forcing it to give way with a shriek of rusty hinges.

The light of the full moon flooded inside, illuminating a strange scene. Belvemar sat on his cot, his hands clutched to his throat. His bedclothes were rumpled and his grey hair stood up in all directions.

I rushed to his side. "Belvemar! Are you all right?"

Between gulps for breath, he gasped out, "Oh, Ruvie. Thank heaven you're here."

"What is it? What happened?" Sweat beaded on his brow, and his eyes nearly bulged from their sockets.

"Someone just tried to kill me!"

"Kill you? How?"

"The pillow…he tried to smother me."

I looked at the pillow where it lay on the floor, reasoning that Belvemar must have flung it there in the throes of nightmare.

I made him lie back and tucked the pillow beneath his head. "No one tried to kill you," I cooed, smoothing his ruffled hair. "You just had a bad dream."

"No," he moaned, struggling to rise. "It was real. A man was here, dressed all in black. He wore a hood. I couldn't see his face. He tried to suffocate me with the pillow, but he must have heard you coming and escaped through the window."

The window was open. A light breeze stirred the ratty curtain. But it meant nothing. Biddy had probably opened it to let in some air before she went home. Two other patients occupied beds at the far end of the room, both snoring peacefully.

I noted that his face bore a purplish tinge. If he'd been holding his breath while asleep, that might produce the sensation of suffocation. Clasping his hand, I murmured, "You dreamt it, is all. Sometimes dreams can seem so real. Go back to sleep."

But the old captain was adamant. "No, it's true," he insisted, squeezing my hand tighter, his voice just a trembling whisper. "There was a man…He tried to kill me! He would have, if not for you."

"Really, Belvemar. Who would want to kill you?"

"I don't know. But you must believe me. You must."

Swallowing my annoyance, I forced a smile. "Would you feel better if I stayed here tonight?"

He glanced around the shadows of the infirmary, then nodded. "I don't think he'll come back if you're here."

Yawning, I dragged over a vacant cot and flopped onto it. I don't know what good my presence might have done had Belvemar's phantom assassin returned. I fell asleep the instant my head hit the pillow.

I slept untroubled until Biddy arrived in the morning, the screech of the door startling me awake. She arched a curious brow, then demanded, "What, may I ask, are you doing here?"

I explained. She did not seem concerned. "It's the medication. It has hallucinogenic properties. Nothing to worry about."

That little mystery solved I returned to my quarters with intent to change my clothes and grab something to eat. But someone sat on the front steps, waiting for me.

Ginger rose to greet me gruffly. "Where were you all night?"

Affronted by the question I snapped back, "I slept in the infirmary. Belvemar had a bad dream." Stepping past him, I added, "Not that it's any of your business."

The mage followed me inside and shut the door. I glared balefully. "I must admit I'm surprised to see you. I thought you were going to spend the rest of the revolt in your quarters."

Ignoring my sarcasm, he said, "I spoke to Sestus. All effort must be made to find the leak and seal it."

I tried to read his expression but it was neutral, as always. "Have you come to interrogate me then?"

"Don't be flippant," he sighed. "Of course I don't suspect you."

"So why are you here?"

"I came to see you last night but you were gone." The mage strode to the window, where he inadvertently stepped on the remains of Repachea's lewd statue. Recognizing it, he stooped to pick up the head, turning it over in his palm as if deep in contemplation. "I couldn't find Ragsey either."

I let the insinuation slide, only because the sword belted at his hip and his travelling garb distracted my anger. "Going somewhere?"

"There's a merchant caravan passing through on its way to Glanshayda.

I'm taking a party to intercept it. We need those supplies more than the Royalists do."

"Is it worth the risk? I mean, shouldn't you remain here? Can Idyll afford to lose you, too?"

A glimmer of defiance stole into his cool grey eyes. "Would it matter? With a spy running around loose it's only a question of time before Valleri finds out where we are and attacks. I want to do him some damage first. He won't be pleased to learn he's lost another caravan."

What could I say? Ginger had suffered one embarrassment after another. First Laurelac. Then Edenwood. Now Killary. He needed a victory, no matter how small, to boost morale and his own confidence. Unlike Sestus, at least the mage wanted to do something to strike back.

But he hadn't answered my question. "Why are you here, Ginger? What has this to do with me?"

"Nothing, I guess." He let the statue's head roll from his fingertips, then straightened. "I just wanted to say good-bye and to let you know I'm sorry about what happened in Edenwood. I shouldn't have argued with you. You were right all along. I behaved like an idiot."

He paused, waiting I assumed, for me to say something. When I didn't, he said, "Look after things while I'm gone," and moved toward the door.

"You're coming back, aren't you?" I blurted.

Ginger turned, one hand poised on the latch as he raked me with those penetrating mage eyes. "Do you want me to?"

What a strange question? "Of course. We need you."

"Then I'll be back."

This time Ginger got halfway through the door before I stopped him. Taking a step forward, I stammered out, "Um…how long will you be gone?"

"Two, three days at the most, if all goes well. I'll be back before Repachea gets here."

An uncomfortable silence descended. Ginger hesitated, perhaps wondering if I would say something more to delay his departure. Finally he just said, "Good-bye, Ruvie."

I leaned against the door, my gaze following the mage as he walked across the compound to the assembled war party, then mounted and rode away. I watched him go with a lump in my throat, knowing I would regret my aloofness forever if anything happened to him.

Something had changed between us. I'd felt it that night camped in the grove with the Shouda. I'd felt it again in the courtyard of the Dragon's Lair, and when we became separated outside the warehouse. Later, after I'd return to the inn, and seen the anguish in his eyes, saw the relief in his smile, I knew he'd felt it, too.

He'd tried to tell me now, when he thought he might never see me again. But his pride, like mine, had gotten in the way.

CHAPTER EIGHTEEN

With Sestus back in charge, I was able to devote more time to Belvemar. His condition improved with dramatic speed. He ate with a horse's appetite and was even strong enough to get out of bed and exercise his flaccid muscles. Slow and unsteady, however, he easily tired himself, even with the aid of a crutch to support his injured leg. Nevertheless, it was an important personal triumph and it heartened him immensely. His commitment to the Crusader cause returned with a vengeance. Despite his limitations, he discussed plots and counterplots with Sestus for hours.

But not even Belvemar's miraculous recovery could erase my anxiety. A week had passed and still Ginger had not returned. There had been no word from him, good or bad. Patrols and scouts reported no sign of him.

Seeking distraction, I locked myself in my quarters and tried to focus my energies on something constructive, such as mending Repachea's broken statue. I spent an entire day sitting on the floor, trying to fit the jagged shards of porcelain into their original shape, though I had no idea how to fuse it all together.

It turned out to be a useless endeavour. There were simply too many shattered pieces to incorporate and I did not possess concentration enough for the task. My thoughts were a tangle, impossible to analyze or separate. Finally, in frustration, I picked up a broom and swept the whole mess into a corner.

I needed to relax, to order my mind. One of Sestus's meditation exercises just might do the trick. So I sat on my bed, eyes shut, legs folded beneath me. It worked for all of five minutes, my body limp, my mind clear, before thoughts of Ginger intruded, along with a hundred questions. I could not shake them, his image constantly drifting behind my closed lids. After a while, I realized I did not want them banished.

I recalled every part of him with startling clarity. His grey mage eyes, piercing and hypnotic. His face, strong and beautiful despite its mutilation by flame. His long dark hair with its sheen of gold. I felt again vivid sensations. Things like our chaste kiss in the courtyard of the Dragon's Lair and his nearness to me on the bench, or my arms around his waist as I rode behind him on his stallion, even the weight of his body as I held him in the grove-his presence a comfort and a curse.

Memories resurfaced unbidden. His valiant effort to save me from that fatal fall in the warehouse. The desperate flight from Fleurry's soldiers and our separation as we were torn in opposite directions. The intensity of our mutual relief as our eyes met again over the crush of the tavern's crowd. The argument on the road from Edenwood, filled with such venom and yet such exhilarating heat.

Such fantasy. The fancies of a young girl, not a battle-hardened general. What did I think? That I could erase all his past hurts? That I could reach deep into that well of agony and fish out the shattered remains of his heart? That with a few sympathetic words and a shoulder to cry on, I could make him forget what happened here, in this very place? Or better yet, what happened in Dundurn?

All these thoughts engulfed me, flowing out to envelop my surroundings without my awareness of it. Suffused with a sense of contentment, I opened my eyes to see Repachea's statue sitting in the corner, whole and solid.

I stared at it in disbelief. It did not seem possible. Only minutes before it had been a heap of smashed pottery. Forcing myself to get up, I walked over to it, then touched it, running my fingers over every curve and cranny. No cracks. No imperfections. It was like it had never been broken. Elation soared through me. I had done it! It had been so effortless, so quick.

But my euphoria at this accomplishment did not last. Mindspells required concentration, serenity, and patience. Ginger had been an irritation to me, a distraction too, but never a source of inspiration. Questions without answers flitted like frenzied moths inside my head. When had my feelings for him changed? Did he feel the same way? And when had he replaced Valleri first and foremost in my mind?

Was it because Ginger appeared so unattainable, so forbidden? Did he pose a challenge to me or a threat? True, I was perversely attracted to him, infatuated with his aura of mystery and danger. Surely not those shallow notions alone could elicit such warm and tender feelings from me. No…he was a kindred soul. We were each intimate with pain and despair and rage. It only made sense that I should be drawn to him in such a manner.

Ginger must never know. It would jeopardize everything I'd laboured so hard to accomplish. I could let it develop no further. First, I must tell him who I am. Once he knows the truth, my breach of trust will ruin whatever fond feelings he has for me. So be it. It is more important to win my throne than to win Ginger-a man I've known for only a few short months, a man with a tumultuous and dangerous past, a man who hates my royal blood and has fought me so tenaciously.

No, I must keep my distance. Because, as we all know, mending a broken heart isn't as easy as fixing a shattered piece of pottery.

I had no sooner made my decision than a charge of horses galloped past my quarters and into the compound. Outside a crowd cheered, welcoming home the riders. I peeked out the window to find that Ginger and his party had returned with the booty of the plundered caravan. Grinning, the mage vaulted from his mount and danced some kind of victory jig with an equally jubilant Sestus while the villagers swarmed around them. The mage's features were smeared with dust and the grit of battle, a triumphant gleam in his eyes. My heart nose-dived into my stomach at the sight of him.

Searching the crowd, he scanned the sea of faces. For mine? I wondered. The urge to greet him was almost irresistible. It took all my willpower to tear away my gaze. Withdrawing from the window, I leaned against the wall for support. My resolve weakened and crumbled.

Let him have his moment in the sun, time to gloat and enjoy his small victory. I could be the Princess Kathedra tomorrow…or perhaps the next day.

I avoided Ginger for the next few days, afraid he would sense all my terrible truths. It was not an easy feat. He seemed to be everywhere I was. I dodged Sestus as well, his reproachful glare reminding me to reveal all before it became too late. Repachea was due to arrive the following week. I decided to wait until his arrival to inform the Crusaders of my deceit, when most of them were gathered in one place.

It seemed the coward's way out. I tried to tell Ginger on several occasions but I always lost my nerve. I could not bear the revulsion I knew I would see in his eyes when he learned the truth.

My only escape was the infirmary, where Ginger and Sestus rarely had time to venture. So one afternoon, I slunk from my quarters to visit Belvemar. "How is he, today?" I asked Biddy.

"Crabby," she replied in her usual snarl. "He's contracted a minor stomach ailment. He vomited all morning."

I peered into the next room. Belvemar had positioned his cot so he could sit on it and lean against the wall, providing himself a view of both the door and the window. He now wore his Crusader's uniform again, and habitually slept with a hand on his sword. I noted a curious absence of pillows.

I strode to the bedside but he did not seem to notice me, too intent on inner thoughts. Smiling, I bent near and murmured, "I hear you're not feeling well."

He grasped the neck of my tunic and pulled me closer. "He's back," he whispered into my ear. "He's smarter than I thought."

Startled, I choked out, "Who's back?"

"The assassin. Poison. It's in the wine."

"Not this again, Belvemar," I sighed. "No one is trying to kill you. There's no poison in the wine. It's just the weather. Lots of people are ill from the heat."

"It's not the heat," he hissed. "I tell you, someone's been poisoning my wine for the last two nights. He knows I'm strong enough now to resist him and so he was forced to seek a new method."

At my skeptical frown, he released his grip on my tunic and smoothed out the wrinkles. "You must believe me, Ruvie. You're the only person I trust."

I looked into his wild eyes, thinking he teetered on the edge of madness. "Listen to me," I said. "There's no assassin. You're hallucinating, is all. It's the medication. Now I don't want to hear—"

He tore his gaze from mine and folded his arms over his chest. "Fine. Don't believe me. But I won't drink the wine. I won't."

There seemed to be no way to convince the man. I glanced at the wine goblet perched innocently on the bedside table. "Look. If it will make you feel better, I'll drink it." Taking the cup, I brought it to my mouth.

"No, don't!" Belvemar shouted, reaching to snatch the goblet, his expression one of horror.

Swatting aside his hand, I drained the cup of its contents. The wine was cool and sweet. In fact, it tasted very good. "There's nothing wrong with it. See? I'm all right."

Belvemar looked at me askance, perhaps disappointed I did not keel over. "Well, it won't kill you instantly," he grumbled. "The dose is too small. But after a few days—"

"Enough," I interrupted. "For the last time, no one is trying to kill you!"

My outburst shocked him into rational thought. The colour drained from his cheeks and his eyelids drooped. Contrite, he asked, "Do you think I'm going mad?"

"Of course not. I just think the strain of prolonged confinement and inactivity is taking its toll. Once you're fully recovered, things will be better. You'll see."

I left him with a reassuring pat on his arm and the promise I would visit again tomorrow.

I returned to my quarters and set about preparing my supper. But I suddenly lost my appetite, as a great weariness swooped without warning upon me.

"Must be the heat," I muttered aloud. Opening the window, I leaned out it and drew several deep gulps of air. A fragrant breeze filled the room, making me realize it was not as warm a day as I'd first thought.

I began to feel a little light-headed. The room spun weirdly. I sank onto the bed, my belly wracked with cramps. I was on my hands and knees when Ginger walked in.

He rushed to my aid. "Ruvie? What's wrong?"

I couldn't speak, couldn't catch my breath, so intense was the pain. Finally I managed, "Fetch a bucket. I'm going to be sick."

I puked until I thought I would die, until I figured death would be infinitely more pleasant, for hours it seemed. Although I'd emptied my stomach long ago, I continued to wretch up bitter yellow bile.

Ginger stayed by my side, afraid to leave, I think, for fear I might expire. Rubbing my back, he steadied me as each convulsion ripped through my body, and whispered words of comfort and reassurance.

When it was over I was too weak to stand. The mage's face must have been as pale as my own. He led me to the bed and covered my chilled flesh with a blanket.

"Belvemar was right," I groaned.

Ginger brushed the hair from my damp brow. "About what?"

"The assassin. The wine was poisoned." I told him about Belvemar's alleged stomach complaint and how I'd drunk from the same cup. "Someone is trying to kill him."

"Kill him? If someone wanted Belvemar dead, why not just stick a blade in him and be done? Why go to all this trouble?"

"Because then it would too obviously be murder. The assassin wants it to appear as though Belvemar died of natural causes, that he succumbed to the severity of his injury. This way, no one will look for an assassin."

"Who would want to kill Belvemar?"

"I don't know. Maybe someone is after his passkey."

"His passkey? To the teleportal? He doesn't even have it now. He turned it over to us following his injury and we destroyed it."

I shook my head, bewildered. "Then it must be someone who doesn't want him to make a recovery." I recalled telling Valleri that night in my room, 'Without its leaders the organization will fall apart.' Who was next? Sestus, maybe? Or Ginger?

Frantic with the thought that this invisible enemy, too, might stalk the mage, I grabbed his arm. "You can't waste any more time. Find out where that wine came from and who has access to the infirmary besides Biddy and me. Ask if anyone saw anything suspicious or someone lurking around. Warn Sestus, but don't tell anybody else. We don't want to scare the culprit away. Post a couple of guards on Belvemar. You might want to get word to Naren and—"

Ginger's frown appeared. "Ruvie…Are you sure?"

Suddenly I knew how Belvemar felt when I refused to believe him. I thrust his hand away. "If you need further proof, next time you drink the wine."

He capitulated immediately. "Very well. I'll see to it. You stay here and get some rest." Risking a sympathetic smile, he squeezed my shoulder and left.

I slept until Sestus awakened me shortly before dusk. He hovered suffocatingly near and pummelled me with questions. "Are you all right? Can I get you anything? Are you hungry? Do you need another blanket? Can I make you some tea?"

I fear I was really quite rude when I told him he should be more concerned about finding the poisoner than inquiring after my health.

"I'm sorry, Little Red," he murmured, flashing those sad puppy eyes. "It's just I feel responsible for you."

"It's not your fault," I said in a milder tone. "It's I who should apologize. I didn't mean to be rude. Thank you for your concern, but I'm fine, really. I'm just a bit edgy."

"That's understandable. It's all very unsettling. I have no idea how all this could have happened. We have safeguards in place, an elaborate warning system, all implemented right from the very beginning."

"Then back to the beginning is where you have to go. Chances are the perpetrator insinuated himself, or herself, way back when. Watch yourself, Sestus. It's likely his mission is to eliminate all senior Crusaders, not just Belvemar."

"I'll take care. I've posted two guards unobtrusively in the infirmary." He fell silent a moment before adding, "Now more than ever, it's imperative that you reveal your identity. When will you tell Ginger?"

"I think it's best to wait until Repachea gets here, that way everyone will be together."

Sestus seemed satisfied. "Probably a wise idea. Repachea will be here in a couple of days, three at the most. No longer, Ruvie."

I caught the drift of his message. He would not allow me to put it off indefinitely.

Once Sestus had gone, I climbed out of bed and freshened myself with cool water from a basin. Then I changed my clothes and pulled on a clean sleeping shift. Famished, I ate a few bland biscuits and some cheese. Feeling the strength flow back into my limbs, I made a pot of tea.

As I sat before the open window, sipping from my mug and enjoying the evening breeze, a knock came at the door.

It was Ginger. "I wanted to see how you were feeling."

"I'm much better," I replied, inviting him inside. "It wasn't a particularly potent poison, but we're lucky Belvemar discovered it when he did. Another day or two and he might have been dead. Any idea what it was?"

He shook his head. "Not yet. My guess is it came from Biddy's medicinal store. "

I offered to share my teapot, but he declined. So we stood there, in awkward silence, me feeling exposed in my flimsy shift and Ginger looking formidable in his Crusader's uniform.

"It's another warm night," he observed, pulling off his coat and tossing it over a chair. He moved to stand before the window where he let the breeze ruffle his hair. He seemed content to stay awhile.

Searching for small talk, I said, "You must be pleased with your raid on that merchant caravan. Some of those supplies we desperately needed, like the grain and cloth. But the luxury items are just as welcome, like those kegs of ale and crates of sugar. How generous of you to share the finer spoils with the villagers. No doubt it put a boil on a few Royalist bottoms."

"What's one more plundered caravan to the Royalists?" he muttered. "I hardly think it hurt them. It is only important to us in the sense it boosts our confidence. It hasn't helped to further our cause. I'm beginning to think nothing we do can hurt the Royalists."

That did not sound like the Ginger I knew talking. Where was the ruthless, cunning mage determined to visit his vengeance upon the house of Gryphon? "What's wrong?" I ventured.

"Everything. We can't stand against the combined muscle of Castle Gryphon. Not with Valleri in command. Once, we had a chance, when the Princess Kathedra lived. She kept the castle in a state of constant vacillation. But Valleri is as decisive as he is ruthless. Any aspirations we had of launching our counteroffensive are dust. We're just rabble. A motley pack of peasants and hearthmages. I realize that now, and how foolish we were to think we could lead any damned revolt. Such grand ambitions we had. What have we become? We've been branded traitors, outlaws, thieves and murderers."

"Not so," I began, trying to lift his spirits. "You've accomplished much. You can't expect change to happen—"

But he cut me off, launching into a litany of self-pity. "The obstacles are insurmountable. Repachea has heavy casualties and Killary is in ruins. Belvemar is crippled. His troops number less than a hundred. Naren is useless in Shanasea. Fleurry has besieged Gregaris in Pixley. Castarr talks about quitting and Idyll is a sitting duck. To make matters worse, the command structure we once considered air tight is rife with holes."

Command did he say? Did Ginger suspect the source of all their troubles was a senior Crusader? That was too delectable a morsel to pass up. "You think your command structure is flawed?"

"Castarr is looking for a way out. He's gotten himself in too deep and isn't committed to the long haul. But that's just my opinion. I've got no proof." He paused to draw a deep breath, raked a hand through his hair. "Don't you understand, Ruvie? Everything we've worked so hard for is about to come crashing down around our ears. We need a miracle."

Is that why he'd come here? To hear a word of encouragement? To blow off some steam? To get a new perspective? Perhaps I could give him that miracle. Perhaps the time had come to tell Ginger the truth. In it he may find new hope. His anger would be swift and fierce, but it would give way to reason. He needed me, the Princess Kathedra, as a symbol for the Crusaders in the same sense as the Gryphon Highlord had been a symbol for the Royalists. He would not be able to deny it, or me. I'd never have him in a better position.

Ginger continued to stare out the window at the darkening sky, his eyes hard like dead stone. How sad he looked, his face awash in the lavender blue of twilight. How hopeless. How terribly alone.

As in the courtyard of the Dragon's Lair, the urge to console him was fierce. I moved to where he stood and rested a light hand on his arm. "Perhaps I can be of assistance," I said, forcing a nervous smile.

"Not unless you can turn back time. Not unless you can wake me and tell me it's all been an awful dream." He turned from the window, his expression softening. "Not unless you can ease my cares with your embrace this night."

My smile disintegrated. His proposal caught me off guard. I stepped back in surprise but he seized my arm, keeping me near. "No, Ruvie. Don't turn away. We can't go on like this, sidestepping each other, avoiding glances, bickering like children one moment then nuzzling like adolescents the next. You can't deny it. You must see in my eyes what I see in yours."

No! This can't be happening. He shouldn't be saying such things. Not now, when I must reveal the truth. I tried to pull away but he held me all the firmer.

"Why am I drawn to you?" he asked, his gaze locked on mine. "Why are you so special? I seek out your voice, your touch, because whenever I'm near you, your presence lends me comfort and strength. How is it when I look at you that I forget Nelia? I forget my obligation to duty. I forget my anger and hatred and all past pains…everything but you."

I understood too well. Whenever I looked at him, I forgot Valleri's duplicity, and my rage fled. I forgot Averi's savagery, and my fear vanished. It was a terrible enchantment he cast over me, this lapse in memory of everything but him. It must be fought. He could not be permitted to exist as the centre of my universe. That is a spot reserved for Thylana.

"Ginger, no. Please. You must listen to me. You don't understand. There is something I must—"

But my protest died as his arms came around me. "What don't I understand? I know only you inspire feelings in me that I've not felt in many years. I know that I like the way you look at me, without repugnance, without distraction. What more do I need to understand?"

His arms were strong, his tall frame sheltering. I returned his embrace and pressed my face to his shirt, where his heart drummed against my ear. "Perhaps nothing," I sighed.

"What is it?" he persisted. "What's wrong? You can tell me anything."

I withdrew just enough to be able to see his grey mage eyes. Can I? I wondered. Can I tell you it is the Gryphon Highlord you hold in your arms?

Ginger smiled down at me, a glorious smile that lit up his whole face, even the part of it that was an abhorrence in other people's sight. Then he pressed his lips to mine in a kiss so unlike the first we shared, one of sweetness and warmth, on a bench in that faraway courtyard. This was all fire and hunger. I lost myself in the moment, swept up in his passionate embrace, and returned his kiss with abandon, forgetting he was forbidden to me.

But desire was fleeting as I recalled how dangerous it was for me to love this man. Recoiling, I tore my mouth from his with a gasp.

Ginger misinterpreted my reaction. His arms slackened and he tilted his head to meet my glance. "Don't be afraid of me, Ruvie," he whispered. "I won't hurt you."

He turned me in the circle of his arms and rested his chin on my shoulder. "I could never hurt you. I'll admit, there were times when you drove me to such fury I yearned to wrap my fingers around your throat and throttle you senseless, like that day we quarrelled outside Edenwood. More so, were the times I just wanted to kiss you, like that afternoon in the courtyard. Times I just wanted to hold you, like you held me after the Shouda attack. I heard you weep. I felt your pain. I did not know how to ease it, so I remained silent. But I swear this to you now, no one will ever hurt you again while I live."

We stood that way at some length, before the open window, the breeze flowing over us, my hands covering his where they were clasped around my hips. I closed my eyes and leaned my head back against his chest, content. Tell him! that nagging little voice screamed. You'll never get another chance.

But I couldn't. It would ruin everything, most especially this moment. I was certain Ginger would never touch me again if I told him. His lips, his hands, felt too wonderful to be turned away now, perhaps forever. Selfishly, I kept quiet.

Finally he said, "Maybe I should go."

"Go?" I asked in alarm. "Why must you go?"

He pulled me tighter. "Do you know how long it's been for me? Not since Nelia. I'm afraid if you ask me to stop I might…" His voice trailed away in an anguished sigh.

I turned to face him. "Don't be afraid," I murmured, plucking at the laces of his shirt. "I won't ask you to stop."

As we fell onto the bed all thoughts of Valleri and Uncle fled. No one existed for me but Ginger. Nothing else mattered. Not the Crusaders. Not Valleri. I would give it all up for the mage, if that's what this one night cost me.

Ginger was a wonder, caressing me with unexpected tenderness, so unlike Valleri's intense passion, yet no less thrilling. Something significant had happened. It was no casual tryst, no idle pleasure. I did not, however, delude myself with the fanciful notion it would last forever. But later, cradled in Ginger's arms, I knew instinctively I would never love any other man. I would be his until time came to a fiery end.

I stirred after dawn, as rays of sunshine slanted across the bed. I pushed myself onto an elbow and glanced over my shoulder in the fear Ginger was gone. But he was still there, beside me, asleep.

I settled on my side so I might better see him, memorizing every detail, afraid I may never be this close to him again. I reached out to stroke the birthmark on his hipbone, then the long white scar emblazoned across his ribs marking the passage of a Royalist blade, and lastly, gently, the puckered and angry skin stretched tight over his left cheekbone and down his jaw line.

An overwhelming sense of grief struck me. He would hate me, I knew with sudden surety, once he learned the truth. How long did I have with him until I would be forced to confess? Two, maybe three days. It would have to be enough.

Ginger moaned drowsily and pulled me closer. I rested my head on his chest and listened to the steady rhythm of his heart. My betrayal of Valleri was almost complete. A twinge of guilt pricked my conscience. It annoyed me. After all, Valleri had betrayed me long ago. Even now, he probably gathered concubines for his royal bed. Perhaps one lay with him at this same moment.

Val's treachery had hurt me deeply, beyond forgiveness. From the beginning Valleri had plotted to seize the throne and murder Uncle, using me in a most vile way. Even though I had come to accept Val was about to steal my crown out from under me, one thing disturbed me, gnawing away at my conviction. If Valleri truly desired to be king, why had he bothered to spare me? It would have been much easier and far more advantageous for him had I died. Could his love for me be that strong? If so, how could I ever ever betray him?

CHAPTER NINETEEN

"What will you do now?" I asked, watching from my rumpled lovenest as Ginger dressed.

He sat down on the bed and pulled on his boots. "Fall back. Regroup. Start over. Once Repachea and Castarr arrive we'll have ourselves a big, noisy brawl and decide where to go from there."

The light of day seemed to have restored his faith, or perhaps it was the magic of the night. His mood had improved considerably. I stretched and yawned. "When will that be?"

"Soon. Tomorrow maybe. Why so curious?"

"No reason. I just want to be kept informed…so I can prevent you from doing something foolish."

He leaned across the bed, lifted my hand and kissed it. "Too late to prevent foolishness now, precious." His eyes glittered, new desire rising up from their cold depths.

I pushed him away and sprawled my most charming sprawl. "Foolishness, you call it. I'll remember that the next time you feel the urge for a bout of foolishness. I may be feeling wise."

It was not so smart to tease Ginger, even in play, now that his long dead ardour had been reborn. His eyes narrowed, ensnaring me in their feral stare. His arm snaked out with lightning speed and curled around my waist, crushing me against him.

"Don't test me, Ruvie. I would stay here and torture you silly with pleasure all day if I could."

With that, he took my face in his hands and kissed me deeply, longingly. Then he strode from the room, leaving me amid the twisted linens, feeling sweetly abandoned.

The door opened behind me and I recognized Sestus's purposeful step. "Come in, come in," I piped, almost singing in all my glee.

He shut the door with a heavy hand. "It's true, then? You and Ginger?"

I turned from the windowsill and the growth of greenery crowding its ledge, to whirl about my tiny quarters, smiling ear to ear. "Is it so obvious?"

"Obvious? A blind man could see it," he snapped, slumping into a chair. "Ginger's going around grinning like an idiot and now I find you dancing a fairy waltz. I put two and two together. This is disastrous. Do you know what you've done?"

I glided toward him on toes ten feet off the ground and fell to my knees before him. "Yes, yes, yes, I know! Oh, Sestus. I feel so alive. So free. Like a young girl again. I love him, Sestus. I love Ginger. I want to shout it to the world!"

"I'm truly happy for you," he muttered, frowning in disapproval. "Only last month you loved Valleri."

Not even the mention of my old lover could dampen my mood. I placed a potted fern in his lap, its bright green fronds reaching for Sestus's beard. "Not so. He lost my love the moment he betrayed me."

"You're fickle," he pronounced, which was a nice way of saying I behaved like a shameless strumpet. "And what am I supposed to do with this thing?"

"Talk to it. It likes that." Back to the matter at hand. "I am not fickle. Valleri was dashing and handsome and exciting. I was in such awe of him. I loved him with the innocence and blind worship every young maiden feels for her very first love."

"Or two or three," he grumbled.

"What I feel for Ginger is deeper, stronger. It will burn inside me forever." I gazed into his stern face. "How can I explain it, Sestus? I would die for this man."

"When Ginger learns he bedded the Gryphon Highlord you may very well die." He spoke directly to the plant, which seemed to perk up at the promise of gossip.

I straightened, my jubilance departing. "You have to spoil this for me, don't you? You just can't allow me to enjoy the moment."

"Kathedra…damn, I mean Ruvie, you're going to break his heart."

"He'll get over it," I growled, turning my back to him so he would not see my quivering lips.

"He didn't get over Nelia."

"That's different. She died."

"It's not so different. When Kathedra is revealed, Ruvie will die…at least to Ginger she will. He won't forgive you this deceit, this betrayal. If you ever had a chance to win his support and trust you've destroyed it."

"Destroyed it how? I took an enemy and made him my friend."

"You took an enemy and made him your lover. You might discover there is no difference between the two once crossed. You have only to examine your feelings for Valleri to know that is true."

Sestus was right, of course. If I could not forgive Valleri, how could I expect Ginger to forgive me?

I drew a deep breath, determined to ignore Ginger until forced to make the inevitable confrontation. I snatched back the plant, stroked its delicate, feathery foliage. "So tell me. Who can I count on to support my bid for the throne?"

Sestus seemed relieved by the change in topic. "Repachea. Belvemar. Gregaris could go either way but he's barricaded inside Pixley. Word can't get in or out, which is probably to your benefit. Naren and Castarr will oppose you. Vehemently, I think."

"Counting you, that makes three. If Ginger gets stubborn and renounces me, at worse it will mean a stalemate."

"Wrong. I don't count. Once the truth is known and my part in your deception revealed, I'll be denied a vote. Ginger will cast the deciding ballot, so to speak. Even if he can see past his anger to do what is best for both the Crusaders and Thylana, I can't promise his endorsement will hold sway with Naren and Castarr. They might say to hell with us and mutiny. If that happens, the revolt will die and you will never be queen."

He shrugged at my wide-eyed horror. "That's the worst possible scenario, I concede. I warned you; there are no guarantees."

"No guarantees," I echoed, realizing the enormity of my mistake. I had knowingly, even willingly, risked Ginger's support. I had not stopped to think he might possess the power of life and death over me. How to undo the damage? I returned the fern to the company of its neighbours, the vigorous henbane and a pot of basil, destined for Biddy's herb bed.

"When the others assemble for their meeting, send for me. I will announce my presence then."

"What about Ginger? Shouldn't you break it to him first?"

"No." I was adamant on that point. "He will learn it with the others. If I tell him beforehand, it will only give him time to ripen his anger."

"Can you be so cruel, Little Red?"

"It's not cruelty. No one knows about Ginger and me save you. Let's keep it that way. It will spare him embarrassment, without compromising his position. I'm only thinking of what's best for him. I can't change last night."

Even if I could, I wouldn't.

Repachea arrived late that same night, rousing the camp with an ungodly clamour. Ginger jerked awake and leapt from the bed as if his tail were afire. "Get up," he hissed, throwing clothes at me. "Get dressed."

Still groggy, I stumbled around in near total darkness and fumbled into a shirt, only to have Ginger yank me out of it. "That's mine."

Sleep and utter contentment had fuddled my senses. It did not seem so important to hide ourselves. With that thought I sagged back onto the bed and closed my eyes, uncaring of the boots that stormed up the stairs beyond the door.

Ginger had worked himself into a lather. Half clad, he dragged me from the bed. "Dammit, get up."

At that moment the door opened. Harsh light from outside torches spilled inside. It cast the intruder's form in shadow and prompted Ginger to pull me against him, hiding my nakedness.

"Well, what do we have here?"

It was Repachea.

"It's not how it looks," Ginger said.

"Really?" Repachea stepped inside and closed the door. "Hell, Ginger," he laughed. "Why so ashamed? I'd be shouting it in the streets. No need to hide her so. I've seen naked women before. Let her dress, then I'll turn up a lamp."

As I struggled, now wide-awake, into my clothes, Ginger muttered a feeble apology. "Forgive me, Repachea. I shouldn't have used your quarters in this fashion. I didn't expect you until tomorrow."

"I can see that," Repachea quipped. "I'm quite unoffended. After all, I did expect to find a woman in my bed. You were the only surprise." Amused, he clucked his tongue. "My, my, my. Ginger, you've shocked me. You've stolen her right out from under me. So to speak. I couldn't be prouder. Ruvie, are you dressed yet?"

I managed an affirmative, mortified beyond intelligible speech. Repachea struck up the lamp, which gave me my first clear glimpse of him. Battered and bedraggled, he appeared in dire need of a bath. A shallow gash decorated his brow and a bloodstained bandage peeked through the tatters of a sleeve. He plopped into a chair and swung his legs onto the table, then favoured us with a sublime grin.

"Well, kids? Is it true love or what?"

Ginger found his shirt, donned it without a reply. I stood there, caught in Repachea's assessing gaze, and blushed. "Just foolishness," I answered.

"Ah, sweet folly," Repachea sighed. "How I wish it were the same for me." His expression clouded and his voice lowered to a whisper. "Oh, Ginger. It was a bloody horror. I can't describe it. I can't even talk about it. It's over. I agree with Castarr. We should quit. I can't watch any more of us die."

"We're not beaten yet," Ginger said.

"What can we do? We can't muzzle a leak we can't find. The bastard feeds Valleri every delectable secret we have. Our plan of attack rested on three teleportals, not none."

"You exaggerate. We can evacuate Idyll and pull Naren out of Shanasea. We'll find new havens and restructure. We can't give up, Repachea. Not now. Don't you want to avenge your dead?"

"Of course I do," Repachea snarled, fury smouldering in his eyes. "I want to tear out Valleri's black heart and shove it down Bertrand's throat."

"Fine. I see you've already decided there's no turning back."

Repachea shifted in his chair. "Yeah, I suppose you're right."

I should have said something then. Indeed I'd opened my mouth, but Ginger's next words struck me dumb. "I promise you, Repachea, you will have your revenge. Our blades will taste of Valleri's blood. Bertrand's too. They will run blue with it. My only regret is they will not drink of Kathedra's."

I cringed at Ginger's gruesome thirst for violence, his undead hatred for me. Is it yet possible my blood will colour his sword? Could he kill the woman he had loved only an hour ago?

Yes, I believe he could.

"Have you heard from Castarr?" Ginger asked.

"He's right behind me. He'll be here tomorrow."

The conversation drifted to the matter of the poisoner and Belvemar's condition as Ginger updated Repachea on all he'd missed. I wasn't listening. I sat on the bed, chewing a nail, wondering whether I should play the coward and steal a horse to ride away from Idyll, from Ginger, from the whole mess, straight to Zigores, Umagi sanctuary or not.

A touch on my arm startled me almost out of my skin. Ginger's brow wrinkled. "What's the matter, Ruvie? You're trembling. Are you cold?"

An icy chill swept up my spine as his fingers tightened around my arm. Though he held me with a lover's gentle hand, it was a hand that could just as easily turn into an enemy's. "Yes. A little."

"Perhaps we should retire to my quarters and let Repachea get some rest."

"No," Repachea said, casting a dubious glance at his tousled bed. "You stay here. I'll take your quarters tonight. I should go greet Sestus, anyway."

When Repachea had gone I crawled back beneath the sheet and curled into a ball, trying to get as far from Ginger as possible. But he snuggled closer and drew me into his arms. At first I shrank from him, stiff with revulsion, but he was tired and wanted nothing except to sleep. His hands were warm, and his body, pressed close to mine, sheltering. Despite my angst I melted into his embrace and fell into a tranquil slumber.

The following day bustled with activity. The infirmary was a busy place, besieged with the survivors of Valleri's rampage. I was surprised to see Belvemar in the exercise yard, wielding a practice blade quite effectively against Repachea. Although Belvemar's leg made him slow and ungainly, his sword arm was in excellent shape. They sparred in vigorous but careful play until Biddy spoiled their sport by stomping onto the field and yelling like a shrew at Belvemar, "Cease your folly, you stubborn old mule!"

Ginger sent a dispatch to Shanasea recalling Naren and his garrison. At noon Ragsey rode in on his roan, fresh from some nocturnal reconnaissance, and announced Castarr's party had been sighted.

Castarr arrived at dusk with a beleaguered escort, having ridden hard day and night. I disliked the man immediately. He was about fortyish, of medium height and build. Unremarkable really, except for his dark, shifty eyes. Arrogant, obnoxious and coarse, he would cause me problems.

The meeting was set for an hour later in the dungeon, giving Castarr time to eat and recover from his journey. They could not wait for Naren. I allowed what I presumed sufficient time for them to assemble, then threw on my cloak.

Before setting out, however, I paused in the doorway, looking at that part of the keep that was just a dark and empty shell. A shiver of trepidation seized me then, though it had little to do about my coming confrontation with the outlaw leaders. There was a distinct and ominous presence to the night.

Earlier, I had moved all my things, including my greenery, from Repachea's quarters to Ginger's. But I had forgotten the dagger that Sestus had given me upon my departure for Edenwood, which I had hidden in the niche beneath the bed. With a potential killer on the loose, I would feel safer with the blade's reassuring weight in my boot.

I hurried across the compound and raced up the wooden steps leading to Repachea's hole in the wall. I had just reached the door when it suddenly burst open, slamming hard into my side and knocking me to the ground as a shadow flew past.

I shook the stars from my eyes; the sound of retreating footfalls faded. "What the hell?" I moaned, struggling to my feet. But as I peered around the open door, the glow of a tipped candle provided the terrible answer.

I ran inside to the man on the floor, his blood seeping between the boards. "Repachea," I gasped. "Heavens above…Repachea!"

Falling to my knees I lifted his head into my lap. Fast flowing blood stained his chest where a blade had plunged into a lung. Miraculously, he still breathed.

"Ginger!" I cried out the door. "Sestus! Anyone! Come quick!"

Repachea opened his eyes, their sapphire depths aflood with pain, their sparkle failing as life ebbed away. They focused briefly, impaling me with a gaze that bore straight through my soul. He was dying, I realized, even as big salty tears spilled down my cheeks.

"Who did this?" I whispered. "Who?"

Sputtering and choking, he tried to tell me. But blood bubbled up in his mouth and with a great strangled groan, Repachea died, just as Ginger and a horde of people stormed into the room.

"No!" I sobbed, falling across Repachea's lifeless body.

I held him tight, heedless of the blood wetting my flesh, and wept for this man who only a few short hours ago frolicked on the practice field, whose marvellous blue eyes I would never see again, a man I would have moulded into one of my most loyal champions.

Sestus collected his wits first. He knelt beside Repachea and felt for a pulse. "He's dead," he pronounced.

Instantly, a flurry of voices crowded into my head, hurling questions too garbled and frenzied to understand. I wept harder, trying to out drown their racket, still clinging to Repachea's warm corpse. Then a man's rough hands took my shoulders and dragged me to my feet, shaking me until I thought my skull would split.

Blurred by my tears, Castarr's face swam into view, a cruel twist to his lips as he shouted in a towering rage. "Damn you, woman, answer me! What happened in here?" His hand swung back as if to strike, but Ginger caught it and shoved him away.

"You handle her, then," Castarr retorted, uncowed by Ginger's fierce countenance. "I have no patience to waste on a hysterical wench. A man is dead."

"Stop crying, Ruvie," Ginger murmured, raising my chin and brushing the hair from my brow. "Tell us what happened."

His gentle ministrations banished my panic, my tears. But when my glance fell once more on poor dead Repachea mindless rage filled me.

"Find him," I hissed, pushing Ginger aside. "Find the monster and give him to me. He will feel my steel. He will watch his blood leak away, and his pleas will fall on deaf ears."

I caught myself just in time to stop the dagger from flying out from beneath the bed and into my palm. Ginger stared at me, his face gone even paler with his shock. He had never seen me behave like this-a bloodthirsty, godless thing. I saw Sestus's warning look, reminding me to get hold of myself. The violence of my words disturbed me greatly, if not for their barbarism, for their resemblance to Ginger's.

"I'm sorry. I'm merely shaken." I took a moment to compose myself, then told them what I knew.

While Sestus had two strong lads take the body away, Castarr questioned me further. His manner of interrogation was sarcastic and brusque. If not for Ginger's presence, I'm sure the fiend would have tortured me into a confession of murder.

"I told you," I snapped, my patience deserting me, "it was too dark to see. He was just a fleeing shadow."

Castarr's brow furrowed with annoyance. "So you say he hit you with the door?" he snarled, implying my story was too incredible to believe. "Did you hear anything when you approached it? A struggle? Voices?"

"No, nothing."

"Why did you come here when you knew Repachea was supposed to be at the briefing?" His tone was accusing.

"He loaned me the use of his quarters since my arrival here. I just came back to get something I forgot."

"C'mon, Castarr," Ginger sighed, stroking the gash above my eye where the door had struck me. "You don't seriously think she killed Repachea, do you?"

"Well, she's as good a suspect as anyone. We know nothing about her. She came here a stranger, claiming to have been waylaid by brigands. What proof—"

Ginger stood, looming threateningly over the shorter man. "Say no more, Castarr. Sestus found her. Biddy can explain to you the severity of her injuries. I will tell you myself how she saved me from being torn apart by a pack of Shouda. So if you're implying she staged this drama after first stabbing Repachea and bashing herself in the head with a door, I suggest you close your mouth right now while you still can."

Castarr was livid. For one tense moment I thought he would call Ginger's bluff and a brawl would ensue. But he held his tongue and stomped from the room.

Needless to say, there was no meeting of Citizens Risen Up to Stand Against a Dread and Errant Regency that night. Ginger took me to the infirmary and tucked me into the last available bed with a draught of Biddy's sleeping potion. According to Biddy, he did not leave my side that night.

The next day we buried the captain on a grassy mound beyond the keep. Resting my head against Belvemar's chest, I watched through a gentle rain as the roughly hewn coffin was lowered into the ground. He was as silent and cold as death itself at the loss of this man who had been like a son. In fact, it had been Repachea who'd hacked his way across that bloody battlefield in Bolta to drag the wounded commander to safety. Awash in sorrow, Belvemar had sat all night on the bed, weeping unabashed tears as he stared at the dark stain on the floor where Repachea had died. Now, he displayed no emotion at all.

Repachea's loss affected everyone in Idyll, for he was an easy man to like. The ladies, I think, would miss him most, although he had been friend as well as protector to everyone. But standing there in the cool drizzle, which so aptly concealed my tears, I mourned Repachea for a different reason. I had lost not only a friend but also perhaps my strongest supporter, a possible champion I had depended upon to save my throne and possibly my life.

CHAPTER TWENTY

After the funeral I accompanied Belvemar to the infirmary, where Biddy put me to work tending Repachea's injured. I toiled well past the supper hour and did not leave until dusk. On my way out, I bumped into Sestus. He was in a foul temper, understandably so. The assassin had not only killed Repachea, but had delivered a near mortal blow to the Crusaders as well. Dissent and confusion reigned. Belvemar was in a state of bewilderment. Castarr and Ginger refused to speak except to bicker. Poor Sestus was at his wit's end, trying to mediate their petty squabbles and hold down the fort. Thus, Ragsey was dispatched to hurry Naren on his way in the hope his influence would restore order and save the revolt from collapse.

"Where's Ginger?" I had not seen the mage since the funeral.

"How should I know?" Sestus growled. "The last I saw him he was threatening to incinerate Castarr's nose hair. Bloody half-wits. I'm seriously considering bundling them up together and leaving them on Valleri's doorstep, for all the good they're doing here."

Through Belvemar I had learned Ginger and Castarr had never been friendly. The enmity between them had been since the start. To be brief, Castarr shared almost the same opinion of the Umagi as Uncle. He too had lost loved ones on the day of Mauranna's miscast spell. A petty lordling, he had chosen to side with the Citizens Risen Up to Stand Against a Dread and Errant Regency due to a dispute with Uncle some years ago over a piece of property to which he felt entitled. When he'd demanded a leadership position, the Crusaders reluctantly gave him one if only because he promised to cut off funds from his hefty war chest.

"You didn't leave them alone together, did you?"

"Of course not." Sestus waved an impatient hand. "I broke it up before anyone got hurt and sent them their separate ways. Ginger mentioned something about cleaning out Repachea's quarters."

I got halfway across the compound when the full impact of Sestus's words struck me. I had left something far more important than my dagger behind in Repachea's digs: the statue. If Ginger found it, whole and restored, after having seen it smashed to smithereens…

Donning my hood, I clutched my cloak tight and ran across the compound, splashing through mud and puddles. Rain pelted my face, plastering my hair to my skin and stinging my eyes, but I hardly cared. All that mattered was the statue. I had to retrieve it before Ginger discovered the truth for himself.

No light spilled from Repachea's quarters; quietly I let myself in. So engrossed in my single-minded mission I did not see the darker shadow parked before the window, blotting out the indigo haze of the rain. As I lowered my hood to shake the raindrops from my hair, I heard the sound of a lamp hissing to life.

Startled, I turned to see Ginger sitting in Repachea's leather chair. In that instant when our eyes met, a wave of malevolence struck me with such force it was as if a physical barrier had sprung up between us. Distorted by the flickering light, his face was grim, and I knew he was enraged beyond any anger I had ever seen in him before.

For a moment only I was confused. Then my gaze fell upon the alabaster statue on the table.

"Is this what you came for, Ruvie? Or should I say…Kathedra?"

I stood rooted to the spot, not knowing what to say, devastated by the realization my world was about to end. It seemed pointless to deny the accusation, equally pointless to verify it. So I said nothing, and steeled myself for his wrath.

He pushed himself to his feet, his expression dark and thunderous. "What a perfect hiding place for a fugitive princess, right under the foe's very nose. How gaily the bards will sing of the deposed Gryphon Highlord finding sanctuary in her enemy's own bed." He clapped his hands to his scalp as if to pull out his hair. "Kathedra. How could I be so stupid?"

Still I said nothing, awaiting the full magnitude of his rage. An almost sentient entity, his anger filled the room. He pinioned me in his feral gaze. "So tell me. Is Castarr right? Did you kill Repachea? Is this all some elaborate scheme to overthrow Bertrand?"

"No," I whispered. "You know none of that is true."

"Do I? Suppose you tell me exactly what is true."

Everything rushed out in a babbling torrent. "I fled Castle Gryphon in fear for my life, unaware Valleri sought to take the throne for himself. Sestus came upon me just as Averi and his men had beaten me nearly senseless. Do you think I allowed that to happen merely to authenticate some grand deception? Ask Sestus yourself. He will validate my story."

"Sestus?" he snarled. "I might have known he was behind this."

"Please don't blame him. He only tried to protect me."

Ginger eyed me suspiciously. "You are adept at lying but not so skilled at telling the truth."

"I am telling the truth. I only lied about who I am. I had no choice. Otherwise, you might have killed me."

"Would have," he corrected, then muttered in an undertone, "Still might."

I held my ground. "I gave you information. I supplied you with numerous opportunities to retaliate against my own flesh and blood. I've even turned on Valleri in order to further your oh-so-glorious revolt."

"For your own purposes. You used us an instrument to seize your throne. You used me."

"Not true. All I did, I did for the good of Thylana. I never ever used you."

"Really? Then why didn't you tell me who you were before you took me to bed? Why did you continue to lie and hide and deceive if not to seduce me into your camp?" His tone was more scathing than his words.

"Seduce you?" I cried in astonishment. "It was you who seduced me. I tried to tell you in this very room, but you wouldn't listen, too intent on manipulating me out of my clothes. So I kept my silence, afraid you might hate me, and you mistook that fear for reluctance because of what Averi had tried to do."

"Averi?" he snapped. "Who the hell is Averi?"

I sighed. "Averi was the flaw in Valleri's plan. He's the reason I am here in Idyll and not in Zigores, my original destination."

"Explain."

I tried. "Fearing my Teki powers had grown beyond his ability to control, Uncle stripped me of my rank and ordered me to marry a distant cousin, Lesuperis. When I rebelled, he imprisoned me. Valleri devised my escape. At the time, I did not suspect he schemed to take the throne for himself. I did not learn that until I went to Edenwood."

His brow narrowed. "Escape? Valleri plotted with Bertrand to kill you."

I shook my head. "No…you misunderstand. Valleri doesn't want me dead. He only wants me out of the way so he can usurp Uncle. He struck a deal with Averi, the officer who led the search party. I believe Val instructed him to retrieve my horse and personal effects, but to let me continue my flight. Then he substituted my body with that of some poor wench with which to prove to Uncle I was truly dead. But Valleri did all this without my knowledge because he knew I would never condone it."

"And Averi double-crossed Valleri?"

"Yes. He took the opportunity to avenge himself for what he considered a past humiliation. Instead of allowing me to flee, he set his dogs loose on me. If not for Sestus, I would be dead."

Unmoved by my horrific tale Ginger stared at me, his face a mask of stone. "So Valleri believes you're in Zigores, waiting to be recalled to your throne? He doesn't know you are wise to his scheme?"

"As far as I know."

He was silent a moment, still battling his rage. "I can sympathize with all you've been through, but your sad story doesn't change the fact you deceived me."

"I won't argue that. I agree I waited too long, but I intended to tell you that night Repachea died."

He tossed his head, agitated again. "You should have told me first."

"When? That day in Sestus's room when you laid your cards on the table, disappointed because you thought my uncle had deprived you of the pleasure of killing me? Or two nights ago, when you told Repachea your only regret is it was not your Crusader steel that had sent me to my death? When, Ginger?" I choked on the words. "When was the safest time to tell you?"

"There was no safe time," he admitted. "But don't hide behind your perception of me as some hideous monster. You know that isn't true. Nevertheless, you didn't confess. Even after our first tryst you didn't tell me. You didn't trust me."

I hurried to explain. "No, you're wrong. I trusted you with Ruvie. But the Gryphon Highlord…How could I? You had sworn to hunt me down, to execute me. Why? Because you condemn me for the atrocities of my uncle…and you can't forgive me for crushing you at Laurelac."

"You didn't crush me," he snarled.

"Well, I most certainly did. You had no—"

"Shut up," he hissed. "I could have wasted you and your entire Royal had that been my wont. I had the chance to take you out on that hilltop and be rid of you for good."

"Then why didn't you?"

He fixed me in a poisonous glare, but instead of answering me he swung away. His arm lashed out, and in his awesome rage, swept Repachea's statue off the table. It crashed to the floor, once more an unrecognizable pile of smashed porcelain.

I cringed, mindful of his powers, which could prove lethal if unleashed, and waited for his fury to subside. The ensuing silence was more terrifying than his wrath. With his back still turned to me, he said brokenly, "I really thought you were the one. The one to mend my broken heart. I bought your act, your whole thing. I really thought I was falling in love with you."

I swallowed over the lump in my throat, anguished by those words I had so ached to hear. "It was no act, Ginger. I never planned any of this. It just happened, which is precisely why I couldn't reveal the truth to you. I didn't want to risk losing you."

His shoulders began to shake and I thought he must weep. But a gust of icy mirth blew away that foolish assumption, and I knew he laughed. He spun around, a glint of madness in his eyes. "You are a greater fool than I am if you think such simple words can right this wrong, milady. Perhaps you were able to control Valleri with your sweet voice and pliant flesh. But in the end, your tame lover betrayed you and stole your crown. Your tender manipulations have gained you nothing, princess."

His mockery irked me. "Are you going to help me or not?"

"Help you?" His face contorted in fury, his mirth vanishing. In a stride he was before me. Crushing me to him, he yanked back my head, his dagger tip at my jugular.

"Help you?" he repeated in a quieter, deadlier tone. "I should help a hateful liar recapture her throne? I should give my sworn enemy what her heart most desires? Instead, give me one good reason why I should not kill you…Kathedra." He spat my name like the foulest of curses.

I tilted my head back further, thrusting my throat at him in foolhardy defiance. "I can't," I replied, forcing the quaver from my voice. "So go ahead. Kill me. If you won't help me, if you rescind your love for me forever, then do it-draw your blade across my neck. Because without you, I don't want to live."

He blinked, startled, I think, more by my bravado than the sincerity of my words. Nevertheless, he lowered the knife. "You're a brave woman to call my bluff. But truly you don't expect me to believe that? You go from man to man, from Valleri to me, seducing whomever you think better apt to secure your throne. You play the whore well."

His viciousness cut deep. "If that's what you think," I managed, fighting back tears, "then you flatter yourself most obscenely. It would have been easier and far less dangerous for me to seduce Repachea. Your ego is beyond belief, but I suppose with good reason. I have given up Thylana for you, even my life, if that is the price you extort. If I am a whore, then so, too, was Nelia. Will you let another woman die because she dared to love you?"

I regretted the barb the instant it flew from my lips. Although my anger at Ginger was justified, Nelia was innocent of any misdoing, and she did not deserve her memory to be so cruelly maligned. I saw the grief in his eyes, and the hurt my harsh words had caused, but it was too late to retrieve them.

Ginger's hand flashed up too fast to dodge or turn aside. The blow struck me hard, connecting with my cheek and snapping my head around. A galaxy of stars spun before my eyes.

I was stunned, dumbfounded. I truly couldn't believe he had slapped me. Me. The Gryphon Highlord. Throughout this hellish long ordeal men had perpetrated unforgivable acts against me. But no man had ever slapped me, as though I were a saucy child in need of a reprimand.

Ginger still gripped my arm, glaring down at me with eyes devoid of remorse. "Do not speak ill of the dead."

"Do not speak ill of the dead?" I cried. "How dare you rebuke me? You did not hesitate to slander and revile my name when you believed me dead."

I fought for control, my indignation refusing to be contained. The first stirrings of a mindspell formed, searching for an unguarded thought. Nothing would please me more than to allow my Teki powers free rein, but I could not risk appearing weak or undisciplined before Ginger. A fragment, however, slipped out, no doubt in response to the flush of humiliation that enflamed me. It flowed forth, surrounding us both in a shimmering wave of heat. The effect was like that of standing too close to a fire. To my surprise, Ginger neither recoiled nor released me, braver or angrier than I'd believed possible.

"Do you think I'm afraid of you?" he taunted. "You, whose fledgling powers are just a fraction of my own? Uncultivated and untamed they are confined to the boundaries of whatever puerile thought enslaves you at the moment. You have much to learn if you hope to achieve absolute control, to possess a power equal to mine."

His grip slackened, and laughing, he said, "You can't hurt me, princess. You don't possess the will."

I twisted away, angered by that truth I couldn't refute. "Don't mock me."

"Your wish is my command." Releasing me, he stepped aside.

"Is it?" I challenged. "I wish to thwart Valleri's plot and restore peace to Thylana. Will you help me?"

"Do I have a choice? It appears we want the same things, if for different reasons. The Crusaders are running out of options. Perhaps with you at our head we can force Valleri into capitulation. But first you must purge yourself of him completely. Otherwise, you'll be as useless to us as you were to the Royalists."

I raised a brow, startled by his favourable disposition toward me. Suspicious, I asked, "What if we succeed? What then? Will you permit me to take my rightful place as queen?"

"That's not for me to decide."

"But if it were?"

He didn't answer. That didn't seem very encouraging.

"What about your friends?"

"It's hard to say," he replied. "I will argue on your behalf for the privilege to reclaim your rank as the Gryphon Highlord, as well as the right to lead us against the Royalists. I will suggest that we announce your return from the grave and reveal Bertrand's failed plot to assassinate Thylana's future queen in the hopes it may incite mutiny in Castle Gryphon. I will also ask to serve as your lieutenant so I may be in a better position to protect you from any opposition. I will do all this because I believe it to be the best way for the Crusaders to accomplish their goals."

"Thank you," I murmured.

"Don't thank me yet. I can't promise my proposals will be accepted. The Gryphon Highlord was never beloved by the Crusaders. It will be difficult to convince them you can be trusted. Our only common ground is we share the same enemy."

Somehow I sensed there was a huge but in all this. "What will happen to Ruvie when the Gryphon Highlord is resurrected? Will you still love her?"

His face softened, and he reached out to stroke my hair. "I still love Ruvie. I always will. But I must say good-bye to her. I know you will argue and say that she and Kathedra are the same. Nevertheless, whenever I look at you, I will see only the Gryphon Highlord, and my eyes will not fall kindly upon her. I can't ignore your tainted blood, the same blood that flows through Bertrand. I can't forget we were once enemies."

Withdrawing his hand, he turned towards door. He paused there, a curl to his lip that might have been a smile. "Repachea should have lived to see this. How he would have laughed at his own arrogance to think he could instruct the Gryphon Highlord in swordplay."

Then he was gone.

So, it seemed I would get what I wanted. I would become the Gryphon Highlord again. I would be given the chance to confront Valleri and wreak my vengeance upon Uncle. My throne lay almost within my grasp. All that remained was the Crusaders' blessing. And I had no doubt I would receive it. Ginger can be most persuasive.

But what a price it had cost me. Was it worth the revulsion and anguish I had seen in Ginger's eyes? Would the reward of revenge take away this pain in my heart? Did I want to rule Thylana at any sacrifice just so I could sit on my throne alone?

There were too many thoughts to sort out, too many emotions tangled together, careening around inside me. My confusion prevented me from thinking straight. I was no longer sure of what I wanted. My desires and needs had changed drastically over these past few months.

I had caged my Teki powers too long. They cried out to be released. I stood in the middle of the room, staring at the door through which Ginger had walked out of my life, and let them come.

Anger, frustration, and grief poured out from me, unleashing the physical whirlwind of thought. At random, the maelstrom picked up books, cups, dishes, and the pieces of the broken statue, all spinning around me in a rush of colour and wind. Even the lamp was swept up into the turmoil, blazing a trail of fire like a meteor in the sky.

The wind roared in my ears, gathering speed. Everything hurtled past me too quick to see, a blur of light that crossed the entire spectrum. I heard the flutter of pages and the whistle of fragmented porcelain as they danced in chaotic flight. Fear, guilt and shame joined in, whipping the tumult into a dizzying frenzy.

The fierce gale lashed my hair, stung my face, but inside all was calm and lucid. Freed of my emotional demons, I soared like a bird as the tempest swirled around me. I let it build and rage until the intensity peaked, then faded and blew itself out. The maelstrom subsided, the flurry dissipated, depositing books, cutlery, everything, in a heap at my feet.

A flood of pride and accomplishment surged through me as I looked at the mess I'd made. While it might seem a childish tantrum or fanciful escape, it was a long overdue catharsis for me. The Teki equivalent of a primal battle cry.

Although their informants reported all was quiet in Castle Gryphon, the Crusaders figured that was sufficient cause in itself to worry that the Royalists were probably up to something. As a precaution, they decided to evacuate Idyll of everyone save its defenders. The idea of closing the teleportal was discussed and rejected. The Crusaders were sticking to their original plan, with a few minor adjustments, the details of which I was not privy.

As we awaited the arrival of Naren, I assisted in the evacuation of the sick and injured. I went about my duties with vim and vigour, sorting medical supplies, filling ration kits, and loading wagons, only because it took my mind off Ginger. He avoided me assiduously. On the few occasions we did come into contact with each other, he refused to speak to me. I was cut off, and it hurt.

Naren and Ragsey finally arrived three days later. My hour of judgment had come. The surviving outlaw leaders assembled in Sestus's quarters, with the exception of Gregaris, who was besieged in Pixley.

I wore my ill-fitting masculine clothes, having failed to establish some pretence of glamour worthy of a princess. I suspect it was a blessing there was no mirror handy for my inspection. The weight of a sword at my hip might have lent me some confidence, but of course that was out of the question. I did not even have the comfort of my dagger. Following Repachea's death, Castarr had ordered his room searched and confiscated the blade hidden its niche.

I donned my cloak and strode into the street, thinking how ironic that after all the lengths I'd gone to in order to conceal my identity, I might actually have difficulty convincing anyone I was truly the Gryphon Highlord. I had more to fear that the Citizens Risen Up to Stand Against a Dread and Errant Regency may execute me as an impostor. I hardly appeared to be a future queen, nor did I resemble the formidable Royalist general the Crusaders had come to respect. I looked and felt like the person I'd become-a fugitive clad in borrowed garments because she possessed none of her own, dependent on the goodwill of others. Insignificant and unremarkable. I had lived with the disguise so long it had grown comfortable, and I was reluctant to exchange it for my former role of commander extraordinaire.

But all that uncertainty and self-doubt fled when I opened Sestus's door and stepped into the lair of my enemies. My old strength and pride returned as my alter ego resurfaced. She was still there, buried but not forgotten, awaiting rebirth.

All faces turned to me. While Belvemar and another man, whom I presumed was Naren, seemed surprise, Castarr regarded me with open hostility. Scowling, he snarled, "Who the hell do you think you are, barging in here like this?"

His arrogance fired my courage. My stance defiant, my gaze unwavering, I replied, "I am the Gryphon Highlord."

Not only did I say it, I believed it as well.

Naren stared, his mouth agape, astonished beyond speech. Belvemar, too, was dumbstruck, although I think deep down he had suspected the truth.

Castarr, on the other hand, was infuriated. He leapt to his feet and dragged clear his sword. Refusing to be intimidated I stood my ground. After all, I had survived Ginger's rage, and he remained the only man I felt I had to fear.

"Don't do it," the mage warned.

"Traitor!" Castarr howled, rounding on him. "You knew who she was from the start."

"Sheathe your blade," Sestus replied. "She's no longer our enemy."

"No," Castarr hissed. "She's tricked you, seduced you." He made a sudden lunge towards me, but Ginger's sword scraped free of its scabbard, halting him in mid-stride.

"Don't take another step, Castarr." Then to me, the mage beckoned, "Kathedra, come."

I went, passing within three paces of Castarr. I almost hoped he would do something stupid. Let Ginger skewer him. But Castarr didn't try it.

Castarr rammed his blade into its sheathe with vicious force. "They've betrayed us," he growled at Naren.

"Don't be an ass," Sestus snapped. "We did no such thing. I wish you hadn't learned it like this but we had no choice."

Naren found his tongue. "I think you'd better explain, Sestus."

So Sestus did.

CHAPTER TWENTY-ONE

"You must be mad!" Castarr was apoplectic. His eyes bulged and the large vein at his temple throbbed.

"She should be executed," he ranted at Sestus, "or at least imprisoned, to be ransomed later should the need arise. But to allow her to lead us against Castle Gryphon is unthinkable. She'll betray us at her earliest opportunity. I'll never consent to it. Never!"

I shifted uneasily where I stood beside Ginger, to be protected by his formidable sword arm if necessary. Castarr himself did not worry me, but I feared the others might find a thread of logic in his heated words and side against me.

"Calm down, Castarr," Sestus groaned. "Nothing like that is going to happen. She switched loyalties long ago, when Bertrand first betrayed her. It's in her best interest to help us. Otherwise, she'll never gain the throne."

"Gain the throne?" Castarr thundered. "Not while I'm alive! You would readily give her what we have laboured so hard to keep out of her hands? You would let our sweat and blood all be for nothing?"

"The time has come to compromise." Although the mage spoke in a calm and controlled manner, his contempt for the man bled through. "We can use her to defeat Valleri. At least this way we can control the throne through her."

"How do you think to control her witch powers?" Castarr sneered. "It is she who controls you. I can understand how our naive and trusting Sestus could be so beguiled-he still sees a three-year-old child. But you, Ginger? Has it really been so long since you had a woman in your bed that you would throw away our lives for a piece of royal tail?"

Without warning Ginger lunged. Castarr met his charge. Fists flew. Poor Sestus took the mage's left hook in his jaw as he made the mistake of stepping between them. With Belvemar's assistance, he separated the grappling men and pushed them to opposite corners of the room.

"Knock it off!" he bellowed, wiping the blood from his split lip. "Has it come to this? Will we turn on ourselves? Why waste energy trying to kill one another when Valleri will gladly do it for us?"

Ginger swore and slumped into a chair, glaring daggers not at Castarr, but me. I could not blame him. Castarr had found us out. Ginger's credibility was ruined. No doubt his comrades would have trouble believing he acted without bias.

Castarr straightened his rumpled clothes. "What do you say, Naren?"

Cerebral, unflappable Naren, who had not said more than five words, who had not moved a muscle during the brawl, still leaned against the door, thoughtful and quiet. He was fair-skinned, slightly built-almost effeminate, but not quite. His pale yellow hair fell past his shoulders, swept away from his forehead. His angular face was naturally gaunt, dominated by large blue eyes that had seen far too much in their twenty-five years. Despite his frail appearance he was an able swordsman, a ruthless strategist, and a superb commander. Men followed Naren because they trusted in his abilities, and because they were mesmerized by the wealth of power emanating from that small, fragile-looking body.

Naren rubbed his eyes with slim, agile fingers, clearly having difficulty standing up. He had ridden non-stop for over thirty hours. Though hungry and tired, he had not allowed his own physical distress to interfere with duty. "I say," he began in a deceptively soft voice, "I have missed much." He spared a swift, curious glance at Ginger and me. "How can I say anything when I don't know half of what you do?"

"That's not an answer," Castarr insisted.

"I know, my friend. Bear with me. I have a lot to catch up on…and I mourn Repachea. It's hard for me to think straight."

Castarr rolled his eyes. "Belvemar? What do you have to say?"

Belvemar, too, had not spoken since my identity had been revealed, busy digesting the revelation. Suddenly, he smiled. "You won't like what I have to say, Castarr."

Castarr's brows narrowed. "Say it anyway."

Belvemar approached me, his hand on his sword hilt. "Princess," he intoned, "you saved my life, and by doing so have earned my eternal gratitude. I swear to you that my men and I will follow wherever you should lead. I will do everything within my power to help you gain your throne."

I swung on Sestus and Ginger. "What about you? Do I have your support?" Both men nodded, one more vigorously than the other. Though I knew full well what his answer would be, I asked Castarr, "Do you also support my quest for the throne?"

"I do not."

I looked at Naren, but he respectfully declined. "Not at this time, milady."

Castarr wore a triumphant grin. "So, all that remains is Gregaris. Maybe he will put an end to this charade."

"Gregaris is irrelevant," Sestus replied. "Nothing he can say or do from Pixley will affect us here."

"He still retains the privilege of casting his vote," Castarr argued. "This concerns him as much as it does us."

"You're absolutely right," Belvemar agreed. "Therefore I suggest you ride directly to Pixley, penetrate Fleurry's siege lines, and scale the city wall to retrieve that vote yourself."

That struck Ginger as wildly funny.

Castarr squared his shoulders, bristling at the mage's laughter. "Very well. I'll concede Gregaris is beyond reach, but Legora can vote in his stead."

Legora was the only Umagi in Idyll anywhere near Ginger's calibre. He had ridden in with Castarr. I presumed he had been responsible for one of the other teleportals, now deactivated until further notice.

"That's ridiculous," Sestus snorted. "Ginger alone speaks on behalf of the Umagi."

"Legora will not speak for the Umagi. He will speak for a Crusader captain."

"Legora will vote against you," Ginger whispered to me on the sly. "He'd sooner kill you than look at you. Umagi, Teki, woman, doesn't matter. You're a Royalist, first and foremost in his book."

"It's out of the question," Belvemar added. "If Legora is permitted to vote in Gregaris's stead, then Sestus should be permitted to vote on Repachea's behalf."

Ginger smiled. "I'll agree to that."

"Absolutely not!" Castarr shouted, his face purpling with rage. "Repachea is dead. We have no way of knowing how he may have voted."

"The same can be said of Gregaris," Belvemar retorted. "I'm merely pointing out the absurdity of your proposal."

"You'll be sorry," Castarr sneered, casting a baleful scowl around the room. "You'll regret you ever trusted her. You'll see how stupid you all are, when the next of us dies with a blade in his heart." Then whirling, he stormed out.

An awkward silence followed his exit.

Finally Sestus said, "Well, gentlemen. It appears that's all we can accomplish tonight." He walked over to Naren and put a hand on the younger man's shoulder. "You must be hungry, not to mention tired. Go and make yourself at home. We can discuss this further tomorrow."

Naren nodded. He spared me a last assessing glance, then dragged himself out the door.

"I'll go with him," Sestus said. "Belvemar, pick two of your best men. I want guards on Naren day and night. He's in no condition to fend off an assassin should one strike."

That left Ginger and me alone.

"Well, I guess that went as well as could be expected," I sighed, perching on the arm of Ginger's chair.

The mage didn't answer. He sat with his fingers steepled before his mouth, pensive gaze on the far wall. At last he said, "What did Belvemar mean by you saved his life?"

"I don't know."

"Yes, you do. You healed him somehow telekinetically, yet you weren't even aware you were doing it."

I hesitated, not knowing how to answer that. "Maybe, maybe not. I hoped he would get better, and he did. But you more than anyone else know that I am too ignorant, too unschooled, to perform such a feat simply by wanting it to happen. If you ask me, it was hope that healed him. Because I believed he would recover, he believed it too, when you and Biddy and Sestus believed he would die."

In my pride I thought I'd mastered my Teki powers. But I did not consider the subtler thoughts that run random, seemingly without purpose. Castarr is right to fear me. If I cannot trust myself to control my powers, no one else can either.

Ginger looked at me suddenly. "And were you casting hopeful thoughts in my direction, too?"

"What does that mean?"

"Until you appeared I never wanted to love anyone ever again. It's too painful. I was so consumed with hatred and rage and hurt there was no room to feel anything else. But your Teki powers kept Belvemar alive and brought me back to life in a different way. They touched everyone you came in contact with, even Biddy and Sestus, without your awareness." He paused, lost in his musings, then wondered aloud, "Can you win a war with wishful thinking, Kathedra?"

I shook my head, pricked by a twinge of sadness. "No. But maybe you can end one with hope."

Ginger stared at me a long moment. "I know that in time," he said, soft venom in his voice, "my anger at you will dissolve and I will forgive your deceit, if only because you won't be able to stifle thoughts of me."

I might have taken exception to his arrogance if he had not been right. As it was, I was simply weary of arguing. "If you would prefer to wallow in misery and guilt, that is your choice. That is the crux of it, isn't it? You have to want the same thought as I do. But you are so comfortable with anger and sorrow that you don't want to feel anything else."

I turned to leave, his bitterness too much to bear, but he rose from his chair and caught my hand. "Don't you understand? I do want this. I want to feel again. That's why when we met on that hilltop in Laurelac I hesitated to kill you. You were my sworn enemy, and yet you were the one person capable of reaching me. In that one instance of weakness, I felt the first faint stirrings of something I hadn't felt since Nelia died, since I joined the Crusaders. Hope. I decided then, as long as that hope remained, I couldn't destroy you."

Swallowing my dread, I whispered, "Do you regret that decision?"

"No. From that very first moment I saw you in Sestus's room, I knew there was something special about you. I knew you would somehow touch me. I felt it here." He tapped his shirt where his heart should lie. "It was the same feeling I had in Laurelac."

"Then…you suspected all along?"

"I suppose, in some part of me. I just didn't examine it closer because I didn't want to believe it might be true. You were right to hide yourself from me. My fury and hatred ran so deep they had to be purged before I could ever love you."

"So I did not deceive you," I said. "You deceived yourself."

Ginger let my hand slide from his. As our fingers fell apart so, too, did something else. "It doesn't mean you are any less to blame. It doesn't make it easier to forgive you."

Ginger did not have to say it. I knew this was good-bye for us. "Come," he said. "I'll show you back to your quarters."

The mage headed out first and I followed, not even aware of where he led. It was good to leave that stuffy room and breathe the fresh night air, to walk the empty byways of Idyll, even if I sensed that my companion wished to be anywhere but with me. "Do you think Castarr and Naren will come around?" I asked.

Ginger's stride stiffened almost imperceptibly, though I did not think it so offensive a question. "Naren will, once given the chance to debate our options. Castarr will need to be…persuaded." His tone was curt, clipped. He did not want to talk about it.

"How will you persuade him?"

"That's none of your concern. I assure you, you need not fear any harm at his hands. Castarr is all bluster and bravado. He's really a coward at heart."

Yes, well I had my suspicions.

I stumbled over a rock, a chunk of rubble actually. Since fragments of broken stone didn't normally litter the way to my quarters I was puzzled for a moment, until I realized the route we took was not towards my quarters, but towards the heart of the sundered keep. Ginger snatched my elbow, preventing a fall, and guided me over the lip of a crumbled wall. "Do you know where we are?"

Wary now, I surveyed the ruins sprawled before me, the wreckage illuminated by a wash of moonglow and starlight pouring through holes and cracks and a vast expanse of open sky. Sadness and a sense of isolation haunted the shattered walls. This was a place the Crusaders took great pains to avoid. A tingle of apprehension raced the length of my spine. "No."

"Below us is the kitchen." He made a vague gesture. "Over there is what's left of the pantry. And beside it, beneath that collapsed archway, is the spot where your cousin died."

I whirled on him, my throat clogged with anger and suppressed grief. "Why did you bring me here?"

"Because there are ghosts here, princess. Ghosts that have followed Bertrand all the way to Idyll." Under my glare, he dropped to his haunches and slid over the wall, turning to extend his hand. "And because I thought you should see it."

Ignoring his offer of help, I started to clamber over the rock myself but

Ginger lifted me by the waist and set me down beside him. Letting his hands linger, he looked down at me, the barest hint of a smile teasing his lips. "You do look like him, you know. Along the jaw line. And the cornflower blue eyes. Especially with your hair cut so short. I see all that now, clear as a bell, whereas I was blind before. I miss Ivor as I would miss a brother. As children we were inseparable. Him. Me."

"And Valleri."

He nodded, his lips pressed tightly together as he struggled with visions of yesterday. I had guessed at that truth some time ago, and he did not seem surprised. The moonlight limning his face lent him a vulnerable quality, revealing every emotion, stripping his soul bare. I reached to touch his cheek, to smooth away the sorrow, but he wouldn't allow it. He withdrew, retreating once more into the shadows, where he was most comfortable.

"We were always together. Shouting. Laughing. Running. Friends forever, we thought. But one is long dead. The other wants to kill me. And with each day that passes, he gives me more reason to want to kill him too."

"Why? Because he is a Royalist and you are a Crusader?"

Head tilted, he gave me a sidelong glance. "How well do you think you know Valleri? I'll wager you don't know him at all. He's a man filled with hate and guilt and anger. Those things can make one unpredictable. Dangerous. Even a bit mad."

"Then I guess I know him about as well as I know you."

His eyes narrowed at that little dig. "I'm nothing like the monster that Valleri has become."

"Well, I'm guessing there's a reason for that. A reason that starts here, in this place. What happened, Ginger, on that day so long ago?"

"That's for Valleri to tell you, princess. Not me."

"Then I see no reason for me to remain." I turned to scrabble back over the wall. I heard the mage clawing his way up behind me. "And stop calling me princess."

"Why not? It's your title, isn't it?"

"I think we have gone beyond the need for such formality," I replied in my driest tone.

"What should I call you then? Ruvie? Kathedra?" He was beside me now, matching my stride as I marched towards my quarters, which I couldn't reach quick enough. "Or will you pick something new? Perhaps Valleri has a pet name for you of which you're especially fond."

"Jealousy does not become you."

"I think, however, Kathedra suits you best. The schemer. The manipulator. The traitor. The liar."

"Stop right there." We had reached the steps to my quarters. I spun, finding him so close on my heels my nose brushed his leather jerkin. I had to shove him away just to meet his gaze. "You are like a wounded dog, lashing out at anyone who comes too close. You can't heal, Ginger, until you let go of the pain."

"Pain?" A howl of laughter, ringing of spite and mockery, pealed out. "What do you know about my pain?"

"I know that whatever is between you and Valleri has nothing to do with me. Now, please go. It hurts me just to look at you."

I closed the door on him, though he'd made no move to leave. But the wooden panel was no barrier against the words he spoke next.

"Not then, Kathedra. But it does now."

CHAPTER TWENTY-TWO

Two days later I awoke with a start at a commotion outside my quarters. Slipping my cloak around my flimsy shift, I ran to the door and flung it wide to see a gang of Crusaders had gathered in the entrance to the infirmary. Castarr and Sestus were engaged in heated debate while Belvemar strove to calm them down. Naren and Ginger looked on impassively.

"You can't just barge in there!" Sestus yelled. "You must reconsider. What you are doing is wrong."

"There is nothing to reconsider," Castarr shot back. "If you don't do something about her right now, Naren and I will pull out of Idyll."

I assumed I was the topic of the discussion. From the doorway, I asked, "What's going on?"

Everyone's attention veered my way. Castarr pointed an accusing finger. "Look! She has the impertinence to pretend she doesn't know what happened."

"That's probably because I don't."

He stalked across the laneway, grim determination in his face. I stepped out to meet him. He could not intimidate me.

The others followed, but Sestus caught up to him first and grabbed his arm. "Castarr, you're behaving irrationally. You know damned well she had no part in Legora's death."

"Legora is dead?" I gasped. Although Ginger had said Legora was a threat to me, I could not rejoice in his death.

"Yes," Sestus snapped. "Strangled in his sleep last night. We found diamond dust beneath his bunk."

Castarr jerked his arm free, to rant at no one in particular, "Everything's ruined! Ginger is the only Umagi left capable of maintaining the teleportals, and he can't possibly operate them all at once."

"I think that's the general idea," Naren remarked. "It's fortunate Ginger wasn't here last night or he might be dead as well."

That surprised me. I had not known Ginger had left Idyll. "Where were you?" I asked.

"Don't tell her anything," Castarr sneered. "She can't be trusted."

"You don't seriously suspect Kathedra murdered Legora?" Belvemar snorted. "That's preposterous. She's physically incapable of strangling a man with her bare hands, even with magebane."

"Search her quarters, then. Something just might turn up. And what about the disaster at Killary? I bet she's responsible for that, too. The Royalists knew the precise location of that teleportal."

"Repachea didn't disclose that information to me," I replied, struggling to remain calm. “And even if he had, how exactly would I get that information to the Royalists? Telepathy? I’m not free to come and go from Idyll as I please.”

But Castarr didn’t care much for logic. He whirled again on Sestus. “I want her locked up. If you won’t do it for our own protection, then do it for hers.”

“Are you threatening me?” I almost laughed at the absurdity. “I warn you, I have the power to defend myself.” Though that remark in itself could be construed as a threat, my indignation would not be contained. I began to wonder half seriously whether Castarr had murdered Legora himself simply to implicate me, so virile is his hatred.

Castarr blustered on, but I sensed his hidden fear. “If you call down your witch powers upon me you will only prove my point. Perhaps if you exercised some benevolence it would work in your favour. If you are truly all you purport to be, then it can do no harm.”

He had ingeniously backed me into a corner.

“Either she is put under lock and key, or Naren and I walk.”

“Don’t do it, Sestus,” Belvemar urged. “You know he’s wrong. Call his bluff.”

Sestus was torn, unwilling to risk Castarr’s bluff, yet unwilling to support the belief I may be untrustworthy. He looked to Naren, who had not openly denounced me, but on the other hand, had not contradicted Castarr. The young commander made no attempt to sway Sestus’s decision either way, his expression bland and unreadable. If I had to make the choice, I would not take the chance he was bluffing.

“Do as he says.”

Sestus turned to the mage, his eyes wide in dismay. “Ginger…not you?”

“Just do it, Sestus.”

Now everyone stared at the mage, including me. “Don’t let them coerce you this way, Ginger,” Belvemar gasped.

“Let’s not argue it further, gentlemen. Sestus, escort the princess back to her quarters.”

Castarr beamed in triumph. “You see, Highness? Not even your own lover trusts you.”

There was no crueller taunt he could have made, the gloating pig. Even Naren had the decency to look ashamed by their petty victory. He would not look at me directly.

Betrayed again by someone I loved.

Sestus approached me, sheepish. “I’m sorry I must do this, Kathedra.” He gestured in the direction of my quarters.

“I understand, Sestus. It’s only your duty.”

I could scarcely believe Ginger would go back on his word. Was this his idea of revenge? Punishment?

As I turned to go I glanced at the mage, hoping to see some hint of remorse in him, yet knowing I wouldn’t. It seemed he stared straight through me, his eyes penetrating like steel. Though his face was set in its customary mask of stone, he could not disguise the anger inside him. He showed no sign of regret, or the love we had shared so briefly. There was no forgiveness in him. Mercy and compassion are not in his vocabulary.

After a thorough but fruitless search of the place, Sestus installed me in my quarters and placed me under house arrest. I don't know what Castarr had hoped to find unless it was his common sense. Two armed guards stood vigil beyond the door, with orders to subdue me any way possible if I tried to escape.

As my jailer Sestus was my only visitor. He brought my meals but did not loiter, always anxious to be gone. He was ashamed of himself, of Ginger, of them all. He avoided all eye contact and conversation. When I questioned him about their grand strategy he sidestepped me with the excuse we were forbidden to discuss such things. That was not the Sestus I knew, the Sestus who had plotted so readily with me to conceal my identity and undermine his fellows.

Something fishy was up. No doubt Ginger had some cockamamie scheme that I was to remain ignorant about until it was too late. He was no different than Valleri. I was a pawn here just as I had been in Castle Gryphon, to be manipulated for someone else's benefit. And again, I was a prisoner.

How long was my incarceration to last? How did the Crusaders plan to defeat Valleri now that they had declined to allow me to resume my role as Gryphon Highlord? Or was I still to be incorporated into their master plan, without my knowledge or consent?

What did it matter? Truly, I couldn't care less about the damned revolt, whether who won or lost, if Valleri was crowned king or that dipshit Castarr. Such things mattered little to me now that Ginger had condemned me, now that he had made it clear how little I meant to him.

Maybe it was simply my just desserts. If I could so easily betray Valleri, then why should I be surprised by Ginger's betrayal? Yet another thought to ponder, to occupy my hours of confinement.

Nevertheless, I clung to the hope that deep down in some small part of him, Ginger still loved me, still believed in me.

On the third day of my captivity, Ginger broke his silence. He stood in the doorway and scrutinized me with those shrewd mage eyes. Meeting their weighty gaze, I tried to manage a defiance but I'm afraid he saw only my despair.

Sombre, almost contrite, he said, "I did not mean to hurt you."

And that's supposed to make it all better?

"Let me explain."

I tried to block him out, but the best I could do was ignore him. Although I had extended no invitation he came inside. "You can't shut me out," he continued. "I know you can hear me."

Though I said nothing, he knew exactly what I was thinking. "I did not betray you."

That angered me into speech. "Don't lie to me," I hissed. I knew I had to control my powers if I wanted to win his trust, but it was an impossible task for me at the moment. Again I tried to close my mind to him, but managed only to slam shut the door.

Ginger did not even flinch. "I know how it must seem to you, but believe me, I had no choice. If we had not given in to Castarr's ridiculous demand, he and Naren would have walked out on us. I had to force Sestus's hand. Can't you understand that?"

In all honesty I could. But it didn't lessen the indignation of being imprisoned like a criminal. "I understand you had a decision to make," I sniffed, crossing my arms. "You chose to dishonour me just to satisfy that swine Castarr."

"I'm sorry you see it that way. Castarr we can do without. In fact, we'd probably be better off had he left. But we need Naren. We need his guile and skill if it comes to a confrontation with Valleri. But most of all, we need to hold the organization together, to present a united front. We can accomplish nothing divided."

My resentment subsided. He had done what he had to do, what was necessary. Devious and ruthless like I could never be. What hurt most was his personal rejection of me. Truth was, I would have gladly suffered this indignity if only I could be certain there was still room in his small, hard heart for me.

"We need you," he added. "The people of Thylana won't want some brash usurper on the throne when they can have you, the rightful heir. Granted, Valleri looks more appealing than Bertrand, but the Princess Kathedra has always been their first choice. Likewise the Crusaders need you, the real Gryphon Highlord, to lead us against Valleri. He will not go without a fight. You must give us strength and leadership. It's a task you do very well."

I gave him a sharp look, trying to gauge his sincerity. "Now you think I should help you, when you are so reluctant to help me? Why, I've been treated abominably! I've been called a lying, treacherous whore. Why should I help you do anything?"

"If you want your throne, you will help. Valleri is your sole obstacle now. You need us to wrest it from him."

Of course when put like that, I had no choice. I lowered my arms, obedient to his will. "Then do me one favour. Shut down your remaining teleportal. If there's a key out there floating around without a minder, you don't want it finding its way into the hands of the Royalists." No one had said either way to me whether or not Repachea's key was missing, but I assumed it was.

"We discussed the matter and decided to keep the teleportal operational. If I close it, it's closed for good. I will be unable to regenerate it on my own. I have no teleportation abilities. That was Legora's specialty. I merely feed it energy when it grows depleted."

"Then you take a huge risk."

"There can be no help for it. We voted unanimously to proceed with our plans. Time is running out for the Crusaders. It's now or never."

It seemed that a plague of illogic had descended upon Idyll, devouring rational thought. Maybe illogic wasn't wholly to blame. Desperation was an element in this, too.

Ginger took a wary step towards me, perhaps fearful of doing or saying something that may drive me further from his purpose. I noticed he held a small, shiny object in his hand. "Here," he said, passing it to me.

I accepted the offering: a silver ring, like a wedding band, delicately scrolled. My heart fluttered. Could it truly be what I thought?

Ginger smiled weakly. "Put it on."

I shuddered all over with delight and slipped it onto the fourth finger of my right hand-the one that girls in Thylana reserve for tokens of love and promise. My first. Women place high store in such things. Even those who lead great armies.

I held it to the light and admired its simple yet elegant beauty. It was a perfect fit! I whirled, overcome with joy, prepared to throw my arms around him.

Then Ginger said a strange thing. "Take it off."

"Take it off?" I echoed. "But, why?"

"Just do it." There was a mournful quality to his voice, a harsh glint in his eyes.

Though disappointed, I obeyed...but the ring refused to budge. How could this be? It had slid so easily over my knuckle. Frustrated, I tugged with all my might.

"Stop it," Ginger said. "You're going to hurt yourself."

"What are you talking about?" I snapped. "What's wrong with this stupid thing? It's like...melded to my finger." I looked up, straight into his steely mage eyes. Then I understood. Silently, I cursed myself for being so ignorant in the ways of magic, for being naive enough to believe he still loved me, if ever he had.

"It won't come off, short of cutting it off-your finger, I mean. If you choose that remedy, I recommend you get a good surgeon."

"You bastard," I whispered.

He was calm. "I'm sorry I had to deceive you this way. The ring is ensorcelled with a spell that will neutralize your Teki powers. You will not be able to manifest your thoughts into anything more substantial than tears. It's a simple binding, however time consuming. It's less detrimental to the body than your tonic and there are no side effects. See how short-sighted Bertrand was to banish the Umagi? Any common hearthmage could have done it."

"You…bastard!" I screamed, at a loss for a more suitable word. I leapt at him, my fist poised to strike.

He grabbed my wrists and held me firm. "I had no choice!" he yelled back. "Do you think I enjoy this? Do you think I want to see you leashed like a dog or caged like a wild beast? But it was the only way Castarr and Naren would agree to our terms. It's only temporary, until they decide whether or not to trust you, until the assassin is caught."

I writhed free of him and spun away to the other side of the room, turning my face so he would not see my tears. So this explained his absence from Idyll, his refusal to discuss how he planned to convince Castarr to accept me as the Gryphon Highlord. The devious, heartless snake!

His impatient sigh drifted over me. "I'm Umagi too, remember? I would hate anyone who attempted to control my powers in this fashion. But I did argue it. I tried to explain that your fledgling powers are no threat to anyone. They wouldn't listen. I had no choice. Please believe me. This isn't personal."

Rage scythed through me, he was so goddamned smug. I had an unkind thought…and was grateful it proved impotent. "Does that mean you don't trust me either?"

"I trust you to do everything necessary to help us if it means you'll wear the crown," he replied carefully.

"Well I won't help you," I declared. "Rot the lot of you. I'd rather relinquish my throne entirely than become a Crusader puppet."

"I'm afraid you have no choice, unless you want to spend the rest of your life like this, your powers fettered, your will restrained by mine."

It would be a fate worse than death, bound forever like a hound on a chain to the wily, perfidious mage. "I hate you."

"I don't doubt that. You trusted me and I was compelled to betray you. I know well the bitter sting of treachery."

He just had to rub my nose in it.

"You have the title of Gryphon Highlord if you want it."

"No, I don't want it," I snarled. "Valleri is the Gryphon Highlord. I am the Princess Kathedra."

"Suit yourself. You are no longer under house arrest."

"Instead I am your prisoner?"

"Don't think of it as such. I don't consider myself your captor."

I laughed, though my tears only flowed faster. "You must find it amusing how you could so easily trick me, even flattering how I loved you so blindly."

"Believe me," he murmured. "This is the hardest thing I've ever had to do."

Perhaps. But he did it so effortlessly. "How is the spell broken?"

"By removing the ring. And I'm the only person who can do that."

"What if something should happen to you?"

He shrugged. "Let's just hope it doesn't."

I was incredulous that he could so carelessly toy with my life. I was not a person to him, merely an instrument to be used and discarded at will. I stared at him, filled with a strange mixture of anger and anguish. "You are no better than Valleri."

Somehow my remark managed to prick him. I saw the dismay plain in his eyes. As he headed for the door he said, "I hope one day you can forgive me. When this is all over, and you sit on your throne, I hope you'll understand."

I flung a curse at his departing back, where it bounced harmlessly off those broad shoulders.

I tried to pull the ring from my finger, attempting in vain to summon my Teki powers. I clawed until I drew blood, until my finger had swollen twice its size, which only served to adhere it tighter to my flesh. I even chipped a tooth in a foolish effort to gnaw it off.

Throughout the long night I wept tears of rage. Ginger, Sestus, Castarr, all of them were no better than Uncle to hold me prisoner, my powers in thrall. The mage was mistaken if he thought I would ever forgive him.

CHAPTER TWENTY-THREE

The next day I strutted around Idyll in my official role as the Princess Kathedra. To my amazement no one objected at my pomposity to stroll through camp like a warrior queen surveying her troops. Instead I was greeted with all the courtesy due a royal personage. Wherever I went, outlaw freedom fighters dropped to their knees, hailing me with 'Your Highness' and oaths of allegiance. Although I wore no elegant gown, no uniform and sword, I tried to muster an appearance of dignity and regal splendour for my supporters. I waved and smiled, pausing often to praise their efforts or simply chat.

As for the Crusader officers, I had a mental grudge-list. Almost every one was on it. Only Belvemar was exempt, and Sestus borderline. I considered Belvemar my sole ally, since he alone had the gumption to defy his treacherous cohorts by defending my honour.

I plied the former mercenary with questions, none of which he could answer. He knew only that Ginger plotted to hatch some grand counterattack against Valleri. The mage had instructed his spies in Castle Gryphon to plant the rumour the Princess Kathedra was alive and well in Crusader territory, having survived an assassination attempt by the Regent, and now prepared to denounce Valleri as a usurper/traitor. Such a juicy tidbit would elicit dissent and confusion within Gryphon's Royals.

Poking around the dungeon did me little good, except to annoy Sestus. Not that he was doing much these days. He spent hours at the worktable, flipping idly through daily reports or building a house of cards in mid-air, the Umagi equivalent of doodling. If he knew what magic tricks Ginger had up his sleeve, he refused to tell. One thing I knew with certainty; whatever the mage had in store for Valleri it would involve me. I'm sure he could manipulate my powers through his sorcerous link to me: the ring. Exactly how he would employ them remained a mystery.

Only Ragsey seemed sympathetic to my plight. We sparred occasionally on the practice field, where he listened and offered his commiseration as I aired my grievances. His skill with the sword was improving, but he had a tendency to lower his guard, a failing for which Valleri had often chided me.

On this particular day, I tapped his ribs as a gentle reminder instead of upending him in the turf as Repachea might have done. "Up, Ragsey. Keep your arm up. C'mon, let's take a break."

We removed ourselves to a stump, which had once been a magnificent oak tree in Idyll's courtyard, to sip water from our flasks. In a matter-of-fact tone, I asked, "What do you know of Castarr?"

He shrugged. "About as much as you do, I'm afraid."

"Do you think he might have killed Repachea?"

"Anything's possible, I guess. Castarr doesn't really like anybody. But not even Ginger kills just because he dislikes a person. If that were the case, he would have planted Castarr in the dirt long ago."

"Hmm, but Castarr might have killed Repachea for the passkey. Maybe to give it to Valleri. Maybe Val doesn't want to destroy the teleportals so much as he wants to use them to lead an pre-emptive strike against the Crusaders."

"All I know is that Repachea's key is missing. But that doesn't necessarily mean it was stolen. Only that no one can find it. But why do you suspect Castarr?"

"For one thing he has no love for the Umagi, Ginger especially. The story goes that he had a falling out with my Uncle, and in a moment of rashness joined the Crusaders to get even. Perhaps he's had a change of heart. Or he hopes that by betraying the Crusaders to the Royalists, he will earn his way back into Uncle's good graces."

Ragsey mulled it over, eyes intent on his fingers where they toyed with the pommel of his sword. After a moment he tipped back his head, and squinted in the bright sunshine. "I see your point. Ginger's never trusted him from the start. Have you told anyone else your suspicions?"

"Like who? No one will listen to me."

"Belvemar might make a good ally. Who better? After all, the assassin had tried to kill him, too. I bet he'd even insist on a search of Castarr's quarters."

"Yes, you could be right." I took a sip from my flask, then traded it for my sword. "Let's get back at it. I hope you're not going easy on me because of who I am," I teased.

Ragsey got to his feet, brandished his sword with a winsome grin. "No, Highness. I'm going easy on you because I am truly an awful swordsman."

"Belvemar, this way," I hissed. "Hurry."

I crouched in the lee of the stables, waiting for the commander to catch up. He materialized at my elbow, huffing a little and grumbling a lot. "I don't see why we have to do this now, skulking about in the shadows in the middle of the night."

"Because if we skulk about in broad daylight somebody is bound to see us. Now pay attention." I patted his bearded cheek and pulled his hood lower over his face. "Do you remember what we're looking for?"

"A bottle of diamond dust, a vial of poison woodroot, and maybe a lock pick. By damn, if that no-good lump of toadshit is the bastard who put rat poison in my wine I'll strip him naked and put him up on a spire for the crows to take their sport with!"

"Shh! Someone might hear. Are you ready?"

At his nod I crept forward, motioning him to follow me.

Why exactly was I out, sneaking like a thief through the broken corpse of Idyll with a grumpy ex-merc captain at my back? My earlier conversation with Ragsey had given me an idea. It made no sense to wait for the Crusader masterminds to get around to searching Castarr's quarters when I could do it myself. Better yet, why not bring Belvemar with me? Then, we could take our evidence and make our accusation together. When Castarr's duplicity was revealed the Crusaders would see how wrong they had been about me and absolve me of all suspicion of treachery. Ginger would then be forced to restore my powers.

Before setting off on our mission, however, I had checked the duty roster and scout reports. At a glance, I knew the location of each Crusader patrol and the time that various couriers had reported in or out of camp. In order to keep the peace, Naren had suggested that Castarr take a perimeter check. Restless and mopish, Castarr had jumped at the idea. He was scheduled to return in the morning. If there was any evidence to be collected, it had to be done tonight. Already misty, predawn light was stealing across the sky.

Situated downwind from the stables Castarr's quarters, assigned by Ginger, were dark and quiet. I tried the door. It slid open with nary a creak. I exhaled a sigh of relief, for I wasn't at all certain I could jimmy the latch with his dagger, though I might have given Belvemar that impression. It had taken some time to convince the commander of my plan and I didn't need him having second thoughts at the last moment.

Duck-walking, we stole inside and paused to get our bearings. Camp cot to the left, trunk at its foot. Table and two chairs to the right. Man crouching with sack directly ahead. Oh, bloody hell.

I froze, there in mid-squat, startled and perplexed. The evidence was there all right, sitting on the floor beside the sack: one lock pick, the vial of poison that Biddy had reported missing from the infirmary, and a tin box such as the kind purchased from disreputable apothecaries known to sell diamond dust.

Despite the man's dark clothing and the gloom, I recognized him, squatting there with sack in hand and staring at me with an expression I expect was similar to my own. He was not Castarr. My perplexity stemmed not from the who or what, but why. Why was he removing the evidence? Surely, not to protect Castarr.

Then the revelation struck me like one of my own thunderbolts. He was not removing evidence. He was planting it.

I felt a nudge in my back as Belvemar bumped into me, unaware I had stopped. "Kathedra, what's-?"

But he didn't get to finish the thought, as the man suddenly sprang, bowling me into the captain and sending us sprawling. I crashed into a wall headfirst. Pain lanced through my temple, stole my breath. Feebly, I struggled to reach something I could use as a weapon but my fingers refused to respond. Next I heard a dull thud and Belvemar's soft grunt as something heavy struck him, repeatedly it seemed, before a second blow to my head rendered me unconscious.

I awoke somewhere cold and damp, unable to move my arms, hanging somehow in mid-air. My skull throbbed like a bellows in Hell's own forge. Pain across my shoulders and a tightness at my wrists told me my hands were bound with rope. Wary, I opened my eyes and squinted into the murk, surprised to find my tethered wrists looped over a hook suspended from the ceiling. Next a glaring torch was thrust before my face as someone lifted me down. But my legs wouldn't hold me and I slid to the floor of the cave, agony shooting through my arms.

"You're too clever for your own good, Highness," a familiar voice sneered, dragging me upright.

"Ragsey?" My wits were as fuzzy as my vision. With swift violence, it all came tumbling back. "Belvemar?" I asked in panic.

"Don't worry about him. He's a tough old fart to kill. I should know. I've tried twice."

I snatched myself away, fought for balance. "Where are we?" I spat.

Ragsey set the torch in a crevice, pulled a dagger from his belt. "On a ridge not far from Idyll." His smile was distinctly unpleasant.

Glancing around the cave, I noticed a couple of things straight off. First, the shaft of daylight just beyond his shoulder and the crates of supplies lining one wall. He was obviously prepared to stay a while. "Why did you bring me here? Do you plan to ransom me to the highest bidder?"

"You flatter yourself, but not without reason." His eyes roamed obscenely over me. "Oh, you are a beguiling temptress. You need only wrap your legs around a man to get what you want. You did it to Valleri and now you've done it to Ginger."

I stared at him, affronted by his scathing gaze. He was not the same man I had met in the infirmary on that long ago day, not the cheerful, charming fellow who had pretended to be my friend. I did not want to believe he was an informant or an assassin. Not that it didn't make sense. As a courier, he came and went from Idyll as he saw fit, ferrying confidential communiqués from one Crusader outpost to another, or transferring them directly into the hands of Gryphon's agents, whichever the case may be. He'd even told me himself that he had been with Ginger almost since the beginning. By earning Ginger's trust, he had also won the trust of the remaining outlaw leaders, if only by association.

"I really would like to believe that you were implicating Castarr to protect me," I managed.

"Sorry, no. I was implicating Castarr to protect myself. And Valleri."

Though I was pretty sure I didn't want to hear the rest of it I asked anyway. "So why don't you enlighten me."

"Very well." He sighed, as if bored. "When Bertrand discovered your powers had grown beyond his control he approached Valleri with a proposition. 'Distract Kathedra. Weaken her will. Make her forget the revolt and the throne. The less use she has for her Teki powers, the feebler they will grow.' In exchange, Bertrand promised him your command."

I felt the blood drain from my face. "I don't believe it."

Although Sestus and Ginger had told me the exact same thing, I refused to believe Valleri had ever conspired with Uncle. Valleri wanted my command and my throne, yes. But it is inconceivable he would stoop so low as to deal with my uncle, a man he hated beyond all reason.

"It's true," Ragsey assured me. "Valleri accepted Bertrand's offer because he found it a perfect opportunity to double-cross him. Valleri tried on numerous occasions to convince you that Bertrand plotted against you, to persuade you to renounce the Regent. But you refused to listen, to act. So when Bertrand retired you and announced your engagement to Lesuperis, Valleri recruited help."

"Averi and Serasteffan," I said.

"Yes. Two of the biggest lowlifes that ever crawled out from under a rock. A decision he's come to regret. Their hunger for wealth and lust for prestige is boundless. They make their outrageous demands and Valleri must yield or brave their threats to reveal his secrets. In order to free himself of your restraints he thought to tuck you away in Zigores. His plan might have worked if he had not placed his trust in that weakling Averi."

"You know about Averi?"

"Of course. Valleri explained to me the elaborate escape he'd devised for you. He believes Averi followed his instructions admirably. The woman whom Valleri murdered to serve as your corpse was an Umagi sympathizer captured at Bolta."

Dagger in hand Ragsey stepped towards me, barring the cave mouth. Still unsure of his motives, I backed away. "So you work for Val?"

"Isn't it obvious? Valleri planted me when the first rumblings of a revolt broke out. Even so early in the game, he recognized an opportunity for self gain. I hooked up with Ginger shortly after Dundurn. He brought me with him to Idyll. Next thing I know you're here, and I realized Valleri's plan had gone awry. When I told him you'd blundered into Sestus, Valleri thought you'd be safe in Idyll under his protection. It then became my job to chaperone you. But I failed. Miserably, it seems."

"Why are you covering for Averi? Why didn't you tell Valleri the truth?" That didn't make sense to me.

"Because Averi's paying me not to tell him." He grinned, flipped the dagger end over end in his palm. "Everything was running smoothly too, until Ginger decided to take you to Edenwood with us."

"That was a ruse designed to lure Ginger to his death, wasn't it? He was never supposed to reach Edenwood."

"My mission was to spy on the Crusaders and assassinate their leaders at the appropriate time. The Shouda were just a horrible coincidence. Truly," he added sheepishly, "I am petrified of dogs. Valleri told me to remove Ginger after Urharde had departed the warehouse. But even after I'd planted the magebane, Ginger managed to escape."

"You fool," I gasped. "Had I been captured, Fleurry would have been alerted to Val's deceit."

"And that would matter to me how? Fleurry would have marched you back to Gryphon, thus revealing Valleri's grand deception and signing his execution. Fleurry would have rewarded me generously for bringing him Ginger and the Princess Kathedra. So generously in fact, I might even now be basking in the sun on a faraway tropical isle. It was a win-win situation."

Maybe for him. My head spun with all I had just learned. I needed to stall, needed time to think of a way to escape. But Ragsey just kept on talking.

"You should be thanking me, Highness. If you had only waited another five minutes before you went poking around Castarr's quarters, I'd have been out of there and you'd be dead or captured. I was going to dispose of the evidence safely, but you gave me the idea to implicate Castarr instead."

Yes, not one of my more brilliants schemes. I lifted my chin, defiant. "I won't cooperate with you or Valleri. I will fight you all the way back to him."

"Too late. He's already here."

A strange mixture of fear and anticipation gripped me at that revelation, laced with overtones of suspicion. "How can that be?"

"Valleri could have put an end to the Crusaders long ago. He needed only to attack Idyll with every man at his disposal, then every last Crusader of note would have fallen beneath his steel. But he hesitated, fearing for your safety. Only when I informed him that you had forsaken him in favour of your outlaw friends did he decide to act. He could not allow it to be revealed you were alive, else Bertrand would have thrown him in the dungeon alongside Arial. As of dawn, Valleri was free to march on Idyll with a fury belittling that unleashed upon Killary."

His lips parted in a wicked grin. "The massacre has already begun."

I shook my head, dazed with horror. "No…no."

Ragsey grabbed my arm and shoved me toward the mouth of the cave. Poised high on a bluff, our vantage provided a clear view of the situation below. "Look. Look at it!" he commanded. "Do you see the fires? Do you hear the screams?"

Indeed I heard and saw everything. Idyll had been besieged and near destroyed. Smoke billowed up in towering black columns from a dozen fires spread throughout the barracks area. Strewn among the human carnage, debris and fallen weapons littered the road leading to the teleportal, which had been cut off by members of the Fifth. A brave group of Crusaders still battled a group of Royalists sporting Urharde's colours on the eastern outskirts of the sundered outpost.

"Val came through the teleportal an hour ago, using the key I took off Repachea after I stabbed him."

My scathing retort was interrupted by a familiar battle cry as a screaming rampager led a cavalry assault down upon the beleaguered Crusaders, the standard-bearer flying my banner. Nay. Valleri's banner now.

The Crusaders scattered before the charge. Withdrawing, they regrouped and opted for a fighting retreat into the trees on my distant right. Urharde's Seventh harried them mercilessly. Numbly, I watched as Valleri whirled his war-horse and raised his fist in victory. Shouts of triumph rose up from the Royalists as the last of the Crusaders scurried into the trees. Recall sounded. Valleri kicked his mount into a gallop and led his Royal to a northern rise where he met Urharde, there to savour their bloody success within taunting distance of the survivors hidden in the forest.

Frantic, I scanned the battlefield for Crusader bodies. But the distance was too great and I was unable to identify any single corpse. Who had fallen? Sestus? Ginger? I was sick with grief and all-consuming guilt.

Ragsey hauled me back into the cave. "You see, Kathedra? It's over. The Crusaders are all but crushed. Valleri is victorious. All that stands in his way now is Bertrand."

The mention of Uncle jarred me back to the situation at hand. "Where is he?" I demanded. "Has Valleri harmed him?"

"Bertrand remains unharmed, for the moment. But he's under no delusions. The rumours that the Regent had ordered your murder have done their damage. Once Valleri returns with news of his crushing victory and his heroic rescue of the Princess Kathedra, Bertrand will be forced to abdicate. Oh, but you know what? Princess or no princess, Valleri will be in control of the throne. So you'd best hope he still cares enough for you to pay me my demands."

I had no intention of being dragged back to Valleri to become his puppet or prisoner or both. Actually I had no intention of being dragged anywhere. Although the idea of bargaining with this contemptible man made my stomach roil, my options were sorely limited. "I can offer you so much more than Valleri can, Ragsey. After all, I am the rightful heir. He is but a brash usurper, a common cutthroat. Help me and I will reward you with riches beyond anything he has promised you."

He stared at me a long moment, contemplating my words. "You can't tempt me," he replied. But his very hesitation implied that I could.

Of course I did not intend to fulfill my oaths. His only reward would be my blade in his heart. "Think about it. You can't go back to the Crusaders and once Valleri learns of your duplicity you'll be a hunted man. There's nothing left for you in Thylana. From where I see it, I'm your only ally."

His hand tangled in my hair, long enough now to become a disadvantage, yanking back my head to expose my neck as the blade came to rest against my skin. His breath fanned my cheek; his lips brushed my ear. "Tell me of these rewards, Highness."

"Gold, if that's what you want. Or a captaincy, perhaps. A Royal of your own."

Turning the blade, he drew its flat along my cheek, relishing my startled gasp. Though his actions belied his intent, Ragsey was receptive to my proposal, and more. He trembled with anticipation, with the effort of restraint. "Is that all?"

"Possibly, but I don't negotiate trussed up like a chicken." He'd made the mistake of betraying his wants, his eagerness, and I could afford this bravado.

His fingers extricated themselves from my hair, glided down the length of my arm to my hand, where they fondled the ring Ginger had placed there. "You're truly helpless, aren't you?"

Well, not completely. He referred to me by name or royal title, concerned only with my Teki powers. He did not remember I was also a soldier, one who had helped Ginger and him beat back a Royalist attack on the road from Edenwood and had touched swords with him on the practice field.

Harsh laughter drifted over me. "I'm not stupid. I'm not Averi." He brought the blade into my line of vision. "If you think to toy with me, Highness, I'll make you rue it. Cross me and I won't hesitate to kill you. Valleri will just have to content himself with a body."

The knife lowered, touched the rope binding my wrists, and began to cut through. My relief was palpable. Sensing it, he withdrew the blade. "Wait. I have a better idea. Let's seal our pact first."

"What?" I barely got the word out, my throat locking tight with dread.

He turned me to face him. His eyes burned a dark fire. I nearly wept when he sheathed the dagger. "Show me you mean what you say, then I'll untie you. Once you surrender all you have, only then will I trust you."

The bastard was playing with me.

But my ploy had worked. Sort of. I was no longer under threat of his knife, and therefore able to resist.

I let him guide me to the wall at my back, just beneath the torch, allowed the press of his body to mine, luring him closer with a pretence of submission. As he bent nearer, I ducked under his chin and rammed his jaw with the top of my brow. The blow snapped his head back, striking the rock face so hard he put a tooth through his lip. Off-balanced, he staggered away, sliding down the length of the wall.

Lifting my bound hands, I grabbed the torch from its cranny and swung to meet him. He'd regained his footing to stand between my only exit and me. "Don't come any closer," I warned with a thrust of the brand.

Ragsey swiped a hand across his bloodied mouth, then drew his sword.

"You little bitch," he hissed. "I'll make you scream for that."

He came at me with an awkward swipe. I dodged it, danced out of his reach. Again he charged, dropping his shoulder and leaving his opposite flank wide open as usual. I swung, aiming for his ribs, but struck his arm instead, setting his sleeve afire. Shrieking, he flung aside the blade and fell to the floor, desperate to extinguish the flames.

At last a chance to escape. I threw down the torch and ran past him out of the cave. The sharp zing of metal scraping stone told me a throwing star had grazed the cave wall.

Outside, blinded by the sunshine, I stumbled towards Ragsey's roan and pulled free its tether. But as I tried to mount, Ragsey staggered from the cave, bellowing in rage. His noise spooked the horse and it bolted, stranding me.

Having no other choice, I plunged down the rocky embankment, skipping and skidding over the loose dirt. I heard Ragsey sliding after me, close on my heels. But without the use of hands to balance me, I slipped and fell, rolling down the last dozen yards to the path below. My pursuer, too, lost his footing, his tumble depositing him in a tanglebush. Flame shot through my shoulders, reverberated along my spine, but I shoved myself to my feet and headed for the trees.

I ran, or hobbled, cursing Ginger for stealing my powers, for so blithely rendering me vulnerable to his enemies. A glance over my shoulder found Ragsey right behind me. Another star whizzed past my temple to bury itself in the trunk of an elm. I screamed, uncaring who heard, friend or foe, although it was possible I had no friends left alive.

Ragsey caught up in no time, tackling me with bruising force. We hit the rough turf together, the impact driving the breath from my chest. He was on me in an instant, his fist hurtling forward. Pain exploded in my jaw. Dazed, I felt his fingers curl around my throat, squeezing like a vice. I couldn't move, couldn't fight, my body trapped beneath his.

"Bitch!" Ragsey raged as throttled me. "I'll kill you first!"

I fought for air, fought to free my arms, struggling to push him away. The world grew dark, silent. Oblivion beckoned.

Then a voice from somewhere behind me said, "What the hell is going on here?"

A crazed look in his eye, Ragsey glanced up at the speaker. "Leave it be, Naren," he panted. "This doesn't concern you."

"Let her up."

Ragsey feigned disbelief, even as his fingers tightened once more around my neck. "But she's a traitor. She's betrayed us to the enemy just as Castarr warned us."

"Get off her, now." Despite the roaring in my head, I heard the unmistakable click of a crossbow cocking.

Ragsey's eyes narrowed. "Are you threatening me?"

"Disobey me and find out."

A sneer twisted Ragsey's face. "You won't shoot me, Naren. You can't. We're on the same side." He drew his dagger. "Surely, you don't suggest we set her free?"

"Put the knife away, Ragsey. Let's not act in haste. We ought to discuss it first. Reasonably."

Of course Ragsey could not hazard the chance Naren would take my word over his. "No!" he roared, raising his knife. "There's nothing to discuss." The blade glinted in the sun as it flashed down. A whimper of fear escaped my lips, the only sound I could muster.

But the blow didn't strike. Instead something slammed into Ragsey with such weight it knocked him clear off me. Sputtering, choking, I gulped in the raw air, my lungs burning, my head buzzing. Someone was yelling; a commotion arose. Closer, the vague form of a man hunched over me, the plethora of spots that swam before my eyes obscuring my vision. I think I may have even blacked out for a moment or two. I heard my name, shouted it seemed from a great distance, followed by a staggering silence as the darkness crawled over me.

CHAPTER TWENTY-FOUR

Ungentle hands hauled me to my feet, forcing me to stand on weak, wobbly legs. Naren retained his grip on my arm, partly to steady me, partly to restrain me. I was his prisoner now. And he was not alone. A beleaguered group of Crusaders, fresh from battle, sat their weary mounts nearby, all just as grim-faced as their leader.

Breathless, dazed, I gasped out, “Ragsey? Is he-?”

“Gone. We lost him in the scrub.”

“Naren…thank you. If not for you he would have killed me. He killed Repachea. He stole the key…gave it to Valleri.”

“Quiet,” he hissed, his fingers grinding into my flesh. “I don’t want to hear it.”

I gaped, distressed by the frosty glint in his eyes. “You don’t believe me?”

Naren made no reply, his mouth set in a taut line as he unbound my hands.

“If you doubt my innocence, why did you rescue me?” I demanded, ignoring his previous order. “Why did you fire on your own comrade if you harbour doubt?”

“Liar or not, you are still Thylana’s princess. It’s not for me or Ragsey alone to decide your fate.” Before I could protest, he swung me onto his horse and mounted behind.

“Where are you taking me?”

“Idyll.” His arm snaked around my midriff, holding me firm while his other hand clenched the reins. “Or rather, what’s left of it.”

I cringed at the reminder. “Your arrival was timely.”

“The two of you made such a racket it’s a wonder you didn’t attract the Royalists’ attention…or perhaps that was your hope.”

“Naren, surely you must be aware I would suffer as grievously as you or any other Crusader should I fall into my enemies’ hands.”

“Even Valleri’s?”

“While I don’t think Valleri seeks my death,” I answered after careful consideration, “I’m quite certain he wants me in no proximity to the throne.”

Naren seemed to accept that.

“What about Ginger?” I asked in sudden panic. “And Sestus? Are they safe?”

“I don’t know anything,” he snapped. Doubtless, he was just as worried for his friends as I was. “Valleri’s attack caught us by surprise. Apparently, Erol’s been in his back pocket all along. We didn’t even get a warning. Once we recovered our wits and restored some order Belvemar, Ginger, and I rode out to meet the Royalists on open ground. Sestus and Castarr remained behind to defend Idyll. The last time I saw Belvemar and Ginger was just before the final skirmish with the Seventh. I have no idea where they are or if they're even alive. I can only hope they made it to the forest. The Royalists have cut off all access to it from this side, making it impossible for us to regroup. But I have no intention of deserting those survivors trapped in the ruins of the keep."

Not that he and a handful of exhausted men could do anything to save them, but brave, noble-hearted Naren was going to try.

Since Idyll had been reduced to little more than a heap of smoking rubble, abandoned by the defenders, the Royalists did not see fit to occupy it just yet. In fact, they ignored it altogether. Valleri and Urharde seemed more concerned with the Crusaders parked in the forest, content to exchange periodic arrow fire. Therefore, we rode unchallenged over the shattered gates and into the main compound, strewn with debris and corpses.

Pockets of flame burned sporadically among the smouldering embers that were once homes to the Crusaders and their families. I recognized a pile of charred timber and crumbled stonework as my quarters. For the most part Idyll was levelled. Again. Valleri was not going to trouble himself by searching the wreckage for survivors.

We dismounted under the cover of half-demolished buildings. Naren left his men to stand lookout. Then he led me by my arm, bruised and aching, through the ruins that were the oldest part of Idyll to a small square door in the ground, and knocked a secret knock. The trapdoor cracked open and an armed guard peered out. Upon recognizing the captain, the sentry waved us down. We descended steep, roughly hewn steps in near total darkness for what seemed a mile, then stepped into the dungeon, where I had spent hours sweeping and filing for the cause of liberty.

Although Idyll's battered survivors greeted Naren warmly, they viewed me with clear hostility. As a second guard guided us through the crowded chamber, I scanned it for faces dear to me…and found none.

We finally arrived at a room in the far rear. There Castarr paced fretfully. Not a hair was out of place. Not a speck of dirt smirched his face. And I did not see a single scratch anywhere on the gutless bastard. He turned at Naren's entrance, surprised and relieved by his friend's advent. Good old Naren would know what to do!

"Naren!" he exclaimed. "Thank heaven you're all right." They embraced with hearty laughter and slapped each other's back, glad I suppose, not to be dead. Then Castarr saw me.

"Her!" he exploded, shoving Naren away. "I can't believe you brought her here, the miserable traitor. She did this to us. She betrayed us to her Royalist lover just like I told you she would."

As Castarr took a menacing step towards me, Naren got between us and recaptured my arm. "Easy, Castarr. We don't know that for sure."

The tension of the moment was diffused as someone arrived with food and water. I drank my fill of the pitcher, then passed it to Naren, never taking my eyes off Castarr. Scowling at my dishevelled appearance, he sneered at the captain, "How did you manage to reacquire her?" He spoke as if I were an escaped criminal.

Naren drained the jug and wiped his mouth with the back of his sleeve. "We were making our way back here when we happened across her in the ravine, locked in mortal combat with Ragsey. He's gone, I think. Or maybe he's—"

Castarr's eyes widened. "She killed him? The murderous whore, I'll—"

"No," Naren interrupted, planting a firm hand on Castarr's chest. "I didn't say that. I put an arrow in his shoulder, but it probably hasn't killed him. He won't get far. Even so I can't spare the men to go round him up."

"You shot him? Why?"

"He was like…a wild man. I can't explain it. I told him to let her go, to put down his weapon, but he refused to listen. I had no choice. I couldn't allow him to kill the princess."

"Why the hell not?" Castarr was apoplectic. When wasn't he? "She's a spy and a murderer! She killed Repachea and gave Valleri his passkey. Ragsey caught her red-handed planting her evidence in my quarters."

I opened mouth to deny the accusation, but Naren nudged me silent. "Not according to Belvemar. He took a pretty hard blow to his head but I believe him when he says Kathedra is innocent. Ginger and Sestus trust her, too. Why shouldn't we?"

"Are you crazy? Look around, Naren! We're crushed, trapped, wounded, and dying. Valleri did this to us. Her lover. Her lieutenant, for God's sake! How can you suggest they are not in league with each other? Ginger was a lovelorn fool, Sestus and Belvemar stupid old men not to see it! I knew we should have shut down that infernal teleportal. I knew it."

Naren was dubious. "Where's Sestus? Perhaps we should discuss the situation with him before we make any snap—"

"Sestus lies near death," Castarr said bluntly. "He was injured when the stable's burning roof collapsed on him. He's useless to us."

Grief assailed me, then rage at Castarr's callous disregard for Sestus's life. "Where is he?" I demanded. "I want to see him."

"Forget it," Castarr snarled. "Biddy tends him, but she's got other patients who require her attention. There's nothing anyone can do for him now."

"Naren, you must let me go to him," I begged, frantic with fear. "Please…he could be dying."

"Maybe later. First things first." He pushed me into a chair, turned to Castarr. "Any sign of Ginger?"

"Nothing. Last I saw him, he went down in a press of Royalist cavalry just outside the village. He's probably fertilizer by now."

Fury unhinged me. I leapt from my chair and dove for Castarr, shrieking, "You coward! You rotten, spineless son-of-a-she-goat! How can you be so smug? How can you be so heartless? I can't believe you just sat here and watched as your comrade was trampled like it's an everyday sport! You pig! You—"

Naren sprang to tackle me, catching my flailing arms lest I scratch out the commander's eyes. Castarr backed away, cowed by the force of my rage. Tears spilled down my cheeks, even as I continued to writhe and buck in Naren's powerful grip. "You bastard!" I screamed. "How can you just stand there and tell me he's gone? You don't even care!"

Sobbing, I fell limp in Naren's arms. "Get a hold of yourself," he whispered between clenched teeth. "We don't know anything for sure. You're not helping your cause by behaving like a lunatic. Let it go."

Let it go? He made it sound so easy. But he was right. Hysteria and anger were not going to win me any friends here. I pulled myself together and pushed him away, calm on the surface while inside I drowned in an ocean of sorrow. I was numb, unable to believe it, unable to believe I still breathed despite the gaping hole in my heart. What if Ginger were dead? What if?

I sank back down into the chair, my legs too weak to support me.

Castarr said to Naren, "Have you seen Belvemar?"

"Not for hours. There's a chance he might be in the forest with the others, but we're totally cut off from them."

They rambled on, but I didn't hear a word of it. My mind was elsewhere. I thought of all the hateful things I'd said to Ginger. I thought of how bitter our last parting had been, and of how I might never get the chance to retrieve my petty words.

I stared down at the silver band on my finger and realized my Teki powers may be lost to me forever. It seemed a trivial matter when compared to the loss of Ginger. I had sacrificed too much in my quest for vengeance, no longer even knowing where to direct it. According to Ragsey, Valleri was the source of all my woes. Not Uncle. Not entirely.

In my reckless ambition I had managed to bring only ruination and death to my benefactors. Nothing I had done had made a damned bit of difference anyway. The throne had never been so far from my grasp.

"Well, what are we going to do?" Castarr snapped.

"What can we do?" Naren sounded calm, resigned to what doom awaited, ever the soldier. "Valleri's in control of the teleportal. His Royalists are everywhere. We'll never be able to evacuate Idyll without being seen, and we don't have enough manpower to provide cover. If we try to leave, it will be wholesale slaughter. We'll just have to wait for a sign from someone. Maybe somebody in those trees has a plan. Maybe Belvemar escaped and will return with reinforcements. For the moment, we're stuck here. But at least we're safe."

"Don't count on it," I interrupted. "Ragsey spied for Valleri. The rat would have supplied him interior plans. Besides, he lived here as a child. You can bet he knows about this place."

Castarr shot me a glower that said he doubted my story. "Then why hasn't he attacked?"

"Your guess is as good as mine." It was beyond my capacity to explain Valleri's actions, his motives. The man didn't make sense to me anymore.

Naren shrugged and exchanged a glance with Castarr. "Well, I suppose we'll find out soon enough."

It seemed Valleri was not without some mercy. He did not make us wait long for an answer.

Naren tended a gash beneath my eye when Jory burst into the room and announced breathlessly, "The Gryphon Highlord approaches. He rides hard for Idyll with the Seventh Royal." He paused to draw air. "I think he means to raze us!"

What? Again?

Hearing this, Castarr leapt to his feet and yanked me away from Naren. "She's our only hope of escape. We can ransom her to Valleri in exchange for our freedom."

"Are you daft?" I yelped, trying to pull myself free. "How do you know Valleri even wants me back? Don't forget it would benefit him if I were dead."

"That can be arranged," he snarled. "Naren, what do you say?"

"Don't listen to him, Naren," I urged. "Valleri won't honour any bargain you strike. You can't trust him."

But to Naren I suppose it appeared they had no other choice. He glanced from Castarr to me. "I should instead trust you?"

He had already made up his mind, but I could see he was not proud of his decision. They were going to hand me over to save themselves. I didn't blame them, of course. But they were fools if they thought my ransom would win their freedom. Naren, however, is no village idiot. He had a scheme, no doubt, to ensure the Crusaders' survival. My sacrifice would buy him some time.

At Naren's nod, Castarr marched me through the dungeon and pushed me up the stairs to the surface. We emerged into daylight just as Valleri and his troops arrived in the compound. As the Royalists drew near, Castarr shoved me ahead of him up the crumbling staircase of a burnt-out building. Below, Naren dispatched the remnants of their forces to various vantage positions, prepared to defend us if necessary.

When we reached the roof, Castarr clasped me to him in the manner of a shield before the advancing horsemen. Squinting through the dust, I saw Valleri rein in hard. I can only describe the look on his face as incredulous. Our gazes locked, and in that moment I knew I stared into the eyes of a stranger.

I sucked in my breath as Castarr brought a dagger against my ribs. "Truce, Valleri!" he shouted. "Or I'll gut her like a fish!" Eloquent as always.

Valleri's officers dragged their mounts to a halt, weapons drawn. Though I recognized Urharde and his second, there was another officer I did not-a slimmer, younger man, clad in foreign colours. Roche's lieutenant, I think. The man I'd bumped into back in Castle Gryphon.

"Weapons down," Valleri barked at his men. But when they only continued to stare dumbly, he snatched Urharde's sword and flung it to the ground. "I said weapons down!"

If Valleri was surprised to see me, then Urharde was positively astonished. "But…but, you're dead," he burbled, his eyes bulging as they gazed upon me. Then he looked at Valleri, and immediately understood. "You!" His tone was accusatory, his expression one of pure outrage. "Bertrand didn't order the princess's murder. You spirited her away."

Valleri levelled his ruthless glare on the captain. "It seems there is doubt as to who is in charge. Bertrand thinks it's him. Well, he's not. I am."

His voice rose to carry to the Royalists in the rear ranks. "The sooner everyone understands that the better…or perhaps I need make an example of someone." His tepid gaze settled on Urharde.

The revelation that the Regent's lapdog had morphed into something deadlier than a Shouda had come as a shock to the captain. He struggled to retain some shred of composure. "Valleri, I assure you," he wheedled, "no one questions your authority. We are obedient to your—"

"Ahem."

The argument ceased as both Royalists turned with an air of irritation to see who had interrupted them. Castarr did not like being ignored. He drew a thin rivulet of blood under my chin to prove it.

Valleri vaulted from his saddle to rush us, but the sound of a dozen Crusader crossbows cocking as they sighted on him brought Val up short. "Unhand her, you whoreson!" he shouted, his face black with fury. "If you touch her again, I'll rip out your throat!"

The force of Valleri's rage was so powerful I felt it like a physical presence. Castarr felt it, too. He cringed and retreated half a step. "Back off. Or I swear, I'll kill her right now!"

Checking his temper, Valleri spread his hands in compliance. "What do you want?" he asked, his voice taut and low with barely repressed anger. "Our freedom. Our lives for hers."

Valleri's eyes flickered to me, hatred in their depths, although I could not say to whom it was directed. My presence here had put him in this predicament. I knew, as did everyone else who stood in the shambles that was Idyll, I was the sole reason why the Crusaders were still alive.

Time passed in agonized silence while the Gryphon Highlord debated with himself. Castarr finally snapped, "You will answer me now."

"Done," Valleri spat through clenched teeth.

Urharde squawked in disbelief. "Are you mad?" he demanded, leaping from his saddle to confront Valleri, heedless of the crossbows swinging to sight him. "You can't allow them just to walk away from here. They're traitors, cutthroats, bandits. I say let them have her. The throne is all but yours. You don't need her anymore."

"I've got news for you," Valleri announced, a smile lightening his features. "I don't want the throne. I never did."

For once Urharde seemed incapable of speech. Therefore, Valleri asked the captain's question for him. "Why did I go to all this trouble, then?" Laughing, he gestured to me. "I did it for her, of course."

A stunned hush descended over Royalists and Crusaders alike. Whether Valleri told the truth or not, his words condemned me as a traitor to Uncle and the Crusaders both. Castarr let out a snort of triumph and shouted down to Naren, "Do you see, now? They were in league all along."

A restive murmur arose from the Crusaders at Castarr's damning declaration. Their hostility focussed on me. Naren looked away in disgust, and I could not tell if his contempt was for his comrades or me. Nevertheless, I could hold my silence no longer.

"Cowards!" I cried, fighting to break Castarr's grip, for he dared not harm me now that a deal had been struck. "It is I who have been betrayed time and time and time again. First by the Regent. Then by Valleri. Now you. You who were so eager to call me Highness, who were so ready to resurrect me as your queen. Where is your loyalty? Where is your honour?"

Castarr struggled to restrain me, but Naren yelled out in a rare display of temper, "Oh, for God's sake, let her speak!"

The captain released me and I stood alone, battling for control of my thoughts, grateful for the ring on my finger, for I know not what chaotic force I might have unleashed. "Traitor," I hissed, meeting Valleri's hooded eyes. "Traitor!" There was no other word for him.

"I'm glad to see you, too, Kathedra."

"You betrayed me. You lied to me. You used me to further your own ambitions. Your little plot to get me out of the way failed. Ragsey's run out on you. He told me everything. Why, Val? Why did you do it?"

"Do you really need to ask?" he retorted, incredulous. "I did it to protect you. If I had not intervened you'd even now be wed to Lesuperis, in thrall to Bertrand. I did it to save your throne."

"You had no right," I spat, my fists clenching in rage.

A flash of anger streaked across his face. "I tried to help you. I had a plan but you messed it up. Do you know how much time and money it cost me to arrange your escape? I had to bribe Averi and his henchmen with commissions and gold to spare you."

"Spare me?" I gasped in disbelief, as memories of that day re-emerged. I strode to the edge of the roof, the closest I could get to him, and sank to a knee. "Do you have any idea what they did to me? They beat me. They would have raped and killed me if not for Sestus. My God! I can't tell you the horrible things they did to me. And I'm supposed to be…grateful?"

Valleri paled, the revelation coming as a complete shock. His brow darkened, and I watched the last glimmer of sanity dim from his eyes. "Forgive me. I had no knowledge of their crimes. My orders were for Averi to retrieve proof of your identity and allow you to go on your way. If I had known—"

He seemed to have difficulty speaking then. Pausing, he took a moment to compose himself. Once more he became the formidable Royalist general. "They shall be executed. I promise, such an act will not go unpunished."

"Spare me your promises, Valleri. Your word is meaningless. It is my privilege to wreak my own vengeance, not yours. Just as it is my privilege to reap my own destiny, not yours to shape it for me. Do you realize what you've done?" I gestured to the carnage and destruction surrounding us. "Look around you, Val. Look!"

He ignored my diatribe, staring at me with a gravity that suggested I had taken leave of my senses. "I'd hoped you would understand."

He turned back to Castarr, abruptly ending our discourse. "The truce lasts until noon tomorrow, at which time this hellhole will be razed to the ground. You will remove your survivors from the area and cross the nearest border, never to return. Be forewarned; if you break this agreement my troops will have orders to eradicate all refugees and renegades in the vicinity."

"That's insane!" Urharde howled, allowing his anger to override good judgment. "They're our enemies. They should be executed as traitors. The princess, too. She's turned against Bertrand. She's turned against you."

Valleri's arm swung out, the back of his hand connecting with Urharde's jaw. The strength behind the blow flung the captain to the ground. "Shut up," Val snarled. "If you touch her, if you utter another word against her, I will plant your skull on a pike. And if you ever think to contradict my orders again, I will cut the tongue from your head."

Never had I seen Valleri so furious. I thought I watched a madman. He rounded on the young lieutenant whose name still eluded me. "If he opens his mouth again, tell your bowmen to shoot him."

His rage vented, Valleri appeared calm and dignified once more. He told Castarr, "I will return tomorrow, at which time you will pass the Princess Kathedra into my hands."

"No," Naren broke in. "Send someone else to retrieve the princess. If we catch wind of you anywhere near Idyll or the teleportal, I'll slice Kathedra's throat."

Valleri capitulated with an ease that told me he had no particular wish to return to this place. "Very well." His shrewd gaze swept over his officers, skimming past Urharde and coming to rest on the young dark-haired lieutenant. "I'll send Saxton. A merc captain, he has no special bias. Is that agreeable?"

Captain? Last I'd seen him Saxton was a lieutenant. That either meant Roche had expired or been shown the door. Valleri had been doing some housekeeping, sweeping out the nay-sayers with the trash.

Naren gave the officer a scathing once-over. "It's acceptable."

Valleri remounted, ignoring Urharde as he struggled to his feet with the aid of his second. Val and I exchanged one last glance of mutual disdain before he wheeled his charger and rode from Idyll, his gold and blue standard fluttering in the breeze.

CHAPTER TWENTY-FIVE

Back below ground, amid the turmoil of evacuation preparations, I had ample opportunity to ponder my impending doom. As my self-appointed guard, Naren dragged me with him from one end of the dungeon to the other, more to protect Castarr from my wrath than to prevent me from making an escape attempt. Not that I had anywhere to go. Everywhere I looked I saw only enemies, whether they be Royalists or Crusaders. I had lost all those most dear to me-Ginger, Belvemar, Valleri, too, who had died for me in a different way.

I wondered what Val had in store for me. I would hardly be more than his captive, for if he thought I'd back his mad quest he was mistaken. No doubt he would dress me in a queen's trappings, place a token crown upon my brow and sit me on the throne, but I would be in all essence his puppet. Despite his claim he'd usurped Uncle on my behalf, I was sure Valleri intended to assume the role of monarch himself. It would be he who shaped Thylana's destiny, governed her people, and exercised her power. Again, as I had been before to Uncle and the Crusaders, I'd be just a figurehead, until it was no longer convenient.

All was not total despair. A spark of hope, a flicker of defiance, still burned inside the Princess Kathedra. I intended to resist Valleri with all my might, even if my rebellion led to imprisonment or execution. My demise would be a quiet affair, for Valleri is a subtle, cunning creature. Once I'd given him an heir, I could see myself perishing in some unfortunate accident or expiring from an inexplicable ailment.

So whatever nasty fate awaited me I probably deserved it. I had failed in everything I'd tried to do. For all my vanity, all my greed, I was about to be punished. But I would have suffered the consequences willingly had all the others only escaped.

Dear, sweet, gentle Naren even tried to comfort me. He joined me where I slumped on a bench out of the general commotion. At his light touch on my back, I lifted my head from my hands to meet his sombre gaze.

"If there were any other way to save what remains of our people I would do it. But there's not."

"Why not shut down the teleportal? Burn it. Deactivate it. I know its drastic, but—"

"The Royalists have it well guarded. We can't get near it. Valleri has patrols posted all over the place. And we don't have the numbers to go against them."

"What about the Umagi?" I pleaded. "Couldn't one of them close it?"

"Only one of the Umagi who originally erected it can do that and as far as I know they're all dead or missing. I'm sorry…" He hesitated, rested a gentle hand on my leg. "About Ginger. I'm sorry. I wish—"

"I know, Naren. I know."

He nodded, having absolved himself of any guilt he might be feeling. A lengthy silence stretched between us. Then in a hushed voice, he said, "Don't give up, Princess. I haven't. It's not over yet."

"What do you mean?"

"I'm not at liberty to explain. I don't want to jeopardize our chances. But we still have one last iron in the fire."

Since Castarr had not seen fit to waste a meal on a prisoner when it could be better spent on a Crusader later, Naren shared his meagre rations with me. Afterward, I cajoled him into letting me see Sestus one last time. He accompanied me to the makeshift infirmary in a corner of the cellar.

Biddy donned a baleful glower especially for me. "Why'd you bring her here?" she snarled at Naren.

"She wanted to see Sestus. And I thought she could be of use to you."

"Hmmph," she snorted, glaring around the crowded sickroom. "Hasn't she done enough already?"

"Biddy, you know you can use the help," he chided.

Unable to refute that, Biddy grudgingly relented. Once Naren had left, she spat at me, "This is all your fault, you know."

I noted her haggard features and weary eyes, feeling sick to my stomach with helplessness. "I did not betray you," I managed in feeble defence.

Raising her chin, she bit back, "I never believed you did. But as the Princess Kathedra it is your duty to protect your people…and you failed."

No argument here.

Without another word on the matter, Biddy led me to the corner where Sestus lay on a pallet. Although most of the more seriously wounded had been loaded onto carts to be transported from Idyll, he still awaited his turn. His right leg had been crushed by the weight of stone and timber under which he'd been trapped when the building collapsed. Despite the swift response of rescuers, he had suffered minor burns to his face and arms before being pulled from the rubble. His raven mane was singed and stank of smoke, his clothes torn and sooty. A patch of blood stained the white scrap of linen wrapped around his head.

Biddy had done all she could for him in the little time she could spare. Because she loved him, because he was an officer, did not entitle Sestus to constant care when so many others had dire need of her skills. Although Castarr and Naren had each brought a physician with him to Idyll, only one had survived the Royalist assault. Together, he and Biddy shared the monumental chore of tending the casualties.

As I watched, Biddy pressed a cool compress to Sestus's brow. He moaned, but she shushed him and said aside to me, "He drifts in and out of consciousness. He's very weak. I fear…" She paused, biting her lip to stop its tremble. "I fear the rigors of travel may kill him."

I tried to console her. "That won't happen. Sestus is strong and healthy. He's too stubborn to die."

Biddy nodded. "Yes, stubborn like an old pack mule." Raising her gaze to mine, she gripped my arm with her stubby fingers. "Can you help him?" she pleaded.

I swallowed over the lump in my throat, shaking my head. "No, Biddy. I can't. I'm sorry." I could not even use the ring on my finger as an excuse. "It just doesn't work that way."

Biddy forced a weak smile. "I understand." She rose stiffly and shuffled away to attend her other patients.

I remained by Sestus's side, mopping his feverish brow and talking to him in the hope he would wake. As I kept vigil, memories from childhood resurfaced. I recalled the day he'd given me my favourite toy: that battered old wooden horse with its mane and tail of real horse hair. I remembered, too, a picnic in the park, with my parents and Sestus, as he bounced me on his shoulders. I heard again the birds chirping on that sunny day, and Mother's cheerful chatter as she set out the food.

Memories flooded me, memories I hadn't even known existed, of ease and joy and love. How I missed those gentle, happy people. They seemed as if from a dream.

"Little Red?" croaked a voice beside me.

Still smiling, I looked down at Sestus to see his eyes flutter open. I clasped his hand as it reached for mine.

"I feared you were dead," he groaned.

"Gallant Naren rescued me." I held a cup of water to his lips so he could drink. Red-faced with shame, I said, "Forgive me, Sestus. I should have listened to you. You were right about Valleri all along. How could I have been so wrong?"

He squeezed my hand, offering me comfort instead of rebuke. "Sometimes we become blinded by our hearts. There are worse crimes."

"It's over, Sestus."

"Nah." He shook his head, wincing in sudden pain. "If I know Ginger, he'll have a back-up plan for his back-up plan."

I battled down fresh tears at the mention of the mage's name, but put on a brave face for the sake of Sestus. I would not divulge his comrades' plans for me. Sestus would fight tooth and nail in my defence, and in his condition, any exertion or upset could kill him.

"I have a question, Sestus, and I want you to answer with the truth." I let out a deep sigh, going over the phrasing in my head, not knowing how to put it into words. "Tell me what might happen if one day a young boy, a young Umagi boy, unskilled and untaught in the ways of magic, was fiddling with a spell, let's say a levitation spell or a concealment charm, and he made the wrong gesture or spoke the wrong word, and it collided with, accidentally of course, a mindspell? What would happen, Sestus? What could happen?"

After a long, long silence, Sestus replied, "I think you know, Kathedra."

A tear leaked out; I swiped it angrily away. "All this, Sestus, over a child's mistake? It doesn't seem possible."

"Of course it's possible. It's just impossible to make sense of it."

And I still couldn't. Not all of it. "Mauranna was Teki?"

Sestus shook his head. "There was a Teki involved, yes. But Mauranna is not the person you want. She was just a simple hearthmage."

"If not Mauranna, then who?"

But my question went unanswered as the porters arrived, which was just as well, for Sestus had begun to drift away on me. I kissed his cheek and whispered farewell, letting his hand slip from mine. As they departed with his litter, he lifted that same hand and waved good-bye.

I pondered the mystery he had left me with. While Ginger is certainly an Umagi adept he is not Teki. If he hadn't miscast the spell, that only left one other person: Valleri. Hardly a logical assumption, it would, however, explain the animosity between him and Ginger, as well as Ginger's cryptic comment in the ruins of Idyll's kitchen. If true, that would mean Val had hidden his powers not only from me but Uncle, too. And for a young, untrained Teki that would be nigh impossible, unless he employed a potion similar to my tonic or a device such as the ring on my finger.

I wracked my brain, ransacking treasured childhood memories for anything that might serve to repress or control magical powers. An amulet, maybe? A bracelet containing a mystical stone such as my amethyst? Was it something he might eat or drink? An herbal infusion in his morning tea or a drop or two of elixir in his wine? What about scars or blemishes on his body, which might indicate some bizarre blood ritual or-

The tattoo. Of course! The imagery seemed obvious now, decipherable even to a novice like me. The wings could easily belong to an owl, a bird long associated with the occult, instead of an eagle. The heart wrapped in chains represented a binding. It's possible he'd received it while still a youth, since I had never seen Valleri without shirt or tunic, as propriety demanded, until relatively recent. The more I thought about it, the more sense it made. Such a device would not only protect him from Uncle's decree but also strip him of raw, unmanageable powers that had already proven themselves deadly. Poor Val. The guilt and grief he must suffer is unimaginable to me. How does one recover from the knowledge that he is responsible for so many deaths, so much destruction? Surely the damage this secret has done to his soul is irreparable. Only someone without conscious, without remorse, would remain unaffected. And yet there were those who might argue, Ginger for one, that Valleri behaved exactly so.

But the revelation did nothing to allay my grief of the moment.

I sought to ease my heartache by lending my modest expertise to the infirmary. A grateful Biddy put me to work dressing wounds and mixing restorative potions. Glad for the distraction, I laboured there far into the night, until exhaustion claimed me, until Naren arrived to physically convey me from the room. He insisted I get some sleep, and despite my protests, I fell into a dreamless slumber the instant my head touched the hard slats of the bench.

Naren roused me just before noon and took me away to await Valleri's henchmen. Castarr, bless his worm-riddled heart, permitted me to breakfast on stale bread and muddy tea. The musty stone rang with an unnatural quiet, ominous in its stillness. The evacuation of Idyll had been completed on schedule. We three alone remained in the dungeon, plus four token guards and a pair of lookouts topside with the Crusaders' mounts.

The minutes crawled past. By the end of an hour, Castarr was pacing. "What the hell is taking him so long?"

"I told you," I said from my chair. "It's a trick. Valleri won't keep his word. The Royalists plot some treachery. I warned you, but you wouldn't listen."

The captain stalked over and made a motion to strike me, but Naren intervened. "Let's try to stay calm."

For all his reasonable words Naren was just as antsy. His fingers raked his hair and his teeth gnawed at his lower lip, his expression one of keen distraction. I could see he had second thoughts about their hasty bargain with Valleri. He hadn't liked it from the start.

"Perhaps we've made a mistake."

Castarr's eyes grew round and big. "We had no choice. It's her or us."

"Ginger wouldn't approve."

"Ginger's dead," Castarr snapped back.

"That's speculation only."

At that moment Jory hurried into the room, diverting my attention. "The escort is here."

Everyone heaved a great sigh of relief. Everyone except me, of course.

Saxton and his escort of twenty armed horsemen sat their steeds as we climbed aboveground. Squinting from the sun's harsh glare after the gloom of the dungeon, I surveyed the foreign colours. I recognized Roche's standard but I could not place the uniforms-a motley assortment of battered helms, unfamiliar surcoats, and nondescript armour. Mercenaries. Hire-swords. Goons-for-sale.

I waited while Castarr and Saxton exchanged terse words, as each party determined whether the other had lived up to his end of the bargain. The nearest horseman was only ten feet away from me. He sat a tall blood bay, its muzzle encased in steel plates. At his subtle cue, the animal snorted and imperiously stamped a hoof.

I cast a sullen glance at the bay's rider, studying me from his lofty perch. He radiated rage and menace. I knew very few of Roche's men and I did not recognize this one's costume. I prayed not all the mercenaries harboured such hostility towards me. Frightful images of Averi resurfaced. Naren stood behind me, his hands resting on my shoulders, and I drew courage from his presence.

At last the formalities were done and Saxton approached me, leading a hardy mare. Before I could put a foot in the stirrup, Naren scooped me up and swung me onto the saddle. "Remember, Princess," he murmured into my ear. "Faith."

I threw him a questioning glare but he had turned away.

At Saxton's command we departed the sprawling ruin of Idyll. My horse started forward and I fell into the middle of my grimly silent escort. We rode at an easy canter along the winding road that led up the gentle rise to the teleportal. We trooped through the barn, iron-shod hooves muted by the hard-packed dirt floor. Upon reaching the far door, Saxton dismounted to insert the key that Valleri had given him, acquired at the expense of Repachea's life. A pair of Royalists from the detachment assigned to guard the teleportal from Crusader sabotage slid open the barn door and waved us through. We emerged on the nether side, into Royalist territory.

As we did so, Saxton leaned down in the saddle to confer with the detachment's commander. I had no trouble hearing what was said; Saxton was not trying to hide what he did. Acting on Valleri's instruction, he ordered the barn to be torched, thereby destroying the teleportal it housed. The merc captain made it clear that the guards were not to return to Gryphon until nothing save ashes remained. Such a directive did not shock me. After all, neither Valleri nor Uncle could allow such a device to remain in place. Nor could I see either one of them ever having the inclination to want to use it to reach Idyll.

The guards immediately set about fulfilling their orders. By the time we had reached the tree line, and I had summoned the nerve to look back, flames had engulfed the building. As tongues of fire licked at the thatch, I thought of those I had left behind. Naren, Sestus, Biddy, and all the rest were hundreds of miles away now, whisked off on the wings of time and space.

We had the road back to the castle all to ourselves. I anticipated no delays or surprises, so when our procession veered from its route and halted in the cover of a stand of beech, I immediately assumed the worst. Saxton was going to finish me himself, here and now. I stared down at the mare's mane, willing myself brave.

Someone said, "It's not over yet, Highness."

I looked at the rider nearest me, but the man had his gaze trained on the gap between his charger's ears, ignoring me. A lot had happened during these past three days. I was numb with shock and fear, steeped in grief over Ginger's disappearance. Therefore, if I did not recognize his voice right away, I believe it was understandable.

"Precious."

Perplexed, I swung to see the bay had trotted up behind me. Panic gripped me at the stranger's approach. Our horses were nose to nose when he drew rein and removed his helm.

Ginger?

He leaned an elbow across his mount's neck and grinned his foxiest grin. "Did you believe you'd gotten rid of me so easily?"

My heart nearly burst from my ribcage. He was alive! Alive. Not dead. I almost pitched off my horse in dizzy delight. My expression must have been comical, for Ginger's grin only widened.

He dismounted and plucked me from the saddle. I clung to him, drinking in the tangy scent of leather, running my hands over his dusty, steel-clad body, unable to believe he truly stood there. I caught a glimpse of Saxton watching us with an indulgent smile.

"Why the ruse, Ginger?" I murmured. "Why all the subterfuge?"

"It was necessary. Castarr wouldn't have given you to me without a fight. It might have gotten ugly." He withdrew to brush away the tears that coursed unchecked down my cheeks. "How could you ever doubt I'd come?"

"I never doubted your loyalty," I sniffled. "I knew you would come for me if you could. Of course, I would have understood if you were dead."

He laughed then, a pleasant sound if unfamiliar, and kissed me until wolf whistles and catcalls rose from our audience.

CHAPTER TWENTY-SIX

Breaking our clinch Ginger introduced me to the merc captain, who dismounted and sank to a knee. Ah! Some respect at long last. "This is Saxton, our most deeply entrenched agent. Not even Ragsey knew about him."

I lifted a brow, impressed. "Please, Saxton," I said, touching his shoulder. "There's no need for such formality."

"Kathedra, come. There's someone else for you to meet." The mage put an arm around my shoulder and led me towards a nearby stump. At his gesture, one of the mercs dismounted to shuffle over, staggering under the weight of his over-sized hauberk, a leather pouch in hand. A little old gnome of a man, he climbed out of his armour and removed his rusted helm to reveal wizened features and a ragged black beard. "Good afternoon, Highness," he said cheerfully, grinning a snaggletoothed grin.

"Good day to you too, sir." I passed Ginger a quizzical glance.

He ignored it. "This is Owyn. An Umagi sorcerer. I've asked him to place a talisman on us for protection from Shouda." To the gnome, now extracting all manner of magical devices from his pouch, including dye pots, herb jars, and delicate horsehair brushes, he snapped, "Let's get to it."

Ginger knelt beside me and placed his arm upon the stump, palm up. I watched as Owyn, puffing on a pipe throughout the procedure, dipped his brush in one of the pots, which contained blue woad, then began to draw on Ginger's hand. Slowly a trisected circle took shape, an Umagi symbol of protection. When that was done, he opened the jar and tapped out a sprinkle of herb onto the still wet dye. I sniffed the air, wondering at the unfamiliar scent, got a snoot full of smoke for my trouble.

"Tarragon?" I queried.

Teeth clamped firmly to his pipe, the gnome replied, "Thyme. It's an anchor. A component to hold the spell in place."

"How long will the charm last?" Ginger wanted to know.

Owyn shrugged. "That depends on what you're paying me."

"How about calling it a personal favour for the future queen of Thylana?"

"You're already getting two for the price of one."

Ginger capitulated with a weary, drawn-out sigh. "Then what will three crowns get me?"

"About three days."

"Good enough."

"Highness," Owyn prompted me, "if you will speak the commands that govern the Shouda."

I glanced at Ginger, and at his nod gave Owyn the information he required. As I spoke, then spelled, each command, the gnome applied a corresponding character less than a millimetre across to the points of his diagram with silver ink from a second jar. As he worked, he began to chant in a language known only to Umagi sorcerers. Time passed, and soon I thought I saw rune-shaped symbols form in the smoke, twisting and writhing in some arcane dance, but I couldn't be sure, for the smoke had a heavy, sweet smell to it and was doing strange things to my brain. My thoughts were fuzzy, indistinct, whether from the incense or the magic weaving around me I could not say.

"You know only seven commands?"

I roused at the jab of Ginger's elbow in my ribs. "Um, yes," I slurred, groggy from the smoke. "Except for disperse." That one still eluded me. I noticed the flesh of Ginger's hand was projecting an iridescent gleam.

Owyn shrugged, opened a velvet packet no bigger than his thumbnail. "What I have is good enough." Holding the packet over the glowing shape, he sprinkled a pinch of gold powder over his handiwork. Then with a flourish, he pronounced, "The spell is sealed." And blew the dust from Ginger's palm.

I looked. I blinked. The symbol was gone. Not a trace of the paint or trisected circle remained. Sounding just as perplexed as I felt, Ginger asked, "How will I know it's still there?"

"You won't. But it's there. You can't have a magic device visible where Royalists might see it, can you?"

Well, no.

He tapped Ginger's palm with the end of his brush. "The charm acts as a repellent against the Shouda. They should not come anywhere near you, but if you stumble upon one by accident, it will bear you no harmful intent. Their behaviour should mimic that of any other dog. To their canine noses you'll smell like any other noxious, ill-tempered biped."

Ginger studied his hand a moment, then rose with a grunt of satisfaction. "Do the same to the princess, and yourself as well. And be quick about it." He left me to Owyn's care to go confer with Saxton, both of them staring off into the distance as if they expected company.

Owyn dipped his brush again into the blue woad and took my hand in his gnarled fingers, surprisingly dexterous for a man of his age. While I had a few moments alone with him I thought to use the time to my advantage. "Owyn, what do you know about bindings, if I may ask?"

He paused in his work to move the pipe, still spewing noxious fumes, from one side of his mouth to the other. "I know some, Highness. But protection spells and curse-lifting are my specialties. Along with male member enlargement." He wagged a cautionary finger at me. "But I must warn you, it is costly and I don't reveal my list of clients."

"Oh. Interesting. I'll keep that in mind. Male member…really? There's a demand for that sort of thing?" Truly I thought he jested with me.

"Very much so, Highness. Before Bertrand outlawed the use of magic I made a decent living in the village of my birth on that alone." He gave me a sly, knowing wink. "The enchantment is not permanent, so it makes for repeat customers."

I gave my head a shake, gathered my regal dignity, certain it was not proper that I should be discussing the matter. The contents of his pipe had gone straight to my head. "Anyway…" I described Valleri's tattoo as best I could, then voiced my suspicions.

He nodded gravely. "Possibly a binding, yes. Though I am unfamiliar with the design. Such a spell is beyond my meagre talent, however."

"Could it be removed?"

"That depends if the enchanter who placed it there put a permanent anchor spell on it or not. Why do you ask, Highness? Would you like one for yourself?"

"No!" I said sharply, startled. "Certainly not." The notion had not entered my mind until he spoke it, and I strove to put it right back out.

Owyn resumed his artistry, along with his chant. Seemingly detached from myself, I floated in the miasma of smoke, lost in the sorcerer's spell. Tranquil, dreamy thoughts meandered through my head, altogether a pleasant sensation, far better than any induced by pretty crystals. No wonder Owyn was so cheerful.

"Highness, I am finished."

"Oh." Reluctantly I stirred from my doze. "Thank you." I reclaimed my palm and examined it. Nothing was there to indicate the talisman's existence. I flexed my hand, feeling no tightness of dried ink. "Splendid work, Owyn. You are a true artist."

"Many women have told me so, Highness," he replied with a saucy wink.

He turned to the task of packing away his supplies while I rejoined Ginger where he shared a flask with Saxton. He passed it to me and I drank deeply, the cool water chasing away the taste of smoke. "Just how well do you know, Owyn?" I asked in my most innocent tone.

"Well enough. He is trustworthy, I assure you. His work is beyond reproach."

"Quite," I agreed, taking another sip to conceal my smile. "I mean from what I have seen of it. Have you, ahem…" The words caught in my throat, still clogged with smoke. "Have you had cause to use his services before?"

He gave me a look of exasperation. "I've gone to him for herbs, ones that Biddy couldn't supply, as well as a few enhancement spells. What's so bloody funny? Did he give you a puff from his pipe?"

Any reply I might have managed through my burst of giggles was interrupted as a lookout shouted, "Riders!"

"Whose standard?" Saxton asked.

"Ours, sir."

Saxton and Ginger exchanged a triumphant glance, before the mage said, "That has to be Naren."

Peering towards the road at horsemen approaching at a hard gallop, I spotted Naren and five sentries from Idyll, plus a dozen more Crusaders disguised as mercenaries, none of them Castarr. "But…how?" I blurted, pointing to Saxton. "I heard him give the order to destroy the teleportal. I saw the Royalists put the barn to the torch. I saw it destroyed."

"It was destroyed," Ginger replied. "But Naren came through the smaller one, our escape tunnel if you will, the broken-down shed nearby. We were counting on the Royalists not being smart enough to fire it, too, and our bet paid off. They're probably six miles out of Idyll by now, looking for a place to camp for the night."

Naren reined in his blowing, sweat-lathered piebald and dismounted before the beast had slid to a complete stop. He and Saxton embraced, laughing and trading ribald jests. Then Naren turned to face Ginger.

All mirth and revelry faded from the mage's eyes. "Castarr?"

Naren, too, had sobered, his previous ebullience gone. A cold expression swept his features. "It's done. As you feared, Castarr refused to surrender his key without a struggle. Jory agreed to stay behind and mind the teleportal. I left him strict orders to open it only to Belvemar or Gregaris."

Ginger nodded, satisfied. "Thank you, Naren. You know we had no other choice. I only regret circumstance elected you."

"It was my pleasure." Naren's hand came to rest meaningfully on the hilt of his dagger.

It did not take a genius to figure out Naren had carried out a death sentence on Castarr at Ginger's order.

"I sent word to Belvemar," Naren continued. "He'll be ready."

"Belvemar?" I interrupted. "He's all right? He's safe?"

"Yes, he's fine," Ginger replied. "He's in the forest with nearly two hundred men."

I was flabbergasted. Someone had a lot of nerve to double-cross Valleri like that. And here I had suspected him of treachery. "If Valleri finds out, he'll have your hides hung from the castle walls."

"So who's going to tell him?" Ginger retorted, a sharpness in his voice I did not recognize.

"Let's move things along," Saxton interrupted. "Valleri will wonder at an overlong delay."

The four of us withdrew to discuss the situation. I asked Ginger, "What happened? Castarr told us you'd disappeared during a Royalist charge."

The mage snorted. "I'm sure he saw what he wished to see, but I was only knocked unconscious. One of my men dragged me to safety. By the time I'd roused, Valleri had already won the skirmish and withdrew. We found a safe place to hole up, then I sent word to Saxton's agents saying we needed him. When the reply came back that Castarr had ransomed you, Saxton and I arranged an ambush."

"So you attacked the escort, then donned their uniforms and armour," I finished. That explained Saxton's delay.

Ginger nodded. "We left behind some men disguised as mercs to inform Naren of our plans and rode to your rescue."

Quite ingenious. Roaming the countryside under Roche's banner and Saxton's leadership, the impostors were safe from Royalist scrutiny.

"In the meantime," Ginger continued, "once the deal had been struck with Valleri, Naren sent out scouts. They found Belvemar tucked away in the forest with his survivors."

Naren added, "When I learned the report of Ginger's death had been premature, I dispatched Jory to inform Belvemar. I left my second behind to see the refugees safely out of Thylana. Sestus has rallied some and Biddy is confident of a complete recovery, but he's still too weak to take command."

"You should know, Highness," Saxton added, "that Bertrand and his Halberdiers have barricaded themselves in your tower. The Regent sensed some time ago that Valleri was about to make his move on the throne. Val's not too concerned about him, though."

I nodded bleakly, out of time and out of ideas.

It seemed nobody knew what to do next. Apparently, my rescuers had not thought the plan through this far. But they agreed on two things: revenge and glory. They still entertained fantasies of turning a victory. As for me, I was just grateful to be alive, that Ginger was alive. I was happy, too, to be free. The urge to turn around and leave with Biddy and the others was tempting. I was willing to admit defeat.

Ginger did not share my sentiment. He sketched out the bones of a hasty plan, the audacity of which petrified me. When I voiced my reservations he challenged me. "Why quit now? The battle is half won. Where's your imagination, Kathedra? Or have you lost your nerve?"

I stiffened at his sarcasm. Our reunion had not necessarily changed things between us. "I've not lost my nerve, mage," I shot back. "But it seems you've lost your wits. Perhaps that blow to your head was a little harder than you realized."

Naren and Saxton glanced away, trying to blend into the scenery.

"Excuse us, gentlemen," Ginger snarled. "The princess and I have a few things to discuss." Snatching my arm, he took me aside and demanded, "Shall we part here? You go your way, I go mine?"

His belligerence put me on the defensive, which was perhaps his intention. He did not want to be the one to give in. "You know that's not what I want. If you'll remember, it was you who rejected me."

"You were not honest with me!"

Ah, this again. "Will you never forgive me?"

"Not as long as you don't trust me."

This seemed to be the crux of it. He could not forgive me and I could not forget. After a lengthy silence, Ginger sighed, "I promise, Kathedra. If you walk away now, you'll never have your throne. This is your last chance to claim it. I say we seize the moment now, when we have Saxton to get us inside the castle."

His plan, I confess, made sense. But it was risky. Strolling into the den of one's enemies is not something to be undertaken lightly. If anything went wrong we'd be trapped inside. The whole thing made me skittish. Feeling threatened, I dug in my heels like a stubborn goat, refusing to see reason, imagining insults and deceits.

"Don't rush me. I need time to—"

"You need a nudge," he interrupted. "See, Kathedra? This is exactly what Repachea meant. Your indecisiveness and vacillation will be the bane of us just as it was the Royalists."

"Oh, so because I don't run off on the first hare-brained scheme which pops into that empty space between your ears, I'm indecisive? I'm gutless?"

I shook my head, dismayed. Ginger and I were such opposites. He was impulsive and bold, almost reckless, willing to do whatever was necessary, no matter the peril, no matter the cost, while I was naturally cautious and patient. I liked order, discipline, direction. Ginger happily courted chaos and danger.

"Do what you want. You will anyway. You don't need my blessing."

He wore a look of abject indignation. "Your ingratitude is astounding. Do what I want? I'm doing this for you."

"For me? Hah! All you want is revenge and you intend to use me to get it." If I had not been so distraught, perhaps if I'd listened more closely, I might have understood exactly what it was Ginger tried to say to me-that he was committed to my cause and supported unequivocally my claim to the throne. But all I'd heard was his bitterness and conceit.

"Use you? Is that what you think?"

"Admit it. You want my powers." Thrusting my hand in his face, I pointed to the ring. "Isn't that why you rescued me? You need my magic to help you reap your vengeance."

His eyes, widening first with disbelief, then narrowing in fury, flickered from me to the ring. "Is it a show of faith you want?" Seizing my wrist, he yanked the band from my finger and hurled it far into the bushes. "How's that? Is that proof enough of my motives?"

I gaped, unable to fathom the mage's latest dementia.

"I don't need your powers to achieve my goals," he hissed, his brow thunderous. "If you want your crown, use your Teki magic to defeat Valleri. Use it of your own volition, with clarity of purpose and deadly force."

"It's not a question of choice," I countered. "It's just I don't know if I can do what you ask. I don't know if I hate Valleri enough to wield my powers against him."

His voice contained a strange mixture of disgust and pity. "That's your biggest problem, isn't it? You let your heart rule your thoughts, your powers. If it is true control, true order, you seek, then you must cast aside your feelings. You must change how you think. Not what you think."

He had a point. Arrogance and ignorance had combined to keep me weak, my powers erratic and limited. Magic wasn't about talent alone. It was about discipline, confidence, determination, things it had taken Ginger years of practice and diligence to acquire. I was but a novice.

Humbly, I said, "So teach me."

"I can't teach you in an hour," he harrumphed.

"I know. I'm asking for as long as it takes, whether that be a year or a lifetime."

Ginger gazed at me for a long moment, his face cast in a deepening sadness. "If all you need is a teacher, you've got the wrong man."

He gave me no opportunity to ponder this new riddle, immediately launching into a fresh tirade. "What do you think to do? Run away like you did before? The Umagi can't protect you. Not from war. Not from duty. Valleri needs you to legitimize his claim to the throne. He will never let you go. Never."

Unfortunately, I knew everything he said to be true. I had to confront Uncle. I had to supplant Valleri. I would not live out my life a frightened, hunted thing, endangering those I loved because I was too scared to act now.

"I must take action," I agreed. "But I have one condition." Not giving him a chance to object, I rushed on, "No harm must come to Uncle or Valleri. They are mine to deal with in any fashion I deem fit."

Even before I'd completed my last sentence I could see Ginger was going to balk. "You overstep yourself, Kathedra," he murmured. "I've waited long enough to serve justice on Bertrand and I won't be denied my due. As for my feud with Valleri, that is between him and me. Stay out of it. I promise you, if either one of them comes within reach of my sword, I'll not hesitate to run him through."

"Ginger, please don't force my hand on this."

"What the hell is that supposed to mean?"

"I know about Valleri. I know what happened in Idyll all those years ago. Hasn't he suffered enough? If I can forgive him, why can't you?"

"Forgive him? Kathedra, you really have no idea what you're talking about."

I lifted my chin, squared my shoulders, dredging up every ounce of courage. He left me no recourse but to prod his failing memory. "Back in Idyll you promised to protect me, to serve me unquestioningly. I beg you to remember that promise now."

He scowled, shocked that I dared issue him an ultimatum, furious that I dared threaten him. Of course, bullying Ginger was probably the wrong thing to do. His pride would inevitably compel him to ascertain the logical, then do the opposite. Nevertheless, I commanded here, by sanction of the surviving officers.

"And if I choose to forget?"

"If you break your oath to me I will charge you with treason. I don't need to remind you of the penalty it carries."

"Then, Highness, on the return of your throne I will present my neck to your executioner's blade."

He was laughing at me, I knew, mocking my authority. He had called my bluff, and if I desired his respect, that of his comrades, and ultimately, that of my subjects, I had to take a stand. I could not back down from Ginger or anyone else.

"Do what you must. But for a broken vow, for disobedience, you will find yourself banished again from Thylana."

That pricked open an old wound, firing his rage anew. "You would exile the man who won you a kingdom? You would banish your own champion? Hah! You don't deserve my—"

Ignoring his tantrum I turned and strode to where our companions waited. I refused to argue with him. A commander need not debate orders with her subordinates. I would not permit my directives to be questioned.

Naturally, Ginger took exception to my curt dismissal. "Don't turn your back to me," he growled. Marching up behind me, he snagged my arm and swung me around. "I'm not finished with you. Listen to me. You cannot afford to show the least mercy to Valleri and Bertrand. If you spare either of them, he will be a nagging thorn in your side forever. Your throne will never be secure. Your life will be in constant danger."

I held his glower, defying his anger. "I will not countenance their deaths. Besides, their fate is not yours to command. It's mine."

Ginger was livid. "This is how you reward my loyalty? This is how you express your appreciation?"

"Enough. You need to forgive them, Ginger. You need to let it go, to reconcile your pain to the past and leave it there. You can't heal inside unless you forgive yourself, and you can't do that if you're holding grudges against everyone."

Still he would not lower that baleful glare. "I know now that I'm not to blame for Mauranna's death, or even Nelia's. But I know who is, and I will make him pay restitution, along with anyone else who dares defend him."

That sounded dangerously like a threat. But Ginger had already spun on a heel and marched off to his horse, making the rest of the Crusaders scurry to mount up in the fear he'd ride off without them.

CHAPTER TWENTY-SEVEN

Knowing a delay would raise Valleri's suspicions, Saxton was on the brink of a faint by the time we finally got moving. The closer we drew to the castle the more Royalists we encountered. Although I thought it strange, it corroborated the theory that with the Crusaders' defeat Valleri would recall his patrols, allowing Belvemar to converge unimpeded upon Gryphon's walls. I had warned Ginger that Valleri wasn't that stupid, whereupon he tersely informed me it would be my task to distract Val if he proved cleverer than the mage believed.

I found myself in a tedious dilemma, caught between a rock and a boulder. On one hand, Ginger expected me to manipulate then betray Valleri. On the other, Valleri expected me to bend to his will and assume my role of puppet queen. But neither was aware he had placed me in the unique position of being able to undermine them both. I would use one against the other in order to achieve my goals, proving myself just as ruthless and shrewd as they.

Oddly enough I grew calmer, more confident, with each step we took towards the castle. I was resolved to my course and so were the men who rode with me. Although fully aware of the possibility they may be riding to their deaths, they did not show it. Regardless of the outcome, whether that be success or failure, these men already considered themselves heroes.

Sighting our party, Gryphon's sentries sounded the alert and raised the portcullis. We clattered beneath the iron gate, Roche's banner snapping above our heads. The castle came to a standstill as its inhabitants paused to gawk at the somewhat less than triumphant return of the exiled Princess Kathedra, or the deposed Gryphon Highlord, depending on one's point of view.

Judging by the taut silence charging the air, the castlefolk did not know whether to hail my rise from the grave with cheers of welcome or gasps of disbelief. My gaze drifted to the east tower, where Uncle had imprisoned himself. The structure projected a sullen malice all its own.

A grisly sight awaited us as we rode farther into the bailey. Testament to Valleri's vengeance had been erected in its centre, diligently shunned by men and beasts alike. Jubilant crows congregated at its foot in anticipation of the feast to come. Above them the stripped and bloodied forms of men were impaled on spikes. I recognized their faces, contorted in expressions of excruciating pain, as those of the soldiers who had belonged to Averi's hunting party so many seasons ago. But their officer was not among them. A few of the bodies still twitched. Valleri's justice had been swift and merciless.

Beside me Naren pretended not to notice, but not even the hindrance of his helm could conceal the fear that drained the colour from his face. I would bet death and martyrdom did not seem so appealing to the Crusaders now. If they failed in their mission they would share a similar fate.

Glancing at Ginger, I tried to gauge his reaction. He seemed more disturbed by the number of Shouda prowling the grounds. Apparently his faith in Owyn's expertise was not absolute. His gaze constantly strayed to his gauntleted hand, as if to reassure himself of the talisman's presence beneath the layers of leather and steel. He had every right to be apprehensive. The mage would forever bear a set of jagged scars as reminders of the wound inflicted by the Shouda's powerful jaws, a wound I knew caused intermittent pain, although he never spoke of it to me.

We had barely drawn to a halt when Valleri appeared. Saxton vaulted from his horse and doffed his helm. Dropping to a knee, he bowed his head. "Milord, I've delivered the Princess Kathedra as ordered."

"As I can see." Valleri gestured the young captain to rise. "What took you so long?"

Saxton rose with a carefully feigned expression of embarrassment. "My apologies, milord. But the princess refused to come peacefully. She made several attempts to escape our custody."

Valleri's gaze sharpened. "I trust she is unharmed?"

"Aye, milord. As you instructed."

At Valleri's dismissal, Saxton and his fellow Crusaders headed for the stables. I felt Ginger's eyes boring into my back in silent warning. Belvemar would arrive with reinforcements tonight. I had only to hold my own with Valleri for a few hours.

Val looked expectantly at me. "Welcome home, Kathedra."

Dismounting, I sniffed, "It's hardly the glorious homecoming I envisioned, being dragged back to Gryphon under the banner of my enemies."

"Enemies? They are allies, loyal to you."

"Loyal to you," I snapped. "There's a difference."

Valleri chose to ignore that. He seemed about to embrace me, but upon glimpsing my expression thought wiser of it. He fashioned a tentative smile. "How's our dear old friend Sestus?"

His casual reference angered me. "He was gravely injured in your attack on Idyll. He could well be crippled for life, thanks to you."

He frowned at the accusation, appearing genuinely distressed by the news, as well he should. As a child Val had been just as fond as I of Sestus. But he would not rise to the bait, seemingly loath to instigate an argument with me. "I'm sorry to hear that. A regrettable mishap. But he shouldn't have stood against me. I would have gladly spared him, otherwise."

I stared at him, trying to measure his sincerity. He was in high good cheer, almost chipper, no trace of his previous enmity evident. He behaved as if nothing had happened to tarnish our rapport. His eyes watched me with that worshipful look of a lost puppy that's found a friend, his manner more attentive and courteous than I could remember.

As he took my elbow to escort me from the bailey I snatched it away. "Lead on. I shall follow."

"As you wish."

Valleri waved an arm at his gruesome monument, scattering the crows with irate squawks. "Would you care to greet our friends?" he asked in the most conversational of tones.

I averted my gaze. "Valleri, you know I cannot stomach cruelty."

"Cruelty?" He laughed, incredulous. "What exactly would you call what they inflicted upon you?"

"Their attack on me was savage and cowardly, yes," I admitted. "Nevertheless, I cannot sanction this barbarism. They should pay for their crimes, I agree. All this time I've fantasized about their punishment, but I'd wanted them alive, or at least cognizant of it. This is not justice, Valleri. This is torture."

"It's nothing less than the whoresons deserve," he hissed, glaring up at the unconscious men. "I promised you restitution and I delivered."

A shudder of revulsion shook me. "That's the whole point. It wasn't your decision to make. I was the one abused and demeaned. Vengeance was mine to take and you deprived me of it."

Valleri actually had the gall to look hurt by my rebuke.

"End it, Val. Please. Do so for me."

"I don't know why it matters," he grumbled. "They're nearly dead already. I promise you may have Averi all to yourself once he is apprehended. He's a canny—"

"Valleri!"

"Oh, all right." His attitude had become that of a spoiled child, miffed because someone had ruined his fun. He signalled to his sentries, who put a swift end to the torture.

Recovering his equilibrium, Valleri said cheerfully, "I have a special treat awaiting you in the dungeons if you'd care to take a tour. No doubt you're anxious to see some of your old friends."

A chill crawled up my spine. Gryphon's dungeons are my least favourite place in the whole world. "Friends?"

"Why, yes. You know, friends like Grezalia and Lesuperis. I assure you, all of those who were ever cruel or spiteful to you now live to regret their disrespect."

I cringed, in dread of the cold and ruthless creature he'd become. "You promised not to harm Lesuperis."

"I promised not to kill him," Valleri reminded me.

"You also promised to let the Crusaders go free. Will you honour that promise in the same manner?"

He seemed genuinely offended. "Of course I will honour it, though it goes against my better judgment." Then his expression hardened as the darkest of suspicions crept into his twisted mind. "Could it be you are merely concerned for your Umagi lover?"

I'd wondered when he would bring that up. I held his stormy glance, filled with remorse at all that had fallen between us. "Val, I'm sorry. It wasn't my intention to hurt you. It just happened. Whatever lies between you and Ginger can still be resolved. Extend the truce. Invite him to par—"

He whirled on me, eyes glittering with rage or malice or both. "Never. There can be no truce between us. Mention his name to me no more. The Ginger I knew died at Idyll over a decade ago."

Though there was more I might say, I held my tongue.

As we entered the castle proper, servants and guards alike greeted me warmly, with an extravagance of curtsies and bows. The unaccustomed adulation shocked me. Neither my earlier incarnations as the Princess Kathedra nor the Gryphon Highlord had ever evoked so elaborate a display.

Valleri seemed pleased, exhibiting no sign of jealousy at the favourable response I'd received. "Aren't you glad to be home, Kathedra? See? Everyone is delighted to welcome you back. This show of affection is all for you."

I remained wary. "How do I know this show is not all for you?"

"I've already told you," he sighed wearily. "I don't covet your throne."

A snort of derision slipped out. "You stole my command, Valleri. You conspired with my own uncle against me. Why should I believe anything you say?"

"I did not set out specifically to seize your command. It was all part of my plan to win you Thylana's throne. I want only to please you, Kathedra."

"Is this how you think to please me? By lying, deceiving, stealing, killing?"

"You wouldn't take steps yourself. You needed someone to act for you. You need me still, to safeguard your rule and put things in order. Once you're ready, I'll gladly place the royal sceptre in your hands. Then you will thank me."

"You expect me to believe you've done all this out of the goodness of your heart, just so you can present it to me like a boxed and beribboned gift? Why? To earn my approval? My love?"

"You act like I've done something wrong."

"You bloody well have!"

He turned smug. "By doing what? Let's see…I crushed the Crusaders, I supplanted the tyrant Bertrand, and I'm about to put the rightful heir on the throne."

"Is that really how you see yourself?" I cried, astonished by his unapologetic arrogance. "As a hero?"

"Really, Kathedra. You make me sound like a rogue. Once Bertrand is gone, you will be crowned queen. Then all the people of Thylana will flock to Castle Gryphon to witness your coronation. We'll have a grand celebration in your honour, with feasting and drinking and merriment. Then…we can be married."

Naturally. That only made sense, along with the rest of it.

I fell quiet, studying the faces we passed, finding something hidden beneath their masks of jubilance and warmth, something like a silent plea for help. Oh, yes, they were happy to have me home again. They saw my presence as deliverance from the madman who ruled this place.

"I have chosen to forgive your indiscretion," Valleri continued. "After all, you were vulnerable and lonely. It would have taken the mage little effort to bewitch you."

"That's gracious of you."

He was so wrapped up in himself he didn't notice my sarcasm.

We came to a stop outside Valleri's private rooms. "I apologize that you cannot have your own apartments but they are otherwise occupied."

He referred, of course, to the deposed regent, who had sought refuge in my tower. "I want to see Uncle."

"I'm afraid that's not possible. Bertrand isn't receiving visitors at the present. Trust me when I say he is unharmed. A little hungry perhaps, but unharmed."

"I want to see for myself."

"We'll discuss it later." He gestured me inside. When I declined to move, he took my arm and firmly guided me into the inner chamber. "Don't be stubborn, Kathedra."

Though I did not mistake his conduct for anything less than coercion, I did not feel physically threatened. Valleri had never manhandled me before, never touched me with violence in his hand. He manipulated with a fleshly glamour Ginger had never thought to try, employing misty eyes, velvet gloves, and silken words, all weapons for which I'd never had any defence.

Val did not immediately release me. He kicked the door shut with his heel and pressed closer, compelling me to back up against the nearest wall. "Later, when you've had time to adjust, you'll see how right I am." He flashed me his most winsome grin and caressed my cheek. "Tonight, you and I will honour your homecoming with a private celebration. In the meantime, I'll have Cook bring you some hot food. You must be famished. How are you managing your Teki powers? Well, I trust."

"Yes, very well, in fact. I've made some progress, with Sestus's help. Speaking of which, I'd like—"

But he wasn't really interested, merely being polite. "That's good news to hear, Kathedra. You can take comfort in the knowledge that I've ordered the Shouda caged, to be eventually destroyed, so there won't be any unfortunate mishaps."

That startled me. "You trust me?"

"Of course. If all goes according to my plan, you shall be queen by the end of the night. Why would you want to jeopardize that?"

It seemed our plans were the same, though they would be achieved by different means.

As Valleri stepped out the door, two sentries materialized. “A precaution is all. There’s no telling what foul temper Bertrand might take once he learns you still live. He’s quite mad, you know.”

The door swung closed with an ominous thud and a bar slid into place. My mad Uncle like hell. In spite of his attempts at mollification, Valleri did not trust me to submit meekly to his will.

Relieved by his departure I sank down onto the bed, one I had shared with Valleri on so many occasions. It was as I’d feared. My Teki blood flowed serene and content, as treacherous as my heart. The sight of Val conjured no ill thoughts of hate or vengeance in me. Even the words he spoke could not move me to want him to come to any harm. And the terrifying thought occurred What if I feel nothing for him at all? But that was wrong. I did feel something for Val that I think was pity.

Sitting there on the bed, I tried to fathom this demon that had so impudently taken possession of Valleri’s body. I sensed Val’s mental fragility, the brittleness of his emotions, which could snap at any time. It seemed that two distinct personalities warred inside him, one sedate and virtuous, the other malicious and out of control. His mood fluctuated inside a broad spectrum of conflicting emotions, all within the blink of an eye. He was attentive and blithe one moment, hostile and terse the next. Actually, when compared to Valleri, Ginger’s quite sane.

He had changed so much since last I’d seen him. Could it be his obsession with the throne had grown to such monstrous proportions it had devoured all rational thought? Or did it all hinge on the past events at Idyll. He seemed driven by his hatred for his Uncle, which was triggered by the slightest affront.

The squeal of hinges interrupted my musings as a sentry opened the door. I looked up, expecting to see Cook, but it was Saxton who entered.

Before the door closed behind him, I saw six Crusaders disguised as mercs outside in the corridor.

I got to my feet, seized by a feeling of dread. It was too early for him to be here. “What’s going on? What’s wrong?”

“There’s been a change in plans,” he replied, his face drawn into grim lines that made him appear much older than his twenty-odd years. “Valleri senses that something’s amiss; he has an uncanny instinct for stuff like that. He’s decided to break with tradition and marry you tonight, before your coronation.”

“Oh, dear.”

“Yes, Highness. We have to act now. I’ve sent Naren out to hurry up Belvemar, but I don’t think they’ll get here in time.”

“Naren? Won’t he be conspicuous? He might be followed.”

The captain shook his head. “He shouldn’t draw any special attention. I have my troops on the walls now. There are patrols coming in all the time and couriers going out. The gate is open more than it's closed. Besides, no one questions my authority unless they wish to answer to Valleri."

"What did Ginger have to say about this new plan?"

"Actually, he's the one who ordered it changed."

Oh, he did, did he?

As we attempted to leave, however, Valleri's sentries refused to let us pass. Saxton feigned sputtering outrage. "Stand aside. I'm here to escort the princess to the Gryphon Highlord, under his direct orders."

The guards exchanged a glance. "Milord did not speak of such to us."

"He didn't have to. He spoke to me." Saxton tried to shove past them but they blocked us with their pikes. Instantly, our mercs drew their swords in response.

"Don't be foolish," Saxton told the sentries. "You're outnumbered."

They didn't budge. Their uncertain gazes flickered to where I stood firm in Saxton's grip. The one nearest me, a sergeant from the Royal formerly under my command, said, "We won't let you harm the princess, nor take her where she does not wish to go. Even if milord Valleri commands it."

Vexed, Saxton roared, "I have no intention of harming her, you stupid ox!"

In an effort to avoid bloodshed I intervened. "I think you'd best do as you are directed, gentlemen."

The second guard stared at me. "But it's our duty to protect you, Highness, to give our lives for yours. We won't—"

Pouncing like a panther, Saxton thrust the soldier up against the wall, blade at his throat. "Where are your loyalties?" he demanded. "Do they lie with Valleri or the Princess Kathedra?"

The guard swallowed hard but managed the retort, "Slay me dead, but we serve the princess."

Saxton released the man and sheathed his dagger. "Then stand aside, for so do we."

It took a moment for Saxton's remark to sink in, but once it did, the two sentries sighed in relief.

"How many more like you are there?" I asked them.

"Two thirds of your former Royal, Highness, would cross to you without hesitation," the sergeant replied. "The rest could be persuaded."

"Good. Round them up and pass the word-there's a coup afoot. When I need you, I'll yell. Try to stall Valleri as long as you can."

Saxton ordered his mercs back to the gatehouse, and the two of us proceeded below ground. "What now?" I asked.

"Nothing's changed except the timetable. You and I will head to the cellar as planned, and don our disguises. Ginger has control of the gate now and will hook up with us as soon as he can."

The original plan had been for Saxton to post Crusader guards under their mercenary guise on the battlements. It was Ginger's task to sabotage the castle's war machines with spells, so no opposition could hamper Belvemar's approach if he were spotted. But now Valleri had forced us to act prematurely. If we went ahead on our own, how long could we survive without Belvemar's assistance?

"Perhaps we should wait for Belvemar. Just a few hours."

"Forget it, Highness," Saxton harrumphed, hurrying us through the maze of corridors. "In a few hours you'll be wedded and bedded by Valleri…and that Ginger absolutely will not allow."

For some unfathomable reason that statement raised my hackles. "Oh, really? Who is he to decide what I shall or—"

"Someone who loves you, Highness."

That silenced me like nothing else could.

"Here's the situation, Highness. Although we'd prefer to avoid a clash of arms with Valleri, if it comes to a conflict we'll have a modicum of inside support. Roche's mercenaries—"

"Kathedra."

"Beg pardon, Highness?"

"Call me Kathedra."

"If you order it so, Highness. As I was saying, Roche's mercenaries, if forced to take sides, will be inclined to cut their losses and run. So far, the Gryphon Highlord's troops are loyal to Val. They worship him as they did you. They are in awe of his battle prowess, basking in victory after victory. His charisma holds them in thrall. In their eyes, he's a hero. But this only holds true while they believed you dead. Their first loyalty has always been to you. I'm confident that if you asked for their support they'd give it, just like the guard said."

Heartening words indeed. "So where does that leave us if Valleri wants to cross swords?"

Saxton frowned. "Lacking, I'm afraid. As you know, Fleurry is indignant at being under Valleri's thumb, but he's still in Pixley with orders to remain there until Gregaris breaks. And Bertrand's Halberdiers, barricaded in the tower, is of no concern. It's Chiverly and Tock we have to worry about."

He paused briefly in our march down the corridor to draw a dagger from his boot and give it to me. "For protection…just in case."

I tucked the blade into my belt, muttering, "Serasteffan really has got to go."

"No argument here, Highness," he replied with a snort. "Serasteffan's leadership has turned Arial's Royal into a pack of bullies. Only Arial himself can bring his men to heel. Stef is Val's faithful minion, make no mistake."

We swiftly descended the stone steps, burrowing deeper into the roots of the castle, past the dungeons and crypt. Taking a torch placed there for us, Saxton pushed open the worm-eaten door to the cellar. An army of furry things fled the torchlight as we crept down the flight of rickety wooden stairs, hoping the contraption would not collapse beneath our weight.

Our descent complete Saxton set the torch in a bracket to have a look around. I found the bundle of clothing atop a crate. With Saxton's help I slipped into my mercenary disguise. As he lifted the finely meshed mail shirt over my head, I asked him, "How in the world did you get involved in all this?"

He shrugged. "Just bizarre timing, I guess. It didn't really start until after the incident in Dundurn. It doesn't really seem all that long ago."

"You were hardly more than a child," I sniffed, donning Roche's black and white surcoat.

"Yes, and a stupid child at that. I left my village a foolish, beardless boy eager to seek his fortune; I grew to manhood fast. I owe my life to a stranger I met on the road, after I'd been waylaid and robbed by a gang of thieves not two days out."

I hazarded a guess. "Repachea?" Wrinkling my nose at some unidentifiable odour, I pulled on the leather coif and tucked every last wisp of telltale red hair inside.

"Naren. An ex-housecarl for some fancy lordling up north. But he was young and bored, and the lord's pay was crap. So he headed south, hoping to hook up with a merc outfit. I was just lucky he came across me on the way. Anyhow, he let me tag along. The first town we came to was Dundurn. We lingered a while because the ale was good and the place was full of Umagi students, some of them female and pretty, gathered there for some kind of protest against the Regent's decree, which banned the use of magic. Before we knew it, Bertrand's troops had arrived to quell the riot. But it wasn't really a riot, Highness. Just a group of over-zealous Umagi and their supporters, a little drunk on ale and the high that comes from defying authority. Then the screaming started, and all hell broke loose."

He lapsed into reflective silence, causing me to prod, "So you were one of the original conspirators?"

"I suppose you could say that. I was present in that room in Dundurn when Ginger carried in Nelia's broken body. He just dumped her on the table in front of me and collapsed on the bench beside her. Her eyes were open but I could tell she was dead. Actually, I though they were both dead. Then people started to crowd into the inn, some of them weeping and bleeding, all hysterical, seeking refuge from Bertrand's troops. Naren took charge right away, calming them down, sorting them out. When the soldiers came, looking for insurgents they said, I had Nelia and Ginger looking like two lovers snuggled by the fire, so Naren was able to convince them to go on their way."

Saxton had told me all this in a dispassionate tone, until he'd come to the part about Ginger and Nelia. Here his eyes grew wide, their whites gone red as they bore into mine, as if he struggled for understanding, his voice betraying his bafflement. "But Ginger just disappeared, wandering away somehow in the commotion in a stupor of grief and hatred. No one saw him again until Idyll, when he volunteered to help erect the teleportals."

He paused to pass me a pair of gauntlets two sizes too big. "To his dismay,

Naren came out of it looking like some of sort of champion to the Umagi and they enlisted him in their cause, which was to force the Regent into capitulation over his decree. With his help, the Umagi were able to persuade two old, worn-out mercs, who'd tired of bleeding and killing for rich people's profit, to join them."

"Belvemar and Gregaris?"

He nodded. "Repachea and Sestus soon followed, outraged by the tragedy at Dundurn. Castarr was the last. Obnoxious and arrogant even then, he was tolerated because we needed his money to finance the movement. Ginger came later, drawn by the rumours of insurrection."

"What about Ragsey?"

"By the time he arrived with the mage I was already gone. When word leaked out from Gryphon that the Regent was hiring mercs to help squelch the uprising, I signed up with Roche. It was my task to undermine the Royalist defence." Saxton favoured me with a sly grin. "It was not solely Roche's fault Church Grove was a debacle."

I took the dented and rusted helm he held out to me, one that my great-grandfather might have worn into battle. I looked but there was no sword. "You had a hand in that?"

His tone turned smug. "The Crusaders planned very carefully right from the start. They realized the advantage of having an insider working on their behalf. So we devised a complicated network of code by which we could contact one another in a crisis…and here I am."

"I remember you," I announced, surprising him and myself.

I recalled a dark-haired youth with soft, compassionate eyes, kneeling in the muck of the soggy road from Church Grove, straining alongside me as we strove to free my charger. The horse was mired in a sinkhole, weighed down by mud and mounds of gear for which he hadn't been bred to carry. It had happened during a Crusader ambush, led by, I was later told, Repachea. Three days of torrential rain and biting wind hampered our retreat. All was panic and chaos, our wagons abandoned in clay-like ooze, our supplies transferred to balky rampagers. Nevertheless, harried by the enemy and drenched by the merciless downpour, I refused to leave behind my stallion, to let him die trapped in the mud. Spying my difficulty, a passing mercenary stopped to help me.

"You saved him…my horse."

Saxton smiled. "I didn't think you remembered. Foolish I know, but I just couldn't bear to see the poor beast struggle." He shook his head at his folly. "You wouldn't desert him and I feared for your life." His eyes met mine and I glimpsed sincerity in their depths. "I'd always tried to protect you, Highness. Through all my deceit and sabotage, it was never my interest to harm you."

I could still picture that day in my mind. He'd had been kicked and bitten and thoroughly abused by the panicked horse as the stallion flailed to free himself. Saxton might have been killed. His efforts had been nothing less than heroic and I'd treated him as if he were invisible. He was a peasant, a merc, an inferior, and I hadn't even bothered to ask his name.

I reached out a hand to touch his cheek. "Oh, Saxton," I murmured, feeling so ashamed I almost wept. "Did I once say thank you?"

He let his gaze slide away from mine, embarrassed I think, to acknowledge this failing in his future queen. "It was enough to see the poor animal pulled free. I've always had a fondness for the noble beasts. Once this is all over, I hope to pursue my dream of breeding and training war-horses. I even entertain the absurdity I might sell a pair to Thylana's queen for her royal stables."

He grinned at me through the grit that smeared his face. "For a small fortune, of course."

I patted the rogue's shoulder, convinced he could sell me the whole damned herd. "I'll take two of every colour."

A voice beside us said, "Well, isn't this touching?"

I whirled to see the mage. He wore a haughty sneer and there was mockery in his eyes. "Are you making this a practice then," I snapped, "sneaking up on me like you do?"

Ignoring me, he shifted his gaze to Saxton. "Are we ready then?"

A mask of granite slipped over Saxton's face. Once more he became the confident, no nonsense soldier I'd first encountered, a guise he could don at will. "How are things up top?"

"Quiet. Chiverly's men are scouring the castle for Averi. Everyone else is on alert. It endangers our plan some."

"What's Val's Royal doing?" I interrupted.

"Nothing special. Just standing around. Why?"

Briefly, I enlightened him. "They won't move against Valleri unless I give the word. Until then they'll follow his orders to the letter to keep him from suspicion."

I tabulated figures. "It's not enough. Sooner or later Valleri and Urharde will find us. We're too short on manpower to offer adequate resistance. We need Arial. We need him free to take back his outfit from that lunatic Serasteffan. We have to get to the dungeons. Our entire plan hinges on that. There's no room for failure."

Saxton agreed. "No trouble. I can bluff a few guards."

"There's only one problem," Ginger conceded. "How do we get Arial out without being seen? We can't stroll blithely through the castle. We'll encounter too many people. And…what if we run into Valleri?"

"That's two problems," Saxton pointed out.

"It's too late to worry about that now." I donned my helm, scooped up an extra uniform and stuffed it under my tunic, beefing up my disguise. "The darkness will work to our advantage. Let's go."

CHAPTER TWENTY-EIGHT

We reached the dungeons without trouble. Guards congregated in the doorway, exchanging idle talk, some of them disgruntled at being relegated below ground to keep watch over a few forgotten prisoners. I counted a dozen at least, probably too many for us to overwhelm without causing an alarm. Urharde himself was nowhere in sight. I identified the key holder, a short, stocky sergeant, then beckoned to Saxton and Ginger crouched behind me.

"Are you ready, Saxton? We'll only get one stab at this."

"As ready as I'll ever be."

We flanked Saxton as he strode towards the guards in the entryway. I tried to walk a little taller, adding a male swagger in the hope I lent an air of arrogance to my disguise. Apparently our facade was rather impressive; as soon as they caught sight of us, the guards bolted for their posts and stood to attention.

We stopped in front of the sergeant. Even I towered over him. No doubt, from his disadvantage, he found Saxton extremely intimidating, especially in his coat of light chain mail, with helm tucked in his elbow. Caught loafing, he made a great show of obeisance. "Greetings, sir," he gabbled at the ground, unable to meet Saxton's withering gaze. "I…we…did not expect to see—"

Saxton cut him short with an impatient gesture. "I've come for the captain. Give me the keys."

Surprised, the sergeant stammered, "Do…do you mean release the prisoner Arial, sir?" He glanced uncertainly around him. "But Captain Urharde didn't mention any of this to me. My orders are to keep one eye on Arial and the other on the alert for Averi."

Saxton took a menacing step forward; the sergeant stumbled back a pace. "Aye, sir," he demurred. "Right away."

I grinned behind my helm as the sergeant removed a set of keys from his belt.

"What's going on here?" came an angry shout.

I jerked my head in the direction of the speaker, none other than Urharde himself. He marched towards us at alarming speed, fussing with the ties at his breeches, his face set in a scowl. Beside me, Ginger muttered, "Rot his eyes, where did he come from?"

My guess was the privy. Leaning close to Saxton, I said, "Just get the damned keys."

The sergeant tried to spit out an explanation, but Urharde talked right over top of him. "Saxton, what are you doing here? You look as if you expect a riot. Do you know something I don't?"

Saxton gave his head an emphatic shake, making his battle gear jingle and rattle. "Tell your sergeant to open Arial's cell. Valleri wants the captain released."

Urharde's eyebrows nearly shot off his face. "What? Why? Valleri was just here an hour ago, telling us to tighten our security."

"Well, obviously he's changed his mind and has decided to execute him instead."

I stifled a yip of surprise. That was not in the script. Saxton what the hell are you doing?

"Oh, why didn't you say so?" Urharde drew his sword, tested its edge with his thumb. "I'll truly enjoy cleaving that self-righteous bastard's head from his neck."

Urharde started for the cells, but Saxton swung out an arm and gripped his shoulder. "No. Valleri wants it public. He wants to make a statement, to send out a warning to anyone who questions his authority."

Urharde hesitated. "If you say so." He sheathed his sword, much to my relief. "Has he decided what he's going to do about Kathedra?"

"How should I know?"

"We'll, he'd better hurry," Urharde grumbled, snatching the key ring from his sergeant. "If he doesn't bring her to heel soon she'll stir up more trouble than he can handle."

"Yeah, well—" Saxton began, but Urharde wouldn't let him squeeze in a word edgewise.

"I keep telling him that he needs to take a heavier hand with her. She's too bold, too independent. Women like her only respond to strong discipline. But he indulges her every whim, showing leniency when he should be breaking her to the bit. Mind you, I'm not blind to her feminine charms, and I admit she must make a delightful mess of his bed. But he can't allow his codpiece to rule his head. Am I right?"

His what?

I couldn't believe my ears. I took a rash step forward, intending to yank out the oaf's tongue through his nose, but Ginger's hand snaked out and rapped my wrist. He could not contain a muffled snort of laughter. No doubt, the mage found the situation vastly entertaining.

"Yes, quite right," Saxton agreed. "He should turn the little vixen over his knee every once and while just to take the edge off her."

I elbowed Saxton's ribs, prompting him to grunt, "Captain, the keys, if you please."

"Saxton, are you sure this is wise? Perhaps you should try to change Valleri's mind. I mean, Arial's pretty popular with the troops. They might start grouching if—"

"Are you questioning Valleri's orders?" Saxton snapped, impatient now. "Do you recall what happened the last time his directives were defied? Why don't you make yourself useful and take your men to aid in Chiverly's search for Averi? I'll handle Arial."

Urharde gave all of us a once-over, but capitulated to Saxton's demands. He may not like the fact that a young upstart like Saxton was Valleri's second, but he wasn't going to jeopardize his own standing with the Gryphon Highlord by flouting his authority. "Aye, sir. Right away." He lifted the ring of keys into the air and let it drop into Saxton's open palm. "Just be careful. Arial still has a lot of fight in him."

"Valleri's counting on it."

Urharde grinned at that, then turned, rounding up his men and heading for the stairs.

Satisfied they were gone, Ginger and I left Saxton to watch the stairs, then proceeded to the cell area. While I had known Arial was not the dungeons' sole prisoner, I was ill prepared for what awaited me. The captain occupied the cell furthest from the door, which forced me to walk the length of the block. Lesuperis had the first cage all to himself. He resembled more a legendary yeti reported to inhabit the northern mountains than the pompous, strutting dandy I recall. More beast than man, he huddled in the shadows, moaning and whimpering to himself, his thin, scab-encrusted arms wrapped around his torso, wracked with shivers.

I moved on, nearly jumped out of my skin as the occupant in the next cell reached past me with a bone white hand to clutch at Ginger's tunic. Startled, the mage had half-drawn his sword before he realized who it was-a middle-aged woman, her iron-grey hair, always so neat and tidy in its bun, now tangled and knotted like the nest of a bird, her simple homespun garment dishevelled and soiled. The stench of her struck me in the face with the strength of an open fist. Her fingers clawed at Ginger's sleeve a moment before slipping free; her pale moon face, drawn and besmirched, loomed against the bars. She crowed at him in her hen's cackle, "Master Valleri, get back to your studies. The tutor is looking for you. You've missed your lessons for the last time. I will see the hide stripped from your back for this insolence."

Ginger leaned aside, just beyond reach of those hag's claws. I felt the weight of the look he passed me, but I couldn't meet it, too saddened and ashamed for poor old Grezalia.

At last we reached the cell at the very end, in near darkness. There was movement, a rustle of straw from the deepest shadows. A voice hoarse but defiant coughed out, "Why don't you tell Valleri to come down here and take me out himself instead of sending in his jackals?"

Though Ginger held out an arm before me, I approached the bars, making sure I stood in the light so the prisoner could see me, and drew off my helm. "Arial. Friend. It's me. Kathedra. I mean you no harm. We've come to free you."

"Highness? Is it really…you?" Slow, uncertain footsteps moved through the straw towards the bars into the weak orange light of the torch, and I saw him for the first time. His auburn, silver-shot hair hung lank and dirty almost to his chest. Thick rust-coloured stubble obliterated his jaw. His soldier's tunic was crushed, tattered, soiled with blood and sweat, the crest of the Gryphon hanging by a thread. A badly healed cut decorated one cheek. His left eye was swollen nearly shut, and he held himself stiffly as if in pain. He looked as if he'd crawled his way out of Hell's innermost pit.

"Yes, it's me. I must say, you look worse than you did at the battle of Storn." The Arial I had known then would have laughed at that, for he and his Eighth had been badly mauled there. But this version of the captain merely continued to stare at me as if he saw a ghost.

"Come closer," I entreated.

He obeyed, reached a grimy hand through the bars to touch my tunic, his fingers crawling up to my chin, then to the strands of my hair, long enough now to graze my shoulders. Beside me, I heard Ginger's indrawn breath at this liberty. "But you are dead," Arial whispered. "I saw your body, saw it draped over your horse when Averi led him through the gates, saw Bertrand fall prostrate with grief over it."

I swallowed hard, gripped his wrist, my throat so clogged with emotion I could barely speak. "No, Arial. Averi substituted a body double. It was all a plan of Valleri's gone horribly wrong." I searched his sea-green eyes, plumbing their depths for understanding. "Arial, believe me. I ordered none of this."

Recognition, or perhaps it was sanity, blossomed then. He withdrew his hand as if burnt, and flung himself to his knees before me in the filthy straw. "General, sir. If I may say so, you are a sight for sore eyes."

"Don't call me that. I'm just Kathedra now." I reached through the bars to take his arm. "Please, get up. You know we have come too far together for that. How long have you been down here?"

He managed a shrug, glancing around the walls of his prison as if he sought insight in their dank stone. "Weeks. Months. I've lost track. When I first fell out of favour with Valleri, Tock warned me to leave while I could, but I lingered. By the time I realized the danger the sentries at the gate had orders to detain me. I was spotted and a gang of Averi's thugs harried me through the keep. I couldn't fight them all…so I ended up here."

"Well, you'll be happy to know Averi's had a falling out of his own with Val. Also, Serasteffan's taken your command."

"I know. The bastard comes down here now and again to taunt me with it." He flicked a glance at Ginger, fitting keys into the lock at random. "Don't tell me you're running with mercs now? You're about as hard up for friends as I am."

"Not mercs, but friends, yes," I replied. "I'll explain later."

The mechanism clicked, and Ginger swung open the door on a squeal of hinges. Arial stepped through it with an air of disbelief, fearful perhaps it might close back in on him. The mage pocketed the keys, said, "Look, if we're going to do this I have to get started. Will you be all right?" He didn't trust Arial. He didn't trust any Royalist.

I nodded. "Go ahead. Let me know when you're ready." Then I grabbed his arm, squeezing it hard. "Look. Are you sure you want to do this? If something goes wrong and Owyn's spell doesn't work, you'll have every Shouda in the place on top of you."

"Yes, I'm sure, Kathedra. There's really little other choice." He left me with the captain and crossed the chamber to the larger holding cells, where he stepped within to set about preparations for the relocation of a teleportal.

"Do you think you can fight, Arial? I really need you able to fight."

The glare he threw me weakened my knees. "You know me better than that, Kathedra." In truth I did. Actually we knew each other better than most people thought we should. But that was a time long ago, before Val, when I was young and frightened, overwhelmed with relief that I had survived my first battle, and filled with too much ale from the celebration that followed. Arial, a lieutenant then, had suffered a broken arm in addition to a blow from a mace that had ripped the iron-winged helm from his head. Ale and head injuries don't usually combine to make good sense.

"Well, you should at least have something to eat." I bade him sit at the table that his jailors had vacated, still loaded with platters of food, some of it untouched. I tossed him a roll of dark bread, pulled the leg off a roasted chicken and placed it before him with a dish of stew. "Eat," I commanded, pouring wine from a flagon into a tin cup.

Arial dived into the fare with abandon. I allowed him his meal in peace while I took plates of food to Lesuperis and Grezalia, shoving them between the bars, a lame attempt to assuage my guilt. I checked in with Saxton, who gave me the all clear sign, then returned to the table, leaving the mage undisturbed.

"Can you tell me what's been going on in my absence?"

"Some. I'm not sure of a lot of it myself." Arial tore into a piece of chicken, crunching through gristle and skin, swallowing it all with a mouthful of wine. "When Averi returned, bearing evidence of your death, a kind of shock settled in. It wasn't until Bertrand named Valleri his heir that things began to get, well, scary. Lesuperis was still here, mooning for his lost bride, or more accurately, his lost tie to the throne. Apparently, he thought his spoonful of royal blood granted him the title of heir. He confronted Valleri, and a fierce argument erupted right there in Bertrand's throne room. All the officers in the castle at that time witnessed it. Lesuperis accused Valleri of vile things, like treason and murder. But Val took it all, I'll give him that much. If it were me, I'd have strangled the young fool on the spot."

I could well imagine the scene he'd described: Lesuperis ranting and raving in his nasal whine, clad in his peacock finery as he strutted circles around the victim of his tirade, and Valleri, so cool, so poised, taking it all with nary a word as he had done from so many others who thought him unworthy of common decency, too smart to be baited into a brawl, too proud to lose his temper. Maybe, finally, he just snapped. There's only so much cruelty, so much harassment, one can endure, until one is reduced to the same level as his tormentors.

"The title of Gryphon Highlord, as you know, gave Valleri newfound power, power to retaliate. He threw Lesuperis in the dungeon, along with your servant woman. Next he ordered all the Shouda released, determined to rid the countryside of Umagi rebels. He perceives threats everywhere, which is how I ended up here and why Roche is napping with the worms. He shows no mercy, no restraint."

"What about Uncle?"

Arial drained his cup, then set it aside to fix me in his level gaze. "In light of everything that's happened you might find this hard to believe, but Bertrand cares about you. Your death did something to him, struck him senseless and impotent. More and more he lost the nerve to defend himself against Valleri. His grief paralysed him, prevented him from taking action to end Val's reign of terror. Not all that long ago I heard the guards talking. The gossip was that Valleri had murdered you, making it look first to be the work of the Crusaders, then the Regent. I didn't want to believe him capable of such a crime. I didn't think he could…I mean, it was no secret that the two of you often shared a bed."

Stifling a burst of hysterical laughter I hung my head, unable to comprehend my own naiveté. For the sake of my shredded dignity, was there anyone who didn't know? But wasn't that Uncle's twisted plot from the beginning? To incite rumour and innuendo in order to discredit me? My romance with Val had never been anything more than a contrivance. I was the only one to be deceived.

I felt Arial's assessing stare, then his fingers on my chin as he tipped it, forcing me to meet his eyes. "Kathedra, I know how painful this must be for you. But the Valleri you loved is gone."

Painful? Try agony. These were not easy things to hear. Not Valleri's descent into depravity, or the reality of my shattered illusion.

He let his hand fall, and a rueful smile skipped across his lips. Pushing away his empty bowl, he crooked his head in Ginger's direction. "What's he doing?"

So cued I filled him in on recent events, including my escapades in Idyll, pushing Arial's Royalist sensibilities to the limit. In his opinion I was perhaps one step behind Valleri on the gangway leading to the ship named Traitor.

"Let me get this perfectly clear," he said, his glance, gone dark and sullen, falling somewhere around my shoulders. "Am I helping you to rescue Bertrand or am I helping you to usurp him?"

"The throne belongs to me, Arial. You know that. Uncle simply refuses to give it up. He had no right to do what he did to the Umagi, to me. I don't know what Val's motives are but they aren't mine. You want your command back, don't you? Or will you leave it to that weakling Serasteffan?"

"You damned well know I want it back." There was no hesitation in his reply, no hint of the uncertainty I was looking for, which, if I'd found, would have led Arial right back to his cell. "I am yours to command, if you'll have me."

"I will."

I rose, withdrawing the extra uniform I'd stuffed under my tabard to lend me more breadth. "Here. This is for you."

Arial fondled the fabric of the tunic and surcoat, his eyes narrowing as they drank in the colours and insignia of Saxton's mercs. He had even less regard for mercenaries than I. A kettle steamed over the fire in the hearth, normally reserved for heating pokers and other instruments of torture, useful now to boil water for Urharde's tea. I filled a bucket and carried it back to the table, where Arial had already begun to strip. I winced at the weals on his wrists, wrought there by chains, my mouth going dry at the whip marks scored into the flesh of his back. His torso was one massive bruise, and he did not bend too low as he scooped water into his cupped hands.

"By the hand of the Fates," I cursed softly. "Arial, your arm, your sword arm. It looks—"

"It's fine. It was dislocated, but I put it back myself." He dunked his head in the bucket, pulled it out with a gasp, whether from the shock or the protest of mistreated ribs. He slicked away his hair with a hand, letting water trickle down his chin. "Don't worry, Kathedra. I can do what you ask."

Perhaps I asked too much. I left him then to his privacy, though modesty hardly mattered to a soldier. His wounds begged attention; I refrained, knowing he would not accept what might seem like pity from me. Instead I joined Saxton by the door, where he was getting antsy. Things were too quiet, he said.

"How long before Ginger's ready?" I asked.

"I don't know. But he's warned me its imperative that he's not interrupted until the spell is complete or it could mean disaster for everyone within a ten mile radius."

He'd barely finished his sentence when I heard it, a thrumming sound, emanating from the very walls. Not really a sound, but a vibration. Like a ripple on still water. For an instant, it felt as if the castle itself shifted, and I reached out to steady myself. The stone hummed beneath my palm, the sensation reverberating all through me. I sniffed the air, but caught no whiff of magical residue, no scent other than the acrid smoke of torches. When I glanced towards the cells it seemed as if I saw Arial and Ginger through a cheap pane of glass.

In the space of an eye blink the moment passed, and all was again as it was before.

I squeezed Saxton's shoulder. He seemed unaffected by the occurrence. Maybe I only observed the advent of the teleportal because I was Umagi. A fissure of alarm snaked through me. What if Valleri had noticed its arrival, too?

Ginger locked the gate to the holding cells with a key from the sergeant's ring then approached me, looking even worse than Arial. Gaunt. Drawn. Weary beyond all care. "Are you sure-?"

"I'm fine. It's just I've never summoned such a wealth of energy before. It took three of us to raise the teleportal in Idyll. I've borrowed the power from the small one we left behind. I hope Naren's through it already. If not, he's coming the long way around. But its very unstable, Kathedra. And it's only temporary. This amount of energy was never meant to be confined under the weight of so much crushing stone. The rock won't let it breathe or settle, not like the barn. Its walls were wood and its roof thatch; it could expand and contract. Magic is a living entity. It hates confinement and will search for a way to escape. You know that as well as anyone. I just don't have the reserves to anchor it properly."

He jerked his head in Arial's direction. "What about the captain back there? Are you sure of him?"

"Sure enough."

"Really? As sure as you were about Valleri?"

"What are you saying?"

"Only that it's a dangerous game you play with men's hearts. There is something between you and Arial."

"That's in the past." A past so far away that it seemed to belong to someone else.

"Make sure it stays there."

He allowed me no time for a rebuttal, snapping, "I have to go open the nether end of the teleportal. Remember, as the decoy you must time it precisely if you don't want to trap yourself. It's one way only. You don't need a passkey because I'll activate it myself. We'll have to hurry. I can't predict how long it will stay open, but it should deactivate once the tunnel door is closed. Meet me at the granaries as soon as the captain's ready."

"Can you find the tunnel on your own? It's a labyrinth in there. About fifty feet in, the passageway forks. Go right, not left. If you go left you'll end up in the crypts, or maybe the library. Damn, I can't remember which. Anyway, at the next intersection you'll see steps. Up leads to my tower, and down takes you to the dungeons. Saxton could show you."

"I'll manage," he said, interrupting my babble. He took my hands, squeezed them tight to stop their trembling. "I saw the maps Sestus had at Idyll. I'll be fine."

He left me with a kiss that told me he would not tolerate rivals, and the memory of his grin.

I went to collect Arial before Saxton hyperventilated. He had cleaned up nicely, his damp hair tied back with a leather thong, a smell about him of wine and vengeance. "Captain, let's go."

"I'm ready." He buckled on his sword belt, and went to a chest built into a corner of the hearth where the dungeon-masters kept a secret stash of weapons for emergency. Withdrawing two blades, he tossed me one, and cut a few awkward slashes into the air with the second.

"Do you want to spar first?"

"No." He slung the blade, gulped down the rest of his wine, and gestured to the door. "I heard your friend. There's no time. Really, I'm all right."

As he moved to go by me I stopped him with a light touch. "Captain, forgive me, but I have to ask. Why would you choose someone like Stef for your second? Surely, you knew what he was."

The look he gave me said that he could ask me the very same question. "Serasteffan wasn't always the monster he is today. I watched him over the years. He was shrewd. Fearless. Ambitious. All traits that can turn a man dangerous and vile when temptation is put in his path. The newly acquired power I gave him changed Stef for the worst. That's all the explanation I have." He crooked his head at Saxton. "We should go."

I went ahead of him, but before we reached the door he took my elbow, turning me so I met his level gaze. "The mage. He's pretty heavy duty, eh?"

He did not refer solely to Ginger's calibre of wizardry. "Yeah, Arial. Does that change anything?"

One shoulder lifted in the suggestion of a shrug, and his wry grin appeared, the one that had so easily charmed me into his tent that night near Storn. "Just the plans for my victory celebration."

A surprise awaited us as we stepped three abreast onto a second level corridor leading topside. I caught a glimpse of the intruder's face in the torchlight as he leapt from the landing, shoving Saxton headfirst into a wall before an arm curled around my waist and a hand clamped over my mouth. It was all done with a speed and efficiency that defied comprehension. The man spun me around to face Arial, who'd stopped dead in the passageway, struck with horror.

The captain raised his hands, palms open. In a calm and steady voice, he told my attacker, "Easy there, now. Don't do anything rash."

The man held me carefully, exerting just enough pressure to restrain not hurt, although in the past he had been anything but gentle with me. Into my ear, he murmured, "Don't make a sound, Highness. Give me a chance to explain."

I had not the slightest inclination to scream. Not when we were so close to the compound that my shout would bring every Royalist in the castle at a gallop. I nodded behind his hand, whispered his name against his cold, grimy fingers.

Arial took a tentative step towards me. "Averi, let her go. If you think—"

"Back off, captain."

I gave Arial a look, tried to impart a warning. Catching my intent, he retreated and crouched beside Saxton lying crumpled on the floor, prepared to shield him if necessary.

"Highness, I just want—" Averi began, but I didn't let him finish. I had spent many a sleepless night in Idyll plotting my punishment for this bastard, for his dogs. Most of my plans were involved and complicated, lasting days or weeks. And I simply didn't have that kind of time.

I conjured a thought, wove it into command. My powers of telekinesis flowed free, unfettered by tonic or ring or even common sense. I opened my hand; the knife Saxton had given me leaped from my boot into my palm with such force it rapped my knuckles against the wall at my back. Averi didn't know what hit him. Quick as a whip, I slashed the blade across his forearm. He released me with a stifled cry and shoved himself away. He stumbled and would have fallen, except the force of my will held him up.

"Please, Highness!" he begged. "You must listen. I'm sorry. I'm sorry for what I did to you. I just want a chance to redeem myself. I'll help you and the captain. I'll help you fight Valleri."

"Only because Valleri is out for your blood," I countered.

Consumed with anger, I summoned power, raw and untamed, hungry for release, for satiation. I wanted Averi bound, helpless before me, as he had once held me. I recalled the strip of leather in Arial's hair and commanded it to unbind itself. It yielded to my will, freeing itself to let the captain's auburn locks fall loose. Another command, wrought by pure thought, picked up the thong and coiled it around Averi's wrists. And when he, in his panic, tried to turn and run, I sent a thought ahead of him, pulling away the laces of his tunic and flinging them to the floor, where they wriggled like snakes, tripping him. Behind me I heard Arial's gasp of awe.

Averi sprawled face first on the stone of the corridor; I was on him in an instant. My fingers wound into his greasy hair, flinging him onto his back. I reached for more power, found it waiting and eager to do my bidding. It encased Averi in a cocoon of paralysis, holding him fast. I straddled his hips, touched my knife tip to his most private of parts.

He sucked in a breath, staring at the blade in blood-draining horror. I took his face in my free hand, forced his gaze to meet mine. I allowed a slow smile, relishing the fear etched onto those fair features. "Say, Averi? Have you ever witnessed the gelding of a horse?"

His terror was such that I nearly laughed. His stricken expression said he recognized in me a glimpse of himself, from not long ago on a grassy hilltop one summer morn. A wicked thrill surged through me. Such power is dangerous, I know. Nevertheless, I won't deny I took pleasure from my cruelty, savouring the heady satisfaction which accompanied that power.

But a pathetic mewl from his lips unexpectedly moved me to pity, and when

I looked deeper into his eyes, I saw myself reflected there, from a time when I had been the victim. Revenge and retribution did not seem so attractive now. My own spite and malice revolted me. I could not justify another's misery inflicted by my own hand, no matter how righteous my motives.

I brought the blade to his throat. "You're a coward, Averi. You deserve a slow, painful death up on those stakes with your friends. But today I'm feeling generous, so I'll give you a quick, easy one on the point of my knife. Better yet…"

I broke off, slit the leather binding his wrists and wrapped the fingers of one hand around the hilt of my dagger. "…I'll let you give it to yourself."

I leaned back, watched the blade respond to my summons. It quivered in his grip, striving to break his restraint. If Averi's desire to fight me had been a fraction stronger, or his belief in himself as a competent, decent human being existed at all, I would not have been able to bat his will aside as easily as slapping down a house of cards. But wasn't that the nature of cowards? They possessed neither the courage nor the inclination to do battle against those stronger than they. Stripped of his self-will, Averi bent beneath my power, and closed his eyes, unable in his cowardice to watch his hand bear the knife forward to slice his own throat.

"Kathedra," came an unsteady voice behind me, one I recognized as Saxton's. "Is it wise of you to employ such power so near to Ginger's device?"

Drat! I hadn't considered that. I recalled a child's misguided spell in a castle not so very different from this one, aware of the devastation such a misstep could wreak. My thoughts scattered, panicked, and the dagger leapt from Averi's hand to skitter down the corridor.

I scrambled after the blade, returned to where Averi quaked on the stones and raised it for a killing stroke.

Then, from out of nowhere, strong arms seized me, pinning mine in their grip of iron, and pulled me off my victim. "Leave him," Arial hissed into my ear. "He's not worth the guilt you'll feel later at killing a helpless man."

I bucked and kicked in the captain's grasp, amazed at his temerity, bewildered by his plea for mercy. "Let me go! Damn you, Arial. I've seen you kill helpless prisoners before. Indeed you've slain them by the dozens. Who do you—"

"Exactly, Kathedra. I know something of what I speak. Do you think I wouldn't take pleasure in running him through myself for all he's done? But listen to me. We can use him."

I ceased my struggles. "Use him? How?"

"Yes, how?" Saxton echoed, tottering up beside me, a hand to the gash in his brow.

Arial set me down, breathing hard, wincing from the pain the effort of restraining me had cost his abused body. "If he wants to assist you so very badly and save his no-good hide he can damn well earn it. Let him be the mage's decoy. Chiverly's men are looking for him anyway. Why risk yourself when you have this miscreant grovelling at your feet?"

The captain had a point. I gnawed a lip, glanced over at the motionless figure sprawled out like a rug. "Can we trust him?"

Saxton offered, "I think we can trust him to do whatever he can to save his own skin."

"I think you're right."

I bent over Averi. He lay so still that I actually feared I had scared the little wretch to death. I knelt beside him, checked for a pulse. Blood beat there, fast and strong. In an effort to rouse him, I started slapping, not hard…well, not as hard as I could have, to no result. It wasn't until Arial planted a boot in his ribs that he groaned and tried to sit up.

Arial got him on his feet. I grabbed the throat of Averi's scruffy tunic. "All right, you scum. You're going to do something for me, and if you mess up or betray me to Valleri, I will sniff you out and make you finish your conversation with my dagger. Distance is no obstacle to me. You won't be able to hide. Do you understand?"

The glazed look in his eye told me he did. He took a big gulp, nodded. "What do I do?"

I told him, reiterating Ginger's instructions to me. Averi's complexion went winter white. Saxton remarked, "He's going to run like a rabbit."

Averi scowled in Saxton's direction. "No, I've got it covered."

The rest of us donned our helms, completing our disguises, weapons at the ready. By the time we got above ground I had gained a whole new confidence in the plan, in myself. For the first time, I had acted by thought and not reflex. But could I do it again?

CHAPTER TWENTY-NINE

We emerged in the bailey via the kitchens, deserted by the servants, and crept into the shadows of the granaries. From this vantage we had a clear view of the yard, including the front gate. The alarm had been sounded. The torch glare revealed soldiers clustered in knots here and there. Valleri had the bailey lit up like the temple of a pagan sun god. The Shouda, confined to their kennels, bayed and howled in a frenzy, throwing themselves at the wire of their cages.

Arial, crouched beside my knee, gestured with his blade towards the furry, four-legged killing machines. "It looks like you and your mage have worked the Shouda into a lather."

That was an understatement. I rubbed the palm stamped with Owyn's talisman. "They shouldn't be able to track us through our protection spells, but I guess we'll see soon enough. Is everybody clear?"

My reply was a clatter of armour and rattle of weaponry, which I took for an affirmative.

Where was Ginger? I hoped we hadn't missed him. This was the appointed rendezvous. Even as I scanned the shadows, a form slunk towards us from the pantry wall. As the mage hunkered down beside me, Averi tried to scuttle back into the kitchen but Arial snagged his jerkin.

"What took you so long?" Ginger hissed at me. "Have you seen Urharde? Or Valleri?" He fired questions like arrows, not giving me time to answer. "And who's he?"

"Slight change in plans. Averi's going to be the decoy."

I saw his face twist in the torchlight, his eyes narrow. He remembered what Averi had done. While he might question my judgment in the matter, time had run out for second-guessing. "Whatever. The teleportal is open and connected to the tunnel. Chiverly's troops are over by the tower. Send out your bait…I mean, your man."

This last he spoke strictly for Averi's benefit. I nudged him. "You know what to do. Remember, don't enter the tunnel yourself. All you have to do is close the door behind them. That will seal the teleportal."

He nodded, and loped out into the open, with only the speed of his legs for protection against Valleri's rage. Averi's mission was to draw the attention of Chiverly's troops, which shouldn't be difficult since they were prowling every inch of the castle for him, and lure them into my secret tunnel. If the teleportal was operating properly and Averi didn't screw up, the tunnel should exit in the holding cells instead of my apartment.

Ginger touched my shoulder. "Shall we?"

We stepped into the bailey, intending to collect Saxton's men with whom to help us reclaim Arial's command, but we got only several yards when a trio of Shouda spotted us. Apparently, Valleri had reneged on his promise.

The dogs headed our way, tongues lolling as their powerful legs carried them at a gallop, their yammer turning all eyes in the compound towards us. I didn't know what to do; neither did Ginger. We froze, in anticipation of the worst, while Saxton and Arial took up a defensive stance before us, swords raised. I opened my palm, expecting to see it filled with dancing runes or mystical radiance, but all I saw was sweat.

The first Shouda to reach us, a brindled male with a ridge along his back, nudged its snout between our protectors' legs to nuzzle my hand. Sinking onto its haunches, it looked up at me with big brown mischievous eyes and tipped its head, panting insipidly. The other two, a pair of small fawn-coloured females, rubbed their flanks against Ginger, the bolder one even throwing herself to the ground at his feet, begging for a belly rub.

I exchanged a glance with the mage, who seemed surprised but not pleasantly so. With a shrug, I surrendered to the male dog's bunting and scratched his huge, shaggy head. "Hello, puppy. Hello, baby. What's your name, big fella? Oooh, that feel good? Want some more? Want a—"

"Kathedra," Ginger snarled. "Just get rid of them!"

"Oh. Sorry."

I tried to shoo the Shouda away, but of course they wouldn't budge. I still lacked the appropriate command, the same one missing from our talisman. Though Arial and Saxton both spat a variety of invectives, none of them worked either. So we resumed our march across the bailey, the dogs cavorting around our legs with playful yips and snarls, the females so insistent, that Ginger finally bent beneath his hatred to drag his fingers through their furry scruffs. "When I see that witchdoctor," he growled, "I'm going to ring his ancient neck."

"Actually, when you think about it, what could be better cover for two Umagi than an escort of Shouda?"

His reply was forestalled as a disturbance broke out behind us. A clutch of Tock's men congregating nearby started yelling and rattling their weapons. We turned to see the cause of the commotion. Averi went flying past as if demons snapped at his heels, pursued by swordsmen in Chiverly's colours. Nimbly dodging a pair of pikemen, he hurtled a cart full of hay and zipped into the alley that led to my tunnel, his pursuers huffing and puffing behind in their mail.

Saxton drew his sword and bellowed at Tock's troops, "After him, you layabouts! A chest of gold to the man who brings Valleri his head!" He answered the look I speared him with a sheepish grin. "The more the merrier."

Excited by the racket, the Shouda barked and yelped but otherwise seemed disinclined to leave us. We were halfway across the compound when a shout rang out over the bailey. "Saxton, wait!"

The voice sent a rush of shivers up my spine. Not only could we ill afford another delay, the last person I needed to see right now was Serasteffan. Saxton, however, couldn't very well ignore his hail. We stopped to wait for him and his core of goons to catch up. I placed myself beside Arial, ready to restrain him if need be. Some of those bruises on his face had been put there by the Butcher, and gleefully so.

Saxton feigned bafflement at the hubbub around us. "What's going on? Why are the Shouda loose? I thought Valleri wanted them kennelled."

The female Shouda circled Ginger's legs, the hair on their scruffs bristling at Serasteffan's approach. One even growled. Spying them, the Butcher didn't get too close. With his closely cropped blonde hair and neatly trimmed beard he was an attractive man, the pale scar slashed across his cheek only enhancing his masculine appeal. But his angelic appearance hid a monster of unspeakable evil. He possessed the viciousness of an Averi and the malevolence of a Ragsey-a deadly combination. All were cruel men, hungry for wealth and power, therefore receptive to Valleri's manipulation. I could not fathom why Val had chosen to align himself with such miscreants. Perhaps that was just it; he'd thought he had no choice.

"They were raising such a ruckus that Valleri figured there must be an Umagi or two around." He tilted his head, his nasty grin parting his lips as he studied Saxton with sly, dark eyes. "I was thinking maybe that they could've snuck in with you and your mercs when you delivered the queen-bitch."

I made a quick movement, my hand darting for my dagger, only to feel Arial's fingers dig into my arm. I smothered a yelp, stilled my palm on my hilt. Serasteffan caught the motion, his hooded eyes shifting to look at me. I met that baleful gaze, though it took all my nerve. I'd seen Crusader prisoners after they'd been entrusted to his not-so-tender care, and later wished I hadn't.

Saxton played it nonchalant. "Anything's possible, I guess. I'm sure the Shouda will take care of them."

Serasteffan's attention returned to Saxton, after wandering first to Ginger then Arial. "Nevertheless, I've got men patrolling the grounds. They may be lurking nearby, waiting to slip out the gate with the next courier or scout."

For some reason, known only to the male mind, Saxton couldn't resist taunting him. "Looks like Chiverly's got your pal Averi on the run. I wonder if Valleri's got a stake picked out for him already."

But Serasteffan never reacts the way one would predict. That's part of what makes him so scary. He laughed, slamming the back of his hand against Saxton's chest. "Sure does. In fact, Val's got one for each of us, just waiting for the moment we'll screw up. But I'll have you know I sharpened the end of Averi's myself…and yours is leaning there against the wall beside it, my friend."

Serasteffan plunked on his helm, turned to go. "By the by, Val's looking for you. He's on his way to collect his princess, wants you to meet him in the Hall."

That was about the time I figured things were probably going to get difficult for us very soon. My suspicion was confirmed two seconds later when, at that inopportune moment, Uncle chose to break out of his prison. A clamour arose behind us as a flood of Halberdiers boiled out from the tower's entrance onto the steps, shrieking battle cries and waving their pikes. Their uniforms were little more than tattered rags and their stench could have toppled an ox. Startled, Serasteffan paused, turned back our way…

To make matters worse, Valleri appeared in the kitchen doorway, in his surcoat of blue and gold, a gang of elite troops at his side. "The princess!" he yelled out. "She's gone!"

Then he spotted us, and comprehension registered on his face as clearly as if someone had thrown a pail of whitewash in it. He looked from Saxton to me, and knew. A mixture of anger and disbelief crossed his face, and deeper, another emotion I recognized as anguish. So, Val? How does it feel to be betrayed by someone you love?

"Stef, seize them!"

Serasteffan whirled, sword in hand, and burbled out an order to his men, even as a severely pissed off male Shouda took his arm in its jaws.

Pushing me aside, Ginger dragged free his sword. As he sprang to meet the first Royalist blade, one of the female dogs leapt for the swordsman's throat, while the second went for his leg. Soldiers closed in. A scream of steel behind me said Arial had entered the fray. As the Shouda wrestled Serasteffan to his knees, a swordsman leapt forward, his weapon driving clear through the dog's flank and pinning it to the ground.

I let out a shriek of rage and rushed in without thinking, only to have Saxton snatch my sleeve, holding me back. Over his shoulder, Ginger bellowed, "You two, get her out of here!"

Saxton tried leading me away but I balked at leaving Ginger alone to cover our retreat. Arial pushed me into Saxton's arms, the sword in his fist already coloured with blood. "Don't worry, Highness. I'll stay." He whirled, his blade driving into another as its edge fell, deflecting it a hair's breadth from Ginger's neck.

Saxton snagged my wrist and spun, his sword cleaving into two of Stef's soldiers stupid enough to stand in his way. Meanwhile, Valleri and his Twelfth fought to stem the tide of guardsmen pouring from the tower. His Royal hacked up a storm, for the Twelfth and Uncle's Halberdiers had always been the fiercest of rivals. So while they were thus distracted, they were useless to me.

A few lucky escapees fought their way past them, however, only to collide with Saxton and me. We ducked our heads and ran, dodging crazed Halberdiers and their halberds. Fortunately, they were not interested in taking sides. They wanted only one thing-out. Earlier,

Saxton estimated their food stores had expired four days ago. Half mad with hunger, they were desperate to escape the castle.

Seconds later an explosion rocked the ground. Torn from Saxton's grasp, I was hurled to the cobbles along with everyone else in the bailey. Two big booms rolled out like thunder, and a cloud of black smoke billowed up, engulfing the entire keep. Choking, I pushed myself onto my elbows only to be blinded by thick, acrid smoke. It burned my eyes and my stung my throat.

At least I no longer need worry for Ginger's safety. Obviously this was his work, a sampling of what might have happened in that warehouse if not for Ragsey's sabotage. Very impressive. Likely Ginger had employed the spell as a diversion to aid our escape rather than inflict damage. Nevertheless, the pewter haze that enveloped the bailey revealed outcrops of fire leaping up all across the yard.

The bailey was strewn with Royalists struggling to pick themselves up, all anxious to collect Valleri's reward for capturing me and slaying my companions. But I wasn't about to lay down arms and surrender. I dragged Saxton back onto his feet and pushed him in the direction of the wall. We didn't get far before soldiers clad in Urharde's colours flew out from the barracks into our path, weapons drawn. We had no choice but to stand and do battle.

A handful of Crusaders had caught up to us and now fought at our side. I threw myself into the melee, exchanging fast and furious blows with a Royalist swordsman. "No, Highness!" Saxton shouted over the clash of blades. "Seek cover! Run!"

I despatched my opponent with a thrust to his shoulder, my steel biting through his leather padding into flesh and bone beneath. As he reeled away, another Royalist took his place, looking to disarm me with a pike. I slid aside, just under his charge, whacking my blade into his torso and knocking him to the ground. "I'm staying!" I yelled back. I was accustomed to fighting, whether my enemy be Crusader or Royalist. I was fed up with running.

I sought out my next adversary; a second Royalist approached Saxton from behind. I stepped in, deflecting a blow that would have hewn the captain in half. Winding up a mighty two-handed swing, I drove my steel into the soldier's hip. He let out a howl of pain and staggered away, falling to the blood-slicked cobbles.

Almost before I could recover, another Royalist blade hammered into mine. I thrust and parried furiously, dispatching foe after foe. Their numbers seemed endless, and we lost two of our own beneath their relentless assault. Saxton and I fought back-to-back, slowly wearing away at the enemy. All around us confusion and chaos reigned, the bailey aswarm with embattled knots of soldiers clad in an assortment of uniforms.

Finally, there came a decline in the amount of Royalists pressing us. As he cut down the last, Saxton bellowed out an order. "Retreat! To the gatehouse!"

Blades still in hand, we turned and ran into the square between the barracks and the keep. Legs churning, arms pumping, we pounded down the stones, bound for the north wall. But rounding the corner I stopped dead, my men skidding to a halt behind me. I had forgotten Tock. He and half his Royal emerged from the square's nether end, blocking our way. I was close enough to the Royalist commander that I could see my expression of astonishment reflected in the polished surface of his breastplate. He let out a shout of triumph and punched aloft his sword, red with the blood of Uncle's Halberdiers.

I motioned the others to go back but as I turned to follow, Serasteffan and his men entered the square behind us. We were trapped.

Before we could react, the Butcher stood among us. One of his spiked gauntlets reached out and swatted the sword from my hand while the other tore off my helm and yanked away my coif. "Traitor-slut," he grinned.

Saxton ran to my defence. "Release the princess, you whoreson!"

Restraining me with an elbow across my throat, my captor laughed and swung me around so I faced my troops, all seven of them. His deep, gravelly voice made each word end in a rasp. I suppressed a chill at the sound of it.

"Put away the blade, boy." He even smiled, so confident was he in his brute strength and ability to intimidate.

Brave and loyal Saxton didn't waver. "Let her go."

"Foolish whelp." Serasteffan's grin widened. I heard the creak of his leather jerkin as he shifted his suffocating hold on me. "How did this happen, Saxton? You were Valleri's pet. His chosen. Do you not know the riches, the rewards, he would have heaped at your feet had you remained faithful? Gold. Women. Lands. Now it shall all belong to me. How did she lure you to her side, or need I ask? She is young, soft, and so very fetching."

Where the hell was Arial? Was he still with Ginger or had Stef carved him up for Shouda vittles? If it were the latter, Saxton and I had waded into deep waters indeed.

Saxton uttered a low threat as Serasteffan proceeded to grope me, there in front of his Royal. "No," I managed from his stranglehold. "Don't listen to his taunts. Don't let him provoke you."

Serasteffan chuckled. I struggled feebly, more to escape his fetid breath than his steel-clad fingers. He was uncommonly strong. I felt the power of his coiled muscles, the tension of his body poised to attack…and more; anger and violence stirred inside him, barely restrained. His petty words and crude behaviour conveyed the extent of his resentment towards Saxton, this man who'd been Valleri's favourite.

Naturally, Serasteffan would take exception to the youth's elevation to so lofty a perch. After all, Saxton had not earned his master's favour by usurping his captain as Serasteffan had. The Butcher nursed a deadly grudge against the young officer. Now he baited him, hoping Saxton would lose his temper and do something foolish.

"This has gone far enough," Tock announced, striding among us. He was an older man, with streaks of grey interrupting his golden beard and hair. Though average of height and build, he wore his scarlet uniform with such a bold air of command that he appeared a giant.

At his tone of authority, Saxton and Serasteffan unlocked their glowers to look at him. Calmly, Tock said, "Saxton, throw down your weapon."

To my surprise Saxton did, gesturing for his men to do the same. Such ready submission indicated Saxton's great respect for this man.

"Insolent pup," Tock snarled as he backhanded Saxton, making him stagger. Fury and disappointment showed in the Royalist's expression, and something else, which might be grief. His voice shook with it as he demanded, "Don't you realize Valleri will have you drawn and quartered for this treachery? And don't you know he'll make the rest of us watch?"

Saxton did not defend his actions. He averted his glance, unable to meet Tock's gaze. I understood his position all too well. It was not easy to betray people you'd come to love, despite your best efforts to see them as your enemy.

"Tock, please," Saxton said, his voice tight with the effort of controlling his anger. "Tell him to release the princess. Whichever side we stand on does not give him the right to manhandle her."

Tock turned his smouldering glare on Serasteffan. "Let her be, Stef. I'll take her to Valleri myself."

Serasteffan balked, reluctant to surrender his prize. His hand slid over the mound of my breast and squeezed it roughly, although my mail shirt protected me from his touch. He defied Tock as a toddler would challenge his father, just to see if he could get away with it. "Now, Tock. Tsk, tsk. Why should you have all the fun?"

Serasteffan grinned at Tock's red-faced indignation. But Saxton did not find the situation at all amusing, outraged more by the insult to Tock than the offence done my royal bosom. With a cry of murder, he lunged.

Serasteffan was ready. He pivoted, placing himself in front of me. His fist catapulted into Saxton's face. I flinched at the sickening crunch of bone. The impact dropped Saxton to the ground.

Tock crouched at Saxton's side, helping him to his feet. "Stef, have you lost your wits entirely?"

The Butcher's only reply was a wild gust of laughter.

A new voice cut in above Serasteffan's mirth. "Stef, unhand the princess."

I wilted with relief. Arial! He'd sure taken his damned sweet time. He stood swaying a little, sword held so loose in his grip it looked as if he might drop it. His helm was lost; a sword-cut to his chin leaked steadily, and sweat plastered his hair to his face, now a sickly grey colour. But his voice was steady, calm, his green eyes clear and focussed. Bloodied and bruised, with his surcoat hanging in tatters and the smoke of sporadic fires rising behind him Arial looked like some vengeful demon coughed up from Hell's own throat, exuding defiance and a hint of madness.

"You?" Shocked as he was to see his former captain, Serasteffan seemed more amused than threatened. "Ho, ho! And if I don't?"

Arial pointed to the barracks roof, where half a dozen snipers from the Twelfth crouched, their crossbows trained on Serasteffan's back. The Butcher snorted. "You're bluffing. You won't risk striking the princess."

"Serasteffan, you oaf," I wheezed, "I'll give the order myself."

I felt his chest begin to vibrate with yet another burst of maniacal laughter when the whine of a missile in flight sliced the air and he flinched suddenly. Shrieking, he shoved me to the cobbles while he crouched to pull free the bolt lodged in his mailed shoulder. It did no real damage to his flesh, but it had served its purpose. I scrambled towards Saxton, who hauled me to my feet.

I turned back to observe the contest. Serasteffan tossed the arrow away and drew his sword, his malevolent gaze sighting on Arial, who responded with a grin of challenge. Arial stepped sideways, began a slow circle, waved him on. "Let's go, Stef. Just you and me. I know you want it."

Taking the bait Serasteffan charged in with all the restraint of a bull, lashing out with his blade. Arial countered the stroke and retaliated with a thrust to the Butcher's flank. Blocking it, Serasteffan swerved and rained a lightning-swift volley of blows down upon the head of his former captain, which Arial easily parried.

Thus it went, each combatant parrying and thrusting, lunging and evading, while the rest of us observed the contest, entranced. Despite his pain and weakness incurred by previous injuries, my fierce captain fought with remarkable agility and stamina, wielding his experience and speed with greater efficiency than his stronger and younger opponent. In fact, I got the impression he exercised considerable restraint. Had it been his wont, Arial could have made minced meat of Stef.

Arial let the Butcher vent his spleen and with it his endurance, then dealt him a solid smack to his ribs, propelling him to the ground. Next he neatly disarmed his fallen adversary, then held his sword tip to Serasteffan's jugular.

Pinned immovable by the blade, Serasteffan spat curses at Tock, who had just stood there and watched his defeat at Arial's hands, smart enough to know that this was not his fight.

Breathing hard, dripping blood and sweat onto the Butcher as he leaned over him, Arial hissed, "You stole my command, you perverted my men. You came down into the dungeons and danced a jig on my face while I stood with my hands chained to the wall. There is a price to pay for that, Stef. Your life is mine, and your soul belongs to Hell."

His hand jerked forward, driving the sword through Serasteffan with such violence, the tip of it scraped the cobbles beneath him.

As Arial bent over the Butcher's body, straining to get air into his spent lungs, the men of the Eighth threw their weapons to the ground in a display of submission, and maybe, a plea for forgiveness.

Arial freed his blade, planted a foot on either side of Serasteffan's body, and addressed his former troops. "You ingrates!" he snarled over their bent heads. "You traitors. Only cowards follow a coward. But if you follow me you need courage. You need honour. On second thought, I don't want you. I don't need you. You're dirt beneath my boots. If you want me back, you're going to have to earn me."

I watched, with a surge of pride, as Arial shamed his men into picking up their swords and falling in behind him. Together, they approached Tock.

Tock held his ground, said without rancour, "Who are you to speak of traitors, Arial?"

"I'll tell you. Valleri discarded me. Bertrand abandoned me. Stef betrayed me. All this happened, while you just stood aside. You ignored it. You ignored me. Then Kathedra rescued me. To whom do you think I owe allegiance?"

"Don't delude yourself. Kathedra sprung you because she needs you. She hasn't any more honour than the rest of us."

Though I strenuously objected to the latter, I could not refute the former. On the other hand, I was not naïve enough to believe that Arial's loyalty had been bought by a single night on a soggy battlefield outside the town of Storn. Betrayed, imprisoned, abused, we each had suffered and survived. If we owed allegiance, it was only to the other.

"Don't try to talk me out of this, Tock. My mind is made up."

"Maybe so, but you're crazy if you think that you, the princess and a pocketful of Crusaders can stand against Valleri."

Arial looked around. "We seem to be doing all right so far."

Saxton stepped in then, cupping his shattered cheekbone. I wondered he could speak at all, but he told Tock, "There are more Crusaders on the way, due here any minute. The smartest thing you can do is lay down your arms."

The captain's eyes narrowed as his gaze swung to Saxton. "You traitor dog. I won't let you usurp the Regent."

"Valleri is the usurper. Can't you see that? In every way but name.

I liked you, Tock. You were always decent to me. More than a mentor, you were halfway a friend. Please, I beg you to step aside."

"Yes, step aside, Tock, as you have always done." Arial motioned to Saxton with his sword. Obeying, Saxton retrieved his fallen blade and began to back away, taking me with him.

"Regardless of what you think," Arial continued, "I don't want to kill you. And I don't think you want to kill me."

"Don't be so sure of yourself." Tock shifted his grip on his blade, began motioning to his men, fanning out behind him, weapons at the ready.

"If you do this, you're only helping Valleri," Arial reminded him. "You're not helping Bertrand."

"We'll see."

As Saxton and I slipped past Arial, I paused, wanting to say something to him but the words escaped me. Thank you seemed inadequate a thing when I thought I probably wouldn't see him again. I touched his arm, began, "Arial, I know—"

"Just go, princess," he told me harshly, his gaze never leaving Tock's. "Just go."

Tock barked out a command to his men. Saxton grabbed my hand and pulled me through the ranks of Arial's men, parting to grant us passage, then closing again to cover our retreat. Behind me I heard Arial's roar of encouragement as he led his Royal against Tock's, and the discordant clash of steel as the two forces met.

We ran into the bailey, where all was pandemonium. Valleri's Twelfth still struggled to contain Uncle's Halberdiers. Fires still burned unchecked throughout the yard, greedily devouring wood and thatch. Squinting against the sting of smoke, I strained for a glimpse of Ginger and spied instead a clutch of Roche's mercs skulking from the main keep, on the very edge of the commotion. The mercenaries had not waited for opportunity to knock twice. Taking advantage of the chaos, they had raided the treasury and other areas of the castle, their loot bundled up in sacks of stolen bedding.

With a yelp of outrage at seeing the family silver lugged off as spoils, I drew my dagger, prepared to give chase. But Saxton had hold of my arm, refusing to let us become separated again. "Forget them. It's not worth your life."

Reluctantly I permitted him to lead me in the opposite direction, my stomach in revolt at the plunder of my home. A glance over my shoulder saw the thieves pounding on the gate alongside a handful of Halberdiers, all bellowing at Ginger's men on the wall to raise the portcullis. The Crusaders ignored them, busy battling Urharde's Royal for control of the gate.

There was no place to run, the bailey clogged with fighting soldiers and maddened horses escaped from their burning stables. A gang of Halberdiers broke free to storm the gatehouse. Veering from their path, we tried to make it to the nearest wall-the south, virtually ignored in the fray-but Urharde spotted us and dispatched a crew to harry our escape. The Royalists intercepted us at the stairs. I had only Saxton's dagger for protection and lost it almost immediately when I drove it deep into a soldier's groin as he made a grab for me. He stumbled away, taking the blade with him.

"Hurry, Highness! Hurry!" Saxton cried, pushing me up the stairs ahead of him as he turned to defend my back. Halfway up I tripped and fell, the jagged stone scoring the flesh of my belly. Saxton backed onto me, nearly crushing me beneath him and the press of soldiers behind but for one hand braced on a step. Trapped, I let him fend off our attackers, his sword arm working feverishly.

Finally, help came from above as the Crusaders on the wall arrived to beat back the Royalists with arrows and blades. Saxton dragged me to my feet and shoved me up the narrow flight to safety. Gasping for breath, we crouched on the battlements, protected by Crusader arrow fire as we watched the fracas below. Then somebody sounded the alarm on the north wall. A great, thunderous knock came from the gate. We had company. Friend or foe, I would not hazard a guess.

"Oh, now who the hell is that?" Saxton groaned to no one in particular, as if he feared nothing more but the advent of an uninvited guest.

To my horror, I saw the portcullis lift but it was impossible to tell whether Crusaders or Royalists, still waging sporadic skirmishes on the battlements, had engaged it. A cheer went up from the mercenaries and Halberdiers below; as one happy crowd they surged past the iron gate to freedom. A heartbeat later, they streamed back inside, trampling my good crockery underfoot, prodded by the lance tips of an invading army.

I held my breath at the sight of the unfamiliar banner. "Saxton?" I whispered. "Who's that?"

Though he, too, stared in amazement, a name slipped past his lips. "Gregaris." Then louder, he said, "By damn! It's Gregaris." Pumping his fist in the air, he yelled to his men, "Gregaris!"

A triumphant roar from the Crusaders reverberated along the walls. Saxton clutched my sleeve and in near drunken glee, exclaimed, "Look who's with him!" Following the point of his outstretched finger I saw Naren at the end of it.

Astride a golden stallion, the man I assumed to be Gregaris entered at the head of the large and boisterous procession, bearing a lance crowned by Fleurry's severed head. My eyes nearly popped from their sockets at the sight of him. A huge, brawny man, he had biceps as meaty as hams and legs as thick as tree trunks. His filthy, carrot-coloured mane and beard flowed in the breeze. Despite his dishevelment, his armour shone like brass. The gaze of a single topaz eye swept the bailey with the glint of a conqueror.

Gregaris dismounted to join the melee, stomping among his enemies like a giant among dwarves. He swung his six-foot battle-axe with deadly speed and accuracy, scything through Royalists with the ease of a farmer through ripe summer wheat. I could well believe this barbarian Cyclops had fought his way out of Pixley with just his bare hands.

Beside me, Saxton watched with admiration as Gregaris and his horde of Crusaders ravaged the Royalists. He leaned forward to tell me, "Gregaris was a free gladiator from Glanshayda. He'd won championships in the sports arena until he lost his eye to a berserker's swordtip, which forced him to retire. Then some crazy fool showed him how to handle an axe." Saxton grinned. "Frightening, isn't it?"

I nodded bleakly, agreeing with his observation on more than one level. With the arrival of Gregaris, there was no longer any question of a victory for me. By rights, I should be delirious with joy. The problem now became how to prevent a massacre and the demolition of my ancestral home. Between them, the warring factions pounded Gryphon to pieces. Sporadic fires still raged unconfined, and rampant horses trampled everything and everyone in their path. I had to end the carnage, the havoc, before it went beyond my ability to control. But how?

To make matters worse, Ginger got into the act. A streak of flame arced into the sky and exploded in a dazzling spray over the bailey, a starburst of violet, fuchsia, and chartreuse. As the shower drifted down, wherever a spark struck, whether stone, steel, or flesh the mote of light swelled until it belched forth a gout of mucous and engulfed its unfortunate host in a glutinous cocoon. Stairs became too slippery to climb, cobbles too slick to tread, and weapons too gummy to wield. It was as if some ailing titan had expelled a glob of phlegm onto the castle.

Once, I caught a glimpse of the mage atop the opposite wall, diabolical in all his glory, as lustrous charges of sorcery darted around him. Periodically, a streak detached itself from its frenetic orbit to hurl itself down into the yard, spreading flame and mayhem wherever it landed. It was a spectacular display of power, of colour, of light. Through my dismay, I was compelled to admit I was impressed. Ginger's magic, albeit barbarous and perverse, was wondrous to behold.

So while I gaped in awe, dithered in confusion, and wallowed in my own impotence, it happened. A stray arrow found my young captain.

Hearing his grunt of pain, I turned to see Saxton lurch, then topple perilously close to the edge of the wall. I reached out to grab his surcoat, a foolish thing, for his weight would have taken me over the parapet with him. My fingertips grazed his sleeve as my hand closed around empty air.

Mercifully, Saxton was dead before he ever hit the ground. I'd seen his eyes as they stared at the nameless shaft impaling him, and there had been no light in them; the arrow had pierced his heart. Now he lay sprawled below on the rocky slope, a twisted and broken doll.

A sob caught in my throat, and I closed my eyes, though they remained imprinted with the image of yet another senseless, wasted death. Reeling away, I sank to my knees upon the battlements, my grief a physical pain. My gallant young captain was dead. I prayed him rest in peace and hoped there were horses in heaven.

CHAPTER THIRTY

"Highness, are you all right?"

A young Crusader approached me where I knelt with my face in my cupped palms. Bolder than his fellows, he extended his hand and helped me to my feet. "Shall I send for Ginger? Perhaps, he can—"

Almost immediately the youth became aware he'd said the wrong thing. I shrugged out of his solicitous grip and swung on them all with a look of such fierceness they stepped back, doubtless to give the madwoman room. In truth, I think I was half-mad, overcome with sorrow and fury and guilt.

Grief assailed me, along with a feeling of panic and failure. My thoughts were in turmoil, all tangled together, confused. I could not contain them, but neither could I organize them into something solid.

Below me on the parapet a rumbling started from deep in the castle, echoing up from the dungeons, from the teleportal itself. Restless at its confinement and captivity, as restless as my own thoughts, the opposing forces of magic collided and clashed. The castle quivered, the bailey shook. A shrill whine, the shriek of iron against iron, began low then rose to a piercing screech. All around me people teetered and fell as the ground slid out from under them with the sway of the keep. The collection of wooden outbuildings threatened to collapse, sagging and leaning like drunken sailors. Everywhere weapons racks tilted, spilling their contents. Lamps tipped and torches toppled, their flames leaping out to devour whatever was handy. The Shouda sent up a frantic baying.

Then Ginger was by my side, kneeling on the stones of the rampart, a fawn coloured Shouda bitch with him. "Whatever you're doing," he whispered through gritted teeth, "stop it."

"I can't," I moaned. "I'm not doing it on purpose."

"Try, Kathedra. Do you want to destroy Gryphon? Turn this into another Idyll and prove Bertrand right?"

That snapped me into clearer focus, almost as if he had removed a blindfold from my eyes. But the damage had been wrought. The castle still shook down to its very roots. I had undermined Ginger's powers with my own, severing what little control he had over the teleportal. "Can you shut it down?"

"Not from here."

"C'mon." I grabbed his hand and hauled him after me from the ramparts, dodging bodies and fallen weapons. Smoke rose skyward in billowing black columns, obscuring the bailey and our descent. Staggering, stumbling, we picked our way over the debris in the compound while the keep shuddered and groaned around us. The Shouda trailed us as far as the stairs, then refused to go any further. Snatching up a torch we descended into the bowels of the castle, leaving the dog behind to whine and pace fretfully.

In a corridor on the second level we bumped into Averi, panicked and disoriented, heading topside at a dead run. He grabbed the mage's arm, swung him to a halt. "What went wrong?" he demanded, his voice high and tremulous. "I did exactly as you said! It's not my fault!"

"Slow down," I snapped. "Do you have anything to report?"

Averi caught his breath, waved an arm in the general direction of the dungeons. "They're all in there. About fifty of the bastards, including Chiverly himself."

"You've done a fine job." I shoved him out of my way. "Come along if you like. We might need a sacrificial victim." I think he half believed me.

Down here, so close to the teleportal, on the verge of self-imploding, the tremble underfoot was so severe we could hardly walk. We inched along the corridor, arms outstretched for balance, not unlike navigating onboard a ship in a storm-tossed sea. Ginger stopped us in the archway that led to the dungeons. "This is as close as I dare."

At his command we sank onto our knees, as much for stability than any ritual of magic. Swallowing my distaste I joined hands with Averi. Together the three of us formed a triangle. Ginger explained, "You two are my anchors. If things get a little scary, hold me down. If you let go, if you break our link, we're all dead."

I squeezed Averi's hand in my metal encased fingers, warning him brave. Ginger began to chant. We felt the power rise and surge against us, trying to barrel a way past us in its struggle to escape the mage's control, to escape its bondage. Ginger tried to contain it, to push it back, but it was like trying to hold up a falling wall. It crushed down upon us, bearing us beneath its weight and ferocity. I felt the mage's hand slip from mine, felt Averi waver on the other side of me. The pressure was too much. Averi was torn from my grip; he did not voluntarily release. He flew across the room, his body striking unyielding stone with a thud.

Ginger and I collapsed together in a heap on the floor. "Kathedra," he murmured, too battered, too exhausted from his otherworldly battle with the teleportal to move. "I can't stop it. It's too far gone, too far out of my control. Run. Go as far as you can get."

I ignored that. From where I sat, or more correctly sprawled, I saw only two choices; let the fight end here, while I stood on the verge of victory, and be buried under mounds of rock and wood and iron that was Gryphon, or try to stop the threat myself.

I staggered onto my feet, turned to peer into the holding cells, my view vaguely distorted. The air before me shimmered, expanding and contracting. I stumbled towards the entity; it had a will of its own, repelling me, keeping me at a distance. The captive Royalists lay on the floor, splayed every which way, knocked cold.

I glanced back once at Ginger, where he lay unconscious. He had said such a force of energy could not be restrained by iron and stone, bonds that did not give or bend. I recalled the strip of leather I'd wound around Averi's wrists, commanded there by thought and adhered by will. I required more flexible shackles, something of unshakable strength but as ethereal as air.

Then it struck me. An earth shattering revelation. Maybe I did not require anything tangible, anything of this world. Maybe all I needed was already at hand.

I shaped thought out of will, wove it strong with fortitude and purpose, more durable than chain, yet soft as cloud. I headed for the teleportal, trailing my mystical ropes of power. Only sheer determination moved my feet forward to the bars of the holding cell. It was like wading through water up to my chest, the tide trying to push me back with each step.

Finally, when I could go not an inch farther, I released my ropes. They slithered and writhed unchallenged between the bars of iron, spinning and twisting as they entwined themselves around the entity pulsing within, where it strained against its stone and iron prison, about to burst asunder in its effort to break free. I wrought more rope, binding my cocoon of power fast. I wove them together, tying up all loose ends, knotting them strong with unbreakable resolve.

The energy shifted, paused. I held my breath, wondering if the entity would fight, if my magic would yield before it. My chains stuck, as strong as my will, formed into substance by my Teki powers. A moment passed, then two. I perceived not surrender or retreat, but a sort of non-resistance, a sense of stability and peace. So delicate, so subtle were these bonds that the elemental force it bound did not even know it was fettered.

But I had no time to marvel over the feat I had wrought. I knelt beside Ginger, deep in his catatonic sleep, and smoothed the forelock from his brow. "I'll come back for you, but first…there's something I must do."

I emerged into the bailey to thunderous cheers. Stunned, I saw the compound ringed with wearied but victorious Crusaders, standing shoulder to shoulder with my former Royal, that of the Gryphon Highlord. Naren approached me, a smile of triumph on that normally stoic face. "It's over. It's done. You did it, Kathedra."

I guess I had.

The hoopla subsided; the keep went unnaturally still. Only a Shouda's plaintive whimper broke the quiet as I looked out over the yard, where the Crusaders seemed to have everything well in hand. According to Naren, the remnants of Roche's thieving mercs had thrown down their swords and pled for mercy. Gregaris had subdued Urharde's Seventh, though Urharde himself was missing. Arial's and Tock's Royals had pretty much obliterated each other. Tock had fought until the bitter end, falling to a well-placed sword thrust. Of Arial, there was no sign.

Victory was mine. I savoured the emotion, having known no deeper feeling of accomplishment. But my elation soon soured, for now the victorious must deal with the vanquished.

I bobbed my head in the direction of the one-eyed giant. "I'm so glad to see you, Naren…and your friend."

Briefly, he explained, "Gregaris had just liberated Pixley when I came across him headed for Idyll. We sent a messenger on to Belvemar, then rode for here with reinforcements."

"In the nick of time," I replied, embracing him warmly. "Thank you, Naren. Thank you."

He hugged me back. "You've won."

Suddenly afraid, suddenly uncertain, I whispered, "But at what cost? I fear I've paid too dear a price. Saxton is dead. He—"

Naren gently pushed me away. "I know. I saw. Don't speak of it now. Time to grieve later. There is still much work to be done."

His smile faded, and once more that mask of gravity settled over his features. "What are your orders?"

I straightened my surcoat, then donned a replica of Naren's stone-sober face. "Have the prisoners taken to the cells below the keep. And send a doctor down to check on Ginger. Keep an eye out for Arial. He's not to be harmed. You can dispatch your couriers at first light. For now, tend to the wounded and start the clean up. I'll handle everything else later. First…there's something I must do."

"Wait," Naren implored. "What about Valleri?"

"Leave him to me."

He seemed about to protest but refrained. "As you wish." He departed with a stiff bow to carry out his instructions.

Confident that Naren and Gregaris had the situation under control, I slipped away to find Uncle. At no time during the battle had I seen him and I feared him dead. The notion did not sadden me, except in the sense I had been cheated of my revenge.

I hurried to the secret passageway, no longer secret if ever it was, and followed it to my apartments, stepping over the corpses of Halberdiers. I opened the hidden panel to see my teak and silk screen in a broken tangle…and Uncle lying beneath it, the far door barricaded against his enemies.

I had heard Uncle had been damned near untouchable with a sword in his younger days, before he'd let himself get fat and soft. Now he'd been forced to take one up again to defend his very life. One fist still clenched the blade while the other clutched at a heavily bleeding wound. It was an effort, in his wretched condition, but he lifted his head at my entrance.

He groaned a single word. "Kathedra." Dropping the sword, he reached out his hand.

The tyrant Bertrand had indeed come to a pathetic end. "Look, Uncle," I sighed, crouching beside him. "Look at what you have done."

He nodded feebly. "I know. It's all my own doing." He clasped my fingers in his and gazed up at me. "Beautiful, beloved Kathedra. I thought never to see you again. I'm so glad you're here."

Awful damned convivial since last I saw him. Perhaps he entertained the hope I would somehow find a way for him to escape his fate. Even now.

"Oh, Kathedra. What cruel punishment you did me," he continued, near to tears. "Had I known you'd leave, I wouldn't have forced you to wed Lesuperis."

Contrite? Tearful? Maudlin? This was not the Uncle I knew. I presumed the severity of his injury had made him delirious.

"I fled for my life, remember? You decommissioned me. Imprisoned me. I believed next you'd kill me."

"Kill you?" he howled in disbelief. "Stupid, faithless wench. Why would I kill you? You are my sole blood heir."

Now this was more like Uncle. "Because my Teki powers had exceeded your ability to control them." I spoke slowly, gently, as if speaking to a dull child. "I had to be removed."

"You had to be rendered impotent, yes. I won't refute it. But I addressed the problem by retiring you and arranging you a marriage. I don't recall signing a writ of execution, although some may argue there is no difference."

That couldn't be a joke. Uncle was not known for his snappy wit.

"You ordered my death," I accused.

"I ordered your capture."

A long pause followed as I attempted to solve this little discrepancy, for until now I had been convinced Uncle wanted me dead.

"How can you believe I'd kill you, Kathedra? I'd not harm a red hair on your head. You are my sister's daughter."

I swallowed back the hurt caused by previous rejections. "Nonetheless, you said some hateful things to me."

"And I regret them all. I spoke out of fear and anger. Can you forgive me?"

"Forgiveness is not something one can deal out like cards." But deep down inside, past all that simmering Umagi blood, a certainty embedded in my bones, I believed his remorse genuine.

Brokenly he whispered, "They told me you were dead."

"Who told you?"

"Valleri and Averi. They said the Crusaders found you first. I saw the body. I…I didn't…" He choked on the words. "I didn't even recognize it."

Sinking to my knees, I lifted his head into my lap. Aware he was dying, Uncle felt a need to confess. He talked and I listened, in a detached sort of way, letting the words drift in my brain until they found a place where they all made sense.

"You had grown proud and wilful, so like your mother. I knew you could not bear to see Thylana in such turmoil; I feared you would try to take over. Each day you grew bolder, more rebellious, your Umagi powers soaring to a level beyond my restraint. I know what I am, a man twisted by grief and hatred. I also know I can't be forgiven for all my atrocities. But I swear, Kathedra, I intended you no harm."

"Yet, you still hurt me."

"In my arrogance and haste, yes. I thought if you had a lover to ease your cares and divert your attention, you'd abandon the revolt, your powers."

"So you went to Valleri?"

"I didn't think any damage could be done by it. I warned him to be discreet, for I did not wish a scandal. As you know, it didn't work. If anything, you became stronger, more determined, and I was forced to take drastic measures. I knew you would not accept retirement easily, so I plotted to marry you off and get an heir sired on you. There would be no time for a new bride and mother-to-be to concern herself with Crusaders or magic. I did not think, however, that you'd buck me so strenuously. When I told Valleri to use the secret passageway to see you, I never dreamt you would use it to escape."

At my expression of surprise Uncle explained, "Yes, I knew about it. Your mother and father employed it often before they were wed, or so I'm told."

I squeezed his hand imploringly. "What happened, Unc? What happened to make Valleri turn on you? It's clear he doesn't covet the throne. What else could he want?"

"I told him if he agreed to help me I would give him your command, once you lost interest in it. But you never did. So when I decided to announce your retirement I ordered him to end the affair, whereupon he could assume your generalship."

"He refused?"

Uncle nodded. "It never occurred to me he might want to marry you himself."

Aghast, I stared at him.

"I couldn't permit that, of course," he babbled. "He's not of royal blood. Indeed his stock is as common as the cook's." Adamant, he shook his head, still unable to comprehend the notion that some people might choose to marry for love. "I told him I had betrothed you to Lesuperis, but Valleri wouldn't hear of it."

My heart contracted in anguish. "Your one mistake, Uncle. Had you allowed Valleri to marry me, he would have stayed loyal forever. Had you allowed us to be together, had you given us your blessing, none of this would have happened."

But it had happened, and because of it the lives of so many people had changed course, their destinies swept in different directions, the fate of a nation--whether for good or bad, who will ever know?--had been irreversibly altered. The past could not be reshaped and the truth was irrelevant.

There was no time for such self-indulgent musings, however. For Uncle lay mortally wounded and someone was battering down the door.

CHAPTER THIRTY-ONE

Valleri stepped over the splintered remains of the barricade, sword drawn. His steely glare swept over me to settle on Uncle, scoring him with twin daggers of hatred and malice

"Come to kill me, have you, Val?" Uncle said with surprising calm.

"Looks like you've done a thorough job of it yourself." Valleri snorted, his gaze shifting to me. "I suppose he's already told you his side of the story. Has he confessed to you all his worldly sins and begged your forgiveness? Did you listen to his prattle? Do you believe his lies?"

"He's dying, Val. Why would he lie?"

"So you'll hate me. He can't bear the thought you might love me."

"I trusted you, Valleri," Uncle interrupted. "We had a deal. You betrayed me."

"Betrayed you?" Valleri snapped. "No, Bertrand. Don't act so outraged. This is all your own fault."

"Your insolence is astonishing," Uncle burbled. "I offered you more than any man of your station deserves."

Pain crept into Valleri's eyes, a pain I had seen many times but had been unable to fathom. Until now.

"A man of my station," Valleri sneered, taking a step forward. "That's always how you thought of me, isn't it? A stray animal permitted to eat the best food out of the finest porcelain, when it should be gleaning scraps out of the gutter. A peasant educated and refined when he should be out labouring in the fields with the rest of his kind. Someone to be pitied and tolerated but never accepted. That's all I ever was to you and everyone else in this cesspit."

"No, Valleri," I whispered, stricken by his bitterness. "You're wrong. You were everything to me."

Ignoring me, he resumed his advance upon Uncle. "But I was useful to you for a while, until you threw me aside, just as you did Kathedra. You denied me what I wanted most. More than the generalship of the Gryphon Highlord. More than the title of your heir. More than even the juiciest morsel you tossed me from your plate when I was a child, as you would a dog."

Though his whole body trembled with anger, Valleri managed to compose himself and point a menacing finger. "I only ever wanted Kathedra for my wife. You promised she would be mine."

In desperation Uncle tried to reason with him. "Only for a short while, Valleri. I loaned her to you for your temporary use. It was not meant to be forever."

Loaned? Temporary? Use? So. I had been reduced from pawn to common chattel. Me. The daughter of a queen.

"Nonetheless, you let me believe otherwise in order to serve your own ends."

Uncle strained to push himself up, fury lending him strength. "Does your greed know no bounds?" he sputtered, struggling onto his knees as if his rage alone were enough to propel his broken body forward. "I gave you more than what was necessary and you readily agreed to the terms. Not only did I give you the rank of Gryphon Highlord, I permitted you the privilege of sating your lust upon royal flesh. You. A man who should have no more been allowed to look at her! You ungrateful cur. What more could you possibly want?"

Silence fell in the wake of Uncle's diatribe. Valleri's face was a mask of hatred. I refused to believe I was the cause of all this. There was another reason that explained why he had done all he did; I could see it in his eyes, something dark and sinister, left festering inside him for too many years…and we were about to find out what.

"This," Valleri snarled, brandishing his blade. A remote smile curved his mouth; anticipation made his eyes glitter coldly. "I want this."

I recognized the look. Bloodlust. I'd seen it in him before, during the heat of battle. Scrambling to my feet, I thrust myself between them. Uncle collapsed to the floor, having great difficulty breathing now. "Please, Valleri," I begged. "Don't do this."

He raked me with a cutting glance. "I've waited a long time, Kathedra. You will not deny me my vengeance."

"Vengeance? Surely not because he refused to let us marry. What is it, Val? Tell me."

"Because he killed my mother."

"Your mother?" I echoed, confused. "But your mother died at Idyll, because a hearthmage's spell had gone awry." I almost said because of you, but refrained.

Val flung Uncle a hideous scowl. "You didn't tell her?"

"I kept my word," Uncle coughed. "Even now. You thankless bastard."

A terrible knot writhed in my belly. Lips trembling, I said, "Tell me what, Val?"

Valleri took a deep breath. "Mauranna was my mother."

I gaped in disbelief.

"Kathedra, I'm sorry you found out this way. I assumed Bertrand already told you. I…I don't know what to say."

"Try."

He shook his head, a rueful twist to his lips. "I was afraid if you knew the truth, you'd hate me because I was her son. Because if not for her, for what happened at Idyll, none of this would have happened, and you wouldn't have had to live your life fettered by your Umagi powers. I agreed to his scheme to prevent you from learning the truth. Then I fell in love with you. But when I asked Bertrand for your hand, he denied me."

"Of course I denied you!" Uncle bellowed. "It would taint the bloodline."

"Quiet, Unc," I hissed, intercepting Valleri as he lunged, sword on the upswing. "You're not helping me here."

I ducked under Val's blade and planted my palms in his chest, holding him at bay. But he easily detached himself, plucking me from him as if I were a gnat. His hand clamped over my wrist, and he dragged me before Uncle. "Ahh, yes. That's your biggest complaint, isn't it, Bertrand? I'm common. I must admit, for a while it was gratifying to see you forced by Kathedra's alleged death to acknowledge a commoner as your heir. I know how galling it must have been for you."

His fist tightened around my arm with crushing force, making me wince. "Val, you're hurting me."

He shoved me aside without heed, his attention never wavering from Uncle. "But with Kathedra out of the castle, I no longer had to endure your taunts, your threats. I could act unimpeded and wait for the right moment to take my revenge. I watched you order my mother's death, I watched her dragged in chains to the site of execution, I watched…" He paused, choked down the grief that strangled his words. "I watched, restrained by your guards, as your executioner's blade cleaved through her neck."

I let the tears flow down my cheeks, distraught to see Valleri in such anguish. In his temper, he hurled his sword across the room and threw himself to his knees, burying his face in his hands as he wept.

So. This was the madness. This was what had driven him to treachery and murder and vengeance: rage and grief bottled up inside a little boy for what must seem an eternity. I could not imagine the horror that child had witnessed, the pain he'd staunchly borne for so long, in addition to the knowledge he was to blame.

The urge to comfort Val was fierce, but I dared not approach him. He was too angry, too unpredictable, and in that moment I feared him. At last, he lowered his hands, and a strange expression crossed his features, something like repletion. Without warning he sprang, a howl tearing itself from his throat. I saw the flash of steel, heard the song of it splice the air. But it all happened so fast I could not move to stop it in time.

Uncle let out a grunt of surprise as the dagger plunged into his shoulder, deflected there by my lunge. "Valleri, please! Don't kill him. I know the truth. I know the truth about you…and I don't care."

Valleri looked at me across Uncle's body, his hand still on the blade, red with the blood of my family. "And what truth is that?"

"That you're Teki, too, just like me. That you were the one in Idyll, who discharged the spell that collided with Mauranna's. Of course you were just a child, untrained, untaught—"

"What?" He staggered onto his feet, swaying over Uncle where he groaned on the floor. "What in Heaven's name are you saying?"

"I'm saying that I know your terrible secret, and it doesn't matter. I am not my uncle. I won't hold you responsible for something you did as a child, for something that was beyond your control."

"Who told you that?" He seemed perplexed, and a little angry.

"No one told me, exactly. I figured it out." I rose, seized his tunic in my hands and ripped it away, exposing the eagle wing tattoo etched onto his skin. "See, Val? I know."

He stared at me incredulous, arms splayed at his sides.

"Shall I leave you two alone?"

I whirled at the sound of Ginger's voice. Having come upon me unawares yet again, the mage stood in the tunnel's entrance, Naren with him, an armed contingent of Crusaders behind them. His timing couldn't have been more fortuitous. Perhaps now the two of them could sift free the pains of the past and put them all to rest.

"Ginger, tell him. Tell him I know that he's Teki. That I figured it out that night in Idyll." I pointed to the tattoo. "It's an amulet to arrest his powers, just like my tonic, just like that ring. Am I right?"

"Hmm, no. I don't think so. It looks to me like an allegiance badge of the Gryphon Royal House. We've seen it on other Royalists." He looked at me, amusement and maybe a hint of pity in his expression. "I don't know what you gleaned from our conversation that night, but I did not mean to imply Valleri was Teki because…well, he's not." Then he fixed his gaze on the man in question. "Are you?"

"You know very well I'm not, you bastard."

How could I have got it so wrong?

Sensing my confusion, Val said, "You're not totally wrong, Kathedra. You just don't have the right person."

I looked at Ginger. He shook his head.

Then who?

At my feet, struggling to sit, Uncle burbled, "Will someone please tell me what the hell is going on?"

"I'll tell you what's going on Bertrand," Valleri hissed, bending near. "That day in Idyll, when my mother cast her harmless hearth spell, another spell, one from a Teki just like your beloved niece, cast one of his own. It spun out of control, collided with Mauranna's and ignited chaos. Your son died on the end of a knife wielded by his own hand, or should I say, his own misbegotten spell."

Shock filled the room, mainly from Uncle and me. Ginger, of course, knew the truth, always had. Valleri pushed Uncle back to the floor, ignoring the pain and sorrow pooling in those eyes. "Yes, Bertrand. Your own son, a fledgling Teki, ignorant of the power, indifferent to the danger, is the source of all that's wrong in Thylana today. And my mother, innocent of all blame, died at your behest."

Uncle babbled, sputtered, overcome with an all-consuming horror. "No. You're lying. How dare you slander my son's name, my dead son's name!"

"I'm not lying. Ivor was Teki. Just like his cousin, Kathedra."

"How can that be?" I whispered.

"Your father was Teki, as you are well aware. But your mother carried the same blood, so too did Bertrand. If you trace if back far enough you'd find Teki mages in the royal family tree. You know that's true, Bertrand. I can see it in your face."

"Ivor would have told me," Uncle insisted.

Valleri snorted. " He didn't tell you because he knew how you'd react, with ignorance and outrage, just as you have now."

"Why didn't you say something?" I asked, incredulous.

"To who? Who would have listened to me, a boy of eleven, desperate enough maybe to say anything to save his mother's life, and after she had begged me the morning of her execution to say nothing, to preserve the love that Bertrand bore his son?"

He crooked his head at Ginger, standing mute with downcast eyes. "Or would someone have instead listened to him, a novice Umagi himself, even if he had not been freshly plucked, delirious and near death, from a raging inferno?"

The full horror dawned on me then, how in jumping to conclusions, both Uncle and I had gotten it all so very wrong.

Valleri reached for his sword, where it lay a hand span away, and rose smoothly to his feet, pointing it at Ginger. "And you. You are as much at fault. You, along with Ivor, who spent that whole summer messing around with powers far beyond your comprehension, too proud to ask for tutelage, too foolish to realize the dangers. Look what your arrogance has done. It cost my mother her life, and the lives of hundreds, no…thousands, thanks to one man's insufferable grief and unremitting hate."

"I know what I have done," Ginger replied, unflinching. "I am reminded every time I see my face reflected back at me. I know what it is to hurt, Val, to lose someone you love. All I can say is I'm sorry. I'm sorry about Mauranna, about Ivor, about everything. But you can't go about exacting your revenge indiscriminately as Bertrand has. You need to go back to Idyll, without your sword this time, confront your ghosts, visit your mother's grave, make your peace with Ivor. You know he didn't do it on purpose."

"Oh, you'd like me to go to Idyll, wouldn't you?" Valleri spat. "Then you could have Kathedra all to yourself."

"This has nothing to do with Kathedra."

"Stop!" Uncle bellowed in a surprisingly strong voice.

We fell silent, turning to look at him as he tottered onto his legs, his hands clapped to his ears. "I won't listen to any more of these lies!" he ranted. "I won't! I'll throw you all in the dungeons and cut out your treacherous tongues before I let you—"

He stopped there in mid-rant, clutching not his wound but his chest, as if in pain. Though his mouth worked, no sound came out. He took a few staggering steps, one arm extended towards me. I went to his side, tried to steady him, but he slipped from my grasp and fell forward onto the cold marble. I felt for a pulse, searched for a sign of breath in him, a sign of life, but there was nothing. I looked up, said, "He's dead."

Valleri had slain him with the truth as surely as if he'd run his blade through his heart.

But not even the death of the tyrant Bertrand could divert Ginger and Valleri from their present course. They resumed their argument as if the Regent of Thylana had not collapsed dead before their eyes. "Tell him to go," Valleri hurled at me. "I promise to spare his life if he leaves now."

I stepped between Val and his intended target. "Valleri, put down the sword."

An answering reply in steel came from behind as Ginger drew his own blade. "Stand aside, Kathedra. I am eager to see just how good a swordsman he thinks he is."

"Are you mad?" I gasped. "Are you both eleven years old again? If you think I'll let the two of you resume your boyhood rivalries while Uncle lies dead on the floor you are out of your mind."

I might have spoken a foreign language for all the response I received. They came together in a clash of steel and wills. Only quick reflexes on Naren's part saved me from harm's path.

They were determined to disobey me. Damn them both. While they claimed there could be no truce between them, they had, nevertheless, united in defiance against me.

Pondering my choices, I watched the two combatants as they circled and lunged, gauging each other's mettle, seeking a weakness. A calculated pounce here, a prudent withdrawal there. Neither wore armour nor mail, stripped down to shirts and breeches. Only blood would satisfy the victor. Each blow was precise yet parried with ease, the next coming harder, faster. Thus they sparred, neither man giving nor gaining ground.

Briefly I considered letting the two of them wear themselves out, since as swordsmen they were about evenly matched. Physically Ginger was exhausted, his struggle with the teleportal having sapped his strength. As for Valleri, he was in no emotional condition to fight. Anger had drained his patience, and whittled away his concentration. If one of them came to any harm at the hands of the other, I would never forgive myself.

I wrenched away my arm, suppressing the urge to conjure a baby cyclone and whisk Naren away in a human whirlwind.

"Stop it," I spat through gritted teeth. "I command here. I say who stays and who goes. You do not possess the privilege of deciding that for yourselves. The Regent Bertrand lies dead and by the law of royal succession I claim his throne. As your queen, I order you to cease this folly and throw down your weapons."

Valleri let loose a savage volley of blows, which Ginger deflected with skill, taking time out to snarl,"I warned you, Kathedra. I warned you not to interfere. But you did, and now you must accept the consequences."

Taking advantage of his foe's distraction, Valleri pounced, his sword flashing up for the mage's throat. Ginger swerved, the tip of Val's blade drawing a rivulet of blood from his brow. Ginger recovered in time to block a forceful two-handed swing, and with tremendous effort thrust Valleri off.

Blade hammered into blade, the discordant notes of steel driving through me with every blow struck. For the sake of my own sanity, I could not let this continue. I recalled the teleportal far below us in the bowels of the keep, bound by its shackles of air, and a similar thought occurred. I called forth power, supple and sinewy, eager to do my bidding. A pair of chains formed out of lightness, forged fast with the strength of will.

Lightning quick the chains struck, lashing out like phantom vipers. The first seized upon Valleri, snaking around his sword arm down to his wrist. He stared at his imprisoned hand, amazement and outrage warring in his expression, and fought in vain to wrest himself free. He was strong, fortified by thoughts of revenge and fury, but in terms of power, they seemed frail and brittle beneath the intensity of my will. I sent forth tendrils of thought, each stronger than the one before it, until Valleri was on his knees, striving to break bonds that were indestructible. At last, the sword clattered to the stones, and Valleri collapsed from the exertion.

Ginger was another matter entirely. Though his arm had been rendered immovable by the chain encircling it, he refused to release the blade. No amount of pressure, wielded by thought, could bend his grip. His will to defy me was stronger than my ability to break it. Apparently he had not spent all his magic on the teleportal. An impasse ensued; I would not yield and he would not surrender.

Losing patience, I snapped, "Ginger, throw down your weapon. There is no one left to fight."

"Except you."

"Why? Why do you have to turn this into a battle of wills? Please, put away your blade."

"Sorry, Kathedra. If you want me to do that, you'll have to break my wrist."

Struggling to raise the sword, his arm quaking from the effort, he rounded on Valleri, where he lay unconscious. I had no idea whether I possessed the strength to do what he said, and in truth, I had no desire to find out. Nonetheless, I would not be coerced this way. Therefore I appealed to Gregaris for assistance.

"Disarm him."

The flame-haired giant marched up to the mage and demanded in a thick northern burr, "Give me the blade, Ginger."

Though Gregaris towered above even Ginger's exceptional height, the mage refused to be intimidated. He glowered up at the burly Crusader with the audacity of a precocious child. "If you want it, you're going to have to take it from me your—"

But before Ginger could finish his sentence, Gregaris had the mage by the collar and the sword yanked from his fist, unimpeded by my ethereal chains. Then, breaking the blade over a knee, he flung both pieces at Ginger's feet and walked back to my side.

"Thank you, Gregaris." I could see such a man would prove handy to have around in the days to come.

"No trouble, Highness."

The chains of thought dissolved, making Ginger staggered under their sudden release. He righted himself, closed his eyes, waiting for his outrage to pass. When his lids lifted next, they revealed a gaze black with fury. It slid to Valleri, his one-time friend come mortal nemesis if only out of habit. "What about him?"

"What about him?" I countered.

"He's your enemy. He can't be trusted. You must take steps to remove his threat."

Certainly if I wanted peace in Thylana I had to do something about Valleri. But I did not consider him a danger. He was beaten, defeated not by an adversary but by his own hand. I knew what I must do. Nevertheless, I would not be commanded by Ginger.

Bobbing my head at Valleri, I said, "Take him to a cell," whereupon Naren dragged Val to his feet and had him hauled away by two husky Crusaders.

Ginger asked, "What will you do?"

I sighed, waving a weary hand. "I won't discuss this with you. Please, just take yourself to the infirmary and get your head checked. You don't look so good."

His complexion was ghostly pale, lines of strain etched into his face. Pain and exhaustion had clouded his judgment. Blood dripped from the gash in his brow. Wincing, he tottered forward. "It's nothing. A scratch," he insisted. "Answer me. What will you do?"

My patience hung by a slender thread. I had not slept more than eight hours in three days nor eaten since yesterday. Fatigue and grief had exacted an emotional toll. "Either take yourself away to the infirmary," I spat, "or I will have you taken there in chains. Real chains. Of iron."

His mouth twisted into a snarl. "Aye, Your Glory. You bellow and I shall jump. Is that how it is to be?" His words were slurred, his eyes glazed. Though I knew it to be the hurt of his injuries and bruised pride talking, the barb stung nonetheless. So I watched, with a certain amount of satisfaction, as he took another wobbly step and fell flat on his face. Had the situation not been so grim and he not so pathetic, I might have laughed had I been able to summon the energy.

"Gregaris?"

At my behest the giant stooped and slung the unconscious mage over a brawny shoulder with no more exertion than heaving a sack of turnips. Relieved, I gazed after Gregaris as he strode away to the infirmary with his burden. With luck, Ginger's injury would keep him on his back for a while and out of my hair. That is not to say I was not concerned about him. His wounds, albeit relatively minor, were the sort that could generate complications. Everything I had gained at so dear a price would mean nothing if I lost Ginger now.

Naren snapped out a command to his men, then gently turned me from the sight of Uncle's body, lying twisted and bloodied amid the wreckage that had been my apartment. Nevertheless, a wayward glimpse brought unexpected grief, not for the Uncle I knew but the one that I had been cheated of by a boyhood prank gone awry, and all the mistruths and misdeeds it had begotten.

CHAPTER THIRTY-TWO

Glowering, I slumped upon my throne, legs outstretched and crossed at the ankles, crown askew atop my dishevelled mane. Though tired beyond belief, I had to attend to this next bit of business before I could seek the solitude and rest I craved. The time for reckoning had come. My faithful would be rewarded and the faithless cast out. I had not even changed my filthy clothes, though I'd taken time to wash the blood from my hands, still clad in my borrowed surcoat and stained breeches. My elbows leaned on the velvet armrests, an empty wine chalice dangling from my fingers. Not exactly a representation of queenly glamour I admit, but I was not much in the mood for regal splendour.

I had left Gregaris in charge of the work details that toiled throughout the keep. Saxton's body had been retrieved and now lay in the Great Hall. Likewise, one small corner of the Hall had been dedicated to Uncle's bier, under heavy guard to dissuade thieves and pranksters. Shredded, broken, Arial languished in the infirmary, clinging to life by a fingernail, too stubborn to accept the grim truth that he was dead. Urharde remained a fugitive in the castle, though every available man was set on his trail.

Only one of my officers attended me: Naren. He stood in mute vigilance at my side as I dispensed justice in Uncle's audience chamber, now mine. One by one an infinite procession of supplicants streamed past the double doors so they might approach my throne and beg forgiveness, plead mercy, or pledge fealty…or any combination of the three.

Gregaris was on housekeeping detail, sweeping Roche's mercs, bereft of their booty, and the survivors of Uncle's Halberdiers, including their captain, out the front door. Chiverly and his men had revived, sending up a clamour in the dungeons, all the while proclaiming themselves loyal to the throne and by extension me. Chiverly, however, was untrustworthy and lazy. I had no choice but to disband his Royal and send him packing. So it went, until the flood became a trickle.

I thrust out my cup to be refilled. Naren leaned over to whisper discreetly, "It's gone, Highness. There's not another drop of wine to be had in all of Gryphon. Gregaris is out somewhere trying to scare up a keg of ale."

If anyone could scare up anything it was Gregaris. But the knowledge did nothing to placate my spleen. Inexplicably, such a triviality infuriated me. My patience eroded. All my frustration bubbled forth. With a savage oath, I threw my goblet against the far wall, where it bounced off the stone and nearly clipped a page's nose.

Leaping from the dais, I stalked to the hearth and leaned my forearms on the mantle, staring down between them at the bright, crackling flames. "Cripes, Naren," I groaned. "All I want is a lousy cup of wine. Is that too much to ask?"

Wise, always intuitive Naren knew my outburst had little to do with absent wine. "Not much longer," he assured me. "Then you shall be able to seek your bed and rest easy knowing that Gregaris and I have everything in hand."

I sighed, grateful. "Thank you, Naren. You're a godsend. I want you to know I will reward you for your loyalty and support. All of you. Gregaris, Sestus—"

The faint hiss of chains and a polite cough interrupted me. I lifted my head from my arms and turned to see that the last supplicant had been brought. He stood alone, his wrists manacled before him, rumpled and begrimed, yet still quite dazzling. It broke my heart to see him bound like an enemy, but on the other hand, Valleri wore iron very, very well. A shadow waited in the corridor, just beyond view, restrained not by chains, but admirable self-control.

Straightening, I pushed myself from the hearth and approached Valleri. Braced for a confrontation I mustered swift courage, for without a doubt, these next words would be the hardest I've ever had to say. Gravely, I intoned, "Valleri, you are hereby banished from Thylana. You will be escorted to the nearest border and sent into exile, never to return. There will be no future contact between us, no written word exchanged. If you step one foot back into Thylana, you risk execution."

Though I tried to interpret his reaction, his face was a blank. "Is there anything you wish to say?"

At last, his vacant gaze sighted on me and he allowed a rueful smile. "Your lenience is touching, Kathedra. Though I deserve nothing less than execution, I am grateful for your act of mercy. Know that I bear you no ill will and shall accept banishment without complaint."

My fierce countenance softened at Valleri's contrition, which I believed sincere. Maybe his stay in the dungeons had provided him opportunity for reflection, allowing him to come to terms with the destiny he'd wrought for himself. He seemed serene and replete, if a bit sombre, his demons finally exorcised. I knew he would not apologize; it was not his way. The title of queen I owed partially to him, but I could not applaud his manoeuvres even if I could rejoice in the outcome. Val would go to his grave believing he had done the right thing.

After a thoughtful pause, Valleri added, "Before I go, I have a last request."

He took a step towards me. Before I could react, Naren had interpreted it as a move of aggression. The Crusader leaped between us, his sword a naked threat.

Valleri is not easily intimidated. He raised his bound hands in a gesture of peace, but did not retreat. "Heel, Naren. I mean Kathedra no harm."

While he lowered his blade Naren did not sheathe it, watching with cold, hateful eyes this man who had killed his friends. "Give me a reason, Valleri," he warned, stepping aside. "For I would dearly love to run you through."

"At ease, both of you." I gestured for a guard to free Val's hands, ignoring the look Naren threw me. "Valleri, speak your piece."

Rubbing his wrists where the iron had chaffed, he said, "I wonder if you might do something for me."

"If I can."

"Sit on your throne for me. I just want to see you on it, if only once. A memory to take into exile."

Naren looked at him as if he were crazy, and suspecting a trick, drew me closer.

I had no trouble understanding Valleri's request. His desire to see me sit as queen upon Thylana's throne had been one of the last things of which Val had spoken before my flight from Gryphon all those months ago. "It's all right, Naren," I murmured, extricating myself from his grip.

I straightened my crown, then mounted the dais. Gripping the ornately-carved armrests, I lowered myself onto the purple, gold-stitched cushion and tried to affect a regal dignity. I realized all too well I did not cut so majestic a figure, clad in ill-fitting soldier's attire, with soot on my face and blood in my hair. Valleri didn't seem to notice. He broke into a radiant grin, his eyes glittering as they fell upon me. "You will make a magnificent queen, Kathedra."

I accepted his compliment with quiet grace, somehow managing to contain my sorrow. Then I beckoned for the guards, declaring in a steady voice, "Take him away."

Painful as it was to see him cast out, it had to be done. I gave Naren orders to install Valleri in his apartments under house arrest, then got to my feet, fully intending to drag myself off to the nearest bed, when the shadow from the corridor stepped inside. Ginger.

Naren slipped from the room to await me without. I sank back down onto the cushion prepared for a lecture on my folly.

"I just wanted to let you know that I've disabled the teleportal. For good. I can't raise another on my own. Belvemar didn't reach it in time, so it's my guess he'll meet up with Sestus and take the long way here. Also, Gregaris believes that Urharde has fled the castle somehow. There's not a trace of him anywhere."

Oh. "Well, yes. Thank you. If that's all—"

"No, it's not all," he snapped. "I also want to tell you what a foolish mistake you've just made."

I presumed he referred to the leniency of Valleri's sentence. I bristled. "Really? I've always been under the impression that mercy is a desirable quality in a monarch."

"Mercy, yes. Idiocy, no. The man is a threat to you, and your attachment to him," Ginger sputtered, "blinds you to the danger he poses.

I heard Valleri himself say he expected execution."

"The man is my friend," I reminded him, then added, though he pretended not to hear, "and yours."

"He is your enemy. You're being completely unreasonable."

I half-rose, my hands clenched around the arms of the chair, fighting to keep my voice calm. "And you're being disrespectful."

"I'll risk it. Damn it, Kathedra! How could you do such a thing? It is inconceivable that you would so blithely grant Valleri his freedom. How can you be certain he won't return some day with an army to challenge you for all that is rightfully yours?"

Naren, too, had put the same question to me, albeit with a degree more tact. I gave the mage the same answer I'd given him. "I saw no other option. I can't kill everyone who opposes me, everyone I perceive a threat, unfounded or not. To do so would make me no different a tyrant than Uncle."

"I respect that. But you are generous and merciful to a fault. I'll concede execution is extreme, but you can imprison him. Let him live out his days in the deepest darkest dungeon or the tallest, most luxurious tower, I care not which. But this?"

He whirled away in a fit of temper. "This is the finest piece of lunacy I have ever seen. Valleri's history only proves his knack for treachery. I can't see him accepting this as over."

"Why not? He has what he wants. Uncle is dead and I have the throne."

"That is not what he wants," he shot back, trembling now with either fury or frustration. "He wants you."

Ah. Now I understood. "Ask yourself this, Ginger. Do you want Valleri dead because you believe him a menace to my rule, or because you believe him a rival for my affection?"

"Don't flatter yourself. I'm trying to protect you."

"Well, I have guards I pay to do that."

"Damn it, Kathedra, you don't have to pay me for anything!"

A hostile silence engulfed us. I stared at my fingers, laced before me on my lap, refusing to yield to his dramatics, unable to fathom his hatred for Valleri. Eyes downcast, I said, "If it will ease your mind, pay Val a visit. Talk to him, talk about what happened at Idyll. Or at least say good-bye. The last time you parted, you didn't get the chance."

My suggestion was met by still further silence.

"Ginger?"

I glanced up to see myself alone in the room. The bastard had not even the decency to slam the door.

Later I learned that Ginger had not gone far. Naren found him collapsed in the outer corridor, too weak to storm any further. He had not fully recovered from his magical battle with the teleportal before exchanging blows with Valleri, thus his tantrum in my throne room had tapped the last reserves of his strength. When Naren took me to see the mage in the infirmary, I found him flat on his back, looking so pale, so drawn I feared him dead. Only his heartbeat against my ear, the whisper of his breath in my hair as I lay next to him assured me he lived still.

The feud with the Umagi was over. Thylana was saved. My enemies had been vanquished and I had my crown. I had achieved my fondest dreams. I should be drunk on the wine of victory. Instead, it left a sour taste in my mouth. The price it had cost me was too dear. I had lost Uncle, Valleri, Repachea, and countless others. I could not lose Ginger, too.

I spent the night there with him on that narrow cot, only to be chased out come morning by the physician, quoting infirmary rules to me…the queen, if you please.

Naren tried to distract me with talk of castle business. Arial had survived the night and was expected to pull through, which I was grateful to hear. Urharde remained on the loose, his ability to escape custody making the walls ring with Gregaris's howls of frustration. And last but not least, the escort that was to accompany Valleri across the border was ready to depart.

"Give me a moment first, please."

He bowed and stepped away, while I slipped back into the infirmary. The female Shouda, the rangy, fawn-coloured one, lay on the cot by Ginger's feet. She lifted her snout from her paws at my entrance and thumped her tail in greeting. I sat beside her, running my hand over her sleek head. "Ahh, so dogs are allowed while the queen gets turned out on her royal rump? Very well. You can stay." Actually I had no choice. The Shouda refused to obey the command to disperse in the presence of Umagi. Owyn's amulets worked a little too well, a glitch he promised to fix once he had revised the charm that would make the effect permanent, all at no small cost in silver to me. The alternative was to destroy the dogs, and looking into the animal's soulful, topaz eyes as she gazed adoringly up at me, her tail beating out a rhythm against Ginger's thigh, I knew I would pay that swindler whatever he asked.

Rising, I cast a last, lingering glance at the mage. A flush of colour had returned to his cheeks and he stirred restlessly, on the verge of waking. My hand lifted of its own volition to smooth away the strands of silky dark hair from his scarred cheek. He moaned at the touch, irritated or pleased. Who could tell with such a prickly man? Satisfied, I left him to the dog's tender watch and rejoined Naren in the hallway.

We entered the compound together, where Valleri and his escort awaited me. Already life in the castle was returning to normal, with repairs well underway. Smiths hammered in their forges, trying to keep up with the carpenters' demand for nails. The gate was open, admitting country folk come to trade their wares with those of the stall keepers inside, as well as groups of wearied refugees who had fled Idyll via the teleportal before its demise.

I approached Valleri, standing unbound beside his horse, buttressed on either side by a pair of guards. Naren, who considered even my shadow too close for comfort, attempted to follow me but I stopped him with a curt gesture. I wished to speak my farewells to Val without an audience, and so dismissed the guards as well.

Clad in travelling gear, Valleri seemed composed, resigned, if a little sombre. I had discounted him as mad, greedy, devious, when in truth he was none of these things. Misguided perhaps. Ruthless certainly. But he had loved me, and I could not discount his heart so easily. My conscience prodded me to ask, "Where will you go, Val? What will you do?"

He tossed me his familiar cavalier glance and crooked smile. "I thought I might travel to Chakan, to offer my services as a hiresword to that desert chieftain who had given Bertrand the Shouda. He is rumoured to reward those who serve him well and faithfully with riches beyond mere mortals' dreams."

I nodded. That seemed a sensible undertaking. The chieftain had refused to become involved in our domestic strife, much too busy himself mediating tribal feuds and foiling murderous rivals to meddle in anyone else's affairs. No doubt he would enthusiastically welcome Val's tactical experience and fighting prowess. And even if by some stroke of stupidity he did not, Valleri could still make himself a lucrative career as a mercenary. I could well imagine him thundering across the dunes on a fleet courser, leading a charge through his enemies and waving a scimitar over his head. Just as easily, I could picture him ensconced in a silk tent, lounging on plush cushions, his every need and want attended to by a bevy of scantily clad female admirers. A life filled with exotic delights awaited him. Desert gold. Beautiful concubines. Countless enemies to slay. What more could a warrior want?

But with that vision a sense of misgiving assailed me. Tactical experience? A rich and powerful foreign ally? I shuddered to think what Valleri could do with such things, and briefly wondered whether I had been too careless with my mercy.

That unease must have shown on my face, for Valleri accurately read my thoughts. "Don't worry, Kathedra. You need never fear I will return one day to make war on you. I don't want Thylana, and I certainly won't help anyone else wrest her from you. You and your throne are safe from me, no matter what rubbish Ginger tells you."

He seemed so sincere, so adamant. But Ginger had planted a seed of doubt in me, and always there would lurk a suspicion in the back of my mind, allowing me no peace. Forcing a smile, I stepped in close to clasp his hands. "I know that, Val. I know. I wish nothing but the best for you."

He bent to kiss my cheek in the formal way. "I'll miss you, Kathedra. But if you ever need me, for any reason, just send word and I'll come. I may be in exile, but my heart is here with you."

Though I'd expected him to be bitter, he wasn't, which only proved how little I knew him.

We embraced, there before everyone, all trying to look busy and sympathetic at the same time. As we drew apart, I swear I saw gnarly old Gregaris brush away a tear.

"Peace, Val."

"And a long and prosperous reign to you."

Even as we parted, I think our fingertips still touched when I heard my name cried out with a note of urgency. "Kathedra!"

Startled, annoyed, I turned to see Ginger had crawled out of his sickbed to rave at me in apparent delirium. Though the look of weakness, of exhaustion, still clung to him, he marched towards us with unwavering stride, purpose and resolve etched onto the hard planes of his face.

"Kathedra, you should take more care," he told me, without trace of mockery. "There is danger here. I sense it."

"Danger from who? From Val?"

"No, not Valleri." He frowned, his gaze sweeping the area. "But nearby." There was an intensity, a watchfulness to him. His jaw was rigid with tension, and perspiration beaded on his brow, not the sweat of sickness but fear. Whatever his discomfiture, it was genuine.

By this time, Valleri had had enough. "Ginger, just what is it that you—"

A shout from above cut him off, and we all craned our necks to peer up at the top of the wall where a man, wrapped in a drab homespun cloak and hood stood. Stunned, I whispered, "Urharde?"

Beside me, Valleri murmured, "No," and took several steps forward, staring at the figure on the wall. "Not Urharde. It's—"

"Ragsey," I breathed. My heart flip-flopped in my chest like a dying mackerel.

Even as I spoke, Ragsey threw off his hood to reveal himself. His clothes were ragged, bloodied, and caked with road dust. He swayed atop the wall, one arm hanging loose, made useless by the festering arrow wound; it was a marvel that he could even stand. Why he was here was anybody's guess. Following his encounter with Naren's crossbow, he must have made his way to the teleportal shortly after we left Idyll, then bided his time until he could slip into the castle disguised as just another refugee.

"You!" he shouted down to me. "And him!" He indicated Ginger with a jerk of his chin. His voice was shrill, piercing, a hysterical edge to it. He was not in his right mind, if ever he had been. Pain and exhaustion and vengeful thoughts had left him mad.

"The two of you have ruined everything!" he yelled. "Valleri was supposed to be king. And with my help he still can be."

While not everyone might agree with his skewed reasoning, technically he was right. No one had thought to revoke Valleri's claim to throne in the event of my death and Uncle's.

Ginger turned to Valleri, demanded, "What treachery is this?"

Just as menacingly Valleri spat back, "I don't know what he plots but I swear I have nothing to do with it."

"What are you going to do, Ginger?" Ragsey cried from his vantage atop the wall, ignoring the sentries who had begun to converge upon him from all directions. "Who will you save? Kathedra or yourself?"

Then his hand whipped out from underneath his cloak and he let fly a throwing star. I saw it coming, the glint of metal against a backdrop of blue sky, heard the whine of it slicing through the air. I started to turn, to lift my arm to ward it off, but Ginger was quicker I bet than even Ragsey had anticipated. With a gesture and whispered command the star that had been spinning toward my throat halted, there in mid-air, to rotate so slowly I could count each blade, tinged with some vile substance, before it dropped harmlessly to the stones with a rattle of metal.

All this happened within seconds, and yet seemed to pass in slow motion. Someone, my ever faithful bodyguard, I suspect, tackled me from behind, bore me to the ground. Even as I fell, I saw with a mind-numbing terror another star hurtle towards the mage. Counting on Ginger's distraction with the first missile, Ragsey had loosed a second. It flew through the air, a deadly spinning disc, bang on for Ginger's heart. Though the sentries sprang to subdue the madman, none of them had reached him in time.

I didn't know whether Ginger had another spell ready or if he even had the strength to invoke it, but it didn't matter…because Valleri was there, stepping into the star's trajectory. The missile struck him square in the chest and penetrated deep, knocking him sideways. He reached out to stop his fall, and found Ginger's arm, his weight dragging both of them to the cobbles.

My cry went unheard in the commotion that ensued. The men on the wall had collared Ragsey, and by the fuss he was making he wasn't going quietly. I wrestled my way free of Naren, climbed onto unsteady feet, staring in horror at the hunk of metal protruding from Val's chest. I froze, watching this nightmare unfold, unable to believe any of it. Ginger was yelling for help, shouting for the surgeon, cursing Ragsey with every oath he knew. He pulled the star free of Valleri's flesh, heedless of its tearing points, used his own hands to stop the bleeding. But even at this distance, I could see it was no good. The poison had already worked its evil. Valleri's face had drained of all colour. His chest heaved as he fought for breath, fought for speech.

I moved to go to him, then stopped myself. I had already spoken my good-byes to Val. It was Ginger's turn.

Valleri batted away his friend's well-meaning hands. "It's no use," he gasped out. Fumbling, he grabbed for the mage, blood-tinged fingers clenching in the folds of his tunic. "Listen to me. The duty of the Gryphon Highlord is to protect the king or queen of Thylana," he paused to draw a ragged breath, "and I can think of no one who can do that job better than you."

Ginger hunched over him, propping Val up in his lap. His voice trembled, threatened to break. "If that were true, then it would be me here lying in your place."

"No, Ginger. It's exactly why you're not. It is I who is unworthy. I see that now. Do you understand?"

"No. Damn you, Val! I don't understand!"

"Promise me you'll take the job. Promise me."

"Job? What job? What the hell are you—"

Val's fingers twitched, drew tighter around the fabric, pulling Ginger closer til their faces were a scant inch away. "Just promise me."

"All right. All right. I promise."

Valleri smiled, closed his eyes and nodded. His hand relaxed, then fell away altogether.

"Val? Val!"

"Cheer up, princess. He'll be back."

I slumped on my stool by Arial's bedside. Ginger was gone, disappearing shortly after Valleri had died. For days I pined, fretted. Until I had word from him I would remain unable to think or sleep or eat. Nothing cheered me. Not the news that Ragsey had expired of gangrene, or the revelation that Urharde had been apprehended, or even the arrival of a messenger from Belvemar with word that Sestus was making a spectacular recovery. I was gratified yes, but not cheered. I haunted the stables, the kennels, hoping to find him there with his Shouda bitch, who'd deserted me also. I spent much of my time in the infirmary, visiting Arial.

It seemed Arial would make a partial recovery, though he suffered great pain from his injuries. His arm worried me most, broken and nearly severed by a sword blow he never saw coming. "How is it today?" I asked, in my ho-hum tone.

"Better some. Yesterday it was agonizing. Today it is only excruciating."

I smiled weakly at his wit. It went beyond my ability to whip up a potion to augment the pain alleviators, which the surgeon had given him. That was just too dangerous a task for me to attempt without the proper training, the required skill. Though Naren had pointed out that I was now free to hire the best damned Teki tutor in all the world, such a prospect held no interest for me.

Despite his own misfortune Arial sought to console me, placing a comforting hand over mine. "I have to admit, for a Crusader/Umagi he's not a bad fellow. Still, I'm murderously jealous of any man who can do this to you."

"Do what?"

"Come now. I don't think all those tears you cry are for my poor arm."

"Maybe one or two."

"Ahh, how generous!" His fingers squeezed mine, reassuring in their strength. "Trust me. Your mage will come back to you when he's ready. He just needs some time to absorb it all."

I supposed that was part of it. I'd finally gotten the truth of what had happened so long ago in Idyll, having learned it one evening from Naren, who grows surprisingly loquacious over a few cups of ale. According to him, Ginger, Valleri and Ivor had come into the pantry after a day's hard play wanting something for their bellies only to be promptly chased out. But boys being boys, they hatched a plan. Ginger was to stand lookout while Ivor distracted the kitchen staff with a spell, at which point Valleri was to sneak in and grab a tray of freshly baked honeycakes. As a result, Ivor's free-flow of telekinesis collided with Mauranna's simple spell to augment the cookfire.

Ginger might have forgiven himself for the events at Idyll, and even forgiven Ivor as well. But he was finding it harder to forgive Valleri, who had kept the truth of it to himself, using his silence as a means to let his hatred for Uncle ripen his vengeance.

A cold wet nose nuzzled my hand. I looked down to see the female Shouda, and knew Ginger must be near by. Pivoting on my stool, I saw him in the doorway. At my smile of welcome he stepped into the room. "Sorry to interrupt. I won't stay. I just wanted to tell you that I don't think I can accept the position of Gryphon Highlord."

My smile faded. Hurriedly, he continued, "I don't deserve such an honour. There are others more worthy than I. Give it to one of them."

I could not fathom what he was saying. While a likely candidate, Sestus was too close to retirement age. Naren would refuse the office, for he had expressed a desire to return to Idyll and restore the keep to its former glory. And Arial? Sad to say, Arial would never swing a sword again.

"Valleri thought you deserved it."

"It doesn't matter what Valleri thought. All that matters is what you think."

I remembered Ginger summoning magic so potent it nearly killed him. I recalled, too, his deflection of a poison-tipped throwing star hurled at my throat. He had even braved a keep full of Shouda, knowing what the price of failure meant. He'd risked his life and the lives of others in order to fight by my side and win me a throne. I understood all this, just as Valleri had.

"Believe me when I say no one is more worthy than you. The position is yours, if you want it."

"Its not that simple, Kathedra. If I accept the role of Gryphon Highlord I want all the titles and privileges that go with it."

"Of course."

"You would agree even though I don't meet all the criteria?"

"Criteria? I don't know what you mean." I glanced at Arial, who seemed equally baffled.

"I am not a member of Gryphon's house."

"Oh." I let out a heartfelt sigh of relief. "That is more tradition than requirement."

He appeared deflated by my answer. "Don't worry," I hastened to reassure him, desperate to make him stay. I got to my feet, faced him from the opposite side of Arial's sickbed. "I won't bind you to me with tedious vows or legal shackles. You will be free to live your life outside the office as you see fit." He had no idea how much that cost me to say, but I did not want Ginger bound to me out of duty or law.

"What if I told you I don't want to be free? That I want to be bound, mind, body and soul to you."

I still wasn't following his thread of logic.

Arial, on the other hand, figured it out. "For heaven's sake," he yelped at me, "he's asking you to marry him!"

It took a moment to sink in. I can be as thick as one of Biddy's bunion creams when the mood strikes me. I had not dared hope for such a thing from Ginger. Elated, I let out a shriek of joy and flung my arms around him, bearing us both down to the cot.

And Arial, bless his sentimental heart, abandoned his sickbed of his own volition rather than be forcibly ejected from it.

www.ingramcontent.com/pod-product-compliance
Lightning Source LLC
LaVergne TN
LVHW010052170826
845678LV00012B/2115